Django Generations

Chicago Studies in Ethnomusicology

A series edited by Philip V. Bohlman and Timothy Rommen

Django Generations

Hearing Ethnorace, Citizenship, and Jazz Manouche in France

SIV B. LIE

The University of Chicago Press Chicago and London

The University of Chicago Press, Chicago 60637
The University of Chicago Press, Ltd., London

Published 2021
Printed in the United States of America

30 29 28 27 26 25 24 23 22 21 1 2 3 4 5

ISBN-13: 978-0-226-81081-2 (cloth)
ISBN-13: 978-0-226-81100-0 (paper)
ISBN-13: 978-0-226-81095-9 (e-book)
DOI: https://doi.org/10.7208/chicago/9780226810959.001.0001

This book has been supported by the AMS 75 PAYS Fund and the James R. Anthony Fund of the American Musicological Society, supported in part by the National Endowment for the Humanities and the Andrew W. Mellon Foundation.

Library of Congress Cataloging-in-Publication Data

Names: Lie, Siv B., author.
Title: Django generations : hearing ethnorace, citizenship, and jazz manouche in France / Siv B. Lie.
Other titles: Chicago studies in ethnomusicology.
Description: Chicago ; London : The University of Chicago Press, 2021. | Series: Chicago studies in ethnomusicology | Includes bibliographical references and index.
Identifiers: LCCN 2021009479 | ISBN 9780226810812 (cloth) | ISBN 9780226811000 (paperback) | ISBN 9780226810959 (ebook)
Subjects: LCSH: Reinhardt, Django, 1910–1953—Influence. | Jazz—Social aspects—France. | Romanies—Music—Social aspects—France. | Romanies—Music—Political aspects—France. | Romanies—France—Ethnic identity. | Music and race—France. | Musicians, Romani—France. | Jazz musicians—France.
Classification: LCC ML3917.F8 L53 2021 | DDC 781.650944—dc23
LC record available at https://lccn.loc.gov/2021009479

♾ This paper meets the requirements of ANSI/NISO Z39.48-1992 (Permanence of Paper).

For Arne Brun Lie

Contents

Notes on Terminology *ix*
List of Figures *xi*
Companion Website *xiii*

Introduction 1
1 Making Jazz Manouche 32
2 Cultural Activism's Living Legacies 64
3 Generic Ontologies and the Stakes of Refusal 98
4 The Sound of Feeling 128
5 Heritage Stories 154
Conclusion 183

Acknowledgments *189*
Appendix 1: Glossary *195*
Appendix 2: List of Formal Interviews *197*
Notes *199* *References* *229* *Index* *253*

Notes on Terminology

All translations from French are my own, and all interview quotations are translations from French to English unless otherwise noted (see appendix 2: List of Formal Interviews). I have chosen to preserve the French letter case of "jazz manouche." I frequently identify Django Reinhardt simply as "Django," as he is referred to by jazz manouche participants. I have withheld some names or used pseudonyms when interlocutors have requested it or when I have felt that it is appropriate to do so. When I cite interlocutors with whom I am on a first-name basis, I use their first names to preserve the character of our relationships. I also do this because many share the same surnames. For example, Reinhardt is a common last name among some French and German Romanies. When any interlocutors are cited as authors, I use their last names for bibliographic consistency.

This book includes a glossary of terms with pronunciations and a link to further information on Romani endonyms and exonyms (appendix 1: Glossary), but I would like to outline my use of a few key terms here. In translations between French, English, and Romani, numerous points of confusion can arise concerning appropriate uses of *Romani* and its synonyms. I use *Romanies* instead of *Roma* as a plural noun partly to avoid confusion with the term *Roms*, which in French typically designates Romani people from Eastern Europe, and partly to include Sinti, who are often designated as related to but separate from Roma. I use *Romani* in the singular as an adjective.

I have chosen to retain the French *Tsigane* in English translations of French passages for reasons of semantic clarity (see Kenrick 1998 and Matras 2015 on the etymology of *Tsigane* and related terms). While in English, *Gypsy* is often considered by scholars and activists to be a pejorative term (though this is obviously not the case among the many Romanies who self-identify as Gypsy), and *Romani* and its variants are generally understood to be more respectful and accurate, *Tsigane* is not directly translatable to either of these terms. Although *Tsigane* is an exonym, it is not always considered as pejorative as *Gypsy* and is used widely among scholars and activists in France. It is also a term by which many French Romanies refer to themselves (on the rejection of the *Roma* appellation by French Romanies, see Williams 2003, 87; Poueyto 2018, 602). *Tsigane* is sometimes spelled as "Tzigane," though the latter spelling is somewhat anachronistic. In Germany, the word *Zigeuner* is widely considered to have racist connotations, owing largely to its use by the Nazis. However, a musical collective to which I refer frequently, Musik Deutscher Zigeuner, was named prior to widespread acknowledgment of these connotations.

In French public discourse, Romanies are typically divided into three subgroups: Roms, Manouches, and Gitans. I use the term *Manouche* to refer to French members of the Sinti subgroup of Romanies. Alsatian Manouches typically have extended family in Germany and refer to themselves interchangeably as both Manouches and Sinti, depending on whom they are speaking with. *Manouche* may also be spelled as "Mānuš" and similar variants.

Gitan may have different meanings depending on the context of usage. *Gitan* can refer specifically to French Romanies with Spanish roots or to Spanish Romanies. *Gitan* may also be used as a vernacular, sometimes pejorative, form of *Tsigane* and thus more accurately corresponds to the English meaning of *Gypsy* than does *Tsigane*. In my translations from French, I preserve *Gitan* when it is used to refer to the Romani subgroup with Spanish roots. When its usage corresponds more closely to the English meanings of *Gypsy*, I translate *Gitan* as *Gypsy*.

Gadjo (n.m.sing.), *Gadji*, (n.f.sing.), *Gadjé*, (n.m.pl.), and *Gadjia* (n.f.pl.) are Romani terms used to refer to non-Romanies (though they vary across varieties of the language). I use these terms throughout this book to refer to non-Manouches, in part because this is how people who identify across this divide refer to non-Manouches in the context of relations with each other, and partly to draw attention to how these groupings are discursively constructed as discrete entities. See Courthiade (2013) for further distinctions in terminology between French Manouches and Gadjé.

Figures

1 Advertisement for *Manouche*: *Les musiques d'aujourd'hui des Tsiganes d'Alsace* (1984) 83

2 Postcard for the 2004 Festival Gipsy Swing 155

3 Ceremony at the grave of Django Reinhardt, Samois-sur-Seine, 1 July 2012 168

4 Map of the Festival Jazz Manouche de Zillisheim 174

Companion Website

Readers are encouraged to access digital materials associated with this book at http://www.djangogen.com. This companion website provides supplementary images, audio, video, and links to further information.

Introduction

A *tarte flambée* is a paper-thin round of dough spread with fine amounts of sour cream, onions, and small pieces of bacon, fired quickly in a very hot oven and served immediately. White and nearly diaphanous, this specter of a pizza is deceptively rich and often consumed with abandon. Along with *choucroute garnie,* white wine, and other gastronomic specialties, the tarte flambée is an important emblem of Alsatian identity.[1] Bordering the west bank of the Rhine, Alsace is a region in northeastern France that, like other French regions, has developed its own brand composed of these and other recognizably rustic features. Despite its status as the nexus of modern European institutions—it is home to the Council of Europe, the European Parliament, and other international organizations—xenophobic and separatist movements have also flourished here.[2] For the right-leaning, overwhelmingly White majority of the region, things like the tarte flambée signify an exclusive ideal of what an Alsatian is or should be.[3]

One March evening in 2014, I accompanied several musicians to a jazz manouche gig at a tarte flambée restaurant in a typically quaint Alsatian village. Like the tarte flambée, this style of music is ubiquitous in Alsace, though its influence extends well beyond the region. Known best for its energetic, guitar-centric swing tunes, jazz manouche is among France's most celebrated musical practices of the twentieth and twenty-first centuries. It centers on the recorded work of Django Reinhardt (1910–1953), a prolific guitarist who rose to fame in the 1930s. Reinhardt belonged to the Manouche subgroup of Romanies, also known somewhat pejoratively as "Gypsies," for whom the genre is named. Alsatian Manouche communities played a central role in the genre's birth and development, so much so that Alsace is often called "the cradle of jazz manouche." A handful of these community members have earned international commercial success and paved the way for other Manouche musicians to cultivate local markets for themselves. Such musicians are regarded as authentic purveyors of the familiar-yet-exotic genre, one in which their alterity is selectively celebrated.

For months before the gig, I worked closely with its organizer and rhythm guitarist, Gigi Loeffler. We had met at a music festival the previous summer: he, an aspiring activist who sought to promote awareness of his Alsatian Manouche background, and I, a US musician and graduate student in ethnomusicology eager to document and participate in his efforts. That night, he arrived looking as he always did for a gig: clean-shaven, hair smoothed, and smartly dressed in one of his signature boldly patterned dress shirts. In his appearance, speech, and musical performance, he wanted to ensure that he would be approachable and taken seriously as a professional.

Gigi was joined by his cousin on lead guitar, a US saxophonist, and me as a videographer. A local non-Manouche bassist new to jazz manouche rounded out the ensemble. In the minutes prior to sound check, the musicians congregated in the back room to devise a setlist, eventually abandoning the idea in favor of selecting tunes in the moment of performance. The bassist had already expressed some anxiety about playing with the group for the first time, so I asked her if she would be comfortable with this level of spontaneity. She responded by saying, "Well, they're Manouche!" and left it at that.

Showtime arrived. Most of the clientele were White locals who had come to enjoy the live performance as an accompaniment to their meals. Gigi kicked things off as the emcee, thanking the audience with his usual warm, gregarious demeanor. The set began smoothly with a few standards in the jazz manouche repertoire, including a rendition of the classic "It Had to Be You" followed by "Blues en mineur," an original Reinhardt composition. Each piece adhered to the genre's typical small-group jazz improvisation form, in which solo instrumentalists introduce the (often loosely interpreted) "head" or precomposed melody, take turns improvising over several choruses (full cycles of the chord progression), and finish with a recapitulation of the head. Throughout these pieces, the bassist and at least one guitarist played chord changes with the percussive bounciness that is characteristic of the genre. Meanwhile, waitresses zipped among tables and in front of the stage with orders of beer, wine, and tartes flambées. In between tunes, Gigi introduced the musicians with praise and spoke about the practice of this "beautiful" music among Manouches. He envisioned this emceeing as a way to promote his community's contributions to Alsatian and French musical heritage and to advocate for intercultural collaboration.

By the intermission, a number of the guitarists' extended family members had filtered into the restaurant and congregated near the bar. They cheered the musicians on, visibly annoying some of the patrons with their enthusiasm and causing one to stand up and complain. In a display of familial solidarity, Gigi invited a few of his cousins up one by one to take turns sitting in on lead and rhythm guitars for the remainder of the second set. By this point, the lead guitarist who had been hired for the gig told me he wouldn't return to the stage, explaining that he felt uneasy about his family's boisterous conduct.

One such family member, Loïc, who had been boisterously encouraging his cousins from the center of the dining room, took the stage on lead guitar.[4] He cued in "Les yeux noirs" ("Dark Eyes"), a timeworn and recognizably Romani anthem with Russian and Ukrainian origins. At the start of the tune, for reasons I could not immediately discern, the bassist had a word with Gigi and stepped offstage. The saxophonist played conservatively over three choruses, then ceded the spotlight to Loïc, who embarked on an extended solo. At each moment of frantic intensity, whether he strummed a prolonged tremolo or loudly repeated a phrase with increasing velocity, his family members and a handful of other listeners cheered and applauded.

As this series of climaxes carried on, Gigi approached me and exclaimed, "Now *that's* Manouche!" Taking in the scene around me, I thought he could have meant a number of things: the tune "Les yeux noirs," the performance techniques, the identity of the remaining performers, the act of spontaneously inviting family members to the stage, or the glee and fervor with which Loïc played—any of these could be considered characteristically "Manouche." I asked, "What's Manouche here?" and he explained that it was the rhythm guitarist's right-hand technique. He then stepped back onto the stage, put his hand on the rhythm guitarist's shoulder, and motioned to Loïc to move on. Following a trick ending, Gigi smiled as he conducted the guitarists in a waltzed, slowed-down, nearly parodic reprise of the piece's theme. This turned out to be the grand finale, after which Gigi picked up the microphone once more to thank the audience and the musicians. Loïc did the same, elaborating on how grateful he was to Gigi for this opportunity, how unplanned his performance was, and how much he loved his family. As Loïc went on, I worried that for all these kind sentiments, Gigi's efforts to cultivate a positive and professional image of Manouches had been undermined in the second set. My apprehensions were reinforced when, as we packed up to leave, the bassist told me that the whole experience was "pretty folkloric."

In the following days, as I ran through what had happened that evening with Gigi and others present at the gig, what struck me most was how divergent each person's understanding of the events could be. It was clear to all that the show had an element of spontaneity and that it was truly a family affair. To Gigi, this amounted to an overall success. He was proud to demonstrate to the audience the joys of improvisation (musical and otherwise), that the musicians were part of a loyal and generous family, and that they were the genuine representatives of a renowned musical tradition. But for others, these same things were not so successful: the musicians' improvisation was disorderly, resulting in a chaotic end to the performance, and their family loyalties took precedence over professional responsibilities. Gigi recognized this too, but explained to me that to *not* invite his cousins to the stage would have violated Manouche social norms. He said he would smooth things over with the restaurant's manager and try to figure out her "interpretation" of what had happened.

My own interpretation of that evening unfolded over the following weeks, months, and years. How did Gigi's approach bode for his advocacy? Why should a restaurant that branded itself as traditionally Alsatian hire Manouche musicians? And what, exactly, was "Manouche" about the performance? Gigi had sought to affirm the value of his people and their expressive practices to Alsatian culture, but multiple, sometimes contradictory readings of this event compromised his goals. Considering the simultaneous reverence and scorn with which many Alsatians, and the French public generally, regard Romanies, it is no wonder that a performance like this should arouse so much ambivalence.

This book explores how a musical genre channels arguments about national and ethnoracial belonging. Jazz manouche is considered a typically "French" music, and Manouches are publicly lauded as some of its most authentic bearers. At the same time, Manouches are widely portrayed as exotic, incompatible with hegemonic French mores, and valuable to the nation only in their musical capacities. In a country that upholds strict ideals of assimilationist republicanism, this music positions Manouches as both integral and antithetical to dominant conceptions of French identity.

I use *Manouches* to refer to a subgroup of Romanies who self-designate as such (or emically as Sinti), who have resided primarily in France at least since the eighteenth century, and who may speak, with varying degrees of fluency, Manouche varieties of the Romani language in addition to French.[5] Historically, Manouches have lived and traveled in various types of mobile housing, but most today are settled in permanent homes. They engage in an array of professions, occupy a wide range of socioeconomic statuses, may marry and have children within or across racial lines, and often identify as Catholic or evangelical Christian. Like other Romanies in Europe and elsewhere, Manouches are frequently stereotyped as alien and mystical—a "'fantasy/escape/danger' figure for the Western imagination" (Silverman 2007, 340)—and as thieving and lazy. They face widespread discrimination from quotidian aggression to lethal violence.[6] According to one study, in 2017, the "tolerance" rate of the French public for Romani populations was the lowest (34 percent) among racial and religious minorities.[7] As "the last minority in Europe that can be discriminated against without limit—shamelessly, and often without punishment," Romanies are subject to what Huub van Baar, cynically drawing attention to this unmitigated racism, calls "reasonable anti-Gypsyism" (2014, 38).[8]

In light of such sanctioned intolerance, the only thing for which French Manouches are widely celebrated is jazz manouche. This is partly because the so-called father of jazz manouche was Django Reinhardt. Django, as he is colloquially known, was born in 1910 into a Manouche family of professional musicians. Despite a caravan fire in 1928 that disfigured his left hand and nearly ended his career, he made his mark in the early 1930s as the front man of the Quintette du Hot Club de France. During his lifetime, he made over nine hundred recordings and performed with some of the most prominent jazz musicians in France, the United States, and elsewhere. He is especially well known globally for his role in promoting the guitar as a solo instrument in jazz. By the time of his death in 1953, he had established himself as Europe's most famous jazz musician, a position he retains today.

In the decades following Django's death, jazz manouche developed as a genre based overwhelmingly on his recorded output. Also known as "swing manouche," "jazz gitan," "Gypsy jazz," and other variations, jazz manouche is performed and consumed by Manouches and *Gadjé* (non-Romanies) alike. The genre is commonly defined by several factors: a mostly string instrumentation centered on one or more (often acoustic) guitars, usually of the Selmer model Django and his accompanists regularly used;[9] small-group improvisation; a repertoire consisting of US swing tunes popular in the 1930s and 1940s and recorded by Django, as well as his own compositions; influences from *musette*,[10] French popular song, bossa nova, and sometimes Hungarian *csárdás*; and a percussive rhythm guitar stroke called *la pompe* ("the pump"), among other characteristics.[11] It is often construed as an authentic hybrid (Taylor 2007) of a now-globalized art form (jazz) with uniquely, but arguably, Romani inflections.

For many Manouche communities, jazz manouche is a deeply meaningful practice that creates and strengthens intra-community bonds. Its significance as an emblem of a minoritized identity also renders it a consumable form of exoticism. At the same time, its nostalgic, playful aesthetic and its use as innocuous background music in cafés and romantic comedies suggest something less than exotic. Jazz manouche has become so naturalized as part of a French sonic imaginary that it also indexes quotidian French Whiteness. Django, in turn, is hailed as a cultural hero not only for Manouche people, but also for French cultural heritage and for jazz guitar aficionados worldwide. His body of work is said to have "generated a musical cult" (Tuzet 2010, 18), apparent both in laudatory discourse about him (Lie 2013) and through the continued, often purist performance of his music. Vibrant jazz manouche scenes exist elsewhere across the globe, including among some Romani communities in Western Europe, but France remains its geographical locus. Together, the genre and the figure of Django are used to represent both Manouche specificity and modern French heritage.[12]

By examining the uses of these musical emblems, this book shows how ideologies of social difference can develop in dynamic relation to an evolving genre. Such ideologies take shape through what I call *ambivalent essentialism*, in which people attempt to reconcile the dissonance inherent to social categorization. I draw inspiration from Paul Gilroy's framework of "anti-anti-essentialism," which seeks to transcend both the essentialism of "those who see [Black] music as the primary means to explore critically and reproduce politically the necessary ethnic essence of blackness and [the anti-essentialism of] those who would dispute the existence of any such unifying, organic phenomenon" (1993, 100). In broad terms, essentialism can be described as a human effort to order the world. It depends on the assumption that social essences exist and are natural or permanent. Essentialism may be directed from members of one social category toward another, or toward one's own category. It may entail complicity and/or confrontation between members of different social categories, and it may be used reflexively and deliberately.[13]

Essentializing maneuvers are performed according to their contexts of use and are thus necessarily selective: a musician might choose to advertise themself as Manouche in order to sell records, but would not do so when seeking other forms of employment.

Ambivalence, argues Zygmunt Bauman, is an unavoidable "side-product of the labour of classification" that appears "as discomfort and a threat" to these endeavors (1991, 2–3). On the one hand, ambivalence means uncertainty. It is the doubt one feels about a choice or a category, doubt that threatens a given social order. People often manage this uncertainty by doubling down on their taxonomies and hardening lines of social difference. They might also question these categories, creating new ones or embracing liminality. Along with doubt, ambivalence involves the lure toward some idealized state of certainty. Ambivalence here is a space between embracing a thoroughly distilled identity and the feeling that there might be a better alternative.

This leads to another sense of ambivalence: the state of harboring contradictory feelings simultaneously. When a Manouche musician markets themself *as* Manouche, an audience member might experience feelings of unfamiliarity with and attraction to the figure of the exotic entertainer. While this dissonance may actually form the basis of the audience member's interest, it poses a special conundrum for the musician. It requires that other facets of the musician's subjectivity (perhaps as French, as middle class, or as a lover of electronic dance music) are bracketed in the service of fulfilling an ideal. According to Asif Agha, essentialization is an "activity or practice that appears to fix the values of complex cultural realities by grouping them into classes and treating some attributes of members (but not others) as necessary or 'essential' to class membership" (2007a, 74). The selectiveness of essentialization—emphasizing "some attributes . . . but not others"—both flattens the complexity of human experience and brings it into relief. The "other" attributes are cordoned off but not erased. For the object of essentialization, then, ambivalence is a reckoning with the demands of differentiation. The Manouche musician may be proud to present themself *as* Manouche, *as* different from some norm, but they might also desire other dimensions of identification that do not align with these ascriptions.

To summarize, ambivalent essentialism is the push and pull at the heart of much social difference-making—a process dependent, in this context, on modern political-economic regularities. Ambivalent essentialism underlies endeavors to construe jazz manouche and Django as emblematic of particular groups. The genre's participants often articulate categorical yet contradictory ideas about what the genre is, whom it represents, and how it should be used. Institutions make similar claims about whom Django's legacy "belongs" to and the sociocultural values he represents. These discourses highlight the struggles of individuals and groups to actualize desired states of belonging, calling attention to how notions of Manouche and French identities are essentialized and legitimized with respect to one another in the service of specific political and economic agendas. In fact, as this book suggests, it is the coexistence of these incompatible essentialisms within jazz manouche practice that render it such a successful, powerful genre.

On its surface, jazz manouche is a lighthearted pleasure, but it is also an industry that advances a political economy of in/exclusion. Aesthetic choices in this music also reflect beliefs about what constitutes "good" music and authentic people. Jazz manouche is an important topic of debate in France that conjoins these aesthetic and ethical concerns. My ethnographic and historical research explores how assessments of the genre correspond to participants' ideological positions as artists and as citizens. By examining divergent claims about where this genre came from, whom it belongs to, what purposes it serves, and just what it *is*, this book provides insight into the politics of recognition, processes of boundary-making, and the capitalist contexts in which culture is put to use.

A Raciosemiotic Approach

The ambiguity of Gigi's exclamation, "Now *that's* Manouche!"—as referring to musical aesthetics, behavior, and/or personal attributes—points to the fact that any definition of racial identity involves an array of interrelated and co-occurring signs whose meanings are produced interactionally in specific contexts (Agha 2007a) and across spatiotemporal scales (Carr and Lempert 2016; Gal and Irvine 2019).[14] Such definitions are situationally variable and may include particular ways of speaking, dressing, learning, relating to others, and performing, among other multisensory cues. Ideas about how these signs work (or should work) comprise *semiotic ideologies*: sets of "basic assumptions about what signs are and how they function in the world" (Keane 2003, 419).[15] A semiotic ideology about a social category (race, ethnicity, gender, etc.) has to do with which signs are thought to authentically represent that category. A semiotic approach to racial identity can account for the intersections and overlaps between signs—including the "bundling" of signs together—and for fluidity between expressive practices such as music and language.[16] It can also shed light on how racial categories become naturalized, especially when their constituent signs traverse the discursive and the somatic.

Music, and sound more broadly, are potent sign vehicles for the construction of racial identity. Although mainstream definitions of race tend to focus on visible attributes, it is also thought to be sonically perceptible (especially in vocal performance). Some genres and styles are also associated with racial groups, such that certain musical and extra-musical qualities, alone and together, are perceived to be representative of these groups.[17] To French listeners, a number of jazz manouche conventions—including solo and rhythm guitar techniques, the use of Django's name and image in publicity materials, and even a pencil mustache, among others—index not only the genre itself, but also the Manouche people with whom it is associated. In turn, narratives about Django and the development of jazz manouche shape semiotic ideologies about Manouche identity and its perceptibility in music, as chapters 1 and 4 argue. I explore how perceivers position themselves as "listening subjects" (Inoue 2006), the "subject position[s] from which the world is heard and reported upon" (Reyes 2017a, 217). By focusing on how listeners make sense of these semiotic configurations, I draw attention to the processes through which race is (re)produced in language, musical sound, and other semiotic modalities.

To account for the multi-modal semiotics of race, I suggest a *raciosemiotic* approach. With reference primarily to constructions of Blackness, Krystal Smalls develops raciosemiotics as a way to address how "a racialized sign, in its co-articulation with other signs, simultaneously racializes other signs while reifying, or restructuring, its own racialized significance" (2020, 237; see also Silverstein 2003). This approach expands upon the work of scholars who have developed the field of *raciolinguistics* in recent years.[18] Raciolinguistics seeks "to raise critical questions about the relations between language, race, and power" by exploring how "racial and ethnic identities are (re)created through continuous and repeated language use" (Alim 2016, 5). Importantly, a raciolinguistic framework interrogates widespread assumptions that race inheres in persons and in words and that language practices are transparent indicators of immutable racial identities. In doing so, raciolinguistics "account[s] for the modes of perception through which bodies are parsed in relation to racial categories and communicative forms are construed in relation to named language varieties" (Rosa 2019, 7). It presumes that race in the modern era is the product of (neo)colonial regimes built on the exploitation and oppression of non-White peoples and that it is historically contingent, malleable, and a major structuring force in human lives around the globe.[19] Raciolinguistics attends to the linguistic processes that, in both subtle and overt ways (depending on who is talking or listening), racialize subjects and reproduce colonial hierarchies. A focus on language practices also highlights the strategies through which subjects navigate, assume, and contest these hierarchies and the terms on which they are racialized.

Similarly, a raciosemiotic approach can emphasize how other semiotic modalities, especially musical performance, contribute along with language to the generation of ideologies about racialized groups. It accounts for how racialized subjects may use language, music, and other semiotic means to critique their own positions within hegemonic structures of difference. It also helps clarify how racial unmarkedness (Whiteness), and thus White supremacy, is constructed and maintained. This approach brings into focus both the structural forces through which race operates and the interactional processes that make and remake race.

Racial Erasure

Rogers Brubaker argues that although the terms *race* and *ethnicity* have served historically distinctive functions, "rather than seek to demarcate precisely their respective spheres, it may be more productive to focus on identifying and explaining patterns of variation on these and other dimensions, without worrying too much about where exactly race stops and ethnicity begins" (2009, 27–28). Both race and ethnicity are overlapping categories of social difference whose valences depend on their contexts of use. For example, Bonnie Urciuoli writes that in the United States, "race and ethnicity are both about belonging to the nation, but belonging in different ways" (1996, 15), such that ethnicized groups are thought to contribute positively to the nation while racialized groups are considered threatening. She frames these terms as "strategically deployable shifters," meaning that "the salient interpretation of [each] term depends on the relation of its user to its audience and so shifts with context" (Urciuoli 2003, 396). In this way, race and ethnicity may be substituted for one another, depending on what a speaker wants to convey about a category of people.

The criteria by which Manouches are said to differ from Gadjé, and the language people use to account for such differences, reveal slippages between what are commonly called "ethnic" and "racial" identities. I find it useful to refer to Manouches as an *ethnoracial group*, or, following David Theo Goldberg (1993, 75), as an *ethnorace*. In France, Manouches have been referred to both as a race and as an ethnicity, though in the past several decades, the use of *ethnicity* has superseded that of *race*. Ethnorace reflects the blurriness between these categories in many of the sources I consult and in everyday discourse as encountered through fieldwork. Furthermore, both race and ethnicity involve assumptions about the roles of heredity and culture in defining one's identity, social position, and life course. These ideas about heredity and culture can be deployed under the guise of race and/or ethnicity, depending on context—whether one wants to portray a kind of person as fundamentally (im)moral or (un)assimilable as a result of genetic inheritance or socialization. Ethnorace captures how race and ethnicity are used as strategically deployable shifters in a range of discourses about social difference.

By calling Manouches an ethnorace, I do not mean to downplay their racialization. To the contrary, I want this term to draw attention to the plural and shifting ways in which Manouches, and Romanies more broadly, are conceptualized and conceptualize their own identities (Potot 2018).[20] In this book, I use both *ethnorace* and *race*, depending on the ascriptive processes I wish to highlight. As I explain below, if ethnicity (and sometimes "culture") are really about race in this context, then ethnorace can help illustrate the stakes of these categories and the dissonances generated in their variable uses.

Race and ethnicity are especially slippery concepts in France. This has to do with the fact that its republican government maintains a longstanding policy banning the official collection of ethnic, racial, and religious demographic statistics (Simon 2008). Defenders of this policy contend that it ensures equal treatment for all subjects of the state regardless of their ethnoracial origins or religious beliefs. However, France's refusal to recognize minoritized groups only renders particular ethnoracial and religious identities—White, European, Christian, secular—normative and protects the state's de facto discrimination against those who are persistently labeled as being "of foreign origin." The liberal embrace of universalism, long used in justifications for colonial rule, assimilationist regimes, and ultimately, racial states (Goldberg 2002), allows for the widespread acceptance in France of White supremacist logics and the synonymization of *French* with *White*.[21] The naturalization of whiteness as unmarked and universal reflects how, as Jane H. Hill argues, "many kinds of silences and inattentions . . . work together to create racist institutions and outcomes" (2008, 29).

The idea that *race* is a dirty word permeates official and vernacular discourse in France, such that talking about race is often considered tantamount to expressing racist beliefs. The pervasive denial of race's existence has resulted in the equally insidious denial of race's effects. In other words, as Crystal Marie Fleming writes in her work on contemporary efforts to recognize the French legacy of slavery, "the dominant mode of 'dealing with race' in France consists of racial avoidance" (2017, 6). Acts of "covert racialization"—such as the refusal to name or acknowledge race—result in the "plausible deniability" of race's real impacts (Dick and Wirtz 2011, E2), amounting to what Eduardo Bonilla-Silva ([2006] 2014) calls "color-blind racism." While many tout France's supposed color blindness as evidence of its progressiveness, those among France's racially minoritized groups often understand this to be a false and dangerous claim.[22]

In light of this discourse on race, French Manouches today usually say they are part of an ethnic group. Compared with *race, ethnicity* is more widely used as a category of social difference in France, often as a substitute for *race*. Alice Krieg-Planque writes that in France, *ethnicity* is primarily a gloss for *race* and is a "synonym for *exotic*" (2005, 153; emphasis in original). For Manouches, self-identifying as ethnic can be a way to acknowledge these covert racializing processes and, simultaneously, to present themselves as racialized in legible, broadly accepted terms. As each chapter of this book explores, it is also a way to claim particular modes of belonging and to develop a marketable brand of music.

Culture serves a similar euphemistic function as *ethnicity*. Manouches and other minoritized groups in France are subject to what Etienne Balibar calls "racism without races," in which the "dominant theme is not biological heredity but the insurmountability of cultural differences" and "the incompatibility of life-styles and traditions" (1991, 21). Bonilla-Silva similarly argues that, as a central aspect of color-blind racism, "cultural racism" captures how "biological views have been replaced by cultural ones that . . . are as effective in defending the racial status quo" ([2006] 2014, 77), echoing Michel-Rolph Trouillot's observations on racialist uses of *culture* (2003, 97–116). It is through cultural racism that race and ethnicity are treated as questions of malleable and voluntary "culture" and as matters of choice or personal responsibility on the part of racially minoritized groups. This position, dominant in France, is assumed to absolve racist beliefs about and actions toward groups such as Romanies. Under cultural racism, denying race's biological reality is touted as the only defensible antiracist stance, rendering suspect any other possible acknowledgment of race. Cultural racism also trivializes the extent to which Romanies have been portrayed as inherently free-spirited, lazy, criminal, spendthrift, and so on. Romanies facing economic insecurity are widely blamed for their own poverty on grounds deemed "cultural," an explanation that elides how racialization, as a justification for (neo)colonial exploitation and exclusion, "is fundamentally pragmatic" (Reed 2013, 49).[23]

The obfuscation of race in France is readily apparent in the state's treatment of Romanies. Lawmakers in the early twentieth century sought to classify Romanies on the basis of behaviors and cultural traits deemed incompatible with republican values and spoke informally of them as a "race" that needed to be controlled. Legislation passed in 1912 curtailed the rights of a new category of citizens, *nomades*, which was meant to connote Romanies without the explicit mention of race. Nomades were required at all times to carry *carnets anthropométriques*, booklets that served as intranational passports and included detailed information about physical attributes such as skin color and skull size, and to check in with the police every three months to avoid fines and/or imprisonment (Filhol 2013). Even "the status of 'nomad' was hereditary: children born from 'nomads' were automatically classified as 'nomads' by the administration until their death, whether they travelled or not" (Olivera 2015, 41).

Under the Nazi occupation and Vichy administration during World War II, nomades faced more explicitly racializing treatment. They were captured and sent to internment camps within France and, in some instances, to concentration camps abroad. Following their release from internment camps (which was not completed until 1946, well after the end of the war), the government made no provisions to aid or reintegrate these former internees, and many settled into slums.[24] Today, many Manouche communities still endure the cumulative repercussions of anti-nomade legislation and internment, including forced sedentarization. As one social worker put it to me, sedentarization "destabilizes everything": it destroys professions that rely on mobility, ensuring economic precarity and thus further stigmatization. It can also undermine intra-community solidarity and morale. The ruptures inaugurated by these policies continue to bear heavily on Manouche communities, sedentarized and mobile alike.

In 1969, policymakers replaced term *nomade* with the more palatable *Gens du voyage* ("Travelers"; see FNASAT–Gens du Voyage 2010). Since then, further reforms to this legislation have eased some restrictions on its target population, though Gens du voyage remains a thoroughly racializing category disguised by the claim that its administrative apparatus mitigates behaviors deemed threatening to the majority population (About 2012; Cossée 2016; Smith 2018). Gens du voyage policy is exemplary of color-blind racism, especially since the very category of Gens du voyage is often considered synonymous with Romanies despite the fact that non-Romanies are also included under this heading. This covertly racializing discourse criminalizes the mobility-dependent livelihoods of some Romanies, reinforcing stereotypes that they are innately vagrant. Furthermore, although most French Romanies today are settled and do not qualify as Gens du voyage, many are paradoxically and persistently designated as "sedentarized Gens du voyage"—a label that unequivocally substantiates and legalizes a specific form of racialization. What is presented as a lifestyle choice, like "culture," is actually a permanent classification imposed by the state.

In light of these rhetorical and legislative contortions, this book examines how ethnorace is (re)produced when its very existence is obscured. How do minoritized groups deal with racism under such circumstances? What resources do people have to articulate, make sense of, and potentially transform their subject positions? If few arenas are available to speak frankly about ethnorace and racism, creative approaches—such as talk about and performance of music—become necessary, as argued in chapters 3 and 4. But these are not merely circumlocutory maneuvers to make up for a lack of effective vocabulary about ethnorace; they are semiotically constitutive of ethnorace itself. What, then, does a semiotics of ethnorace look, sound, and feel like in these contexts?

Defining Citizenship

As Gens du voyage legislation demonstrates, racist ideologies have always accompanied, if not undergirded, the French policy of color blindness. This was made especially clear in the "multiculturalism" debates that arose in the 1970s and 1980s. In the years following decolonization, public debates ensued over how to incorporate immigrants from former colonies into metropolitan French society. Nationalist politicians argued that postcolonial immigrants—non-White, and many of whom were Black and/or Muslim—were culturally incompatible with French values and needed to "assimilate" in order to become legitimate French citizens. Since the 1980s, a "neorepublican discourse" that "blames the cultures of immigrants for any failure to assimilate" (Beriss 2004, 18) has dominated public discussion, fueling xenophobic attitudes toward ethnoracially and religiously minoritized groups, immigrants and non-immigrants alike. For example, the rights of Muslim women are continually thrown into question with bans on the niqab in public spaces and on religious symbols in public schools, among many other insidious forms of Islamophobic discrimination.[25] Much of this discourse has been aimed at people of North and West African descent, though it has also been mobilized in recent years against Romanies, especially those who have (im)migrated from Eastern Europe.[26] It rests partially on the idea that ethnoracial and/or religious "communitarianism" would proliferate if multicultural policies were enforced and would thus threaten the cohesion of the nation. Although a range of public programs have been implemented to address the needs of minoritized groups and to promote cross-cultural "tolerance," neorepublican discourse ultimately endorses the White, Christian, and/or secular identity of the ideal citizen.

Debates surrounding what French identity is, or should be, can be framed in terms of *cultural citizenship*. Whereas formal citizenship is one's legal status as a citizen of a state and the rights and duties entailed in that status, cultural citizenship encompasses the many other dimensions of belonging to a nation. My thinking here is informed by Jean Beaman's work on cultural citizenship among children of North African immigrants to France, in which she writes that "Insofar as cultural citizenship is a claim, it is a claim to full societal belonging by fellow members of one's community rather than a claim to a specific set of rights" (2017, 24). I am also informed by Renato Rosaldo's formulation of cultural citizenship as "the right to be different (in terms of race, ethnicity, or native language) with respect to the norms of the dominant national community, without compromising one's right to belong, in the sense of participating in the nation-state's democratic processes" (1994, 57), as well as by Aihwa Ong's further assertion that cultural citizenship is "a dual process of self-making and being-made within webs of power linked to the nation-state and civil society" (1996, 738). Cultural citizenship is thus both a sense of inclusion within a larger national community *and* a project into which subjects of a nation-state are compelled. Dominant ideals of French cultural citizenship, framed in terms of universal values and norms, privilege the racially unmarked individual subject. This requires the exclusion of minoritized ethnoracial groups from any broadly shared conception of what it means to be French. Members of such groups are expected to endorse the norms of French cultural citizenship over their own ethnoracial identities, at least in the public sphere.

While much literature on cultural citizenship in France has focused on the experiences of immigrants and children of immigrants, very little has addressed the Romanies who have been French citizens for generations. Throughout European countries and especially in France, Romanies have long faced barriers to both formal and cultural citizenship as, for example, Ioana Szeman (2018) details in Romania. French Romanies are often characterized as being culturally incompatible with dominant norms of timeliness, industriousness, and education, especially when they are categorized as Gens du voyage. They are always in, but not of, their nation (Hall 2003). Some Manouches insist that they can never be "both" French *and* Manouche. In fact, the term *Gadjé*, while technically meaning "non-Romani people," is often used interchangeably with *French* (*les français*) and almost always in reference to White people. Like the Gadjé who exoticize them, these Manouches conceive of two separate and irreconcilable Gadjo and Manouche "worlds."

Other Manouches articulate collective goals toward inclusion in the French nation. In formal terms, this means group-specific demands to cultural, legal, and political institutions; for example, petitioning for a settlement's access to municipal electricity and plumbing, or advocating for equal voting rights for Gens du voyage.[27] In informal terms, this means making appeals to their broader inclusion in, and recognition of their contributions to, French society. They may privately reject the dominant standards for French cultural citizenship while outwardly performing their adherence to these standards. For these Manouches, cultural citizenship has to do with the extent to which they feel they can legitimately call themselves "French" without contradicting their own backgrounds, values, and practices.

Django Reinhardt has long been the key figure through which Manouches make claims to French cultural citizenship. Django is considered "a hero of the Gypsy people" (Antonietto and Billard 2004, 20) and the sole person to positively represent Manouches on such a public scale. More broadly, though, his status as France's most famous jazz musician has earned him a privileged place in modern French cultural heritage. Many Manouches recognize Django's value to France and consider him their entry point to societal inclusion. One early encounter in my fieldwork exemplified this phenomenon for me. On a July evening in the summer of 2013, I joined Gigi, his partner Laetitia, and one of his guitar students for dinner at a rather upscale restaurant in central Strasbourg. I had first met Gigi just a few weeks prior and was visiting Strasbourg to find an apartment for the year. That evening and for years to come, Gigi would pour his heart out to me about the importance of Django and jazz manouche to his family, the struggles Manouches have faced in France, his aspirations for professional success, and his dreams of being accepted by French society. Over escargots and a foie gras terrine, he looked straight into my eyes and announced, "You're going to think I'm crazy, but: Django didn't revolutionize music." He threw his hand over his mouth in mock surprise. "He revolutionized a people. That was his real impact. Before, we didn't go to fancy restaurants like this. We didn't fly in airplanes. Django changed all of that." Indeed, there Gigi was, enjoying fine wine and appetizers in the company of three Gadjé with whom he might not have entered into close contact were it not for his role as a jazz manouche musician.

Later, Gigi would tell me that he considered his guitar to be his "passport" to the Gadjo world. This metaphor of music-as-passport, or musical performance as proof of citizenship and enabler of mobility, encapsulates the role of jazz manouche within France. Considering all the ways in which this music indexes Django—as a world-renowned jazz musician, as an artistic pioneer, as a representative of French heritage, and as a Manouche—it is a potent means for performers and listeners to articulate their relationships to French society, actual or hoped for. By emphasizing the Frenchness of Django and jazz manouche, they express a sense of belonging, or desire to belong, to the French nation, an assertion of cultural citizenship on widely sanctioned terms.

Django's international fame has also enabled the genre's participants to understand themselves as part of a global jazz community. Since its early days, jazz has developed in place-specific ways both within the United States and as part of international musical networks, giving rise to "transnational jazz narratives" (Wilson 2015) among many musicians. As chapter 3 explores, many musicians typically associated with jazz manouche insist that their music is simply *jazz* and therefore an inherently ecumenical expressive form, a claim that aligns with the supposedly universal tenets of French identity.[28]

Simultaneously, some participants hear this music as an expression of non-White racial consciousness. Much recent scholarship on jazz has centered on the music's racial politics, addressing how musicians and listeners relate musical aesthetics and practices to various racial imaginaries.[29] As chapters 1 and 4 discuss, Django's contemporaries and jazz manouche participants have drawn parallels between Manouche and African American experiences of racialization and the ostensible audibility of such experiences in jazz, similar to what some African American jazz listeners identify as a "blues aesthetic" (Jackson 2012; see also Monson 2007; Porter 2002). While Romani and African American histories are obviously quite distinct from one another, such comparisons are considered useful among those seeking to articulate a felt sense of racial differentiation.[30] By emphasizing Django's ethnoracial background, and how jazz manouche might reflect specifically Manouche values and practices, these participants indicate desires that do not align with dominant conceptions of French cultural citizenship. They may suggest that Manouches are indeed a world apart from French society and might never truly belong to it—or, more optimistically, that the hegemonic terms of cultural citizenship can and should be transformed.

As Ingrid Monson writes, jazz "tends to be cast as either universal or ethnically particular, colorblind or fundamentally black, with many jumping from one side to the other depending on the contextual situation" (2007, 71). The multiple valences of Django and jazz manouche provide ways to maneuver within the constraints of French republicanism and, ultimately, to envision a society that could transcend these very constraints. Mame-Fatou Niang calls this ideal "the democratisation of the universal," one that challenges how contemporary French "universalism preserves such a degree of innocence, ignorance and arrogance that there is little room for the Other" (2020). The various approaches to portraying Django and jazz manouche with respect to essentialized national and ethnoracial identities—as more French than Manouche, as more Manouche than French, or as some harmonious combination of the two—constitute efforts to reconcile the contradictions of racial markedness in France. Under current conditions, these approaches may seem at odds with one another, yet each is also situationally contingent and deployed at different times and places depending on the desired outcome. Gigi's passport metaphor suggests that while Manouches might be foreign to the (French) Gadjo world, they may also be part of it, thanks to the opportunities enabled by musical performance.

Putting Jazz Manouche to Use

It was nearing midnight at the brasserie where I had gone to hear a jazz manouche concert. For an hour or so after the final set, I drank beers with the Manouche musicians' entourage at the tables near the stage. Given the late hour, I decided to take my leave and approached one of the performers, Pascal, to say goodbye.[31] I had gotten to know Pascal over the previous several months, and he knew I was conducting research on the political implications of music-making for Manouches. Upon noticing me, he took me aside from the throng of people. Locking eyes with me, he declared that he was "not into politics" and that he only wanted to "do business." He pleaded with me to "show the positive, not the negative," and not to get him "involved with all this political stuff." Although I had long sensed some reluctance on his part to engage in the politically minded, pro-Manouche musical activities for which others had solicited him, this was the first time he ever stated his position so bluntly to me. I told him I understood that he did not want to portray himself or his family publicly as victims of racism, to which he responded with relief, saying, "You know me!" He then returned to the bar to order the round of drinks he owed his cousins and continue what would surely be a much longer evening than mine.

A few weeks later, I recalled this encounter as I listened to Pascal perform with some local musicians at an exhibition of Romani arts in Strasbourg. The exhibition was sponsored by several prominent political and cultural institutions and featured works by Romani artists from all over Europe that addressed issues of Romani marginalization and inclusion. As part of its opening events, the exhibition's organizers, based at a foreign university, had decided to program a concert to represent their commitment to involving local artists within this context of pro-Romani activism. But, having translated between the English-speaking organizers and the French-speaking musicians in their contract negotiations, I knew that Pascal understood his purpose there differently than the organizers did. While he told them that he was completely on board with their activist vision, he considered this to be merely one gig among others. It didn't matter so much that he was hired to represent Alsatian Manouches to an international audience; his main concerns were to earn a good salary and to gain some high-profile exposure.

Each party's understandings of what music was supposed to *do* in this context diverged, though they did not appear that way to others. Pascal was acutely aware of—and frustrated by—the fact that his music was being politicized, even if that politicization helped him reach his own goals of financial security and publicity. He was reluctantly willing to associate himself with this kind of event only to the extent that the payoff outweighed what he saw as a compromise to his artistic reputation. The organizers, on the other hand, had the impression that Pascal deliberately served as a representative of his Manouche community and was taking on this performance as an act of pan-Romani solidarity. They thought that paying him was a gesture of appreciation—and thus they, too, became frustrated when, during the contract negotiations, Pascal asked for a higher salary than they had offered.

This situation is just one example of how individuals manage their ambivalence about the *uses* of jazz manouche. For its participants, jazz manouche is an inherently pleasurable and rewarding practice. It can be a vessel for cultural memory and intergenerational transmission, and a way to generate affective bonds within and between communities and individuals. It can help improve the self-esteem of music learners and bolster senses of ethnoracial, regional, and national pride. Importantly, it also generates profits for an array of individuals and organizations, from entrepreneurial musicians to businesses to state-sponsored cultural institutions, and it can be used in the service of both pro-Manouche and pro-French political agendas.

The multiple pragmatic uses of jazz manouche point to what George Yúdice calls *the expediency of culture*. Yúdice argues that, under neoliberal regimes, culture has become "a resource for both sociopolitical and economic amelioration" (2003, 9) that is "located at the intersection of economic and social justice agendas" (17). Similarly, John L. and Jean Comaroff (2009) suggest that the political and economic functions of ethnic branding tend to be synergistic, while Morgan Luker writes that we live in an "age of expediency" in which multiple "musical values, meanings, and uses" are continually renegotiated to serve a variety of needs (2016, 11; see also Quintero 2018). Drawing on these authors' arguments about cultural expediency, in this book, I show that ideas about Manouche culture become expedient for Manouches, their allies, and French music and heritage industries. In particular, I focus on how jazz manouche is used to achieve shifting and overlapping antiracist, community-building, identity-affirming, and profit-making ends.

The uses of the genre arise from, and give rise to, its polyvalence: as representative of the classed, racialized, and gendered identities linked to Manouche culture, French heritage, and global jazz. That is, jazz manouche is expedient in so many ways because it entails so many different meanings.[32] Each use of the genre distills a particular set of meanings while ignoring or downplaying others. When certain uses come into conflict with each other, it is also a conflict of what jazz manouche means (or should mean). This friction between semiotic ideologies, even when overtly about musical aesthetics alone, is really about the kinds of people thought to legitimately belong to an ethnorace and/or a nation, and to have the rights and privileges accorded to such statuses. It is also about what music is supposed to do in the world and on whose terms music should be valued. Putting jazz manouche to use—to political, economic, social, and/or affective ends—is how people both enact and work out ideological conflicts about the genre and its semiotic affordances. As I explore throughout this book, it is the means through which people make claims to cultural citizenship and what that citizenship can or should sound like.

In addition to its community-building and economic functions, for decades, music has played a role in European pro-Romani political mobilization (see, e.g., Brooks and Collins 2017; Kovalcsik 2010; Lange 1997; Silverman 2012; Szeman 2018). Beginning in the 1970s, a number of organizations emerged to address the injustices faced by Europe's Romani populations on local, national, and transnational scales. These initiatives have been especially prominent in countries where Romanies faced increased marginalization following the collapse of socialism in the early 1990s. Many organizations have highlighted expressive practices as ways to counter racism and to raise awareness about Romani struggles. For example, as Adriana Helbig (2005, 2009) documents, nongovernmental organizations in Ukraine have promoted Romani musicians to bring visibility to their activism, even as doing so re-entrenches class divides among their constituents and reproduces stereotypes. Indeed, numerous scholars (e.g., Canut 2019; Lemon 2000; Olivera 2011; Surdu 2016; Vermeersch 2005) point out the counterproductive consequences of efforts to define and consolidate Romani "identity" in the name of activism. And, as Carol Silverman notes, the popularization of Romani musics "rarely changes the structures of inequality" (2013, 192). While endeavors such as these tend to reinforce the racializing logics that undermine necessary transformations in policy and economic infrastructures, they are still used to challenge some essentializing ideas about Romanies and to garner public support.[33]

In line with these mobilization efforts, jazz manouche has been used as a means of *cultural activism*. My conception of cultural activism draws on the work of Faye Ginsburg, who writes that "cultural activism calls attention to the way that people engage in *self-conscious mobilization of their own culture practices* in order to defend, extend, complicate, and sometimes transform both their immediate worlds and the larger sociopolitical structures that shape them" (2004, xiii; emphasis in original). Through musical performance especially, "people who historically have been marginalized from institutional power create self-representations of their groups—both idealized and accurate—to counter widely disseminated negative images, the absence of images, and images produced by outsiders" (Mahon 2000, 470). Cultural activism in jazz manouche can take diverse forms, ranging from awareness-raising stage banter by an individual musician to large-scale music festivals. Those who engage in cultural activism through jazz manouche understand the genre to be 1) a way of building self-confidence and group consciousness among Manouches; and 2) an emblem of ethnoracial identity geared toward a general public.

One of the clearest instances of this cultural activism took shape in the work of a regional pro-Romani nonprofit organization, L'Association pour la Promotion des Populations d'Origine Nomade d'Alsace (known as APPONA), which I detail in chapters 1, 2, and 5. APPONA foregrounded Manouche music as part of its multifaceted strategy to mitigate racism and to more fully incorporate Manouches into Alsatian and French societies. Other initiatives have also promoted jazz manouche as a form of cultural activism, such as the Festival Gipsy Swing (discussed in chapter 5). In addition to these collective endeavors, some musicians use performance as a platform to raise awareness about their communities without reference to a specific political agenda or organization. Especially in the wake of APPONA's closure in 2002, this relatively diffuse mode of cultural activism has become more prevalent than organized action. It reflects the fact that overt political mobilization among Manouches today is minimal compared to decades past. In the absence of a clearly defined collective political cause, individual cultural producers tend to act in their own self-interest, gesturing toward vestiges or visions of ethnoracially centered political consciousness.

Other jazz manouche musicians are disinclined to politicize their work in the first place. To reiterate Pascal's stated anxieties about cultural activism, a number of performers are just "not into politics." As another musician told me, politics can get in the way of "doing [my] gigs," an unnecessary (and even detrimental) influence on his public profile. Similar to the Romanian Romani musicians Margaret Beissinger describes as "rejecting Romani ethnic politics for their occupation" (2001, 48; see also Stoichita 2016), musicians like these prefer to develop reputations as professional artists, not as activists. This points to a broader sentiment shared by many, if not the majority of, jazz manouche producers and consumers: that this music is for pleasure, not politics. They refuse to recognize its expediency, understanding it as an aesthetically pleasing, and perhaps culturally meaningful, practice (though this, too, is itself a form of political positioning). Oftentimes, the genre is explicitly politicized not because its producers intend this to be the case, but because others project their own activist visions onto it. This may lead musicians to feel exploited or misrepresented. Furthermore, some Manouches may feel that since *they* are the targets of racism, it should not be their own responsibility to educate the public about their struggles.

Yet even those who disavow the cultural activist uses of jazz manouche can still benefit from them. Pascal's case is exemplary: he does not want to politicize his music, but this politicization opens up more opportunities to gig. This situation reflects the fact that much of the genre's political and economic expediency hinges on its ethnoracial branding. In *Ethnicity, Inc.*, Comaroff and Comaroff write that "[ethnic] identity is increasingly claimed as *property* by its living heirs, who proceed to manage it by palpably corporate means: to brand it and sell it, even to anthropologists, in self-consciously consumable forms" (2009, 29; emphasis in original). The second half of the name *jazz manouche* is an overt appeal to the marketability of alterity, a way for Manouches to stake a claim to a musical practice when other kinds of economic opportunities are limited. In promoting the genre *as* uniquely Manouche, cultural producers become "ethno-preneurs" (29), a label applicable to all who work to profit in some way from ethnoracial branding.[34] It is through this commodification that the political and economic uses of jazz manouche—its activist and profit-generating potentials—become mutually reinforcing, necessarily so within neoliberal regimes that render entrepreneurship the normative mode of subsistence. Ethnoracial branding can be a boon to cultural citizenship for Manouches within France because it is profitable and may position them as productive citizens. In valorizing Manouche culture, it can also promote a transformative vision of French cultural citizenship that supports ethnoracial diversity. But it is also a barrier because its very (exotic) appeal can reinforce the idea that Manouches are incompatible with the hegemonic norms of French society.

Driving the utility of jazz manouche *as* Manouche are both its historical associations with Manouches (which I explore in chapter 1) and the perception that there is something especially Manouche about the sound of the music itself (the subject of chapter 4). Although much of the genre's selling power may depend on a performer's ethnoracial background, Gadjo musicians can also profit from this branding by marketing themselves using stereotyped discourses and aesthetics of Manouche identity.[35] As one musician complained to me, "There are some Gadjé who become more Manouche than some Manouches!" Given the limitations of public discourse about race in France, this is not widely viewed as problematic (except by Manouches and their allies). At the same time, the genre's associations with French Whiteness afford its Gadjo players flexibility in their self-presentation. They may dabble in exoticism while performing what is understood to be a fundamentally French music and never risk compromising the security of their own cultural citizenship. As chapter 3 details, Manouche musicians, too, can draw on the genre's French associations in order to strategically position themselves as cultural citizens. The extent to which musicians align themselves with the genre's Manoucheness and/or its Frenchness depends both on how they envision its expediency and on the social mobility to which they have access.

In addition to its potential to further pro-Manouche causes, jazz manouche is expedient for the purposes of national and regional branding. This dimension of expediency often centers on narratives about Django that present him as integral to the development of French jazz.[36] Such narratives rely on the nostalgic appeal of swing-era Paris for their efficacy and are mobilized in the service of present-day political and economic agendas, especially to bolster the French heritage and music industries. They also tend to selectively downplay his ethnoracial background, treating it as secondary to his French citizenship and to his membership in a cosmopolitan jazz community. Insofar as he is portrayed as an exceptional figure in French history, it is mainly because of his artistic genius and the fact that *despite* being Manouche, he achieved such success. At the same time, Django's Manouche identity is sometimes played up, either to promote an image of diversity and tolerance or to infuse these portrayals with an alluring twist. The various, sometimes contradictory narratives about Django's relationship to his ethnorace and to his nation offer tools for French municipalities and institutions to craft their public images in contexts such as music festivals (the subject of chapter 5). In turn, the extent to which jazz manouche is characterized as a distinctively French music shapes Manouche claims to cultural citizenship: it is a question of how expressive practices might be considered simultaneously of a minority and of the majority, and how minoritized identities might be tolerated or incorporated within dominant conceptions of cultural citizenship.

Methodologies and Organization

Historical narratives are never just about "what happened" in the past. Their power comes from how they are shaped and wielded through the present (Trouillot 1995). By intertwining ethnographic and historical analysis, I show that the force of jazz manouche transforms across temporal and social scales, from the early twentieth century to the present day and from everyday interactions between individuals to broader political-economic structures. This book's title is meant to reflect two senses of "generations": first, as contiguous historical periods representing values, practices, and aesthetics that change over time. As chapter 1 details, Django's reputation has undergone a series of transformations between his lifetime and present-day commemorations, while it took decades for jazz manouche to become codified as a (still-developing) genre. Treating "generations" in this way also underscores the fact that this genre is an intergenerational practice within and beyond Manouche communities. Second, and more broadly, "generations" suggests that jazz manouche is *productive* in several ways: of ethnoracial difference and ideologies of cultural citizenship, of profits, of community, of affective states, and of histories. Countless threads emerge from, break off, and are reincorporated into the jazz manouche story, from facts and myths about Django and his entourage, to the individuals and communities who took inspiration from his music in myriad directions, to his cultural and commercial impacts worldwide. Simultaneously, these threads are woven into narratives of Manouche and French identities. This book produces a "history of the present" (Foucault 1977, 30–31) that foregrounds the continuing legacies of French racism under new guises, as well as Manouche efforts to contend with these circumstances. While this history is selective by necessity, it accounts for some of the most pressing implications of music for the in/exclusion of a marginalized population.

Because this book is centrally concerned with how social difference is generated, maintained, and challenged, I am just as interested in what defines (publicly exoticized) Manouche identity as I am in what defines (publicly normative) French identity. One model for thinking through this process of difference-making is *Gadjology*, a term coined by Romani ethnomusicologist Petra Gelbart. Drawing on Whiteness studies, and in response to a legacy of scholarship that treats Romanies more as objects of study than as agentive subjects, Gadjology—the study of the "Gadjo"—represents "a minority-centric perspective (which need not come from a minority author) [that] can hold up an ethnographic mirror to society as a whole" (2010, 188). Gadjology in this sense serves as a tongue-in-cheek corrective to a long history of academic "Gypsiology." While I situate my own analytical framework in terms of racial (un)markedness more broadly, I use *Gadjology* to refer to the everyday practice through which people theorize about Gadjé. The vast majority of my interlocutors, Manouches and Gadjé alike, articulate their own Gadjologies through discussions of ostensibly Manouche and Gadjo behaviors, values, and musical expressivity. Although "Roma do not live *between* 'two worlds' but *in* one world of many overlapping spaces" (Lemon 2000, 211; emphasis in original), people still often speak of distinct Gadjo and Manouche "worlds." As one Gadjo put it, "[Manouches] are our Martians, and we are theirs!"

Theorizations of how "we" differ from and are similar to "them," from the perspectives of Manouches, Gadjé, and those who see themselves as somewhere in between, suffuse the ethnographic data of this book. At the same time, I follow Romani anthropologist Anna Mirga-Kruszelnicka who, in critiquing the racializing scholarly legacy of "Gypsylorism," argues that it is imperative for scholars and activists to emphasize Romani identity as "dynamic and multi-dimensional" (2018, 23).[37] I also follow Alaina Lemon, who writes that since "It is usually not Roma who find 'hybridity' problematic, but non-Roma" (2000, 212), we must attend to how actors manipulate ethnoracially distinguishing terms that necessarily "index *contingent* social configurations" (201; emphasis added). That is, while my attention to how people essentialize themselves and others might be construed as reifying hegemonic social categories, to the contrary, I aim to show that different types and degrees of essentialization are performed strategically, often in tension with or in contradiction to one another (Silverman 2012), as necessitated by overarching political-economic orders. I resist the urge to resolve these tensions and contradictions, focusing my analysis instead on how people make them work.

To be clear, I am not of Romani background myself. I started learning about Romanies in my teens when, as a classically trained violinist and violist, I tried my hand at jazz. While I studied anthropology as an undergraduate at Boston University in the mid-2000s, my improvisation teacher at the nearby New England Conservatory guided me through recordings of Django and the Quintette du Hot Club de France.[38] I soon became personally fascinated with Romani history, political struggles, and musics. In 2010, I decided to enter the Ph.D. program in ethnomusicology at New York University to pursue research on the cultural politics of jazz manouche. By this time, I had become fluent enough in French to conduct this research, thanks to twelve years of language study and familial connections to France. In parallel with my graduate studies, I befriended and worked closely with Petra Gelbart on various educational and activist projects, such as the Initiative for Romani Music at NYU and advocacy for Romani Holocaust recognition. As the daughter of a Norwegian resistance member who survived Nazi concentration camps, I felt personally invested in the struggle for recognition of Holocaust victims and survivors and in understanding the ramifications of such atrocities in the present day. Although the Romani Holocaust is not an explicit focus of this book, knowledge about it has been one motivating factor in my decision to undertake this research, especially as it has shaped my understandings of Romani racialization.

I began to explore jazz manouche ethnographically through the genre's scene in New York City and through "Django in June," known informally as "Django Camp," which occurs annually in western Massachusetts. My first research trip to France took place over two months in the summer of 2012. I established initial contacts with people in the

French jazz manouche scene through email and social media, by showing up to performances and festivals, and at a serendipitously timed conference on jazz manouche at the University of Angers. Afterward, I met most of my interlocutors through ones I already knew. I had originally planned to conduct all of my fieldwork in and around Paris, but early on I was repeatedly told to just go to Alsace, where I would find "real Manouches" and "real jazz manouche." I also learned that some of the most concerted pro-Manouche cultural activism in the country had thrived there. I spent about a year between 2013 and 2014 conducting the most intensive phase of my fieldwork in and around Strasbourg, followed by several shorter trips between 2015 and 2018, in addition to continuous online fieldwork on social media since 2011.

My primary in-person fieldwork methods have been participant observation and audio-recorded interviews (sixty-four in total, not all of which are referenced in this book; see appendix 2: List of Formal Interviews). Participant observation includes, among other activities, attending performance settings from small rehearsals to large festivals; performing with other musicians, onstage and off, as a violinist and vocalist; offering help and expertise in various capacities, including translation, cooking, booking gigs, grant writing, and childcare; and joining in activist endeavors. In addition to venues for music performance and rehearsal, my fieldwork has taken place at sites such as family celebrations, exhibitions, public presentations and debates, private meetings, and interlocutors' homes. Some of the close friendships I developed are reflected in the pages of this book, while others are less obvious. My partner, Davindar Singh, moved with me from the United States to France and sometimes participated in the in-person phases of this research. At the time, he was a professional saxophonist who gigged regularly with a handful of my interlocutors in addition to his other colleagues.

I treat the jazz manouche scene as an "art world," or "the cooperative networks through which art happens" (Becker 1982, 1), which includes an array of participants: professional performers, their families and friends, teachers, scholars, critics, concert and festival workers, instrument makers, music industry representatives, managers, social workers, and fans, as well as nonprofit organizations, public institutions, and commercial enterprises.[39] All of these individuals and entities play important roles in the constitution of jazz manouche writ large. The genre's performance circuit is overwhelmingly male-dominated, though women are involved in many other aspects of its art world. Accordingly, most of the musicians represented in this book are men (with the exception of chapter 2, in which I discuss my experience singing in a women-centered choir). Partly by choice and partly by circumstance, the most central figures in this book are those who consider themselves to be "between" so-called Manouche and Gadjo worlds: Manouches whose relationships and aspirations extend well beyond their ethnoracial communities; Gadjé who are deeply involved with Manouches as professionals, friends, and life partners; and those who may not fully identify with one or the other category. I believe that their reflexive awareness of being in between or on the margins of these worlds has helped illuminate much for me in terms of how people in this scene negotiate difference and belonging.

In addition to the traditional, physically situated sites of ethnography, I have also conducted ethnographic research via internet-based communications. Online research has allowed me to more comprehensively account for the transnational dimensions of jazz manouche and to carry out my study longitudinally. Another cornerstone of my methodology is archival research. I draw primarily on APPONA's official archives at the Archives de la Ville et de l'Eurométropole de Strasbourg; the private collection of archives compiled by APPONA's former secretary, Stella Funaro; the collections at the Centre de Documentation of the Fédération Nationale des Associations Solidaires d'Action avec les Tsiganes et les Gens du Voyage, curated by Evelyne Pommerat; the digital repository of the Bibliothèque Nationale de France; and other, more informally collected materials.[40] I have looked at concert and festival programs, newspaper and magazine articles, advertising, press kits, contracts, correspondence, budgets, photos, project proposals, and other traces of jazz manouche production. In addition to making my own audiovisual recordings, I obtained recordings directly from interlocutors, purchased them in stores and online, and consulted the holdings of several of Strasbourg's municipal *médiathèques*.

A few comments on positionality and research ethics are in order. I am well aware of the issues that my various identities raise in the context of this project. I navigated the challenges of being a woman in a male-dominated musical environment. As a US resident—and even more so, a (now former) resident of New York City—I have often been an object of curiosity and considered a potential resource. Some interlocutors have said that they attribute their relative ease in building trust with me to my US nationality, citing their misgivings about European researchers (despite the fact that I am also a Norwegian citizen), and even to my Jewish background. This all has to do, of course, with the long history of violence perpetrated against Romanies by other Europeans, especially the ongoing trauma of the Holocaust. The eugenicist research of anthropologist Eva Justin is of particular note; as part of her dissertation fieldwork on Romanies, she earned the trust and learned the language of her research subjects, after which they were sent to concentration camps (Rosenhaft 2008).[41] Another reason why members of the Manouche communities I have worked with are rightly skeptical of ethnographic research is because they want to have a say in how they are represented while maintaining their privacy.[42] These concerns were not lost on me, and I have taken steps to ensure the respectfulness and transparency of my work. Among Manouches, it is generally considered inappropriate for Gadjé to speak Romani (Lie 2017). Although I did learn some Romani vocabulary, since I am not Romani, I spoke only French or English. Where appropriate, I have anonymized people and changed or obscured details of events. At times I forewent formal interviewing because the process put some people ill at ease. My ideas were developed in frequent consultation with several interlocutors, a few of whom provided feedback on my writing. I recognize that not all those I have consulted throughout my research will agree with every one of my analytical approaches, and I take full responsibility for the claims I make in this book.

The chapter following this introduction examines the historical development of jazz manouche in relation to ideologies about ethnoracial identity between the mid-twentieth and early twenty-first centuries (chapter 1, "Making Jazz Manouche"). In the decades after Django's death in 1953, some Manouche communities adopted his music as a familial practice. Simultaneously, critics, promoters, and activists extolled the putative ethnoracial character of this music, giving rise to the "jazz manouche" label as a cornerstone of both socially conscious and profit-generating strategies. Drawing on analyses of published criticism, archival research, and interviews, I argue that these ethnoracial and generic categories have developed together, each informing and reflecting ideologies about ethnoracial identity and its sonic expressions. Jazz manouche grew out of essentializing notions about Manouches, while Manouches have been racialized through reductive narratives about jazz manouche. This chapter traces the historical reception of Django and his cohort to arrive at the living history of jazz manouche in contemporary France and globally.

Chapter 2, "Cultural Activism's Living Legacies," centers on the life and afterlife of the nonprofit organization APPONA to show how jazz manouche emerged as a resource for pro-Manouche cultural activism. APPONA was founded in the 1970s out of serious concerns over violent racism against Manouches as well as anxiety about Manouche cultural loss. The organization subsequently built the economy of public Manouche musical production in Alsace as a means to combat racism and to integrate Manouches into the workforce. Its leaders promoted music professionalization as a technique of entrepreneurship while valorizing aural pedagogies as emblematic of Manouche alterity. By examining how these aims evolved over time and manifest in Alsace today, I show that ambivalent essentialism necessarily underlies cultural activism for French Manouches. In its growth, demise, and living legacy, APPONA exemplifies the fundamental contradiction of cultural citizenship in France: how to construct ethnoracial singularity as an asset while working toward inclusion in an assimilationist nation.

Chapter 3, "Generic Ontologies and the Stakes of Refusal," explores the question *What is jazz manouche?* Through close readings of ethnographic encounters and interviews, I show that interlocutors' endeavors to define and situate themselves in relation to genre also give shape to complex political stances. In talk about music, how do speakers intersubjectively develop ideas about ethnorace and citizenship? Most speakers critique the very notion of jazz manouche. Refusing this generic label is one way to address the tension between identifying as Manouche and as French: to have it subsumed by the supposedly universal nature of jazz, or to position the genre as quintessentially French. Yet many simultaneously embrace the genre's exoticizing connotations, and some use it to reshape dominant ideas about Manouche identity. Apparently contradictory stances reflect the continuously shifting, dialogical unfolding of subject positions.

Chapter 4, "The Sound of Feeling," delves further into the subjective experience of ethnoracial identity to examine how difference is naturalized through language about instrumental sound. In talk about the sensory impressions made by jazz manouche guitar performance, speakers invoke qualities such as rawness, loudness, and "feeling" to describe both the sound itself and the person producing it as palpably Manouche. In doing so, they render Manouche identity a perceptible sensation, like the adjacent qualities used to describe it. I argue that claims about the *in*describability of a uniquely Manouche sound constitute an effective strategy for conveying affective intensity. I propose the term *ethnoracialness* to account for the sensorial dimensions and often ineffable character of ethnoracial identity, as well as the ambiguity of ethnoracial differences as inherited and/or enculturated. A focus on how people claim to hear identity reveals continuities between individual sonic perceptions of, and broader semiotic ideologies about, ethnorace.

Bringing together key tensions of the previous chapters, chapter 5, "Heritage Stories," explores how festivals enact discrepant ideals of cultural citizenship. Throughout France, annual festivals dedicated to Django and his legacy are coordinated by an array of organizations. These festivals typically foreground Manouche performers and/or so-called Manouche aesthetic traits, resulting in both empowerment and exploitation of Manouche artists and their communities. I outline how endeavors to engage (or exclude) Manouche constituencies at several festivals reflect contrasting political and economic agendas, from those that seek to meaningfully involve Manouches to those that serve mainly to promote tourism. As frames for developing emplaced narratives about belonging, festivals materialize a variety of localized, future-oriented social imaginaries. Such visions for the future may seek to preserve the status quo of interracial power relations, or to reimagine the very terms of French cultural citizenship.

Challenges to the French disavowal of a racial order are mounting (Fleming 2017; Niang 2020). In France and many other places across the globe, far-right nationalism continues to gain influence, basic social protections are eroding, and calls for economic and racial justice persist ceaselessly. Considering these ever-present yet shapeshifting conditions, it is important to understand how expressive practices like jazz manouche are central to processes of ethnoracialization. This seemingly innocuous genre offers compelling opportunities to make, remake, and unmake all kinds of narratives about ethnorace, from those that champion the dignity of minoritized populations to those that deny them a sense of cultural citizenship. This is why, once opened up to interpretation, "Now *that's* Manouche!" is such a powerful phrase to keep in mind. With its potential to signify in so many possible ways, it distills the ambivalent essentialism at the heart of identity-making endeavors.

ONE

Making Jazz Manouche

Contemporary jazz manouche narratives tend to rely on a compelling and improbably coherent story that begins with Django Reinhardt's first forays into the jazz world. In the 1930s, Django became Europe's most illustrious jazz musician, thanks primarily to his leading role in the Quintette du Hot Club de France and his development of guitar soloing techniques.[1] As popular lore has it, Django was musically inspired by his Manouche Romani roots. Thus, it was only natural that his extended Manouche family would carry his musical torch after he died in 1953. Since then, according to this narrative, generations of Manouches have sustained an ethnoracially distinctive jazz tradition that Django self-consciously invented.

This chapter tells a different story. Jazz manouche is the result of several decades of selective reinterpretation of Django's work by both amateur and professional musicians, stylistic influences from the Romani communities that took up his music, and promotion by nonprofit and governmental organizations as well as the music industry. Nearly two decades after his sudden death, groups of Manouche musicians began performing jazz and jazz-derived styles inspired by his recordings, spawning an intergenerationally transmitted community practice. This practice became popularly known as jazz manouche only from around the early 2000s as a result of increasing commercial success. Although the genre remains grounded in Django's recordings, including an emphasis on recreating his improvisational techniques, it has also evolved into a practice quite distinct from what he performed during his lifetime.

Despite the fact that Django considered himself a jazzman with little, if any, stylistic influence owing to his Manouche origins, critics have tended to project ethnoracial qualities onto his music and his persona. These descriptions helped lay the groundwork for future slippage between Manouche musical production and ideas about Manouche identity that show remarkable continuity from the 1940s through the present day. For example, journalist Michael Dregni recently wrote that at the moment Django recorded a version of "Tiger Rag" in 1934, "so Gypsy jazz was born: a wanderer's music," resulting from the guitarist's "Roma sensibility [that] savoured minor keys and favoured emotional intervals" (2018, 655–59).[2] In addition to linking Romani stereotypes with musical sound, temporal conflations like this reflect what Givan calls a "presentist" perspective (the improbable narrative just described), as opposed to a "historical" one in which the chronology of Django's music is understood as distinct from the advent of jazz manouche (2014, 26–27).

Taking such a historical approach, this chapter explores how jazz manouche evolved in tandem with the development of ethnoracial discourses about Manouches in France. I argue that these ethnoracial and generic categories have developed symbiotically, each informing and reflecting ideologies about ethnoracial identity and its sonic expressions. The coalescence of jazz manouche as a practice and as a generic label depended overwhelmingly on its associations—forged by music industry representatives, critics, historians, audiences, and musicians themselves—with Manouche ethnorace.[3] In turn, conceptions of Manouche ethnorace have also been shaped through discourses and practices of jazz manouche. I draw on scholarship that shows how genres are continually negotiated (Brackett 2016; Briggs and Bauman 1992; Holt 2007; Lena 2012) to illustrate the historical contingency of both genre and categories of social difference. Examining ideas about the genre and those who perform it helps differentiate between ethnoracial imaginaries and the people onto whom these imaginaries are projected. Ethnorace, constituted through discourse and cultural practice across semiotic modalities, is used to unite, distinguish, and segregate populations—processes observable in a wide variety of music genres and exemplified in jazz manouche.

In this chapter, I account for the sociopolitical and economic contexts that galvanized the coalescence of jazz manouche, including the pro-Romani identity politics that emerged internationally in the late 1960s and 1970s and the development of a "world music" market in the 1980s and 1990s. Two related processes were especially crucial to the growth of jazz manouche as a community practice in Alsace, the region on which I focus: the adoption of Django's music by a West German Sinti musical collective (Musik Deutscher Zigeuner, or "German Gypsy Music") and the promotion of Django-inspired music by French pro-Romani nonprofits such as L'Association pour la Promotion des Populations d'Origine Nomade d'Alsace (APPONA) as a means of cultural activism. Both the producer of the *Musik Deutscher Zigeuner* album series and APPONA's leaders promoted Romani alterity as an expedient force: celebrating Romanies for their uniqueness was a way to combat discrimination, to prove the value of Romanies to the majority society, and to sell records. As such, the work of artists, activists, and entrepreneurs has given rise to a dynamic process in which ethnoracial difference and musical genre are co-produced.

As described in the introduction, French Romanies are subject to what Eduardo Bonilla-Silva ([2006] 2014) calls "color-blind racism." The republican mechanisms that claim to ensure equality among citizens actually render White supremacy normative, reproducing racial *in*equalities and casting cultural difference as a barrier to inclusion in the nation. While most scholarship on Manouche racialization in France focuses on legislation and other forms of governmental control, little work has shown how Manouches have been racialized historically in the media. Close readings of media portrayals of Django and jazz manouche practitioners can illuminate important parts of the historical foundation upon which Manouches are popularly racialized today. By tracing how the raciosemiotics of Django's musical legacy and his background evolved historically, I offer new contributions to understandings of genre, identity, and national belonging through music.[4]

This chapter draws primarily on research in public and private archives and published critiques of Django, jazz manouche, and related musical practices. Supplementing critical appraisals of musical performance with interview excerpts and ethnographic observations allows me to provide a holistic assessment of the genre's historiography and its present. I focus on the development of jazz manouche as a community practice among Alsatian Manouches, though overlapping processes among Romanies have occurred elsewhere in France and in Germany, Belgium, and the Netherlands (Antonietto and Billard 2004; Awosusi 1996). I also touch on Django's status as a major figure in nationalistic conceptions of French jazz, though I further explore the implications of his belonging to multiple heritages in chapter 3.[5]

In the following pages, I progress from the historical reception of Django and his cohort to the living history of jazz manouche in contemporary France and globally. The first section describes how Django was racialized in popular media from the 1940s through the late 1950s, followed by a brief section on how his music became discursively linked to actual Romani musical collectivities. The next sections describe how West German Sinti took up and transformed Django's music, leading to its adoption by Alsatian Manouches as a community practice. I then examine how the Alsatian nonprofit APPONA cultivated this music as a means of cultural activism, reifying links between Manouche identity and particular forms of musical expression, followed by a section on how the commodification of jazz manouche solidified its reputation in French popular media. This narrative is necessarily incomplete and fragmented, but it sketches the contours of a specific ethnoracial imaginary relevant to current understandings of cultural citizenship in France.

Racializing Reinhardt

There exists no documented evidence for popular use of the term *jazz manouche*, nor that of its English equivalent *Gypsy jazz*, until well after Django's time. According to Givan, "Reinhardt himself had no conception of 'gypsy jazz,' and even if he had lived to witness it, he would likely have had little interest in it" (2010, 6). However, in a wide variety of publications, Django is credited as the "founder" of jazz manouche, with the likely implication that his music was understood to be ethnoracially inflected during his lifetime. Even Patrick Williams and Alain Antonietto, the two most reputable French scholars of jazz manouche, misleadingly titled a coauthored article "50 Years of Gypsy Jazz" (1985), suggesting that the genre had existed since Django's first major successes in 1935 (though this was probably meant to be tongue-in-cheek). In contrast, guitarist Matelo Ferret, who knew Django since the early 1930s, once claimed, "People say Django plays Gypsy style. He doesn't play Gypsy style. He plays a style that's only his" (quoted in Jalard 1959, 57).[6] In part because Django was notoriously averse to giving interviews, his own opinions on the possible Manouche character of his work remain mostly undocumented.[7] Additionally, most of what is known about Django's personality comes from secondhand sources, many of which describe him as unreliable, errant, obstinate, and childlike (even while, according to some, he carried himself with a royal elegance; see Fry 2014, 175–76).

Attributions of an ethnoracial component to Django's music tend to result in the conflation of individual creativity with presumed cultural traditions (or even genetics). Such conflations influence not only narratives about Django, but also understandings of Manouches more broadly. Historian Elizabeth Vihlen McGregor argues that critics from the mid-1950s through the 1980s "betrayed their own understandings about [Django's] ethnic group and their belief that gypsies were not only culturally but also sometimes racially distinct from the French. According to these writers, this difference contributed in large part to Django's musical talent" (2016, 168). Extending McGregor's argument, I suggest that the attribution of racial elements both to Django's music and to his persona—by musicians, Reinhardt family members, and others in addition to critics—gave rise to flawed narratives about Django and jazz manouche while shaping subsequent understandings of Manouche alterity. Antonietto writes that racial characterizations of Django

> [deny] the great Manouche (as incidentally they still regularly deny his racial brothers) the faculty to set a personal goal and to undertake an intensive effort to reach it. Unfit for any personal endeavor as for any collective project, the image of the indolent and irresponsible Tsigane remains alive in our society. Nothing is more wrong. . . . We have been told ad nauseam that [Django] was born a musician, and for many this explanation suffices: *Tsiganes, don't they have music "in the blood" after all? As Blacks have rhythm?* We know the refrain of this oblivious racism that attributes to heredity what it denies to intellect: one is born a Tsigane musician as one is born a hunchback, it's destiny, by Jove! (1984, 77; emphasis added to indicate reported speech)

Antonietto's frustration with the tendency for many Django listeners to project racialized qualities onto his music, and to attribute his musicality (and that of other Manouches) to racial determinants, reflects the pervasiveness of these sentiments. "The image of the indolent and irresponsible Tsigane" has suffused much commentary on Django since the 1930s and well beyond the publication of Antonietto's critique from 1984.

Within ethnoracially inflected narratives of Django's life lie the roots of jazz manouche. If the genre is so profoundly centered on Django's music, retrospective projections of ethnoracial qualities onto his musical sound, as well as a focus on his Manouche identity more broadly, have contributed significantly to the ethnoracialization of the genre. While several critics have repudiated claims that Django's ethnorace played a measurable role in his musical style, others—especially those writing well after Django's death and who contributed to the creation of jazz manouche as a concept—have supported such claims. Furthermore, posthumous emphases on Django's connections to his Manouche community, as propagated by critics and others in the media industries, set a precedent for the transformation of Django's work into a Manouche-specific community practice. These retrospectives reinforce present-day popular notions that any personal and aesthetic links between Django and jazz manouche are a matter of ethnoracial significance. Although Django is consistently portrayed as a singular genius, his Manouche roots have come to bear strongly on his biography—in the words of Hot Club de France leading member and Django biographer Charles Delaunay, Django was considered both "primitive" and an "artist" (1954, 36). Below, I offer a sketch of Django's life and musical output together with ethnoracializing appraisals thereof in order to show how ideas about Django's relationship to his Manouche background directly shaped the decades-long evolution of jazz manouche.[8]

Django was born in Belgium but grew up primarily in France. From an early age, he became well versed in the popular musics of his time, learning to play the violin, the banjo, the banjo-guitar and, eventually, the guitar.[9] According to anthropologist Patrick Williams (2000, 410), the Manouche milieu in which Django was raised had no ethnoracially distinctive musical tradition to begin with. Along with Gitans (a name for a Romani subgroup associated with southwestern France and Spain), Manouches started to become prominent performers in the *bal-musette* dance hall scene beginning in the early twentieth century (Roussin 1994, 135).[10] This was the professional environment into which Django entered in his early teens. Musette guitarist and amateur historian Didier Roussin (1994, 139) cites several well-known musette performers of the time who were astonished by the young Django's talent and credits him with popularizing the use of guitar instead of banjo as the musette accompaniment of choice.

A devastating accident set the course of Django's life and later popular fascination with it. As Givan writes,

> On the night of October 26, 1928, the eighteen-year-old musician returned from a playing engagement to his caravan . . . outside Paris. As he prepared to retire to bed, a candle's open flame accidentally ignited a large pile of celluloid flowers that Bella, his first wife, planned to sell the next day. Bella escaped from the blaze with minor injuries, but the right side of Reinhardt's body was burned so severely that a surgeon at the Hôpital Lariboisière recommended his leg be amputated to prevent gangrene. Reinhardt refused. (2010, 7; see also Delaunay 1954, 29–30)[11]

Following an eighteen-month period of convalescence, during which he retrained himself to play guitar with his newly deformed left hand—

the scarring from the fire had rendered his third and fourth fingers virtually unusable, requiring him to rely overwhelmingly on his index finger, middle finger, and thumb (Givan 2010, 7)—he only joined the occasional musette gig (Roussin 1994, 139).[12]

Delaunay (1954, 31–32) writes that Django first encountered jazz as a near-religious revelation upon hearing a record by Louis Armstrong in 1930. Django's big break into jazz occurred when Hot Club de France member Pierre Nourry enlisted him and his brother Joseph to perform guitar with the club's ensemble (36–37). Django had met violinist Stéphane Grappelli in 1931 while playing in a band under the direction of bassist Louis Vola, and in 1934, the Quintette du Hot Club de France (hereinafter the QHCF) was formed with Django, Grappelli, Joseph Reinhardt, Vola on upright bass, and guitarist Roger Chaput (Grappelli 1992, 79–80).[13]

Many of Django's best-known recordings of the 1930s were made with the QHCF, which performed on and off and with various personnel changes until the late 1940s. The ensemble's first recording session with Odéon in 1934 was deemed by the record company's executives "too modern" for release, but after a successful concert, Ultraphone agreed to release two QHCF records (Delaunay 1954, 37). In addition to his work with the QHCF during the prewar period, Django performed and recorded with other ensembles and musicians in France, among them US musicians Coleman Hawkins, Rex Stewart, and Benny Carter. His career flourished under the Occupation, but it was not until the end of the war that Django engaged again with musical developments across the Atlantic. He embarked on a US tour with Duke Ellington's orchestra in 1946 and subsequently recorded more prolifically than ever before, drawing on the musical influences he was exposed to in the United States (especially bebop).[14] During this postwar period, he played on both electric and acoustic guitar and infrequently as part of an all-string lineup. He died suddenly of a brain hemorrhage in 1953 at the age of forty-three.

As a Manouche, Django inhabited an ambiguous position in the racial politics of mid-twentieth-century France. On the one hand, during this time, Romanies were often considered a distinctive racial category in the French popular imagination at this time. As described in the introduction, although it was (and continues to be) illegal for the French government to collect statistics about the state's racial, ethnic, and religious demographics, and to enact legislation pertaining specifically to such groups, French lawmakers have devised ways to target Romanies for race-based discrimination. On the other hand, Romanies were not always considered entirely distinct from White racial identity, at least not to the extent that African-descended peoples were.

Jazz critics tended to racialize Romanies in relation to Whiteness and Blackness. In mid-twentieth-century France, racial considerations in jazz criticism were overwhelmingly situated along a Black-White binary (although there was no clear consensus among critics as to the relevance of race to musical style or talent).[15] This occurred in the context of discussions about the role of jazz in constructing modern French national identity. As several scholars have shown (Braggs 2016; Fry 2014; Jackson 2003; Jordan 2010; Perchard 2015; McGregor 2016; Tournès 1999), in the early to mid-twentieth century, jazz became a focal point for anxieties about nationalism, globalization, and modernity in France and channeled "ambivalent desire" (Berliner 2002) for racialized "Others." Jazz's newness, as well as its origins and development among African Americans, represented both a promise of cultural invigoration and a threat to "true French culture" (Jordan 2010, 58). Within this context, Romani racial attributes were identified relationally in terms of Whiteness or Blackness and all of the primitivist assumptions such racial distinctions entailed. It was likely convenient for some advocates of French jazz to describe Django, the most vaunted jazz musician France could lay claim to, as White and thus as a legitimate representative of French ethnonationalism.[16]

While Django was sometimes identified as White in jazz publications during his lifetime, by the mid-1940s, commentators often highlighted his Manouche background as an explanation for the allure of his musical style. The writings of Hugues Panassié, a co-founder of the Hot Club de France, reflect this tendency. In identifying Django as White and Romani, Panassié articulates Django's racial ambiguity, and that of Romanies more broadly: "Django, one of the rare white jazz musicians comparable to Negroes, belongs to a race which has remained very 'primitive,' for in truth the gypsies' lives and customs are closer to those of the Negroes than those of the whites" (1942, 162). To Panassié, Django was proof that at least some of the desired "primitive" qualities of jazz did not depend on a performer's African descent. Django's expressive capacities were simply mystified as part of his ethnoracial characteristics. Considering that by the 1940s, Panassié's mission was to promote what he thought of as "real" jazz—that is, jazz performed in a "hot" style as opposed to "straight," which he associated with Blackness and Whiteness, respectively—Django's ostensible similarities to Black performers would have rendered him a more plausible "hot" performer than other

White musicians (see Panassié 1942, 1946). As McGregor contends, to these critics, "the gypsy in Reinhardt gave him his musical talent, while the Frenchman in him allowed jazz fans to focus on his French national belonging . . . and to promote him as the most important French jazz musician" (2016, 168).

A number of writings published during Django's lifetime make passing mention of his Romani background, such as an Air France promotional magazine that identifies him as a "French guitarist of Gypsy origin" ("Cannes" 1948, 9) and a feature in the popular magazine *Paris-Match* bearing the headline "This disabled Gypsy is one of the kings of Jazz" (Giacobbi and Descamps 1950). Other publications that invoke his Romani identity in more detail tend to portray Romanies as nomadic, free-spirited, marginal, and even primordial.[17] In a historical overview of the QHCF, Delaunay refers to Django as an "impenitent nomad" (1948, 12). Pierre Bonneau's biographical portrait of Django in *Jazz Hot* magazine imagines the guitarist's early life "within errant families," stating that he was "like all the subjects of his race, incapable of settling down and living randomly on the road in traditional *roulottes*,[18] parking at the gates of cities" (1945, 13). Jean de Trazegnies, writing in 1945 for the Belgian magazine *Jazz*, extends Romani qualities to the music and personae of both Django and (the non-Romani) Grappelli:

> Musicians who received your talent from the depths of time, Reinhardt, authentic and tanned Tsigane, Grappelli, Tsigane soul and dreamer-adventurer; both magnificent bohemians, I hope that civilization never spoils and corrals you. . . . Remain yourselves in your music, do it only for those of your errant race and for those who know how to understand it, as they understand nature and the healthy bitterness of wild fruits. (1945, 17)

Here, Trazegnies attributes Django's and Grappelli's musical allure to the former's Manouche "race" and the latter's "Tsigane soul" (suggesting that Grappelli, though not technically belonging to a Romani "race," shared its supposed behavioral and spiritual traits). He both conflates and essentializes alleged personal characteristics and artistic output while further typifying Romanies as "errant" and uncivilized. Django's perceived "tanned" appearance underscores his racialization, also pointing to his ambiguous position in binarized popular understandings of race and jazz in the French imagination.

Although many critics analyzed Django's music independently of ethnoracial considerations (e.g., Hodeir 1962), discursive connections between Django's ethnoracial origins, his persona, and his music intensified precipitously starting in the 1950s (after his death). Among the critics who drew the most attention to Django's background was Delaunay, though he did not explicitly attribute Django's musical style to his Manouche background. Immediately following Django's death, Delaunay actually refuted these perceived associations, writing in the June 1953 edition of *Jazz Hot* that

> Some jazz critics have reproached Django for the Tsigane character of his music. Without denying his origins, it seems to us that the connection is, to say the least, fortuitous, and at most motivated by the nature of the instrument. . . . His taste for the arabesque remained in the purest tradition of artists such as Benny Carter, Barney Bigard, and Eddie South, whom it would be difficult to consider as musicians of Tsigane essence! (1953, 11)

However, in his full-length biography of Django, Delaunay resorts to racial stereotypes to explain his eccentric behavior. Though at times he treats Django's idiosyncrasies as entirely his own, he refers numerous times to the "primitive" character of his nomadic "tribe" that gave rise to his personality, characterizing them as a paranoid, superstitious, "backward," "medieval" people who have "oriental traditions" and a history of stealing children (1954, 13–14).[19] Delaunay speculates that had Django been raised among Gadjé, had he "opened his mind to the mysteries of a modern civilization, he might have lost his purity and the richness of his gifts for invention" (14), yet he rejects the notion that "all his racial brothers are natural musicians" and asserts that Django's "glory belonged to him alone" (16). Still, he emphasizes Django's fidelity to his ethnoracial group and his fundamental, enduring Romani character (14). As the most comprehensive biography of Django written by someone who knew him intimately, Delaunay's book has significantly influenced popular understandings of Django's persona and ethnoracial background, especially in terms of continuities between the two.

Years later, Panassié similarly described Django as "essentially a Gypsy" (Panassié and Casalta 1975, 211) who "was what one calls in English a 'natural' musician. He was also a 'primitive,' in the good sense of the word. He was a Gypsy, and he had these qualities" (210). It is unclear here whether Panassié still believed at this point, as he had in the 1940s, that Django's Romani background could be heard in his music. In the same piece, Panassié also says that Django expressed a strong sense of "solidar[ity]" with his Manouche community (211), an aspect of his biography that he had not mentioned in writings published while the guitarist was still alive.[20]

Both Delaunay's and Panassié's accounts point to an important shift in narratives about Django: while his Manouche background was invoked before and after his death as an influence on his *individual* character, attention to his relationship with a Manouche *collectivity* became more pronounced posthumously.[21] Perhaps public fascination with Django's premature death and initiatives to memorialize him galvanized a desire for knowledge about his kin. In addition to the release of Delaunay's book detailing Django's relationships with his immediate and extended family, there was the nine-part serial publication of "La Légende de Django Reinhardt" by Yves Salgues in *Jazz Magazine* from 1957 to 1958. A work of historical fiction, the series makes frequent reference to the behaviors of Django's "race" or "tribe" and recreates intimate moments between the guitarist and his family members as well as interactions with hordes of his Romani "brothers." In the final part of the series, Salgues attributes Django's musicality to racial determinants, writing that "music [and] jazz had brought Django to his race. His race brought Django to music, to jazz. Born like that, not otherwise, he lived like that and not otherwise. Perhaps never before was such a good destiny dedicated to such a powerful atavistic inevitability" (1958, 32).

The 1958 historical fiction film by Paul Paviot, *Django Reinhardt*, draws similar connections between Django's ethnoracial community, his personality, and his music. Much of the film juxtaposes images of Romani caravans and gatherings with a soundtrack of Django recordings and voiceovers (narrated by Chris Marker) describing Django's devotion to the Manouche people. An early scene shows images of Samois-sur-Seine, Django's home in the 1950s and final resting place, accompanied by a romanticizing description of how he was drawn to "the elements, water, clouds, all that is moving and unstable like his race." The final scenes of the film feature clips of Romani children, Django's brother Joseph, his widow Naguine, and his son Babik passing in and out of their roulottes on the dingy outskirts of Paris, accompanied by the following narration: "Perhaps a legend will develop about the Gypsy who had accepted this incredible adventure to go live in the city, and it will appear as fascinating to young Manouches as to us, Tarzan among monkeys." Near the film's closing, the narrator states that an objective of the film is "to recover, through the memory of Django, and through all that which is Gypsy in us, the rhythm of a life and of a freedom that he brought to fruition with the candor and the stubbornness of a gentle beast" (Paviot 1958).

This objective—to awaken a sense of "life" and "freedom" through a racially inflected homage to Django's life, his music, and humanity's inner "Gypsy"—invites viewers to understand Django's legacy as sonorously uniting Django with Manouches, Manouches with each other, and the viewing public with an otherwise disdained population. This was not lost on critic Michel-Claude Jalard, who wrote in a 1958 review of the film:

> *Django's creation is inseparable from the Tzigane race from which he came,* whose sensibility he had, whose spirituality he shared and for which his art, because of his greatness, represents one of its best chances to communicate with the hostile world on whose margins he lives. In sum it was necessary [for the film] not only to render the work of Django present, but to make [the audience] feel that in recognizing itself in [the music], an entirely misunderstood and scorned people becomes present to us. (1958, 13; emphasis added)

Testimonies by Django's immediate family members after his death have reinforced public understandings of Django's significance to his community and the significance of his ethnoracial background to his music. In an episode of the television program *Sept jours du monde* (1964), Naguine Reinhardt is interviewed about her late husband in the midst of a tightly packed group presumed to be her Manouche family, complete with several musicians performing Django's famous composition "Nuages." And Babik Reinhardt's foreword to a published collection of Django-related memorabilia states:

> My father was, of course, a giant of the jazz world and all his admirers know that he was Tsigane. But many people don't recognize the enormous effect that being Tsigane had on his music, which, in fact, transcended jazz. . . . Above all, my father was a Tsigane. (1994, 1)

In the decades after Django's death, commentaries that drew explicit causal links between his music, his ethnoracial roots, and his broader Romani community (like Babik Reinhardt's homage above) flourished in books, magazines, films, and other media; it is possible to cite only a small fraction of these.[22] In addition to the French sources addressed here, English-language commentaries to the same effect abound.[23] Some of the sources dating from the 1980s and later highlight the fact that jazz manouche remains an important tradition among numerous Manouche communities. However, many of these sources tend to conflate Django's music with jazz manouche, relying on ethnoracially tinged presumptions that reinforce ahistorical conceptions of Django's music and its supposed continuity with jazz manouche.[24]

I have focused primarily on accounts generated in the decade or so following Django's death in order to demonstrate how the beginnings of such ethnoracializing narratives set a precedent for the emergence of jazz manouche. These narratives would later allow musicians, nonprofit organizations, critics, and others in the music industry to frame Manouches as the natural inheritors of Django's legacy and to capitalize on an exoticized identity in the marketing of jazz manouche. Django would be exalted as a "hero" for Manouches from both emic and etic perspectives (Williams 2000; Antonietto and Billard 2004). Although Django's musical styles never displayed any discernibly Manouche influences, listeners from various backgrounds came to retroactively project these influences onto his music anyway, further cementing its putatively ethnoracial character in the popular imagination (Williams 2015, 117–18). Django's musicality is now frequently perceived as a product of, simultaneously, his incomparable genius *and* his (innate and/or inculcated) Manouche expressivity, eliding any distinction between the artist and his art, a stance that often exhibits the "oblivious racism" Antonietto once decried (1984, 77).

Articulating a Collective Practice

The first known reference to an emergent practice based on Django's music dates only from 1959, when the critic Michel-Claude Jalard published his article on "the Tsigane school of jazz."[25] He writes that "by jazz tsigane, we mean jazz music created by musicians of the Tsigane race. It is really about a race" (1959, 54). After speculating for several paragraphs about what may be particularly "Tsigane" about this "school," he concludes that

> neither the [musical] tradition, nor the Tsigane condition [of oppression] imply, in parallel to the rise of Black jazz, the advent of a jazz tsigane. But the one and the other reflect characteristic elements that were Django's to crystallize [through] his prodigious talent: the Tsigane milieu that manifests such a particular expressivity, the destiny of the Tsiganes that orients them toward an art of improvisation, the conjunction of the one and the other that fixes these musicians on certain instruments, the violin and especially the guitar. (1959, 56)

Jalard's hypothesis that Romanies inherently possess "characteristic elements," chief among them "expressivity," links Django's musical genius to ethnoracially determined factors ("the destiny of the Tsiganes" to improvise on certain instruments). His speculation about Romani "expressivity" is central to his definition of jazz tsigane, as is the identification of Django as the catalyst that gave rise to it.

Jalard divides the Tsigane school into two groups: the "followers" who imitate aspects of Django's music and the "continuers" who seek to innovate upon the stylistic precedents set by him (1959, 66),[26] referring to the groups as representative of "folklore" and "art," respectively (73). Though he demonstrates a clear preference for the latter group, he claims that the two are aesthetically united by their ethnoracial identity:

> Django's musical universe is for them a common language because in addition to his art, and through him, they discover an instrumental lyricism that speaks to their own sensibilities. This "ethnic supplement," if one can say that, means that Django is not only the master of a conception of the guitar . . . but truly the leader of a Tsigane school of jazz. It explains how [this school] *coincides almost exactly with an ethnic group*. . . . (72; emphasis added)

After Django's death, his guitar accompanists continued to perform his music in and around Paris. Some took inspiration from his late work and developed styles that followed modern jazz trends of the day. Others, such as Matelo Ferret, gravitated more toward *swing musette*, a style of jazz-infused, waltz-centered musette. Although the musicians in Jalard's original "Tsigane school" built on Django's success and were strongly influenced by him, they branched out in idiosyncratic directions that did not, on their own, cohere into an independent genre called "jazz manouche."[27]

Jalard was one of the earliest critics to speak of a "jazz tsigane," and the first to publish a detailed treatise arguing that the essences of both Django's music and that of other Romani musicians were contingent upon ethnoracial belonging. Although the musicians Jalard identified in his 1959 article did not subsequently form the core of the jazz manouche genre, his writing marked a consequential moment in the discursive linkage between musical style and ethnoracial identity to which future writings on the genre would refer.[28] For example, in several articles, social worker and prominent jazz manouche festival organizer Michel Lefort draws on Jalard's article to support his descriptions of the contemporary jazz manouche scene, writing that for Manouches in the 1990s, jazz manouche had become "a sign of recognition, internally (between members of the community) and externally (in their representation to the Gadjo world)" (1991, 114; see also Lefort 1990, 1994, 1997). Other key figures in jazz manouche scholarship and popular media from the 1980s onward, such as Alain Antonietto and François Billard (2004) and Patrick Williams (1998, 2000, 2004), also refer to Jalard's article as an important discursive turn in the genesis of jazz manouche.

Ultimately, the jazz manouche genre that came to be associated with French Romanies would adhere to the imitative, "folkloric" model outlined by Jalard. This genre developed only after the adoption and specialization of QHCF-style jazz by French Manouche communities. Jalard's notion of "jazz tsigane" as an expressive approach to jazz would later give way to a much broader recognition of "jazz manouche" (sometimes also called "jazz tsigane") as a codified tradition with explicit ties to such communities.

Jazz, Sinti Political Consciousness, and Musik Deutscher Zigeuner

Jazz in a QHCF style might not have become such a widespread familial practice among French Manouches were it not for both the mobility and the religious practices of the families of Jalard's "continuers." In the 1950s and 1960s, French Manouche and Gitan musicians mingled with their West German Sinti cousins during trips to places such as Lourdes, France, primarily as part of Christian pilgrimages or conventions.[29] A "Tsigane and Gitan gala" organized by the pro-Romani journal *Études tsiganes* in March 1967 was also an important occasion for West German Sinti musicians to encounter French Manouche and Gitan jazz musicians from Django's inner circle, in addition to musicians, dancers, acrobats, and animal trainers from various other Romani subgroups (Vaux de Foletier 1967).[30] In conjunction with the circulation of Django recordings, jazz inspired by him and the QHCF spread through these encounters as a performance practice among Romani groups beyond Paris.

Among the West German Sinti who participated in the 1960s pilgrimages and performing at the 1967 gala were a violinist and singer named Schnuckenack Reinhardt and his cousins. In a 1997 interview with Michel Lefort, the West German Gadjo student-turned-entrepreneur Siegfried Maeker describes his spearheading of the *Musik Deutscher Zigeuner* album series with Schnuckenack as the front man, beginning in the 1960s.[31] Maeker's objectives were both entrepreneurial and political: in developing a new market niche for Sinti music, he aimed to increase the visibility of Sinti cultures and communities. After befriending several Sinti musicians, Maeker organized concerts to "document" and showcase the music they played for themselves and had never performed for a general audience (Lefort and Maeker 1997, 19). This music comprised numerous styles, including those learned from the Polish and Czech Roma whom Schnuckenack had encountered in Nazi concentration camps, as well as jazz inspired by the QHCF and Django's prewar recordings. Maeker emphasizes that although they were familiar with some of Django's music from recordings, West German Sinti desired to learn to play it via personal contact with those who had been close to him. As a result of this "direct" transmission during pilgrimages and other travel opportunities, "Django's music entered the repertoire of German Sinti and became a sort of folkloric music. . . . They knew all the melodies *without knowing where they came from*" (Lefort and Maeker 1997, 20; emphasis in original).

However, the more traditional Romani styles remained fundamental to the Musik Deutscher Zigeuner collective (hereinafter MDZ), especially considering Maeker's vision of "documenting" the familial musical practices of the Sinti he knew. For the purposes of generic categorization, I will call these traditional styles *csárdás*, since the majority of the pieces in question can be stylistically classified as such and are referred to collectively by Manouches and Sinti as "Hungarian" (even though a number of pieces exhibit possible influences from other Central and Eastern European styles). MDZ's sonic signature became not a true fusion but a *juxtaposition* of csárdás with QHCF-inspired jazz. For example, the first MDZ album (known as *Musik Deutscher Zigeuner 1* following the release of subsequent MDZ albums) includes three tunes that are most accurately described as the *friss* (fast) sections of csárdás, as well as nine jazz tunes (seven of which are jazz standards recorded by Django and two of which he composed) and two waltzes. The principal distinction between the jazz and csárdás repertoires is rhythmic: the jazz pieces swing using the QHCF-associated pompe technique on the rhythm guitar, whereas the csárdás pieces are played straight, usually in an offbeat-dominant 2/4. Waltzes are more closely affiliated with the jazz repertoire, as they come directly from the swing musette tradition represented by Matelo Ferret and others with no discernible influence from any Eastern or Central European genres.

The combination of jazz and csárdás could simply mean an alternation between jazz and csárdás within the same piece, such as in the song "Lass maro tschatschepen" (composed and sung by guitarist Häns'che Weiss). However, their jazz tunes often exhibited distinctive csárdás elements, such as heavier, brisker rhythm guitar strokes than one would hear on Django's recordings. Later MDZ albums would exhibit a greater degree of crossover between the styles within pieces, especially in original compositions with sung lyrics in Romani. Schnuckenack's csárdás-grounded violin style remains fairly consistent across the MDZ repertoire, characterized by fits of scalar and arpeggiated runs that push ahead of the beat with heavy legato bowing; frequent use of intense, consistently paced vibrato; and conspicuous slides and ornamentations, especially trills, among other features.

Despite MDZ's transformation of jazz into "a sort of folkloric music," Maeker believed that jazz had the potential to afford far more cultural and social capital to West German Sinti than the traditional Romani musics they were familiar with:

> Another thing that was important to me at the start: Sinti musicians always wanted to put on the little Hungarian folkloric jacket [i.e., to play the part of the "traditional" Romani musician]. I said to them, "No, [that's] a cliché in the mind of the ordinary German for whom Tsigane music equals Hungarian music, operetta . . . who thinks that the Tsigane plays for the eyes of the clientele of good restaurants, a servile thing." I told them: "It's better if you earn money without doing that, with a little more pride, with dignity." And they followed this advice . . . and felt that it was very well accepted by the public. (Lefort and Maeker 1997, 21)

By performing Django's music in addition to the stereotypically "Tsigane" styles MDZ musicians already knew, the demeaning, metaphorical "little Hungarian folkloric jacket" could be tossed aside. As Maeker suggested, incorporating jazz repertoire allowed the musicians to present themselves as modern, innovative, and respectable. Music inspired by Django and the QHCF appeared to offer these Sinti an antidote to degrading stereotypes and greater opportunities to be taken seriously as artists.

This appeal to artistic (and social) legitimacy coincided with the leftist political sentiments of the time, as Maeker recalls: "It was the era of the student revolts in '68 and these [students] invited Sinti musicians [to perform]. It was right in line with their political agenda to defend the rights of minorities" (Lefort and Maeker 1997, 21).[32] The formation of MDZ was also directly related to a growing Romani rights movement in West Germany, which had begun quietly in 1956 and gained public momentum in the late 1970s (Margalit and Matras 2013, 110–11). As Maeker recounts, "We were ten years before the beginning of the *Civil Rights Movement of the Gipsies in Germany* [*sic*]. . . . We were a little avant-garde in a political sense" (Lefort and Maeker 1997, 21; emphasis in original). Maeker was especially concerned with the failure of West German society to adequately recognize that Romanies had been racially targeted for persecution and extermination. Yet his intended audience was not only West German: a 1969 promotional article in a French journal lists the various West German, Austrian, and Swiss cities in which MDZ had performed and provides short biographies of MDZ musicians, describing the experiences of those who had survived Nazi concentration camps (Maeker 1969, 13–15). Maeker advertised MDZ's ethnoracial specificity as an asset, promoting the "ancestral tradition" of German Sinti music whose only outside influence was "that of 'hot' jazz, which the glory of Django made popular, beginning in the 1930s, among all the musicians of his race" (14).

Although MDZ's music rarely communicated any overt political appeals—the major exception being the aforementioned 1977 recording "Lass maro tschatschepen" (Romani for "Let's Take Our Rights"), in which Häns'che Weiss urges Sinti to abandon their silence about the atrocities of the Holocaust and to demand recognition of their plight[33]—it was important to showcase this distinctively Sinti music in the context of pro-Romani political efforts. MDZ's unique combination of traditional and (relatively) modern musics allowed them to assert a novel aesthetic conception of Sinti identity: one that reflected both adherence to familial heritage and adaptability to new influences, and one that indexed a transnational ethnoracial affiliation with their French Manouche "cousins." Maeker and MDZ members self-consciously cultivated this performance style not just as a commercially viable strategy or as a genuinely pleasurable musical experience (though it certainly was both), but as a means to draw attention to the political struggles of German Sinti while articulating a new, relatively cosmopolitan conception of Sinti identity.

Alsatian Manouches and the Discovery of Django

Several of my Alsatian Manouche interlocutors have told me that Django's music was not well received by many Manouches during his lifetime and for some years after his death. At least, Manouches at this time were reportedly not eager to listen to it in group settings, let alone reproduce it as a community practice; jazz was deemed too "modern" for their tastes. Alsatian Manouche accordionist Marcel Loeffler told me that growing up in the 1970s, older members of his family "said they liked Django, but at the same time, we knew that it wasn't their preferred music. For them, Tsigane music was the music of Eastern Europe that came mainly from Hungary."[34] This included recordings by Hungarian violinist Yoska Nemeth and Romanian violinist Georges Boulanger, "great violinists like that. They played csárdás, 'Dark Eyes,' violins [that made you] cry." In part because Alsatian Manouches were already fond of such music, typically performed by violinists whose techniques and repertoires resembled those of Schnuckenack Reinhardt, MDZ's generic amalgam provided a model and an entry point for these Manouches to explore jazz performance.[35]

Alsatian Manouches experienced a revelation of sorts when they first heard Schnuckenack and his quintet at a performance near Strasbourg in December 1970. In an article on the history of music among Alsatian Manouches, Patrick Andresz, a history teacher and guitarist intimately connected with the Alsatian jazz manouche scene, describes the concert:

> On stage, Schnuckenack, bursting with charisma, sings and plays violin. The solo guitarist is the young virtuoso Häns'che Weiss, while the bassist, Hojok Merstein, will be the pillar of the quintet for years to come. It is the first time that an orchestra composed of Sinti musicians takes to the stage in Alsace. . . . These German Manouche musicians have just unveiled a new horizon. In Alsace, the shake-up is going to be important. (2015, 136–37)

In personal conversations with me, Patrick has gesturally described the reaction of the numerous Manouches in the audience as lifting off their seats in astonishment. He writes that the first Alsatian Manouches to publicly perform Django's music were a guitarist named Poro Reinhardt and his family members, who performed in a Strasbourg café in the early 1970s. Unfortunately, their success was confined to this venue and they left no recordings, so the birth of this practice in Alsace remains sonically undocumented (Andresz 2015).[36]

In an interview with me, Mandino Reinhardt, one of the most celebrated Manouche guitarists in Alsace, recalled taking up the guitar right around this point of transition, at the age of fifteen in the early 1970s: "in the heart of the [Strasbourg] neighborhood where we lived . . . one day, [the chaplain] Marcel Daval brought the sons of Piton Reinhardt, who was Django's cousin, and they played so wonderfully that I decided, all of a sudden, that I wanted to do that."[37] Mandino noted that he had already known about Django through his grandfather, who knew a few Django tunes, but that this music did not truly impact Manouches in the region until Schnuckenack and his quintet came to perform: "it's thanks to him that many people today play this music. . . . Thanks to Schnuckenack, we *really* get in touch with Django, in his music, and we say to ourselves: 'What a genius!'"

As a result of their live performances, recordings, and Maeker's intensive promotion efforts, MDZ spurred a "rediscovery" of Django's music as performed by Manouches, inspiring some to proclaim, "we have our own music!" (Williams 2000, 415). Alsatian Manouches began to see and hear themselves in the music of MDZ and to develop associations between their musical aesthetics and a sense of ethnoracial belonging. For these Manouches, MDZ recordings were soon supplemented by an influx of reissued Django recordings that enabled musicians to learn his jazz from the original source. Musicians would listen repeatedly to, and imitate, these vinyl records, a process later facilitated by the introduction of cassette tape technology (Williams 2000, 415). Cassette technology also allowed musicians to produce and circulate their own recordings, further enhancing familial transmission. They were primarily concerned with reproducing (and in some cases, simplifying) musical material from Django and the QHCF's pre-1946 recordings. Within a decade of Schnuckenack's first performance in Alsace, a repertoire combining MDZ and Django's music had become both an emblem of ethnoracial identity and a cultural practice among Alsatian Manouches. Over time, musicians' grounding in their own traditional (so-called Hungarian) music and their affinity with MDZ would give way to a much stronger emphasis on QHCF-style jazz, though the significance of MDZ currently persists among (mostly older-generation) Alsatian Manouches.

APPONA's Cultural Activism

By the time Alsatian Manouches began performing jazz in the MDZ model, an international pan-Romani rights movement had taken shape, with the first Romani World Congress taking place in London in 1971. In France, although very few Manouches participated in this nationalist movement, local and regional associations formed around the same time to address the needs of Romani populations facing poverty and racial discrimination ("Les Associations Membres par Région").[38] Also around this time, French nonprofit organizations and pro-Romani publications began to promote jazz as a distinctive Romani performance genre, in addition to other, more traditionally recognized Romani musics. Journals such as *Monde Gitan* (published quarterly by the Association Notre-Dame des Gitans, a Catholic organization) and *Études tsiganes* (an academic and activist journal now edited by the nonprofit La Fédération Nationale des Associations Solidaires d'Action avec les Tsiganes et les Gens du Voyage) printed reviews of French and German Romani jazz musicians alongside scholarly and advocacy-oriented articles about French Romanies. Maeker's 1969 promotional article for MDZ, which communicated his activist aims in West Germany to a French audience, as well as synopses of Jalard's writings that linked Django's music to French Manouche communities, were among these.

One nonprofit organization, the Association pour la Promotion des Populations d'Origine Nomade d'Alsace (APPONA), was an especially decisive force in the development of jazz manouche in Alsace and beyond. Run mainly by Gadjé but with a limited degree of Manouche leadership, APPONA was founded in 1974 following a spate of discriminatory actions, some violent, against several Alsatian Manouche communities. Until its closure in 2002, APPONA undertook a variety of projects aimed at countering anti-Romani racism and bettering the lives of Romanies, primarily Manouches, in Alsace. In addition to facilitating access to adequate housing, education, healthcare, and employment, APPONA sought to enhance public opinion of and engagement with Manouches by promoting its constituents' artistic practices. Music in particular was seen as a way to bolster self-confidence, to build relationships with Gadjé, to mitigate what APPONA called the "ethnocide" of Manouche culture, and to develop an economic niche for Manouche performers. APPONA organized concerts, festivals, recording projects, professionalization programs, and even its own music school with Mandino Reinhardt as the longtime principal instructor. According to Andresz, APPONA founders were inspired by "the spirit of May [19]68" and realized that "social action and music could be complementary" (2015, 138).

The earliest documented cultural promotion project that APPONA spearheaded was the tour of a roulotte over two weeks in August 1974. The tour, called "Le Voyage en roulotte," brought five young Manouche musicians and three chaperones through a handful of Alsatian villages to perform their music in hopes of generating intercultural dialogue. The culminating performance took place in the Polygone, the Romani-dominated section of the low-income, ethnoracially diverse neighborhood of Neuhof on the southern edge of Strasbourg. Following the tour, APPONA president and founding member Marcel Daval wrote:

> Alsace, which has demonstrated time and again a veritable racism [toward Manouches], showed this time that it also had a heart sensitive to their music and to their issues. Racism often results from ignorance of the other; this is why it is preferable to show to Gadjé the other side of the Gypsy world, before hostilities are unleashed. (1974, 14)

Another such early endeavor aimed explicitly at Gadjé was the "Tzigane Cultural Week" in 1977 featuring musical performances, film screenings, art exhibitions, and a conference intended to "overcome prejudices." As one Manouche participant explained, "we are proud of our race and we would like to make [others] understand this sentiment" ("Musique, films et artisanat" 1977). Projects like these sought to mitigate anti-Manouche racism both by emphasizing the common humanity of Manouches and Gadjé *and* by glorifying Manouche difference as expressed through music. Celebrating Manouches for their ethnoracial alterity was, somewhat paradoxically, a way to productively fold them into majority society: as a marketable asset, it could become a resource for economic incorporation.

Other archival materials further demonstrate that APPONA sought to define Manouche ethnorace in opposition to a normative and unmarked Gadjo population. APPONA literature frequently makes reference to a Manouche or Tsigane "world," implicitly characterized as self-contained and alien to Gadjé, existing in or alongside but not of the Gadjo "world." APPONA's vision was to "integrate" Manouches into majority society in a way that protected certain cultural specificities that the organization deemed worthy of "saving"—namely, artistic practices, language, methods of generating income, and mobile residences. This integration, in turn, would require change within the majority society such that these cultural specificities would be accepted as constituting part of—not contradictions to—the social fabric of Alsace and of France more broadly.

Musical performance was considered an ideal means to achieve integration in these respects. On the one hand, it was a form of skilled labor that, with proper guidance and cultivation, could generate sustainable income and renew a sense of self-sufficiency among Manouches. On the other hand, it was deemed a "universal language," one that would facilitate widespread acceptance of Manouche people into local communities. For these reasons, APPONA privileged music over other Manouche cultural practices in the fight against ethnocide, as captured in a 1997 project proposal:

> Contrary to what people habitually think, Tsigane society is heterogeneous[;] there are the same sociological strata, as in all societies, poor, middle class, comfortable, rich. But all, whether sedentary or itinerant, find and recognize themselves in music. During a concert [or] a festival, when the Tsigane orchestra is on stage, it is the entire Tsigane people that is on stage.[39]

By unambiguously using musical performance in the service of non-musical activist objectives, APPONA rendered music expedient.

Music was also regarded as the quintessential expression of an inalienable Romani essence. In 1978, APPONA member Georges Kautzmann wrote in APPONA promotional materials that Romani music was "free language or the shout of the socialized man" and "more instinctive than interiorized, more natural than civilized."[40] The same year, an anonymous author wrote in the region's largest daily newspaper *Dernières nouvelles d'Alsace*, "Music gives rhythm to the journey of the Gypsy people across its history, as if it were the heart of it" ("Concert pour une symphonie tzigane" 1978). Throughout APPONA's documentation, music—and in particular, Romani music—is described as an affective link between the lived present moment and a past otherwise lost to history (see chapter 5 for more on these temporal contiguities). Parallels between cultural purity, nature, travel, memory, and music are drawn and redrawn with varying degrees of essentialization. According to this discourse, Manouches are closer to nature than Gadjé and their culture is defined by freedom (both in terms of literal, physical mobility and in more figurative, spiritual terms). Echoing Jalard's and others' descriptions of Django and his milieu from the 1950s, these Manouche qualities are presented as finding their purest, most potent manifestation through music. Through these emphases, APPONA attempted to override negative stereotypes with another essentializing cultural discourse. Ethnoracially specific musical practices were considered worth salvaging for the benefit of all, Manouches or Gadjé, but more importantly for the survival of Manouche culture itself.

APPONA also promoted music as a vital, structuring element of contemporary Manouche life and culture and as a meaningful practice aside from any expediency it may have offered. In the above-cited newspaper article, Mandino is quoted as saying, "The music that we feel, it's our entire life, and we express our life through music in celebration. Django Reinhardt gave us a lot in allowing us to express our freedom" ("Concert pour une symphonie tzigane"). For Mandino, jazz inspired by Django is the ultimate means to "express" a great deal about a shared Manouche identity (notably, through non-discursive semiotic modalities). He reiterated this sentiment to me in a 2014 interview, saying that Manouches "feel the [cultural] root through the music of Django. It's first of all for that that we play." The music school he led was a principal means to ensure intra-community social cohesion—a necessary precondition for outward-facing cultural activism, and an objective in itself—as he told me: "the first step, the first concern for APPONA, was to reintegrate music into Manouche families. First, the familial recognition of [this music], its belonging. And then sharing [it], then opening [it up to the outside world], of course."

While APPONA initially promoted other musics performed by Manouches, jazz eventually became the preeminent genre. Concert and festival programs from the late 1970s and 1980s advertised performances by local Manouche musicians of "traditional Tzigane music" as well as "jazz," and sometimes both within the same ensembles. Texts such as the following in APPONA brochures of the 1970s and 1980s presented jazz as a music inherently appropriate to Manouches:

> Django Reinhardt [was] the founder of the [Quintette du] Hot Club de France,[41] the leader of French jazz, a Tsigane, a Sinto, like them. [Tsiganes] had learned his tunes and they played them trembling, so [powerfully] did they tell of the life of their people, their freedom. Jazz [had] its roots in Negro spirituals, prayer, the shout of black slaves in America. Django had also unleashed his own shout, around the 1930s, unsettling traditional Tsigane music, renewing the language of his ancestors, recounting in his own way the long tragedy of his people across history. (Daval 1982, 6)

It was (and is) not uncommon for some to draw parallels between the Manouche experience in France and the African American experience in the United States, however dissimilar these situations have been, and to portray jazz as the natural, historically rooted musical expression of both oppressed racial groups (a subject further explored in chapter 4). Problematic as these comparisons certainly are, APPONA leaders saw them as a means to articulate the importance of music for Manouches in the struggle for social change.

Other sources also document this shift toward jazz. In a 1989 coauthored article, longtime APPONA employees Marcel Daval and Pierre Hauger list a number of musical genres that the Manouches they worked with "like[d] to listen to and to play" in the mid-1980s, including "traditional music for violin of Hungarian inspiration (csárdás) or, more generally Balkan," "waltzes," "classic jazz: swing, middle-jazz, up to certain aspects of bebop and 'cool' style," and "classic Brazilian bossa nova," among others (1989, 480–81). The authors note that by the time of their article's publication, the number and proportion of performing ensembles devoted to jazz had increased conspicuously: "[In 1966,] 5 out of the 9 [Alsatian Manouche] ensembles . . . played primarily variety music. . . . By contrast, all [17] current ensembles practice jazz, with 3 among them incorporating Hungarian-inspired music, and only 1 [incorporating] variety music" (484).[42]

By the 1980s, jazz had become a familial practice that adults transmitted to children. Gigi Loeffler and fellow Manouche guitarist Billy Weiss once told me that growing up in the 1980s and 1990s, they listened to Django's recordings with awe. When they heard their family members playing similar music, they realized, "Wow, we can do this, too!" For them, Django's music was not confined to mythical recordings, but was something children could actively participate in. The immersive, community aspect of musical performance among Manouches was an important factor in the younger generations' adoption of jazz. Daval and Hauger write that in the 1980s, the musical practices of typical Gadjo children were "less skillful and rich in potential developments than the jazz on which young Manouches cut their teeth" (1989, 479). In part, the recognition of this distinction between the musical practices of Manouches and Gadjé, and of Manouche processes of musical transmission, allowed Manouche communities to build reputations as notable jazz musicians.

Developing the marketability of this music was a chief concern for APPONA. The shift toward jazz was shaped by the organization's encouragement of QHCF-inspired jazz as the most prestigious ethnoracially specific—and the most commercially viable—Alsatian Manouche music.[43] Daval and Hauger (1989, 483–84) write that there was a stronger demand among more affluent Gadjo audiences for jazz than for other musics, a demand to which Manouche ensembles adapted (see also Andresz 2015). Around the inception of APPONA's music school in 1978, Mandino's oral method of instruction was hailed as traditionally Manouche and the "authentic" way to learn jazz, an advantage that Manouches held over Gadjé. Other APPONA members sought to teach students extramusical skills such as advertising and time management. Through initiatives aimed at professionalization, guided by a neoliberal ethos of entrepreneurialism and self-sufficiency, students would learn to become good performers and to build sustainable careers as musicians (see chapter 2).

One of APPONA's "success stories" is Francky Reinhardt, a Manouche guitarist who currently leads the jazz manouche ensemble Di Mauro Swing. In an interview with me, Francky stated that he had enrolled in the school at age eleven as part of its first cohort, beginning with instruction on rhythm guitar. Early on in his instruction, he still "followed the traditional thing more." When I asked him what he meant by "traditional," he responded, "Everything that's violin. In the old days, we listened to a lot of csárdás. Especially at birthday parties, you saw that, too. We played live, without microphones." Mandino introduced students to Django compositions such as "Minor Swing," which Francky enjoyed upon first hearing; he told me, "I still play it now, because I adore it," and that "[we students] learned slowly, but well." After a few years of studying Django's music with Mandino, and after the gradual adoption of jazz by his own community as well as the rise in popularity of QHCF-style jazz among paying audiences, Francky dedicated the rest of his professional career to, as he called it throughout our interview, jazz manouche.

The text of a mid-1980s promotional flyer for Francky's ensemble at that time, Le Quartet Reinhardt, reflects this reorientation toward jazz:

> Outside the bounds of formal musical institutions, and under the legendary auspices of Django Reinhardt, Manouches continue to teach each other and to bring their music to life. The Quartet Reinhardt is part of this new generation of guitarists for whom swing and the sense of improvisation are like a native tongue. What they propose to us is a musical itinerary: first, that of the Hot Club of the 1930s, where swing and Parisian popular music took root together, but also an original, unprecedented approach to more recent and diverse musical universes (bossa nova, bebop), as well as remarkable personal compositions.[44]

By referring to "swing and the sense of improvisation" as "a native tongue," the text naturalizes jazz as a longstanding Manouche performance practice. While the advertisement focuses on the influence of Django on a "new generation of guitarists," its reference to other "musical universes," and to the versatility of these musicians, points to the parameters of a nascent genre. Bossa nova developed after Django's death and, together with several other styles not represented in his recorded work, became incorporated into jazz manouche as it was later conceived.[45]

A trio version of Francky's ensemble is included in a 1987 APPONA project proposal to perform at a Romani music festival in Hungary along with two other ensembles that grew out of the music school. In presenting these musicians, the authors of the proposal write that while it may seem "problematic" to include jazz musicians at such a festival, this is "justified" if one recognizes that these musicians "best illustrate the current state of the most authentic Manouche musical tradition."[46] They state that jazz manouche "has well and truly become a distinctive genre: for any attentive listener . . . jazz manouche is not the jazz of European or American Whites, and its particularities tend to bear more resemblances to other Tsigane musics."[47] The authors argue that, if what matters in the definition of a traditional Romani music is not so much its content as its approach, and if Romani music is characterized by a history of borrowing, then jazz manouche must in itself constitute a Manouche tradition. Furthermore, "simply because it fulfills the necessary function of a traditional mode of transmission and musical practice"—oral, immersive, community-based learning—"'jazz manouche' . . . should be considered traditional."[48]

It is especially remarkable that this 1987 proposal offers the first evidence in APPONA's archives of the use of *jazz manouche* to refer to a singular genre. By the early 1990s, the term *jazz manouche,* along with *swing manouche* and *jazz tzigane,* had begun to appear frequently in APPONA's promotional materials and in press about the organization, with the majority of local Manouche musicians categorized under these headings. APPONA documentation from the 1990s through its official closure in 2002 indicates that not only was *jazz manouche* used to classify what its musicians were performing at the time; it also retrospectively described the QHCF-inspired jazz that they had been performing since the 1970s. Although APPONA was probably not the first to use *jazz manouche* in reference to a specific genre, the term helped APPONA crystallize the Manouche musical brand it had been developing since the organization's establishment.

Thanks largely to APPONA and its educational and promotional efforts, Alsace remains one of the premier regions in France for Manouche-led jazz manouche production, though similar endeavors have also flourished elsewhere.[49] As part of his work as president of a government-funded agency that provides basic services for Gens du voyage in the Angers metropolitan area (southwest of Paris), Michel Lefort organized small-scale jazz events throughout the 1980s. Lefort expanded these concerts into the Festival Gipsy Swing, held almost annually from the mid-1990s until his retirement from social work in the mid-2010s (see chapter 5). Among other genres, this festival promoted musicians from Manouche backgrounds across France, including Alsace. Lefort wrote in 1991 of jazz manouche that "the public dimension of this music—professionals, concerts, recordings—is but a glimmer illuminating access to a musical and human universe that vibrates and warms itself by the thousand fires of an indescribable expressivity" (1991, 101). Lefort acted simultaneously as Manouche-serving social worker, as author of numerous articles on Manouche jazz practices (cited several times in this chapter), and as festival promoter. It is probably no coincidence that jazz manouche emerged as a genre closely associated with Manouche communities and Manouche expressivity around the same time that he engaged publicly in all these activities at once.

In addition to Lefort's efforts, APPONA's embrace and promotion of jazz manouche solidified the role of this music as an emblem of ethnoracial identity, both for Manouches themselves and for the wider public. The adoption of this music by Alsatian Manouche communities thus has a much more complex history than one of direct transmission from Django to his extended Manouche family. Attention to the wider social context of genre formation elucidates the processes by which ethnoracial identity, and the expressive forms that represent it, come into being, especially concerning the roles of ethnoracial outsiders. Gadjé such as Siegfried Maeker and Lefort, numerous members of APPONA, critics, managers, audience members, and others were crucial forces in this respect. Gadjo authors have emphasized the importance of music, and specifically of jazz manouche, as representative of Manouches: Django is "at the same time unique and other, himself and his people" (Antonietto and Billard 2004, 15); "this invention [jazz manouche] reproduced more or less literally has become an emblem of identity for Manouches: the music that is their music" (Williams 2000, 409). In everyday discourse, these kinds of statements are often made under the assumption that ethnoracial "identity" is necessarily a concern for those to whom it is ascribed. Such a "concern for the affirmation of [group] identity" (Daval and Hauger 1989, 483) may have arisen partly from Manouches' own anxieties about the fate of their communities, but this was not a purely internal phenomenon. Gadjé shared and shaped an interest in defining Manouches as a distinctive group, manifested through the cultivation and promotion of particular musical practices as a form of cultural activism. Some specific concerns about "identity" were just as invented as the tradition of jazz manouche itself.

Marketing Difference

Thanks in part to the promotional work by nonprofit organizations, and to the inclusion of Romani musics in a nascent French "world music" industry (Warne 1997), the term *jazz manouche* started to gain traction in French media. It began to appear in France's major newspapers in the 1970s (e.g., Marmande 1978). From the early 1980s up through the 1990s, a number of artists, especially those of Manouche background, advertised their music as "Manouche" and variations thereof. Examples include the albums *Manouche partie* by Jo Privat and Matelo Ferret, *Swing 93* by Gypsy Reunion, *Gypsy Music from Alsace* by Note Manouche,

Aimez-vous Brahms? by Les Manouches, and *Gypsy Guitars* by Ensemble la Roue Fleurie, among numerous others. Still, occurrences of the phrase *jazz manouche* and its analogues (various combinations of *jazz/swing* and *manouche/gitan/tsigane*) were rather infrequent in French music publicity and press before the early 2000s.

Around the turn of the millennium, jazz manouche quickly gained popularity with the French public as a genre in its own right. Michel "Mitch" Mercier, a guitarist who worked for over a decade at Universal Music France in Paris, explained the timeline of the genre's explosion to me:

MM: [In the early 2000s,] there was no Gypsy jazz.[50] You would go into the record shop, like FNAC,[51] and there was one record by Moreno, two by Romane, one by Angelo [Debarre], and one by [the] Rosenberg Trio. It was really nothing. And over the years, you could really see the shelf expand. Now you have, I don't know, three hundred references.

SL: And so back then, when it was still very small, where would you find these records, like in what categories?

MM: You had to ask the merchant. So it was sometimes in world music, sometimes in jazz. But now you have a dedicated shelf, "jazz manouche." . . . [Starting in the early 2000s, jazz manouche albums went from] five records to a hundred and fifty. It took five or six years.

Other factors in the rise of the genre's popularity included Woody Allen's film *Sweet and Lowdown* (released in the United States in 1999, and in France as *Accords et désaccords* in 2000), a fictional account of a swing-era guitarist who idolized Django. There was also the release of Tony Gatlif's film *Swing* in 2002, which stars Mandino Reinhardt and fellow Manouche guitarist Tchavolo Schmitt in the story of a young Gadjo who befriends members of Strasbourg's Manouche community. In the early 2000s, the acclaimed Alsatian Manouche guitarist Biréli Lagrène, who began his career performing jazz as a teenager in the late 1970s and quickly became internationally renowned across several genres, returned to his roots in Django's music and released the *Gypsy Project* and *Gipsy Project and Friends* albums.[52] Furthermore, the increased availability of recordings and information enabled by improved internet access bolstered interest in jazz manouche, especially among Gadjé who learn it as amateurs and who develop careers teaching and performing in the genre. Today, Mitch says, "in France, [the genre] has a status. People know what jazz manouche [is]. Even if they don't like it, or they don't know it very well, they know. But ten years ago, they didn't know. It was only for, you know, aficionados."[53]

Various publicity materials from the 2000s attest to the popularity of jazz manouche as well as the polyvalence of the term. The latter is used to denote jazz performed in a QHCF style and as a synonym for Django's music itself. An undated promotional brochure produced by FNAC is titled "Jazz Manouche: The Inheritors of Django" and lists twenty-five albums, including six reissues of Django recordings. The rest of the albums listed, including the motion picture soundtrack to *Swing,* were released between the early 1980s and the early 2000s. This means that the brochure effectively categorizes four decades' worth of music—the aforementioned late twentieth-century period and Django's recordings from the mid-1930s to the early 1950s, thus spanning seven decades—as jazz manouche. The selection of albums is fairly representative of the genre's most acclaimed stars of the 2000s, including Babik Reinhardt, Angelo Debarre, Mandino Reinhardt, Marcel Loeffler, Biréli Lagrène, Romane, Tchavolo Schmitt, Moreno, and Patrick Saussois, among others. A similarly broad assertion is made in the web publicity for the CD *Swing manouche: Anthologie 1933–2003,* which describes the release as representing "a panorama of all the Gypsy jazz recordings produced or re-released by the La Lichère and Frémeaux & Associés labels between 1933 and 2003."[54] A review of the album published on the same web page clarifies that the first disc of the collection spans the years 1933 to 1947, while the second begins in 1989 and "present[s] musics more or less influenced by Manouche music and sometimes very little by jazz," yet all such recordings are still grouped under the heading of "swing manouche." By 2007, jazz manouche was so well established that it could be spoken of as a style to be "enriched" and "enlarged" upon, as Benjamin Goldenstein and Patrick Frémeaux write on the web page for an album by the ensemble Gadjo Combo.[55]

As Mitch's account and these marketing materials suggest, the success of a jazz manouche industry correlated with the genre's increased recognition and consumption by a relatively wide audience. Keith Negus identifies this as a process in which "*an industry produces culture* and *culture produces an industry*" (1999, 14; emphasis in original; see also Taylor 2014). Negus writes that although the recording industry does not monolithically determine popular musical tastes, the notion of industry producing culture captures "how the music industry shapes the possibilities for creative practice and how this intersects with broader historical, social and cultural processes" (1999, 129). Complementarily, he refers to culture producing an industry in order to describe how music production occurs "in relation to broader culture formations and practices that are within neither the control nor the understanding of the company" (19). As I have shown, jazz manouche was not simply a label invented by music industry representatives. It was an extant phenomenon that gained popularity in a national and international marketplace through interactions between industry and culture, one whose "possibilities for creative practice" have been shaped, though not determined, by its small- and large-scale commodification. The widespread recognition of jazz manouche is thus due in large part to market demands on cultural production.

Reckoning with Ethnorace

Although not all French Manouches perform or listen to jazz manouche (Poueyto 2015), and although Manouche musical tastes are necessarily diverse and fluid, many Manouches (especially those in Alsace) consider it to be the most representative music of their communities. This remains the case despite a gradual decline in jazz manouche practice within Manouche communities across the nation. In France, the genre's popularity peaked in 2010 with the celebration of what would have been Django's one hundredth birthday, complete with festivals, album releases, and other promotional events and campaigns that drew on his cultural cachet. Since 2010, such attention has subsided somewhat in France, though the generic category remains highly recognizable. Today, "jazz manouche" is more likely to evoke a particular set of aesthetic elements than the Manouche communities indexed by the term.

Waning popularity notwithstanding, connections between the genre, its progenitor, and its namesake communities remain steadfast and simplified in French (and global) ethnoracial imaginaries. After Django's death, his ethnoracial background was transformed from a simple fact of his biography to a consequential personal trait, becoming ever more tightly bound to his musical aptitude and expressivity and leading some commentators to generalize about Manouche musicality more broadly. As Manouches began to perform music inspired by Django and the QHCF, associations between particular musical aesthetics and ethnoracial backgrounds were discursively naturalized, flattening out a history of musical transmission, concerted pro-Manouche advocacy, and marketing strategies into an essentialized continuity of inherited taste and talent. Ahistorical correlations between Django's music and its adoption as a Manouche practice became attractive both for Gadjo consumers of jazz manouche and for Manouche communities themselves.

This outline of the history of jazz manouche has shown how the genre, as well as ethnoracial imaginaries about Manouches, have informed one another since Django's postwar fame. More broadly, I have shown how genre and ethnoracial identities develop in tandem: both arise as convenient categories into which messy, disjointed histories can be distilled. Retrospective appraisals of Django's music, and the production of music inspired by it, reflect a great deal about how race and ethnicity are constituted in public spheres, pointing to the contingent and constructed nature of ethnorace globally. In the next chapter, I delve deeper into the story of APPONA and its living legacy to show how genre and ethnorace are also constituted through efforts to redefine cultural citizenship.

TWO

Cultural Activism's Living Legacies

In 2011, Mandino Reinhardt and Stella Funaro proposed an idea to the music school of the Social and Cultural Center of Neuhof, a neighborhood on the outskirts of Strasbourg. They wanted to establish a choir that would include Manouche women and others in the area. Stella and Mandino worked in Neuhof: she, for a youth nonprofit, and he as a guitar teacher. Both had long been concerned about the status of women in Neuhof's Manouche community, in which Mandino himself grew up. The choir was meant to provide local Manouche women with both an expressive outlet and a break from their domestic obligations, if only for an hour each week. By and large, Manouche women in Neuhof (as in many Manouche communities elsewhere) are expected to devote themselves to their husbands and children, leaving little time to pursue their own interests or to socialize outside the domestic sphere. They are also discouraged from performing publicly unless accompanied by a male family member, usually a spouse. Given that few opportunities exist for these Manouche women to branch out from such constraints, Mandino and Stella thought that a choir—one that, at the initiative of locally respected figures, publicly valorized their talent and knowledge—would help bolster women's senses of self-worth.

The choir was named the *C(h)œur des Femmes,* a pun meaning "choir (*chœur*) of women" and "heart (*cœur*) of women." Stella told me that from the start, "diversity" was a central concern, so the choir also included *partenaires*:

Gadjo teachers, social workers, and others who already worked with Manouche populations in some capacity. Despite the choir's name, it also welcomed a handful of men, including one Manouche man, to fill out the lower voices.[1] Since its inception, the choir has been directed by Anne Huber, a professional jazz and cabaret singer, and rehearses in Neuhof's music school. The repertoire typically consists of US jazz and gospel standards, popular French songs, and, importantly, jazz manouche tunes with lyrics in Manouche. These latter songs showcase Manouche members' talent in jazz vocals as well as the language itself, which few members of the Gadjo public are likely to hear in a musical setting. These songs also provide opportunities during rehearsals for Manouche choir members to give translations to Gadjo members, to coach the director and other singers in pronunciation, and to explain other linguistic features. In doing so, Manouche members exercise a degree of agency within the choir, foregrounding the value of their own language and their authority over its use.

After attending one of its concerts in December 2013, I joined the choir in January 2014 as a second soprano. In the six months during which I was a regular member, the choir rehearsed weekly and performed in public several times, including at an International Women's Day celebration, a charity event at a bank's corporate office, the end-of-year concert of Neuhof's music school, and, most significantly, the massive annual Romani pilgrimage to the southern French town of Saintes-Maries-de-la-Mer. In rehearsing and performing with the choir, and in socializing frequently outside of normal choir activities, I became close with several of its singers. Considering that most of my fieldwork was in the heavily male-dominated, professionally oriented world of jazz manouche, my time with the choir gave me a very different perspective on Manouche-Gadjo relations and on the lives, concerns, and aspirations of the choir's eclectic membership.

My participation in the choir also offered a window into the afterlife of the nonprofit organization L'Association pour la Promotion des Populations d'Origine Nomade d'Alsace (APPONA), which operated officially from 1974 until 2002.[2] Both Mandino and Stella had been leading figures in APPONA: he, the principal teacher of its music school, and she, the organization's secretary. The very inception of the choir represents a continuation of APPONA's socially progressive objectives well after the organization's demise, as Stella often pointed out to me. In fact, she told me on several occasions that APPONA "lives on" in the work of its former members and constituents. They endeavor to improve the material conditions of Manouche communities, to solidify inter- and intra-community bonds, and to project positive images of Manouches to the public.

This chapter explores the life and legacy of APPONA, from its activist origins to its present incarnations in initiatives such as the C(h)œur des Femmes. Propelled by racist actions against Alsatian Manouches in the early 1970s, a collective of Manouches and Gadjé established APPONA in 1974. For nearly three decades, it undertook a variety of projects aimed at countering anti-Manouche racism and improving the living conditions of Manouches in Alsace. APPONA members—leaders, volunteers, and employees—included both Gadjé and Manouches, though its volunteer base and much of its leadership tended to be predominantly Gadjo. They worked tirelessly to secure Manouches' access to adequate housing, education, healthcare, and employment, in addition to fostering stronger relationships between Manouches and other Alsatian populations.

Like some Romani cultural activists (e.g., in Hungary; see Kovalcsik 2010; Lange 1997), among others, APPONA also understood music to be an expedient means to achieve these social, economic, and political objectives (Yúdice 2003). It organized a plethora of concerts, staged one of the most renowned recurring music festivals in Strasbourg, enabled the production of several albums, founded a still-running music school, and logistically supported local Manouche musicians and ensembles, among other music-related activities. As detailed in chapter 1, these efforts were integral to the establishment of jazz manouche as a cultural practice among Alsatian Manouches and to the development of an Alsatian jazz manouche economy. This chapter further explores APPONA's cultural activist endeavors with regard to their long-term effects on musicians and their communities, institutional partnerships, and Manouche-Gadjo relations.

APPONA fully recognized the devastating economic effects that racializing governmental policies exerted on Manouche populations. I must stress that the majority of its efforts were designed first and foremost to alleviate poverty in sustainable ways. Its cultural activism often complemented these efforts, especially when it helped build the confidence of some constituents and strengthen senses of intra- and inter-community solidarity. However, this cultural activism relied at times on reductive conceptions of Manouche identity, such as the sonic "ethnoracialness" I detail in chapter 4. Adriana Helbig writes that pro-Romani nongovernmental organizations generally tend to promote "an essentialized, performance-focused identity" of their heterogeneous Romani constituents (2009, 170; see also Lemon 2000, 97). Similarly, APPONA tended to construct public images of Manouches as entertainers and as bearers of tradition whose value to society consisted primarily in these capacities.

This essentializing approach to cultural activism often took the form of what John L. and Jean Comaroff call "ethno-preneurialism," which "entails the management and marketing of cultural products and practices, *qua* intellectual property, as sources of value—indeed, as monopoly capital—inseparable from the being-and-bodies of their owner-producers" (2009, 51; see also Brubaker 2004 on "ethnopolitical entrepreneur[ship]"). Comaroff and Comaroff argue that, on the one hand, such branding need not reduce ethnoracial identity to an instrument of profit (2009, 26). On the other hand, an intensive focus on ethnoracial branding, even as a means of activism, can also reinforce the ethnoracial logics that antiracist efforts are meant to dismantle while obscuring the socioeconomic inequalities that enable and perpetuate the conditions of poverty endured by many minoritized populations (142).

Taken together, APPONA's programs reflected a complicated stance toward cultural citizenship in France. APPONA promoted an ethnopreneurial ethos to carve a place for Manouches within the nation. With its emphasis on cultural difference, this strategy appears antithetical to republican values. However, one of APPONA's aims was to render Manouches legible to the state as productive citizens under France's growing embrace of neoliberalism. APPONA imagined both a French society whose policies would make accommodations for Manouches as an ethnoracial group *and* a Manouche ethnoracial group that would adopt certain elements of entrepreneurial individualism in order to thrive within French society. That is, APPONA sought to realize a *dialectical model of cultural citizenship*. But, as I show in the pages that follow, APPONA's branding strategy could not fully achieve this vision. This was not because French republicanism was necessarily impervious to change. Rather, an ethnopreneurial approach perpetuates the idea that marginalized ethnoracial communities can achieve equality by conforming to the profit-centered demands of capitalist economies—a system at the root of modern racial logics and the disenfranchisement of minoritized populations. Ethnopreneurialism could both harden presumed lines of ethnoracial difference and overshadow pressing appeals for sustainable socioeconomic justice across French society (Olivera 2011; Surdu 2016; Vermeersch 2005, 2006).

Considering the limitations of cultural activism and ethnoracial branding, as well as the possibilities they enable, this chapter asks: to what extent can such strategies both empower and disenfranchise the populations for whom they advocate? In the context of assimilationist France, how can ethnoracial singularity be cultivated as an economic and political asset? More broadly, how do actors navigate the political and economic instrumentalization of ethnorace with respect to other individual and collective aspirations? To address these questions, the next two sections of this chapter summarize the socioeconomic conditions that led up to APPONA's founding and the political contexts in which the organization took shape between the 1970s and the 1990s. This allows me to explain the evolution of its approaches to music-focused cultural activism and economic development. I then explore the afterlife of APPONA and the work of its splinter organizations, circling back to the C(h)œur des Femmes. The various initiatives that remained or arose in APPONA's wake can serve as barometers of its continued relevance. In its growth, demise, and living legacy, APPONA exemplifies some fundamental contradictions of cultural citizenship in France with regard to minoritized groups. Ultimately, this organization and its inheritors have rejected the dominant terms of French cultural citizenship, envisioning a different kind of France, yet the imperative to work within existing structures to achieve tangible benefits means that such a vision remains elusive.

By critiquing APPONA's approach, I do not wish to discount or misconstrue the important roles music played within the organization. The pride with which musical activities were documented and the warmth with which members reflect upon them have given me pause each time I question the appropriateness and effectiveness of this approach to activism. It would be a cynical overstatement to conclude that APPONA was wrong to engage in musical cultural activism, and I intend for my assessment to be more nuanced than that. I hope that APPONA's former members read this as a commemorative, yet cautionary, account of how cultural activism can play out in the long term.

Setting Antiracist Agendas

An abundance of internal memos and reports from APPONA, as well as numerous newspaper articles, document acts of antagonism, neglect, and overt violence toward Manouches during the 1970s and 1980s. These acts were carried out on the part of civilians and municipalities alike. For example, a Manouche community was forcibly expelled from a small village, and subsequent pleas to local officials for explanation and assistance went unanswered.[3] APPONA was officially established in 1974 following outcry over the particularly brutal municipal treatment of a

Manouche family.[4] At the first General Assembly meeting on 29 November 1974, Father Marcel Daval, one of the key founders of APPONA and the organization's president for much of its existence, bluntly summed up the situation of Alsace's Manouches. In addition to being plagued by explicitly racist violence and discrimination, he said that the thirty settlements in the region were "more or less unsanitary slums," that the "Gypsy economy" was in a state of "continual failure because it is not financially viable," and that "the cultural problems and the destruction of the *milieu* have led to significant delinquency."[5]

The precedent for such a dire situation was clear. As I explained in this book's introduction, legislation that restricted the movement of Gens du voyage, the majority of whom were Manouche, made it difficult for them to maintain itinerant livelihoods. With the burdens of obtaining official approval to park their caravans in each new municipality, and of getting their *carnets de circulation* stamped by the police at regular intervals under threat of fines and imprisonment, sedentarization became the alternative to these onerous regulations. As both a cause and an effect of sedentarization, Manouche economies underwent drastic changes. Bertrand Routhier-Faivre, a former employee of APPONA who went on to work for the Gens du voyage affairs division in the administration of the Bas-Rhin (then one of Alsace's two *départements*, or regional subdivisions), explained to me that sedentarization "destabilizes everything." Mobility-dependent trades that once developed bonds between family members through intergenerational transmission lose their viability and are eventually phased out.[6] With all the difficulties of adjusting to these new social and economic configurations, he called sedentarization "a kind of failure in [Manouches'] minds."

Meanwhile, municipalities justified their continued subjugation of Manouches for reasons of "inadaptability," much as governments in other European countries have also done with their Romani populations (Trehan and Kóczé 2009, 55). This approach generated a snowball effect in which Manouche hardship, as well as mutual distrust between Manouches and Gadjé, increased as municipal neglect continued. Patrick Maciejewski, a former president of APPONA and current president of AVA Habitat et Nomadisme (an organization that develops housing for low-income Manouches and other settled Gens du voyage), told me that municipalities' strategies for dealing with sedentarized Manouche populations led to further intolerance. As he explained it, in the immediate postwar years, "locals thought [the Manouches] would leave, but then they didn't leave. Thus, the strategy was to make life as difficult as possible. No access to water, no access to electricity, no access to a real house, a livable space, really.

But instead, the more [the municipalities] made life difficult . . . the more [the families] became sedentary [and] impoverished."

In the absence of social services equipped to address the historical and cultural specificity of these predicaments, concerned members of some Alsatian nonprofit organizations joined forces with local Manouche representatives to form APPONA. The organization coalesced on the heels of new antiracism legislation passed by the National Assembly in 1972, following advocacy by the *Mouvement contre le racisme et pour l'amitié entre les peuples* (a national organization to combat antisemitism) that drew attention to a sharp increase in racially motivated hate crimes.[7] Building also on the momentum of the nascent Romani rights movement and the first Romani World Congress of 1971, APPONA articulated its antiracist mission during its first few years of existence.[8]

APPONA's development paralleled other antiracist organizations that arose in the late 1970s and early 1980s in France to address the struggles of immigrants from former French colonies following decolonization in the 1950s and 1960s and the global economic downturn of the mid-1970s. These organizations, along with politicians from the left, championed a platform of the "right to difference" (*droit à la différence*) starting in the late 1970s, arguing that extant assimilationist policies were discriminatory and inappropriate to the needs of growing immigrant populations in France. Though the majority of France's Romani populations were not composed of immigrants, APPONA understood their struggles against racial discrimination to be similar. In the early 1980s, politicians of the far right, led by Jean-Marie Le Pen and his National Front party, coopted the "right to difference" rhetoric to claim that the White French population also had the right to defend its own cultural identity, and that immigrant cultures (especially Islamic ones) posed a threat to national unity. This xenophobic line of argument caused the left both to abandon the phrase and to shift away from a pro-multiculturalism position toward a pro-republican, quasi-assimilationist one (Weil and Crowley 1994). However, the more militant antiracist organizations, including APPONA, continued to advocate for the rights of ethnoracially minoritized groups, though they too backed away from using the phrase "right to difference." According to Adrian Favell, by the late 1990s, "the multicultural social movements [had] faded or tamely given in to endorsing more universalist and republican rhetoric" (1997, 184; see also Silverstein 2018, 131). In line with these developments, APPONA's cultural activism navigated between promoting ethnoracial singularity and embracing universalist values.[9]

Integration, Insertion, and Neoliberal Accommodation

APPONA's cultural activism, as well as its other economic and advocacy projects, were largely based on the models of *insertion* and *intégration* that arose in the 1970s. A policy of insertion emphasizes the rights and responsibilities of individual citizens, whereas a policy of integration prioritizes the economic, political, and social inclusion of entire groups (Loriol 1999, 7–8). Insertion and integration have often been conflated in French literature and policy, their definitions interchangeable depending on the interests of political factions (Gaspard 1992, 15–18).[10] Insertion is usually used in reference to employment, but sometimes can mean "inserting" an individual's own cultural identity into French society (Hargreaves 2007, 183). Integration, too, can be understood as "a euphemism for assimilation" by those on the political right, and "as a more palatable term for something akin to insertion" for those on the political left (184). Further complicating this terminology is that while integration is often understood to apply to immigrants, since 1990 the term has officially referred to any population marginalized within French society.[11] The definition of such a population also relies on a normative conception of White French identity, often framed in racist terms as *Français de souche* ("of French stock") (Bertaux 2016, 1501). Meanwhile, insertion has come to include all socioeconomically disenfranchised individuals, immigrant or not; hence the establishment in 1988 of the *Révenu minimum d'insertion* (RMI), a welfare program geared toward under- and unemployed French residents regardless of nation of origin (Paugam 2003).[12]

APPONA documentation states that the organization's "official theory is that of integration."[13] Whereas integration was sometimes considered the antithesis of cultural survival—as one journalist put it, for Romanies in France, the "choice" was between integration and the "development of cultural particularism" (Reinheimer 1979, 2)—APPONA also conceived of integration as a more holistic endeavor to shape French society, not just a synonym for assimilation. As Weil and Crowley argue, organizations like APPONA thought of integration as "an interactive, rather than self-evidently one-way, process" (1994, 115). Integration thus meant both folding Romanies into French society *and* changing French society to welcome Romanies more fully—as I have called it, a dialectical model of cultural citizenship. Daval wrote in the *Rapport moral* (President's Report) for 1991:

> All that is done so that Tziganes [can] have a little more of a voice in our society that is barely used to listening to minorities, all that is undertaken so that employers learn within the Tzigane world, so that Tzigane teachers work toward the promotion of their own people, all that goes in the direction of a broader assumption of responsibility, all [this] brings hope for the future.[14]

Building on this dialectical understanding of integration, APPONA sought to redefine the terms of cultural citizenship for French Romanies.

While APPONA leaders understood *integration* to be the organization's ultimate objective, they saw *insertion* as a practical means to achieve this objective. Its insertion-oriented strategy focused on developing professional skills in a variety of careers, especially artisanal trades and music performance. Insertion meant both working with institutions to gain access to resources and cultivating economic self-sufficiency among its Manouche constituents. As Daval wrote in the 1986 President's Report, "to allow someone to earn his living is also to engage him in a dynamic process for a better quality of existence[;] it is to put in his hands the means to get out of the situation of misery and marginality in which he lives."[15] Although this "situation" for Romanies in France long predated the rise of neoliberalism, APPONA's philosophy of self-reliance aligned smoothly with the neoliberal regime for which the groundwork had been laid in France since the end of World War II and that became the cornerstone of extensive economic reforms starting in the mid-1980s.[16] To compensate for the large-scale unemployment and precarity spurred by privatization, the French government implemented job training programs and augmented social services (Evans and Sewell 2013, 54). The "neoliberal social imaginary" of "entrepreneurship, self-reliance, and sturdy individualism" (37) aligned with France's republican emphasis on individual rights and responsibilities, albeit with the retention of a social safety net.

APPONA's professionalization programs of the mid-1980s built on this spirit of entrepreneurship.[17] A musician would be trained in self-presentational, promotional, managerial, and technical skills, or as Bonnie Urciuoli calls it, a "worker-self-as-skills-bundle" (2008, 211). APPONA's professionalization programs offered extensive logistical support while upholding the idea that musicians should be "personally responsible for skills acquisition, to the point of self-commodification" (212). The success of these programs, in turn, depended on APPONA's promotion of Manouche ethnorace *as* valuable, and of Manouche music as the authentic manifestation of Manouche heritage. Together, these professionalization and promotional strategies constructed "the entrepreneurial (singular) and ethno-preneurial (collective) subject" (Comaroff and Comaroff 2009, 141). This process is captured in the 1991 President's Report, which states:

> A successful insertion occurs through an adaptation to the modern world, to which the keys are found in [Tzigane] heritage and in the expression of their cultural identity. The challenge of APPONA is to transform a population [labeled as] problematic into *agents of its [own] promotion*. Tziganes, as individuals and in relation to [their] group, are capable of modifying their social environment.[18]

The implementation of the RMI welfare program buttressed APPONA's professionalization efforts. As a strategy of insertion, professionalization offered a promising path to economic self-sufficiency. Furthermore, the promotion of ethnoracial singularity—while, on its surface, antithetical to French republican ideals—could in theory *facilitate* Manouche integration within the French nation, as it allowed Manouches to become entrepreneurs within an increasingly dominant neoliberal context. That is, the incompatibility between Manouche ethnorace and French cultural citizenship could be partially resolved through the cultivation of competent ethno-preneurs. However, this strategy could not be wholly sustainable, in part because it depended on a static and essentializing model of ethnoracial identity and, importantly, since musicians' livelihoods depended largely on market forces well beyond their control. Its success as a source of pride and cultural activism also hinged on the extent to which Manouche communities and their audiences understood cultural commodification to be a necessary step in the struggle against so-called ethnocide.

A Manouche "Brand Image"

At the outset, APPONA's principal goals were explicitly socioeconomic. It sought first to "rehabilitate the Gypsy economy" and to secure adequate housing for its constituents, with the corollary aims of improving schooling rates, literacy, and health, as part of a "comprehensive [plan of] action" (APPONA 1979). APPONA's founders believed that a strong media campaign was a vital component of their action plan. They wanted not only to bring attention to problems facing local Manouches, but also to combat hostility toward, and negative stereotypes of, Manouche populations. They saw music, among other artistic practices, as a way to raise the public profile of Manouche communities without victimizing them.

Though music was valued as an important practice in and of itself, APPONA also considered it a means to achieve other objectives. As stated in one project proposal, "If music is the object of instruction, it is also the pretext [by which] we address other realities and necessities, such as reading, writing, negotiating a contract, presentation and clothing onstage, obligatory legal declarations, etc. . . . [we must] consider this useful work as a means to fulfill a dimension of citizenship."[19] In turn, the cultivation of good (French) citizens was construed as beneficial for more than just individual Manouches. It was good for the images of their communities, improving possibilities for wider social acceptance and participation in the political and economic realms from which they were excluded. APPONA thus promoted music as the respectable public face of Manouches and used it to advance its multifaceted agenda.

APPONA's leaders began soliciting Manouche musicians to perform publicly as part of the organization's awareness-raising endeavors. Its first musical project was a two-week tour called "Le voyage en roulotte" in 1974 (see chapter 1). The tour's final concert, in Strasbourg's predominantly Manouche and Gitan neighborhood of the Polygone, garnered attention from local newspapers. One headline read "The party of the Gypsies tonight in the Polygone: An encounter, beyond the seductions of exoticism" ("La fête des Gitans ce soir au Polygone: Une rencontre, au-delà des séductions de l'exotisme" 1974). The journalist described that evening's affairs in optimistic terms, stating that the concert was a "symbol of a long hoped-for friendship, possible now more than ever" between Romanies and Gadjé. While the author portrayed Gadjé as responsible for having "erected" social barriers between the communities, Romanies were still a source of "culture shock" for Gadjé. The celebratory tone of this piece and its emphasis on Romani-Gadjo "encounter" are representative of much of the press garnered by APPONA's cultural programming. As Marie-Christine Hubert (2003) and Jean-Luc Poueyto (2003) have written, efforts to publicly recognize Romani cultures and histories are often conducted more in the service of transforming Gadjo views on Romanies than speaking to Romanies themselves. This newspaper article treats the encounter as one-sided, an event "especially, maybe, for the [Gadjo] others," though it is not clear by whom the promised "friendship" is "long hoped-for."

This account reflects how, through concert and festival organization and through the press surrounding it, APPONA sought to construct a Manouche brand that would foster prejudice-abating "encounters." In an internal document, an anonymous author sums up the goals of another APPONA project, the 1977 Tzigane Cultural Week: it was to be "a full program whose objective is to present the Gypsy world in all of its aspects. But whose goal is also especially to give back a brand image [*redonner une image de marque*] to Tziganes, and to show that they have something to bring to us [Gadjé]."[20] One way to convey this "brand image" to Gadjé was through live performances. These offered important opportunities for face-to-face interaction, as Mandino told me in an interview:

> When you're onstage, you feel that something is happening in the communication with others, with the Gadjé. I know that when I still performed, for me it was something very, very important, to create a bridge, to say, *voilà*, we're not only that, we're not only in the offbeat [section] in the newspapers. Right? "Come find us after the concert, we'll talk, and then *voilà*, we're like you, after all." That's kind of my approach, which was very important.

Media promotion was even more crucial to music-focused Manouche brand promotion than these interpersonal interactions. For example, in an internal memo dated 11 September 1994, Stella (as APPONA's secretary) asked the administration for permission to allow a filmmaker to shoot footage of Manouche musicians that autumn. Subsequently, a detailed four-day schedule was drawn up for the filmmaker, during which he would meet and film several Manouche members (at APPONA headquarters, on a Manouche settlement, and at the Council of Europe) and attend concerts performed by some of APPONA's most prominent musicians, among other activities. It appears that this schedule was intended to provide the filmmaker with reputable Manouche representatives and with an adequate breadth of exposure to various aspects of this Manouche community.[21]

APPONA developed a strong public relations arm, especially for the promotion of Manouche musicians. Its members provided materials and spoke to the press about concerts, festivals, and other musical engagements. Many newspaper and magazine reports on Manouche musical activities included information on APPONA's social, political, and economic endeavors and objectives. For example, an article appeared in a 1987 issue of the newspaper *Dernières nouvelles d'Alsace* with the headline "Tsiganes in Alsace: Two musical ensembles invited to Hungary" (Brassart-Goerg 1987). The first third of the text describes these performances at festivals in Hungary. The rest of the article describes the founding of APPONA, its sources of financing, the hardships Alsatian

Tsiganes endure, and how APPONA addresses these problems. Only at the very end is music invoked again, this time as another iteration of APPONA's economically focused "politics."

Widely distributed newspaper articles such as these enabled APPONA to inform the public about the realities facing Manouche communities and to disseminate its broader mission. Through these promotional mechanisms, Manouche music and musicians came to be associated with, if not representative of, issues well beyond the scope of musical performance. Musicians were foregrounded as the good, respectable face of Manouche communities, while the communities at large were portrayed as victims of poverty and deserving of help. Because of APPONA's public relations strategies, Manouche music was rarely (if ever) represented as a politically disinterested art form. In the media, it became a practice inextricably linked to its sociocultural context.[22]

Building Cohesion and Pride

In addition to projecting a positive image of Manouche musicians to a Gadjo public, APPONA worked within Manouche communities to develop musical practices as a source of pride and community solidarity. This rendered music not just a pleasurable and meaningful experience for Manouches, but a practice that could be harnessed to further other social and cultural objectives. Pierre Hauger, an APPONA social worker who coordinated cultural activities and was a key force in the organization's music professionalization programs during the 1980s and early 1990s, told me, "In order for [Manouches] to be invested, they had to be interested [in APPONA's work]. And in order for them to become interested, they had to feel recognized as such, and celebrated for what they love." He said that at this point in time, appealing to musical culture was one of the most effective means to encourage a sense of dignity in a hostile climate, and to ensure that APPONA's work would be meaningful to Manouches beyond the delivery of social services. Music was not only a way to draw the attention of Gadjé to APPONA's cause; it was also a way to bring Manouches to their own cause (as defined by the organization).

APPONA's leadership (which consisted mostly of Gadjé) understood music to be crucial in the prevention of Manouche cultural "ethnocide," a threat it thought would unravel Manouche communities altogether. For APPONA, the state of Manouche musical culture could serve as a litmus test for the cultural health of the Manouche population in general. APPONA leaders attributed the decline in so-called traditional Manouche musical practices partly to the increased availability of *other* musics to both Manouche and Gadjo consumers, characterizing supposedly traditional Manouche music as something that was "missing" or was being "lost" in the face of new technologies. On the one hand, Manouche communities embraced many new technologies as well as new popular musics (as they continue to do), recognizing these as positive changes. On the other hand, as APPONA leaders insisted, such loss constituted part of a cultural upheaval brought on by broader social and economic forces. With APPONA's interventions, the impending death of uniquely Manouche musical traditions—even those that had been recently adopted, such as jazz manouche—stood in for the death of the culture itself.[23]

APPONA leaders regarded music as the quintessential expression of an inalienable Romani essence, a perspective that sometimes entailed primitivist conceptualizations of Romani cultures as premodern, in contrast to intellectually and technologically advanced but spiritually alienated Gadjé. A professionalization project outline from the late 1990s stated, "Music is one of the cornerstones of Tzigane culture. It has always been, and is still, at the base of the survival of this community."[24] APPONA explicitly framed the need to preserve music as a preventative to ethnocide by comparing the fate of Manouches to other ethnoracialized populations: "Who is not troubled today by the disappearance of Indians of the Amazon and their culture, who is not troubled by the destruction of the Inuit people of the Grand North[?] The same destiny is in store for the Tziganes."[25] Here, APPONA called on Gadjé to redirect their concerns for faraway groups under threat toward one that was much closer to home.

While APPONA espoused an ideal of self-empowerment for Manouches, its leaders took a decisive role in outlining the terms of ethnocide prevention. In order to establish "social links" with the rest of French society, "it depends on us (social, cultural, and political actors) to inscribe [this question] into an issue of minority culture."[26] This was necessary because, allegedly, "the Tzigane people have never claimed anything, no territory, no particular recognition, has never demanded a specific status for its language."[27] Treating this supposed lack of political mobilization as a failure among Romanies, the document insists on the need for assistance from an organization such as APPONA to access the benefits due to them. However, it claims, there was a clear solution to this predicament: "the only language they have to express who they are, to say that they exist, is music. Over the centuries it has been their only means of being recognized, the only [practice] through which all Tsiganes recognize each other."[28] Essentializing Romanies as capable of legible self-expression only through music, APPONA saw this as the only viable recourse to cultural recognition and thus to the mitigation of ethnocide.

One concrete strategy of ethnocide prevention was the establishment of a music school for young Manouches.[29] A 1998 document detailing the history of the school states that it could preserve the "ardent flame" of culture and "could be for [Manouches] a means of survival."[30] The school was initially open only to young Manouche students of the Neuhof neighborhood, who would be led by a Manouche teacher from their own community. As Stella told me in an interview, learning to play music had once been a source of intergenerational bonding within Manouche communities, but this practice was dying out. According to her, it was crucial to link social objectives (such as building community solidarity) with cultural valorization "from the very beginning." This was so important that the first salaried position APPONA created was for a guitar teacher. Mandino, who by 1978 had trained extensively as a jazz guitarist, was appointed to this position. In 1987, a piano teacher was hired, largely for the benefit of Manouche girls, for whom playing guitar was not considered culturally appropriate at the time.

In order to assure the continuation of both the music itself and its means of transmission, the guitar section of the music school was committed to "respecting to the fullest the traditional characteristics" of Manouche music pedagogy, meaning "no keys, writing, classification, but [rather] orally transmitted rules," as determined by Mandino.[31] This aural method was intended to reproduce as closely as possible the "traditional" transmission of musical knowledge from older to younger generations through mimesis virtually devoid of formal music theory. By encouraging this practice, APPONA sought not only to preserve tradition for its own sake, but to resuscitate a means of social solidarity perceived to have slipped away over time. Engé Helmstetter, a Manouche guitarist and eventual leader within APPONA, later wrote in a newsletter that in the Manouche method of transmission, "One listens, one looks, one reproduces, one practices, where the warmth of the group [and] friendship [have] a place just as important as music. . . . Can one imagine a better [kind of] social insertion?" (Helmstetter 2000, 5). Here, he articulates one of the organization's core principles: that dying Manouche cultural practices should not be revitalized merely for the sake of preventing ethnocide, but that their preservation should also be in the service of *other* objectives such as intra-community social cohesion.

The development of musical skill was meant to boost the self-esteem of students, while the exaltation of Manouche music in particular would encourage youth to take pride in their cultural backgrounds. Early on, APPONA leaders had identified the risks male youths faced in terms of crime, substance abuse, and other issues. In a 1985 interview, Marcel Daval stated that Manouche youths' participation in the school could "prevent them from doing stupid things. . . . By positively rediscovering his culture, the young Tsigane rediscovers himself 'clear in his mind.' We often see evidence of this" ("À la recherche" 1985). Especially in cases where young Manouches refused or were unable to attend school consistently, musical practice (although no substitute for formal schooling) provided one way to keep boys out of trouble. This was, according to an internal review of the school's progress, largely successful: "In a neighborhood where nearly all the youth are delinquent, as in the Polygone of Strasbourg, the youth of the [music] school are not delinquent."[32] Additionally, the older youths of the school served as role models for the younger ones, becoming teachers' assistants "without problem."[33]

APPONA leaders wrote that one major source of delinquency among youths was a sense of alienation both from their own community and from the outside world into which they were expected to integrate. According to Hauger and Daval, emphasizing traditional music could bring to a precariously situated young person "a rewarding recognition, both within his own community and with his Gadjo entourage," and a means of expressing himself in a musical "language respected by the community" (1983, 5). Hauger and Daval insist that what they call a "pedagogy of success"—a pedagogy developed and advocated by Gadjé according to a Gadjo definition of "success"—cannot possibly achieve this outcome (5). A Manouche-specific pedagogy, enacted by Manouche teachers, was therefore needed. To further facilitate solidarity between Manouche youth and their non-Manouche peers, by the late 1980s the school was opened to all of Neuhof's youth.

Music Education and Civic Legitimacy

The revitalization of Manouche music pedagogy was meant to build social solidarity and morale within Manouche communities. This revitalization was also intended for Gadjé, who would comprise the supporters and consumers of Manouche music. The continued viability of the school depended on both the success of its students and its recognition by outside institutions. Support from governmental and nongovernmental sources enabled the school to finance its projects while conferring a degree of *civic legitimacy* the school might not have been able to achieve on its own. By civic legitimacy I mean the public validation afforded by the official endorsement of one or more established, external organizations, especially governmental bodies. Civic legitimacy can be understood as a component of the French cultural citizenship that APPONA sought to cultivate for Manouches, and one that entails both symbolic and material benefits.

One notable example of civic legitimacy occurred in 1986 when Rigo Steinberger, a founding APPONA member and then its vice president, was conferred the title of officer of the order of arts and letters by the former minister of culture, Jack Lang. The chief of Lang's cabinet, Gilbert Estève, presided over the ceremony, and stated in his speech addressing Steinberger, "Since the creation of APPONA in [19]74, Tzigane cultural values have come out of the ghetto. You were one of the principal instigators of the first Tzigane cultural weeks in Strasbourg that served as a model for other events elsewhere."[34] On this occasion, Daval remarked, "This is a day of celebration for us, since this honor confirms the recognition of a culture."[35]

Civic legitimacy was both generated by, and necessary to obtain, the funding to develop educational projects. The earliest available evidence of APPONA's concerted effort to secure civic legitimacy is in the 1987 President's Report, which outlines a plan to establish a "Maison des Musiques" in Neuhof through a partnership with the City of Strasbourg and the Social and Cultural Center of Neuhof. Collaborations with institutions such as these were meant to bring outside investment into Neuhof through APPONA and other local organizations while laying the groundwork for even more extensive projects. According to the 1991 President's Report, the project was delayed indefinitely, but it was eventually brought to fruition in 2010 with the opening of the Espace culturel Django Reinhardt (detailed later in this chapter).

Although the ambitious vision of building a Maison des Musiques took decades to achieve, the outreach APPONA engaged in with local institutions was a pivotal step in establishing its civic legitimacy. By developing and proposing these plans, APPONA showed that the music school should be taken seriously as an important and promising element of Neuhof's community-building programs. These institutional outreach efforts also helped legitimize the music school's unorthodox pedagogy. APPONA saw the involvement of local cultural authorities as an endorsement of their pedagogical methods. For example, the 1998 President's Report states that, following visits by a municipal official and the director of another music school, "this year the music school has been confirmed in its specificity, its credibility, and in external performances."[36] In 2000, Engé Helmstetter wrote that the school had grown from humble beginnings in 1978 to its recognition "by the city of Strasbourg, just like the other [local music schools]." This recognition, he claims, was remarkable because it validated "the indispensable place of music for the Tsigane people, an original and atypical method of teaching" and, by extension, "the ways in which Tsigane families and groups function" (Helmstetter 2000).

To Helmstetter, this represented a potential shift in governmental recognition of Manouche musical arts. With the official municipal endorsement of the music school as credible "like the others," Helmstetter, on behalf of APPONA, interpreted this as a gesture of inclusion into the city's social and cultural fabric. This ostensible legitimization of various aspects of Manouche culture and social norms signaled two potentials: that the status of Manouche communities might improve in the public imaginary, and that Manouches might begin to enjoy a heightened sense of cultural citizenship. APPONA regarded this pronouncement as an important source of civic legitimacy that paved the way for a larger public profile for the organization, for an expanded Gadjo audience, and for increased funding.

From Students to Professionals

The conferral of civic legitimacy onto APPONA's music school had direct implications for students' career potential. Developing the marketability of jazz manouche had long been a chief concern of APPONA even near the inception of the music school. Through initiatives aimed at professionalization, students would learn to become good performers and to build viable careers as musicians. Although APPONA assisted musicians at virtually every step of their development, it aimed to cultivate professionals who would be as self-sufficient as possible. This, in turn, would contribute to the broader economic goals APPONA envisioned for Manouche communities.

In addition to regular group and individual guitar lessons, APPONA instituted structured programs to foster a range of professional skills among its students. These would often take place as part of intensive workshops over the course of a weekend, or as a *stage* (training course) over a longer period of time. For example, the 1985 stage took place over three months and aimed to teach students skills in instrumental performance, composition, arranging, sound technology, public relations, negotiating contracts, accounting, licensing, and managing performances. Under the supervision of eight teachers, these objectives were pursued through lessons with Mandino, numerous concerts in the region, a trip to Hungary during which they performed and met various Hungarian Romani musicians, and a large end-of-stage concert at one of Strasbourg's most prestigious venues. The seven young Manouches who participated were chosen on the basis of their potential to develop careers in music, for whom the stage was "a step toward insertion into [French] social and professional life for a group of youths united by the same passion."[37] This approach to insertion for a select group of youths, in turn, was meant to be one step toward a larger goal of Manouche integration.

The path to professionalization often required students to acquire musical skills not germane to the aural pedagogy APPONA endorsed. By 1987, some students asked for training in solfège, to which the school responded by setting up special class sessions in formal music theory with a local improvisation-centered music school.[38] That this step was taken at the initiative of students themselves indicates their growing awareness of the practical demands of a professional career in music. It may also indicate students' ambivalence toward APPONA's privileging of "traditional" music and its attendant "traditional" transmission. Though this directly contradicted the earlier pedagogical philosophy of the school, APPONA conceded to these needs, prioritizing the students' preferences and their professional success over the retention of less expedient pedagogical approaches.

APPONA also sought to expand students' learning and performance opportunities in terms of instrumentation and genre, for example through saxophone and double bass instruction.[39] Growth in these areas would enable versatility and would bring students into closer contact with individuals and organizations outside their own communities. Since one of APPONA's main concerns about Manouche youth was that they remained too closed off socially from Gadjé, these strategies meant that youths would necessarily come into sustained contact with other players (and potential role models) in Strasbourg's diverse musical community. Over the years, students also traveled to Paris, Italy, and Hungary. These trips gave students opportunities to leave the havens of their own communities, which APPONA characterized as "secure but rigid and marginalized."[40]

After students graduated from the music school, they continued to benefit from APPONA's professional support, which included publicity, management, and for some, record production (including the 1984 re-

Figure 1 Advertisement for *Manouche: Les musiques d'aujourd'hui des Tsiganes d'Alsace* (1984). Image courtesy of Stella Funaro. Illustration by Torino Zigler.

cording, production, and distribution of an album called *Manouche: Les musiques d'aujourd'hui des Tsiganes d'Alsace*, in partnership with Radio France Alsace). Even musicians who did not attend the music school had access to APPONA's services. Fabrice Steinberger, who was active in APPONA before becoming an artists' manager, insisted in our interview that having an agent allows Manouche musicians to "appear more serious." APPONA continued to fill the role of manager as needed because its organizers were perceived as more reliable than the artists. This perception was likely due to the fact that APPONA was an "official" organization composed largely of Gadjé. Audiences and concert organizers who held unfavorable impressions of Manouches' trustworthiness could thus feel assured that the musicians would deliver. With such representation, Manouche performers could enlarge their possibilities for employment and even mitigate negative stereotypes of Manouches as unprofessional.

Because APPONA's nonprofit status restricted some of the commercial work it was legally allowed to carry out, and in order to facilitate specialized profit-generating activities, in 1992 it established a separate organization with which it retained close ties (Moog 2003). The mission of Les Ateliers Manouches d'Alsace (ATEMA) was "to prolong and potentiate some economic activities encouraged by APPONA," with the primary objective of "professional and social insertion of those excluded from the world of work" and who were beneficiaries of the RMI welfare program.[41] Initially, ATEMA trained Manouches in manual and artisanal labor (primarily street cleaning, basketmaking, chairmaking, and construction) and helped them develop the professional skills needed to secure and maintain employment. In the late 1990s, ATEMA took on music production activities, including artist management and album production. It released CDs by Note Manouche (*Note manouche*) and Tchavolo Schmitt (*Miri familia*), and co-produced an album by Dino Mehrstein with Djaz Records (*Point de départ*). It also opened a storefront from which consumers could purchase these albums in addition to other artisanal products. Whereas APPONA oversaw a wide array of Manouche musicians and ensembles, ATEMA was focused on those whose careers held the most potential.

While making these forays into the music industry, APPONA leaders did not lose sight of the organization's broader socioeconomic objectives. A spreadsheet in the President's Report for 1994 reflects such concerns.[42] The first column lists all of the ensembles APPONA represented in any capacity, with individual members named just below the ensemble titles. The next column grouping, "Status of musicians," indicates each person's employment and benefits status: whether each received welfare payments, earned government subsidies for professional performance work, and/or fulfilled "other" criteria (e.g., if they were a student or received disability benefits).[43] The last column grouping, "Promotion and training of musicians," indicates whether each musician received musical training through APPONA, whether the organization produced a press kit for them, how many concerts they performed in that year, and whether they had received any media coverage.

As Stella told me, this spreadsheet was made to document how musical performance and education could be used to fulfill aspects of welfare beneficiaries' contracts, in which they were required to seek employment and/or job training. She described this as a "creative" approach to fulfilling these obligations, one that was fortunately accepted by the state and served as a model for other French Romani organizations. The spreadsheet also suggested who was most in need of APPONA's support, placing measures of each musician's financial dependence on the state alongside measures of their professional success in terms of gigs and media exposure, as well as their training or lack thereof through the music school.[44] By detailing each musician's socioeconomic status, it accounted for the relative needs of its musician-clients to earn money through performance. Additionally, the inclusion of "other" statuses such as "student" and "regularly employed" indicates upward social and economic mobility on the part of these musicians.

One project explicitly aimed toward welfare recipients was the "Project [of] Insertion through Work." The project proposal, conceived on the heels of APPONA's 1997 music festival, proclaims that "if a concert [and] a festival are really acts of insertion, this is not enough to destroy prejudices. It is essential to transform these attempts and to transport these successes into the quotidian."[45] Observing that "among the beneficiaries of the RMI [welfare program] served by APPONA, there are a number of musicians among whom some have a real potential," the document proposes that a music professionalization program that operated within welfare regulations could be the key to both social and economic insertion. Resigned to the notion that "everyone knows that the Tsiganes will never have regular employment," the author(s) insist(s) that Tsiganes should privilege work that is "useful to others [and] to society" over that which is "productive," and that "music . . . can be this useful work."[46] The project would then fulfill the state-mandated requirement for some welfare recipients to engage in professional training. Following a format similar to the music school *stage* of 1985, but more comprehensively outlined and addressing more concertedly the needs of adult learners, the project proposed to train participants in instrumental techniques, repertoire, technical logistics, promotion, and legal issues.

APPONA regarded these professional skills both as the foundation for viable careers in music and as "a means to fulfill a dimension of citizenship."[47] Professionalization projects thus aimed to cultivate the educated, competent, hardworking, outward-looking Manouche ethno-preneur: an ideal neoliberal subject. Behind this logic is the notion that an entrepreneurial citizen is a good cultural citizen, capable of insertion, integration, and complying with the demands of the market and the state.

Decline and Afterlife

Recognizing that much of the impetus for cultural activism had come from its Gadjo members, in the late 1990s, the organization put more Manouches in leadership roles (though some Manouches, such as Rigo Steinberger, had held influential leadership positions since the 1970s). However, according to some interlocutors, conflicts within the leadership threatened APPONA's stability, and financial institutions may have regarded the loosening of Gadjo control within the organization and its internal rifts as liabilities. In the early 2000s, faced with insurmountable financial difficulties attributed largely to debts incurred from the production of its music festivals, and with the election of a more conservative and less sympathetic local government, APPONA shut down.

Although APPONA sought to create self-sustaining entrepreneurs, most of the musicians it trained relied on support and resources from the organization and its subsidiary ATEMA. Some interlocutors have emphasized to me that Manouche musicians depended so much on APPONA for their livelihoods that in the organization's absence, their careers collapsed. These musicians often spoke nostalgically to me about the days when gigs flourished through APPONA's support. Now that the organization is defunct, it has become much more difficult to secure performance opportunities. Dino Mehrstein, who was a student in its music school's early incarnation, exclaimed to me, "It rained! The concerts, they rained [down]!" Commenting on APPONA's support of young musicians, he said, "When you're young, you have to believe that you're going to succeed. [There were] journalists, television, radio, nothing but that, throughout my youth. . . . How could you not believe [that you would succeed]?" In contrast, numerous musicians have struggled to find work in recent years.

APPONA's promotional activities for musicians did not end entirely with its closure, nor was the closure absolute. In 1994, an organization called APPONA 68 was established as "an antenna of APPONA" in the Haut-Rhin *département* and, following the official closure of its parent organization, it became an independent structure.[48] APPONA 68 operates solely in the Haut-Rhin, doing much of the same work on housing, healthcare, education, employment, and cultural activities that APPONA undertook. In 2015, it obtained the official status of a sociocultural center and currently engages in some music-related activities, though the scope of its music programming is much smaller than that of the original APPONA.

In the Bas-Rhin département, where Strasbourg is located, a number of splinter organizations were established and/or joined by APPONA members to continue the specialized work that APPONA had carried out, both prior to and following its closure. These include AVA Habitat et Nomadisme, described earlier as a housing and social service provider; Jeunes Equipes d'Education Populaire (the Young Teams of Popular Education), also known as "the JEEP," an organization that serves the educational and counseling needs of youth in Neuhof; the Association pour une Recherche Pédagogique Ouverte en Milieu Tzigane (Organization for Open Pedagogical Research in Tsigane Populations), which focused on education among Gens du voyage in the Strasbourg metropolitan region; and others.[49] Stella, who works at the JEEP in Neuhof, told me she took the job because she was already familiar with the neighborhood through her work with APPONA, and that her presence drew "a strong proportion of Manouche families" to the JEEP's services.[50]

Another organization that involves former APPONA members is Lutte pour une Vie Normale (Struggle for a Normal Life), better known as Lupovino. Lupovino has been an especially crucial resource for Romani communities in Strasbourg's Polygone neighborhood, whose inhabitants are primarily low-income Manouches and Gitans. Officially established in 1995 by several women from the Polygone, Lupovino provides administrative and educational support to the neighborhood's residents.[51] In addition to helping them secure basic services and playing a key role in the construction of public housing, it periodically programs cultural events that it says "make the cultural richness of Tsiganes visible to an uninitiated, but curious and often passionate, public" ("Grands événements" n.d.). These have included two music festivals, each in 2010 and 2011, featuring both jazz manouche (representing the Polygone's Manouche inhabitants) and, to a lesser extent, flamenco (at the request of the Gitan inhabitants).

Lupovino's longtime president Eric Faure told me that its festivals were held at locations in central Strasbourg to attract a broader swath of the public, and because some residents were hesitant to hold the festivals in the Polygone due to insecurities about bringing outsiders to their neighborhood. To help counteract the idea that Manouches are respectable only as musicians—that the public "likes musicians when they're behind their guitars, but as soon as they're in front of their guitars, likes them less"—Eric told me they wanted to "get the Gadjo public to *meet* Tsiganes. So [at the first festival] we had a conference, a debate . . . with different journalists, writers, and historians, who spoke about the internment and the deportation of Tsiganes" during World War II. While the bulk of Lupovino's work is geared toward the Polygone community itself, he considers its public outreach important as well, especially if it can help build pride within the neighborhood.[52]

Like APPONA, Lupovino strives to promote both the singularity of Romani cultures and the inclusion of Romanies into the broader community of Strasbourg. However, the terms on which the Polygone's residents actually desire such inclusion remain uncertain. The addition of flamenco to Lupovino's second festival caused some uproar among the Manouche inhabitants, reflecting ongoing intergroup tensions between them and their Gitan neighbors, as well as disputes about how to represent the Polygone to a general public. Residents have also been ambivalent about the construction of new public housing: while some welcome the improved amenities, others complain that its design is sterile and impedes sociality between units. They also resent the destruction of the homes many built for themselves.[53] Eric says that despite these disagreements, "if [Lupovino] were not in step with the population, [the organization] would have disappeared a long time ago." He added that its collaborations with outside entities have helped residents combat the neglect to which they have long been subjected. The cultural and socioeconomic programs that Lupovino has spearheaded or facilitated continue to be sources of debate among residents, as their needs are neither monolithic nor easily negotiated. Their situation reflects the difficulties of achieving the kind of integration APPONA envisioned, as well as the transformative potential enabled by these efforts.

The Espace Django and the Neuhof Music School

In 2010, the Espace culturel Django Reinhardt, also known as the Espace Django, officially opened its doors about one kilometer south of the Polygone. It is now one of Strasbourg's premier venues for "musics of the world."[54] In addition to its ticketed concert series, which consists of dozens of concerts between September and July, it also sponsors a variety of educational and outreach activities geared especially toward children and residents of Neuhof. The Espace Django is funded through both public and private institutions, including the City of Strasbourg, and maintains partnerships with other local cultural organizations. Thanks to its robust marketing efforts, and to the expansion of the municipal tram line into Neuhof in 2007, it attracts audiences from various parts of the metropolitan area who would probably not venture into Neuhof otherwise. In a 2013 interview, the Espace Django's director at the time, Jean-François Pastor, told me that while audiences for most of the venue's concerts come from outside Neuhof, Manouches make up a significant portion of the audiences for its jazz manouche concerts.[55]

In addition to housing the neighborhood's local library branch, the Espace Django is home to the École de Musique du Centre Social et Culturel du Neuhof, which I will call the Neuhof Music School. Stella and Mandino, in partnership with the JEEP (the youth nonprofit for which Stella works), brought the idea of the music school to the Neuhof sociocultural center prior to the establishment of the Espace Django. They proposed to essentially reincarnate and expand APPONA's music school several years after its dissolution, with the Espace Django providing the space and the organizational structure for it to flourish again.[56] Laetitia

Quieti, who became the director of the Neuhof Music School in 2010 after completing degrees in sociology and flute performance, told me that she thought the job would be a great way to apply her expertise in both fields. She explained that the school is designed to serve all the youth of Neuhof, which in addition to Manouches includes various North African, Middle Eastern, and Eastern European immigrant communities. For this reason, the course offerings range well beyond jazz manouche guitar, though it remains one of the most popular instruments. When the school opened, most of the jazz manouche guitar students were Manouche; within a few years, more non-Manouche students registered for jazz manouche guitar, one-third of whom were not even residents of Neuhof. Since it is the only music school in Strasbourg to formally offer jazz manouche lessons, it has been a magnet for interested musicians from across the metropolitan area.[57]

Laetitia told me that, beyond music instruction itself, the music school serves an important social function within Neuhof. With so many youths in the "precarious" situations that tend to afflict low-income communities, the school provides a haven where students can develop their confidence and social skills. Private lessons, Laetitia said, "are sometimes a way for students just to have someone [to talk to] for half an hour. . . . Our main goal is really to bring something to the student: to be a social tool, to let them encounter new people, to expand their horizons, to put them onstage, and if one day they have a [job] interview, they'll be used to self-presentation." Social gatherings organized by the school, including students' concerts, also provide convivial settings for Neuhof residents to interact. Jazz manouche concerts are especially opportune events to bridge social divides: "When we throw jazz manouche parties, there aren't real boundaries between Gadjé and Manouches. Everyone eats together afterward."

Laetitia also emphasized that earning the trust of Neuhof residents has been crucial to the school's success. In addition to her explicitly collaborative approach with its constituents, she said she got along very well with the Manouche instructors from the start, and that this was a gateway to building strong ties between the school and other local Manouches. These instructors include Mandino and his nephew Francko Mehrstein, who specializes in rhythm guitar. As a child, Francko took lessons with Mandino through the APPONA music school, and after it closed, he started to build his career performing and recording with family members. Eventually, he became a rhythm guitarist for renowned guitarist and violinist Dorado Schmitt and now tours regularly with the Schmitt family, including annual trips to the United States.[58] His regular employment, however, is with the Neuhof Music School, where he teaches dozens of students. Mandino remained the principal guitar teacher of the school until his retirement in 2018, at which point another nephew, Dino Mehrstein (quoted earlier in this chapter), took over as lead guitar instructor.

In interviews with me, both Mandino and Francko made it clear that they still embrace the same aurally centered pedagogy that Mandino developed and that APPONA promoted as integral to Manouche culture. They and other jazz manouche musicians I have spoken with also recognize the utility of music literacy for students who wish to pursue careers in jazz, and other teachers at the school espouse music-literate pedagogies. Yet, as Laetitia told me, professionalization is not the school's main concern. Unlike APPONA's music school, which stressed the social functions of music education in tandem with its potential for Manouche insertion into local economies, the Neuhof Music School privileges the social aspects entirely. This means embracing various pedagogical approaches and musical traditions according to student desires. Variety in these approaches is a crucial part of the school's ethos. In addition to fostering relationships across ethnoracial lines and helping fulfill the school's mission of serving community needs, such variety represents an alternative to France's assimilationist music education system. The endorsement of musical epistemologies that diverge from "official" French frameworks provides a space for students to question how they are expected to think and behave as French citizens and for them to generate different models of cultural citizenship.

"Where Is the Line between Integration and Genocide?"

In addition to her role as director of the music school, Laetitia also manages the C(h)œur des Femmes. In 2014, she and Stella organized a weekend trip for the choir to the annual festivities in Saintes-Maries-de-la-Mer, also known as "Saintes-Maries," that May. Saintes-Maries is a massive annual gathering of Romanies in Western Europe: a pilgrimage to honor Saint *Kali* (Romani for "Black") Sara and to socialize over music, dancing, and food for days or even weeks (Wiley 2005). Although the event is not customarily attended by Alsatian Manouches, the Helmstetter family was an exception, having made the trip each May for years. Their matriarch, Louise "Pisla" Helmstetter, who had been deeply involved with APPONA for a time and who was revered as an outspoken advocate for

Manouche culture in Alsace, had passed away in 2013.[59] This year, the Helmstetter family planned the trip in her honor with a performance by the C(h)œur des Femmes as part of the commemorations.

This would be the first visit to Saintes-Maries for any of the choir's Manouche members, and for most, their first time on an airplane. Stella and Mandino envisioned the trip as a special occasion to travel and experience other facets of Romani culture, and as a way for the women to take a break from their domestic obligations for a few days. Early on a Friday morning, we met at the Strasbourg airport and departed for Saintes-Maries, arriving just in time to join the Helmstetter family for the festivities at their campsite. With instrumental accompaniment by Engé, his nephew Railo Helmstetter, and their bassist Perry Lamielle, we performed a few tunes, including Mandino's composition "Mer Djina," a song about honoring elders.[60] It was a large, joyous celebration of Pisla's life, intended primarily for family and friends, though it was also documented by a crew from the France 3 television chain.[61]

A great deal of coordination had gone into this project. For example, Laetitia launched a campaign on the French crowdfunding platform KissKissBankBank, which advertised the choir as an effort that "allows women of the neighborhood a respite from the difficulties of their daily lives." The campaign text emphasizes that the choir aims "to break down barriers between people and to create trusting relationships," depicting the Saintes-Maries pilgrimage as "a very important cultural event for Manouches" that would also help "promote" the choir.[62] In addition to raising funds, this campaign aimed to bring further visibility to the choir and its mission to promote singers who were doubly marginalized (as Manouches and as women within their own communities). The trip, therefore, promised not only to be an especially meaningful experience for the choir's Manouche members, but to draw attention to the social work its leaders already engaged in.

As this campaign suggested, the choir foregrounds two aspects of APPONA's cultural activism—the promotion of jazz manouche as evidence of Manouche value, and advocacy for women's rights—in a novel combination. It seeks not only to instill pride in Manouche culture, but to champion women's agency, which necessarily challenges gender norms within their communities. While these dual aims could be considered contradictory to APPONA's goals of preventing Manouche ethnocide, since social life within Manouche communities is largely structured around specific codified gender roles, the C(h)œur des Femmes actually reflects one of APPONA's overarching goals: a dialectical model of cultural citizenship in which both French society and Manouche culture would adapt to each other. Friction within Manouche communities may be seen as a necessary part of working toward this vision.

At the same time, the choir's public-facing cultural activism is relatively benign. Its goals are to bring women out of their households, to foster positive interactions with people outside their community, and to recognize Manouche singers' abilities and cultural knowledge for their own sake. There are no expectations that members of the public will rally around any particular political cause, nor that singers will develop into professionals. Singers show improvement in their technique, but this is a secondary objective. Laetitia told me that since the choir began, "people say that the women have really progressed, in their voices but especially in their self-assurance. The women hold their heads higher, whereas they kind of hid themselves before. I think that they really accept the fact of being in public now, of singing in front of a lot of people, of taking time for themselves." Through my participation in the choir and conversations with members, I too observed Manouche singers become more outwardly confident.

Like the Neuhof Music School, the choir's main function is a social one geared toward the community itself, with external recognition serving as a welcome source of encouragement (and funding). Driving these efforts is a vision of cultural citizenship that is not predicated upon being accepted by or folded into a dominant conception of French identity, but one that serves as a modest challenge to this conception. This entails a rethinking of what it means to be properly French *and* what it means to be properly Manouche. In some ways, the emphasis on women's agency falls perfectly in line with ideals of individualist republicanism. In other ways, the emphasis on ethnoracial singularity calls for an interrogation of these ostensibly color-blind ideals.

At one point during the weekend in Saintes-Maries, as we waited for a bus, Stella started complaining to me that religion is at the root of much conflict and intolerance in the world. Stella, an atheist, regularly challenges some devout Catholic Manouches on their unequivocal orthodoxy, so this was not a surprising comment. "But have you heard of the Freemasons?" she asked. The Freemasons, she told me, operate as a quiet force of good in the world, "in the shadows," to advance humanistic causes. That, she said, is how she thinks of APPONA's legacy. She then recalled how, at Pisla's funeral the year before, Engé's father had expressed to her how nostalgic he was for the organization. She reassured him that, in fact, APPONA lives on through the work of its former members and the associations of which they are a part.

APPONA's impacts on Manouche populations and Manouche-Gadjo relationships in Alsace were broadly transformative in a number of domains, from improving access to housing, education, healthcare, and employment, to cultivating renewed senses of community pride, to increasing the visibility of Manouches in French society. It was largely responsible for the creation and development of an Alsatian jazz manouche scene, helping lay the groundwork for an international boom in the genre's industry in the early 2000s (ironically, around the same time that the organization collapsed). APPONA was also a pioneer in pro-Manouche cultural activism. By linking musical performance with activist projects, it constructed enduring associations between Manouche music-making, ethnoracial identity, and socially conscientious objectives.

One important aspect of this activist legacy is that now, more Manouche musicians speak out publicly. Mandino told me that when he first started performing, he had his Gadjo friend do all the talking onstage because he was "too shy. . . . But I'll say that in becoming aware of all the negative things society thought about us . . . maybe it was then that I freed my word, [that] I spoke more easily." In part because of his willing participation in cultural activist projects, Mandino became a role model to young Manouches. Over the years, other Manouche musicians such as Engé Helmstetter, Dorado and Samson Schmitt, Francky Reinhardt, and Gigi Loeffler have also risen to the occasion and speak out as representatives of their communities onstage and elsewhere.

In the years since APPONA folded, public discussions about minoritized populations in France have both changed and remained the same in many respects. The riots of 2005, the Sarkozy-led national identity debates of 2009–2010, the terrorist attacks of 2015 and their backlash, and the death of George Floyd in 2020, among other events, have all catalyzed national discussions about racism and xenophobia.[63] With the resurgence of the National Front (now the *Rassemblement National*, or National Rally, under the leadership of Marine Le Pen), it is clear that France still has a long way to go with respect to its minoritized groups. Ongoing debates around these issues prove that France is a color-blind nation only in name. Meanwhile, the actors of APPONA's legacy have continued to highlight various facets of Manouche ethnoracial singularity while simultaneously advocating for Manouches' compatibility with the republican ideals of national identity. Other Romani nonprofits pursue similar political agendas, in which Romani cultural difference is affirmed alongside advocacy for human and citizen rights.[64] In Alsace, APPONA set an enduring precedent for the need to navigate between particularism and universalism.

The uneven outcomes of APPONA's cultural activism illustrate the possibilities and limitations of commodifying and politicizing social difference. While such activism can be an effective means of drawing attention to economic and political struggles, it can also feed into the same logics that serve to oppress ethnoracially minoritized groups. As Comaroff and Comaroff write, "it is yet to be seen whether ethno-prise actually *will* increase the general prosperity, the commonweal, of those who look to it for a panacea—or whether it will exacerbate, even reinvent, long-standing forms of extraction and inequality" (2009, 142; see also Surdu 2016, 99). Indeed, Andresz maintains that with regard to the material concerns of Alsatian Manouches, "of course, [APPONA] was not the universal panacea. At certain times, Sinti had the impression that their free will had been confiscated by a[n institutional] structure" (2015, 140). Ethno-preneurialism entails buy-in to the promises of neoliberal entrepreneurship which, when conjoined to a political agenda of antiracist mobilization, can result in what Adolph Reed Jr. calls "a neoliberal ideal of social justice" that spurs "a retreat from political-economic interpretations of the bases of racial inequality and [moves] toward an individualist, psychologistic perspective focused on racism as prejudice, bigotry, or intolerance" (Reed 2016, 311; see also Blake, Ioanide, and Reed 2019; Chun 2016). This approach does not concretely envision an alternative to the ethnoracializing processes that are reinforced as part of an inherently stratifying neoliberal political-economic regime. The success of a small handful of Manouches as musical ethno-preneurs does not translate, as some cultural activists might hope, into material benefits or political leverage for Manouches more broadly.

It is worth emphasizing that the economic precarity most Manouche musicians find themselves in is not a direct result of an imperfect cultural activist program, but is built into the music industry itself. If one is committed to pursuing a career in music, certain risks are known and borne, and ethno-preneurialism may become one of the most viable marketing strategies to which a musician has access. The rise of neoliberalism has compelled members of some ethnoracially minoritized groups to commodify their cultural practices in hopes of surviving under its demands. The fact that only a few Alsatian Manouche musicians have developed sustainable careers is not necessarily a sign of failure on APPONA's part—if anything, its professionalization programs helped cultivate a variety of skills that could facilitate entry into the workforce, even in non-musical domains—but is symptomatic of the vagaries and impenetrability of the music industry. As Dino Mehrstein put it, it may have "rained" gigs during APPONA's time, but for some the subsequent decline in performance opportunities had just as much to do with their reliance on APPONA as with forces inherent to the market.

A further source of frustration for some Manouche musicians is the politicization of their musical practices. They may bristle when music is rendered expedient toward political ends, a process that, arguably, can compromise the politically disinterested value of music to themselves and to their communities. They may also perceive professional risks in aligning themselves and their music too overtly with political projects (a stance explored further in the following chapter). APPONA created an environment in which Manouche music became so closely associated with activist objectives that, to a certain extent, it predetermined how Manouche musicians would be politically positioned, vesting their performances with intentions that they did not necessarily embrace. But in APPONA's absence today, apart from the handful of those who use the stage as both a musical and a political platform, jazz manouche is now minimally charged with publicly recognized activist objectives (especially in the wake of the genre's commercial boom in the 2000s).

Part of the ambivalence Manouches face with regard to the commodification and politicization of their music has to do with stances toward Gadjo intervention. When music becomes instrumentalized in these ways, it can exacerbate extant anxieties about co-optation and exploitation by Gadjé. This, in turn, stokes mistrust of nonprofit organizations, including those whose key mission is to benefit Manouches, as well as suspicion of ethno-preneurial Manouches and of Gadjé in general. While the retrospective assessments of APPONA's activities I have elicited from many stakeholders, Manouches and Gadjé alike, have been overwhelmingly positive, opinions on contemporary organizations (including those that descended directly from APPONA and whose missions remain largely similar) are often skeptical. Leaders in the Romani nonprofit world are subject to allegations that they seek political and economic gain off the backs of those they represent. When organizations use musical performance as part of their cultural activist repertoire, they are sometimes met with the same suspicion as any entrepreneur whose primary goal is profit.

Compounding skepticism of nonprofit organizations is ambivalence about one of APPONA's foundational approaches: working toward integration while promoting ethnoracial singularity to prevent Manouche "ethnocide." "You have to be careful," Marie-Hélène Gille, now retired from decades of social work with Manouches (including with APPONA and, most recently, at AVA Habitat et Nomadisme), told me:

> One of the first things I wrote, when I was young and unafraid, [was] "Where is the line between integration and genocide?" When you're between the two, it's difficult. If you integrate [Manouches], make them function like us, they cease to exist! . . . [You have to question] how far you can go. And how far *they* can go. And how far they *want* to go.

Denouncing the hegemony of French cultural citizenship, she lamented, "We're still in a logic of normalization: enter into the world, or die!" If people like Marie-Hélène fear the total assimilation of Manouches into mainstream French society, ethno-preneurialism appears to be a viable means to both cultural survival and integration. It disintegrates "the line between integration and [ethno]cide," rendering the former possible without the latter.

Yet even if we bracket the question of which aspects of Manouche culture are worth saving, or what actually constitutes Manouche culture to begin with—questions that are also sources of anxiety among Manouches—we are still left with the apparently paradoxical ideal of a French society that both upholds assimilationist republican values and makes accommodations for the cultural specificities of minoritized populations. I have called this ideal elusive because APPONA's ethnopreneurial strategies could not actually fulfill it. By foregrounding the value of ethnoracial singularity as the means to achieve integration, APPONA compromised what might have been a more effective and sustainable class-centered agenda. This is not to say that promoting Manouche music was entirely counterproductive, for the reasons listed above. Ultimately, however, the success of APPONA's goals to enact two-way transformations between Manouche populations and French society—a dialectical model of cultural citizenship—hinged more on advocating for Manouches as worthy of equal treatment as French citizens than on celebrating their (changeable, disputable) ethnoracial difference.

Perhaps APPONA's legacy reflects progress on this challenge, since for most of the organizations and initiatives that followed in its wake, resolving socioeconomic concerns such as access to housing, employment, education, and healthcare is foregrounded as a pathway to integration. With less of an emphasis on ethnoracial singularity, this focus helps spare Manouches the ambivalent essentialism that ethno-preneurialism obliges. Appeals to cultural citizenship for Manouches in France are thus predicated less on monolithic notions of cultural distinctiveness—which can carve a slippery slope into racialization—and more on the needs of a population striving for socioeconomic justice. Even the C(h)œur des Femmes, though it celebrates Manouche musical culture, is much more focused on building solidarity across presumed cultural divides and strengthening women's confidence. If anything, by encouraging Manouche women in these ways, the choir aims to de-essentialize the boundaries of Manouche ethnorace. Initiatives like this are modest steps toward a different horizon of cultural citizenship, one whose realization depends on broad political mobilization with others who share similar socioeconomic interests. In the next chapter, I turn to talk about jazz manouche to show how the genre's participants also envision different ways of belonging ethnoracially, nationally, and transnationally.

THREE

Generic Ontologies and the Stakes of Refusal

For me, jazz manouche doesn't exist, in fact. It's a fiction.
CHRISTOPHE ASTOLFI, GUITARIST

[Jazz manouche] necessarily exists because everyone talks about it.
DAVID GASTINE, GUITARIST

To you, what is jazz manouche? Throughout my fieldwork, this was a question that never got old. At face value, it seems straightforward. Jazz manouche can be defined simply in terms of its aesthetic parameters: small, mostly string ensembles featuring at least one Selmer-style guitar, a repertoire drawing primarily from 1930s and 1940s swing tunes, and the famous pompe rhythm underlying improvised solos inspired by Django Reinhardt. When these conventions are sounded together, they typically index jazz manouche for knowledgeable listeners. On this, few in the genre's scene would disagree. But unless they wanted to get rid of me, most of my interlocutors did not take the easy way out of this question. Many times, I didn't even have to ask the question outright; they would willingly bring up some version of it. Their multifaceted responses were what made me come back to the question again and again.

Take, for example, an interview I conducted with the Manouche guitarist Billy Weiss. In the summer of 2012, I traveled to a multi-day jazz manouche festival in Salbris, the village in central France where, in 1943, Django married his second wife, Naguine. My status as a young doctoral student from New York was enough to merit a backstage pass, so I spent much of my time socializing with the festival's organizers, volunteers, and musicians. During the afterparty on Saturday evening, I met Billy, who had performed earlier that day with his eponymous trio. Not wanting to waste a fieldwork opportunity, I asked if he'd be willing to do an interview with me on the spot. Fortunately, his curiosity about the endeavor matched my eagerness. We sat down at a table and were soon surrounded by other revelers and musicians, including Billy's brother Gaga (a guitarist in his trio), who was apparently fascinated by the exchange taking place between us. Early in the interview, I asked the question:

SL: How do you define *jazz manouche*?

BW: I'll say this. So, jazz manouche, for me—it's personal. Jazz manouche, for me, is not jazz manouche.

SL: And what does that mean?

BW: Listen, for me, it's *jazz*. Because Django, when he invented this music, it wasn't—it was French jazz.

Billy's first reaction is to deny that jazz manouche really exists, claiming that the music called "jazz manouche" is *actually* just "jazz," or more specifically, "French jazz"—but not "manouche." Billy credits Django with inventing the music he plays, situating it as temporally continuous with the era in which Django performed. Immediately after Billy's answer, Gaga interjects (brackets indicate overlapping speech):

GW: It's a blend of musette, [a blend of Gypsy music]

BW: [*yes* no, no, no]

GW: [it's the first genre of music]

BW: [yes yes yes] no no—but people say, "why this, jazz manouche," because Django created it. But in fact, it's French jazz. It's French jazz.

Unlike Billy, Gaga does not deny the existence of jazz manouche. Instead, he points to its stylistic diversity stretching beyond jazz. For Gaga, it is a concrete genre, its roots and influences attributed to other nameable genres, including an ethnoracialized one ("Gypsy music"). Billy's reaction to this is ambivalent: an alternation of "yes" and "no," finally resolving back to his initial stance that the music in question is nothing but French jazz. I push him on the matter:

SL: So why call it jazz manouche?

BW: Bah, because it's Django who invented it, and because he was a Manouche, so they said it was jazz manouche, therefore—in fact, it's French jazz, because it was Django who brought it to France, and it's French jazz. Why suggest that it's jazz manouche?

Billy's response here encapsulates the sentiments of many other jazz manouche musicians to whom I later posed the question. They are frustrated with the fact that the music they perform is labeled "Manouche"—that their music, and that of Django, would be attributed so blatantly to an ethnoracial character they claim is minimally present, if at all. Billy feigns bewilderment as to why *jazz manouche* even exists as a term in order to reinforce its apparent absurdity. Like Billy, many musicians resent the fact that they are considered to be playing something *other* than jazz, and specifically, a genre that would not explicitly align them with their own national heritage.

At the same time, Gaga's interjecting voice and Billy's hedging reaction to it represent a persistent contradiction that musicians must regularly navigate. Gaga confirms the existence of jazz manouche and its connection to Romani culture, situating himself and other musicians in a tradition at once part of and separate from French jazz. By emphasizing its roots in both musette (a distinctively French genre) and Romani music (which, for French listeners generally, is *not* considered traditionally French), Gaga attempts to nuance Billy's more categorial understanding of the music they play. Billy surely knows there is *something* linking this music called "jazz manouche" to his Manouche community, but after a few moments of wavering, he doubles down on his denial. Given the opportunity, Billy would rather proclaim his music's (and, by extension, his own) belonging to the French nation than to his ethnoracial community.

Instead of responding to *What is jazz manouche?* at face value, this chapter asks: what are the stakes of responding to the question? I argue that in defining and situating themselves in relation to genre, speakers give shape to complex, often ambivalent political stances. During my fieldwork, I persistently asked "What is jazz manouche?" not because I was truly unsure of what constituted the genre, but to elicit the various responses that would disclose each interlocutor's aesthetically informed opinion on the politics of French citizenship and minoritized identities. To them, jazz manouche can be considered a subgenre of jazz, a subgenre of Romani music, both, or neither. When speakers state any of these positions on *genre*, they simultaneously express positions on *ethnorace* and *cultural citizenship*. In doing so, they necessarily engage in acts of ambivalent essentialism: What does it mean to categorize a music as jazz? As national? As ethnoracial? As a combination of the three? And what does it mean to reject generic categorization altogether?

I center my analysis on the most prevalent response I have encountered to the question *What is jazz manouche?*: that the term *jazz manouche* falls short. This type of response takes various forms: music called "jazz manouche" is really "Django-style jazz," "French jazz," or simply "jazz"; when understood as "folklore," jazz manouche limits artistic possibilities; and jazz manouche reinforces ethnoracial stereotypes and sectarianism, among other complaints. While Fabian Holt argues that genre can be "a tool for essentializing connections between ethnicity, place, and music" (2007, 172), in critiquing jazz manouche, musicians can render genre a tool for *de*-essentializing such connections implicit in the second half of the genre name—in other words, a means of what George Lipsitz has termed "strategic anti-essentialism" (1994; see also Briggs and Bauman 1992). Depending on the context of their utterances, musicians' stances may move between the essentialist, the anti-essentialist, and the anti-anti-essentialist (Gilroy 1993).

In practice, musicians performatively index their critiques by incorporating musical techniques that elide the genre or challenge its boundaries, by using images that index cosmopolitan ideals, by affiliating with artists outside the genre's boundaries, and by performing in diverse contexts. Critiques of the "jazz manouche" label range from implicit, such as avoidance of the term, to explicit, in outright denunciation of its meaning and denial that such a music even exists. Here, I focus on speech about jazz manouche in order to ask: How do speakers reflect on the significance of their own performative gestures in relation to the genre? How do they construct indexical relations between the idea of jazz manouche, its instantiations, and its political implications? What are the semiotic ideologies (Keane 2003, 2018) at play? Through talk about music, how do speakers intersubjectively develop ideas about ethnorace and citizenship?[1]

Both the rejection and the embrace of jazz manouche can index particular claims about cultural citizenship. Recall from this book's introduction that under French republicanism, while members of ethnoracially minoritized groups may be citizens legally, they might not be considered citizens culturally. One way for Manouches to forge a sense of national belonging is to treat jazz manouche as a form of *French* jazz. The use of the term *French jazz* as a synonym for *jazz manouche* privileges jazz manouche more as part of a national, rather than an ethnoracial, heritage. This nation-oriented framing resonates with sociologist Jean Beaman's argument that when ethnoracially minoritized French people "seek to be viewed as French by others, they are ultimately making a claim for cultural citizenship—a claim to be regarded as a legitimate member of the French mainstream or a part of French culture" (2017, 23). Such claims can be performed through various semiotic modalities, including music and language, in subtle and/or overt ways. Manouche musicians may use the "French jazz" label not only to avoid the marginalizing potential of "jazz manouche" but also to suggest that they are indispensable elements of a French cultural fabric.

There are other reasons to critique the "jazz manouche" label. Both Manouches and Gadjé take issue with the fact that the label is understood to inhibit certain artistic liberties and to exclude them from a wider jazz world. They may resent how jazz manouche is perceived as imitative, simplistic, and naïve. Talk about the genre allows speakers to voice frustrations with the music industry and with how others construe their artistic visions, frustrations that have less to do with questions of national belonging than with the professional implications of presenting oneself through a certain generic lens. These sentiments recall Kevin Fellezs's work on how 1970s fusion musicians contested both the presumed limits of their creative choices and the limits of the sociocultural boundaries that generic boundaries connoted (2011, 7). Like those who challenge ideas about which genres are appropriate for African Americans to participate in (Mahon 2004, 2020), Manouche musicians may use music to contest assumptions that homogenize their cultural identities and deny them artistic agency. Musicians who choose to bill themselves as "jazz" more than "jazz manouche" also create new narratives of jazz history, challenging the margins on which they often find themselves. In Sherrie Tucker's view, such efforts reflect musicians' "desires mapped onto representations of and narratives about jazz and the connections and disconnections between them and jazz practice" (2012, 279).

Within the jazz manouche scene, it is the *manouche* part of the genre label that is typically the object of complaints, not the *jazz* part. When speakers reject this component, they are often suggesting that ethnorace is a barrier to their professional and artistic goals. Taking issue with the *manouche* part reinforces a widespread notion that Manouche identity is necessarily marked, whereas jazz is not. Jazz is understood to afford musicians a degree of prestige, class status, and creative autonomy that ethnoracial markedness—especially the stereotypes that Romanies are poor, uneducated, and criminal—would inhibit. This dichotomy reflects a paradigm in which the supposed "universality" of an expressive practice such as jazz, despite broad recognition of its African American origins, represents the ostensibly race-neutral ideology of French republicanism.

In their criticism of jazz manouche, musicians call attention to how they envision themselves as artists, as members of ethnoracial communities, as citizens of a nation, and in terms of other artistic, class, and social affiliations. By refusing jazz manouche—as an ontological fact, as a set of stylistic parameters, or simply as a restrictive label—speakers challenge essentializing assumptions that cement ethnorace to aesthetics. In doing so, they attempt to broaden the artistic, social, and political opportunities available to them, enacting anthropologist Carole McGranahan's conceptualization of refusal as "generative and strategic, a deliberate move toward one thing, belief, practice, or community and away from another" (2016, 319).[2] For Manouches especially, to refuse the "jazz manouche" label is not only to make a claim to French cultural citizenship but to challenge the very terms of cultural citizenship as they are and to imagine a society in which ethnoracial difference is conceived and valued otherwise.[3]

At the same time, repudiation of the "jazz manouche" label is not just a matter of trading one term for another, nor is it a refusal to associate the music with Manouche ethnorace entirely. Many who critique the label also emphasize the music's ties to Manouche individuals and communities. As Manouche guitarist Yorgui Loeffler once put it to me,

> Jazz manouche is a style of music, like other styles of music. People call it jazz manouche, but for me, it's jazz. . . . At the same time, [Manouches] are a community that's a little separated from the rest of the world, who have a different culture. And, well, if we can be known thanks to [jazz manouche], then that's very good.

Here, Yorgui conceives of the genre as "jazz" instead of "jazz manouche," implying that he sees himself as part of a national and transnational jazz musical community. But he also acknowledges the advantages of using the "jazz manouche" label for the purposes of cultural recognition, a label from which he and his extended family have often benefited. To positively construe the genre as distinctively Manouche can be understood in several ways: it may be a challenge to hegemonic conceptions of French identity; it may be a rejection of assimilationist compulsions; it may be a gesture toward transnational, pan-Romani identity formation; it may be a strategy to reap the economic benefits of autoexoticism; and it may be any or all of these things at once.

I cannot say for sure which of these positions, if any, Yorgui takes with the above comment, and that is perhaps the point. In one breath, a speaker can both refuse and embrace the label. This mode of ambivalent essentialism opens up a space to negotiate one's own uncertainty about what it means to be Manouche and what it means to be French, and about how to navigate market demands and artistic goals for oneself. An individual may adopt seemingly contradictory stances depending on which audience they are addressing and which goals they seek to fulfill (see Marković 2015; Stoichita 2016).[4] Such context-dependent positions reflect how identities come into being through "situated social action" (Bucholtz and Hall 2004, 376); we are "interpellated" into them as "the forms in which we are obliged to act, while always knowing that they are representations which can never be adequate to the subject processes that are temporarily invested in them" (Hall 1995, 65). By examining holistically, through ethnography, the multiple stances an individual may hold simultaneously, this chapter treats apparent incoherencies as generative and imperative in the struggle to make sense of one's place in the world. When Billy and Gaga verbalize different understandings of what jazz manouche is, they are not necessarily at odds with each other; when Billy says, "Yes—no no no—yes yes," he does not necessarily contradict himself. Individually and together, speakers like Billy and Gaga dialogically participate in an ongoing process of meaning-making, an unfolding and continual rearranging of subject positions that underlies expressions of ambivalent essentialism.[5]

The following parts of this chapter analyze some of the most prevalent stances—complementary and seemingly contradictory alike—on jazz manouche as described by those in its scene. Each section illustrates a different kind of response to the "What is jazz manouche?" question. "Jazz high and low" presents the insistence that the genre should be understood as "jazz" *tout court*, followed by "Refusal to autoexoticize," in which Manouche musicians seek to avoid detrimental ethnoracial stereotypes associated with the genre. "Striving for inclusion" addresses how certain Manouches frame jazz manouche as integral to regional and national heritage, and "Redefining Manouche freedom" shows how play with generic boundaries reflects, and even generates, plural conceptions of Manouche identity.

With all its semiotic complexity, jazz manouche refracts an array of political beliefs and conjoins aesthetic and ethical discourses. Though indexical relations are never fully determined, their meanings never fully discernible (to speakers *or* to analysts), attention to these very uncertainties is productive (Nakassis 2018). The multiple and always shifting indexical meanings of "jazz manouche" are fertile ground for analysis. They reflect the messy process of metapragmatically working out one's own positionality. But the inconclusiveness of these indexical relations is felicitous not only for social scientists. For speakers, discussions about jazz manouche are often seen as appropriate, accessible means for articulating even the most inchoate stances on ethnoracial politics and national belonging. The polyvalence of jazz manouche offers potent opportunities for developing these kinds of stances.

Jazz High and Low

As I described in chapter 1, in popular discourse about Django, speakers often attribute Manouche qualities to his music. Some listeners tend to conflate contemporary jazz manouche with this music and then retroactively project an ostensible "Manouche sound" onto the original source material. For example, jazz critic Frank Ténot once mused, "the music of Django is the result of the meeting of Tsigane heritage and jazz from the 1930s: folklores born in the ghettos at the margins of official culture" (1988, 851–52). But beyond the string-based instrumental tradition in which he was raised (Williams 2000, 410), it is difficult to argue that Django preserved any musical techniques unique to his ethnoracial group. This is due to the lack of (known) recordings and transcriptions of his milieu prior to his own recording sessions. Patrick Williams writes that although Django's "style is also marked by a certain number of methods associated with Tzigane music" that are "aimed at sonorous expressivity," these very methods "also exist in jazz: emphatic vibrato, multiple ornamentations, virtuosic traits" (411). Williams argues that one should not distinguish these qualities as uniquely Manouche as opposed to jazz conventions of the time. Similarly, Alain Antonietto and François Billard acknowledge that the history of Romani music-making has been characterized by mixture, adaptation, and transformation, but caution that this "does not allow one to automatically endow Django with a Tsigane 'soul' that would ideally be affirmed thanks to jazz!" (2004, 387).

While some of my interlocutors claim to perceive certain Manouche expressive qualities in Django's music, many have expressed frustration upon hearing assessments like these. They continually emphasize that "he was a *jazz* musician," arguing that his style was all his own and not necessarily representative of his Manouche background. One memorable instance of this took place during an interview with Michel "Mitch" Mercier, whom I introduced briefly in chapter 1. I first learned about Mitch online—he is a moderator of and frequent contributor to the popular French jazz manouche forum GuitareJazzManouche.com—and met him in person at one of the jam sessions he regularly organized in a Paris bar. I later joined him for an interview at the Paris headquarters of Universal Music France, where he had worked in marketing since the early 2000s. When I asked him, "In your opinion, what is jazz manouche?" he responded affably,

> Ah! [*laughter*] It's interesting because, for example, here in my work, I had some disagreement with people [who] wanted to label Django as jazz manouche. I don't agree at all. So I [told] them that Django is a jazzman, a jazz player. He was Manouche, okay. But jazz manouche is something else.

For Mitch and others, the distinction between labeling Django as a "jazzman" as opposed to a jazz manouche musician is important, not only because of the chronological impossibility that his music and jazz manouche could be one and the same. By emphatically characterizing Django as a jazz musician *without* regard to his Romani background, they situate him as an extraordinary, creative individual, not as a representative of any particular ethnoracial heritage. Mitch's aside that Django "was Manouche, okay," imputes nothing more to his Manouche background than a biographical fact. Later in the interview, he remarked, "[Django] was a living legend, and he was Manouche, so [*laughter*] they called it jazz manouche!," suggesting that the label was coined as a matter of convenience and not as the consequence of a uniquely Manouche musicality.

Many musicians revere Django as an artistic role model and wish to dispel notions that his level of musicianship could be anything but the product of hard work, collaboration, open-mindedness, and creative vision. Construing Django in these terms also indexes how they *themselves* want to be understood along similar lines: as serious jazz musicians. Even those who claim to hear some kind of Manouche expressivity in Django's music privilege his status as a renowned jazz musician above anything else. This insistence may be in part because, unlike music labeled "Manouche," jazz enjoys a certain "legitimacy" as a "high art" form (Lopes 2002).[6] Musicians endeavor to earn this level of prestige and sometimes feel that labeling themselves as "jazz manouche" can compromise such efforts.

Unlike some US musicians, such as Max Roach and Nicholas Payton, who have been among the most vocal critics of the term *jazz*, many in the jazz manouche scene embrace it.[7] The defense of Django's identity as a jazzman also speaks to the transnationalism and supposed universality of jazz (which, I should note, can also be linked to the universalist discourse of French republicanism). Philip V. Bohlman and Goffredo

Plastino write that "jazz is the art of the intimate," yet it also "finds its place everywhere in the world" with "the force of a musical lingua franca" (2016, 1). In emphasizing Django's jazzman status as a model for themselves, contemporary musicians articulate their own desire to participate in a musical world beyond ethnoracial or national boundaries while demonstrating "a willingness to accept a unifying ontology of jazz" (6). They endeavor to engage in the "jazz cosmopolitanism" that, as Steven Feld writes, is understood as "the agency of desire for enlarged spatial participation [which] plays out in performances and imaginaries of connectedness" (2012, 49). At the same time, by imagining jazz as color-blind and transcendent across geopolitical and cultural boundaries, and by downplaying the situatedness of their own musical production, musicians may also try to depoliticize the music they produce (cf. Monson 2007). Excising the *manouche* part of the "jazz manouche" label allows musicians to consider themselves more as "world citizens" than an ethnoracialized, or even national, genre label might afford. Their stated priority is art for art's sake.

Extrapolating from the fact that Django was a jazz musician, a number of musicians argue that jazz manouche should be recognized as *jazz*, simply put. One reason why jazz manouche musicians feel the need to justify their music as "jazz" is that they are often excluded from or considered marginal to jazz writ large. This is partly because jazz manouche is founded on the close reproduction of Django's solos and techniques. While it is common practice in jazz study to learn the solos of master musicians by rote, this is usually done in the service of developing one's own improvisational style, not as an end in itself. In jazz manouche, however, players tend to strive for close reproduction of Django's style.[8] This goal is sometimes mocked by musicians in other jazz subgenres who characterize jazz manouche players as uncreative. Benjamin Givan writes that "although both jazz manouche and jazz (each of which are, naturally, far from monolithic) share certain basic idiomatic features, such as improvisation, swing rhythms, and repertoire, their differences remain considerable" (2014, 26). Givan considers jazz manouche to be a genre distinct from jazz because, he argues, it has developed somewhat apart from other jazz practices and because it tends to privilege the preservation of strict musical parameters over innovation and generic evolution. As he puts it, "Reinhardt's jazz-oriented impetus toward individual expression has been subordinated, in jazz manouche, to principles of imitation and adherence to an invented tradition" (27). François Billard similarly describes jazz manouche as a "folklore" (2011, 819), though not necessarily in contradiction to its "jazz" status.

Performers recognize the preservationist character of jazz manouche in both critical and celebratory ways. During our interview, Mitch blithely told me that "we only try to copy what Django and [violinist] Stéphane Grappelli did. And it's amazing to see that it has become a real folklore, just on the style of two persons." He later added, "If a guitar player asks me, I will tell him, 'Yes, I play jazz manouche,' or 'Django style,' because we copy Django. That's all we do." It is common for jazz manouche participants to glorify Django as a "master" or even a deity and to treat his works as sacred elements of an incontestable canon, as one musician did in a public Facebook post: "Today I say happily that our master showed us what jazz manouche is. Thanks to you musicians for staying in line and for not deforming his works, and [for] keeping them the way Django Reinhardt created them." These interlocutors identify Django's style as the epitome of their own aesthetic ideals and consider fidelity to the source materials to be a worthy goal in itself. Jazz manouche is also considered much more accessible to a wide public than, for example, bebop and free jazz, subgenres of jazz that may appear illegible and elitist to uninitiated audiences. This is both a point of pride for jazz manouche participants and an object of derision by others.[9]

When contextualized within discourse about Manouche performers, the genre's conservatism takes on further, ethnoracially inflected meanings. As the most public-facing aspect of Manouche communities in France, jazz manouche is often understood by Manouches and Gadjé alike to distill the core characteristics of Manouche culture. This stereotyping entails a process of iconization (Irvine and Gal 2000, 37–38) between the aesthetic qualities of jazz manouche performance and perceived Manouche cultural traits: simplicity, lack of sophistication, and rote reproduction in the genre are understood to signify simplicity, lack of sophistication, and rote reproduction in Manouche culture.[10] I broached this subject in an interview with Eric Faure, president of the pro-Manouche organization Lupovino introduced in chapter 2. He spoke of the genre's accessibility and attributed this to a Manouche sense of anti-elitism, saying that Manouches

> have a jazz audience that is not part of the kind of group [*shifts to a snobbish register*] of people who are supposedly cultivated, who listen to jazz, and who speak seriously—[*he returns to his normal register*] I'm just kidding, but . . . it's true that [Manouches] are really the only people who can frequently attract an audience that's not [already] passionate about jazz. [People] who still like to listen to jazz manouche, even though they won't go to a concert to hear John Coltrane['s music].

By associating jazz manouche with certain behaviors and values attributed to Manouche ethnorace, Eric interprets the genre's distance from "serious" jazz in a positive way. He emphasizes what he perceives as the unpretentious, candid character of Manouche musicians, which he says is expressed in the simplicity of the genre: "[In jazz manouche,] there's nothing intellectual. It doesn't claim to be intellectual. To the contrary, it's profoundly Manouche in the way it's played." Eric's comments suggest causal links between Manouche heritage and musical preferences, and between ethnorace and class status.[11] In this way, jazz manouche is heard as a naturalized expression of lowbrow Manouche values, a welcome counterpoint to musical elitism.

In contrast, some Manouche musicians take pains to advocate for jazz manouche as "serious" jazz. This strategic anti-essentialism is performed in response to perceived links between Manouche ethnorace and jazz manouche's supposed naïveté, the genre's relative emphasis on reproduction as opposed to innovation, and its status as a folkloric tradition. One such musician, Gigi Loeffler (described in this book's introduction), explained to me countless times that this was a crucial impression to make publicly. Early in my fieldwork, Gigi became one of my closest interlocutors. He believed strongly in the importance of my research and took me under his wing, securing an apartment for me and my partner in the same building as his and treating us like family members. He was also remarkably forthcoming about his strategies for professional development and his vision for pro-Manouche activism in his home region of Alsace. He enlisted my help and expertise in several ventures, including public speaking engagements, plans for a documentary film about Alsatian Manouche musicians, and a jazz manouche school, among others. Although many of his ideas never came to fruition, he was consistently determined to avenge the injustices he and his family had faced as a result of anti-Manouche racism and to prove that jazz manouche was a crucial part of Alsatian and French heritage.

Echoing the motivations of Black US musicians who emphasized modernist aesthetics in jazz as part of a broader political struggle (Monson 2007), Gigi often insisted that framing jazz manouche *as jazz* was the only way for Manouche musicians to be taken seriously by potential audiences and employers. Over one of our many morning coffees in his kitchen, he rejected the possibility of playing at a Romani music festival, saying, "We [Manouche musicians] have nothing to do with Eastern Europe. We need to make a *jazz* festival, so that Manouches have an open door to jazz. Jazz manouche is part of jazz." To him, even participating in jazz manouche–specific festivals could send the wrong message. In order to prove Manouche competency in jazz, he said that "we need to get out of" these festivals and "go elsewhere." While Gigi still had to rely on these festivals and other Romani-themed events as sources of income, he strove to participate in jazz festivals and to market his music as jazz while simultaneously emphasizing his Manouche background onstage and in publicity materials. By arguing that jazz manouche shares the forward-looking ideals of contemporary jazz, Gigi also made an argument for the inclusion of Manouche culture within progressive conceptions of regional, national, and transnational cosmopolitanism.

The refusal of the "jazz manouche" label can be as subtle as the substitution of the term *Gypsy* and its variants for *Manouche*. Adriana Helbig writes that a Ukrainian Romani jazz ensemble chooses to label itself as "Gypsy" "because it is an English term. It linguistically invokes a larger global context and modernity in the postsocialist space. It supersedes locality and sounds cosmopolitan and hip to Ukrainian citizens in its invocation of the West" (2005, 11). Although in the situation Helbig describes, the ethnoracial term *Gypsy* is chosen as an alternative to the regional term *Carpathian*, a similarly global-minded approach informs the use of *Gypsy* by jazz manouche musicians. This use suggests cosmopolitanism as opposed to provinciality, especially when used in conjunction with other English terms recognizable in French, such as with the Manouche-led ensembles "Gipsy Liberty" and Gigi's own "Gipsy Feelings." During my fieldwork, when Davindar, my partner of Indo-Fijian background, joined the latter ensemble on saxophone, Gigi invented a pun to further emphasize the international relevance he aspired to. He decided to replace "Feelings" with "Filja," both to use the Romani term for "feelings" and as an (albeit far-fetched) orthographic nod to the addition of the Pacific Islander to his ensemble.

Gigi's brother Yorgui, quoted in the introduction to this chapter, also shares concerns about how his music is labeled. Yorgui ranks among the most well-regarded jazz manouche lead guitarists in France, with several albums to his name and frequent domestic and international engagements. As an accompanist, Gigi used to perform sometimes with Yorgui at high-profile gigs and invite him for cameo appearances at the smaller gigs he organized himself. One evening, Gigi, Yorgui, and I met at my apartment to discuss the possibility of organizing a tour to the United States with them and a cousin. Since they wanted to spend most of their time in New York, I suggested they consider playing at the Golden Festival in Brooklyn, an annual event that often features various Romani-influenced musics. While Gigi, in his eagerness to secure gigs abroad, was enthusiastic about the idea—perhaps this signaled a change of heart about performing in "ethnic" contexts—Yorgui argued that the festival would be too "folkloric" for him. He wanted to prioritize playing at *jazz* venues and festivals, especially in Manhattan, where he hoped to build his reputation as a jazz musician.

For musicians such as Gigi and Yorgui, it is often important to advertise themselves as jazz musicians in their own right. As Manouches, they are especially aware of the ethnoracial stereotypes potential audiences may attribute to them along with the "jazz manouche" label. They need not disavow their roles as jazz manouche musicians, but in order to overcome negative assumptions about their creative capacities, they endeavor to identify with a higher-prestige art form. In doing so, they may assert the status of their music as a "legitimate" art form as opposed to the "folklore" slot that so often frustrates them. As with other jazz manouche musicians, Manouches and Gadjé alike, framing jazz manouche contextually as part of a broader jazz world allows them to voice how they would like to be seen as artists and as citizens.

Refusal to Autoexoticize

Dino Mehrstein, introduced in the last chapter, is among Strasbourg's better-known guitarists. As the nephew of Mandino Reinhardt and brother of Francko Mehrstein, he is part of an important Manouche family of musicians. On a brisk January evening in 2014, I caught up with him at a US-style, 1950s-inspired diner in Strasbourg. He was eager to share with me his thoughts on French jazz manouche and on his own music. Once our sodas arrived, I clicked on my recorder and eased into the interview with a couple questions about his musical background. As he explained Django's influence on him, I prepared myself to bring up some more contentious questions—such as "What is jazz manouche?"—when he beat me to the punch:

DM: People know France for its poets, for its wine, for its gastronomy. But damn, back in the day, there was Django, and he was recognized as—he was part of *French* heritage! So what did they call it back then?

SL: What he played?

DM: What we play today, jazz manouche.

SL: Well, they didn't call it that.

DM: Voilà.

SL: And why, in your opinion, does this term exist now?

DM: [*pause*] I don't know. I want to say people have been talking nonsense.

Dino then let this question go, but a few minutes later, in the course of describing how APPONA supported him early in his career, he lamented the fact that the organization had insisted he market his album as "jazz manouche":

DM: I released a CD, and in making this CD, I really pushed what I wanted—*not* what other people wanted! Not swing! But it was called that. It was called jazz manouche. I was *never* okay with that.

SL: So you don't want [to use] this label?

DM: Well, of course not, I never wanted it. I always said that would fit people's expectations. Jazz manouche—you *don't* hear jazz manouche [on that album]! You hear a Manouche musician behind it, okay. But strictly speaking, that's all. You don't hear a guy who only plays that. Or who wants to *sell* that, who puts *that* front and center. No.

While about half of the tracks on the album *Point de départ* indeed fit the technical parameters of jazz manouche broadly conceived—a pompe driven by Francko Mehrstein and accompanied by Gérald Muller on double bass, Dino's solo guitar improvisation, and standards of the jazz manouche repertoire—others, including several tracks with funk or bossa nova rhythms and Dino's original compositions, fit less clearly within a jazz manouche idiom. Dino's frustration with how the album was marketed not only stems from how the "jazz manouche" label flattened out the artistic diversity of his music; it also reflects his refusal to put his ethnorace "front and center" and to instrumentalize ("sell") it.

Taking Gigi's and Yorgui's efforts to move beyond the "jazz manouche" label a step further, musicians like Dino strive to prevent their ethnorace from influencing how they are marketed and how audiences perceive them. This represents an unwillingness to "autoexoticize" (Savigliano 1995) and to commodify ethnoracial identity (Comaroff and Comaroff 2009), strategies that some minoritized groups have otherwise used to their advantage. A musician might avoid acknowledging their Manouche background in biographies and interviews and might choose album cover designs and other visual materials that make no explicit reference to their ethnorace. Some musicians have little to no say in how they are marketed but may, with varying degrees of reluctance, consent to being labeled as "Manouche" in publicity materials. Privately, they sometimes voice ambivalence about being marketed as such, or in Dino's case, express outright repulsion at the idea of using their ethnorace for marketing purposes. Refusing to be labeled as "jazz manouche" is one way to express their discomfort with autoexoticization, and by extension, their desire to be understood as regular citizens.

For some Manouche musicians, avoiding the "jazz manouche" label also allows them to circumvent a fraught terrain of Manouche identity politics. Considering that appeals to ethnoracially associated cultural production can be both economically *and* politically expedient, the assertion of a Manouche identity through music can easily be read as an endorsement of a pro-Manouche political stance—a stance with which some musicians do not want to publicly associate themselves. Musicians often articulate their aversion to using their music to advocate for Manouches through variations on the phrase "I just want to play my music."

I was not surprised to hear this sentiment in an interview with Biréli Lagrène, by far the most internationally famous French Manouche person other than Django.[12] Biréli is particularly well known as a guitarist who has easily and fruitfully crossed generic boundaries throughout much of his career. Narratives of Biréli's musical development typically compare his grounding in jazz manouche to the other influences he has exhibited, evaluating his degree of connection to Manouche ethnorace by measures of his adherence to jazz manouche stylistic parameters. After gaining recognition as a child prodigy for his interpretations of Django's music in the early 1980s, he blossomed on international stages in the 1980s and 1990s playing in other jazz subgenres and crossover genres such as jazz fusion. He then publicly returned to his "roots" in Django's music around the time of the jazz manouche boom in the late 1990s and early 2000s and continues to perform today, primarily in jazz manouche contexts.

Biréli's professional success, unparalleled by any Manouche musician other than Django, is one indication of his capacity for exceptional generic flexibility and virtuosity. He has the choice to autoexoticize or not, as he pleases, whereas most Manouche musicians cannot market themselves in such versatile ways. Biréli's privilege in this respect is an object of emulation for musicians who wish to transcend generic boundaries as well as the limitations of ethnoracial identification. They see Biréli as a Manouche who can afford *not* to promote his Manouche identity, while simultaneously lauding him for his role in popularizing jazz manouche.

Although Biréli certainly recognizes his status among Manouches and the esteem in which he is held, when I asked him whether his ethnorace might impact perceptions about Manouches, he demurred, saying, "No, because I didn't, I don't fight for that. I mean, [I say] 'I don't fight for that.' I don't think of it as that. All I think about is that I'm just a regular musician that does his gigs." By calling himself "just a regular musician," Biréli disavows any desire as a high-profile artist to represent or to "fight for" Manouches. He added that, because he was raised in a "nontraditional" way for a Manouche—in a house, financially stable, and well accepted by his Gadjo peers—"I have never been confronted [with] that problem, the fact of being a Gypsy." Biréli might find it disingenuous to involve himself in the politics of Manouche representation when, by his account, he has led an atypical life for a member of his ethnorace.

While Biréli has the option to politicize his music without seriously compromising his career, other Manouche musicians are concerned that doing so themselves could entail unwanted professional risks. For example, in 2010, Billy and Gaga Weiss (described in this chapter's opening anecdote) were recruited by their half brother Mickaël Stoll, a choreographer, to play guitar in *Samudaripen. Samudaripen,* conceived by Stoll and the director and dramaturg Yan Gilg, is a theatrical production that depicts the Nazi persecution of Romanies during World War II. It premiered in 2010 and aimed to raise awareness about Romani Holocaust survivors and victims through a combination of hip hop dance, spoken word, concentration camp imagery, sound art, and live jazz manouche performance.[13] Several years after *Samudaripen*'s initial run, Billy told me that he had been somewhat hesitant to participate in the project and now wanted to distance himself from it. He said he did not want to be publicly known as "the Holocaust play musician." Like Biréli, and like many other musicians, Billy does not want his artistic reputation to be influenced by how he is politically positioned—especially because, in the case of *Samudaripen,* he has little say in what kind of message his participation broadcasts.

Another professional risk musicians bear by publicly emphasizing their Manouche identity has to do with professionalism itself. As we developed plans for a documentary film Gigi wanted to make about Alsatian Manouche musicians, he told me that it has to "come from a Sinto—it has to be a Sinto who speaks," but that it was also necessary to involve "professionals like you" (meaning a Gadji with academic affiliations) to lend credibility to the project.[14] He told me that framing his music as "jazz" signals "professionalism" much more so than "jazz manouche" does, suggesting that the latter term carries with it the baggage of stereotypes he prefers to avoid.

My Manouche interlocutors are especially aware of how assumptions about the professionalism of Manouches can compromise relationships with Gadjé who employ them. Gadjo concert and festival organizers have described to me in detail how Manouche performers cannot be trusted to show up on time (or at all) or to fulfill contractual obligations. These organizers also complain about Manouches demanding cash advances, asking to be paid off the books, drinking excessively during gigs, and generally being difficult to work with, as if these were ethnoracially distinctive behaviors. This makes it ever more difficult for Manouches who do not engage in such behaviors to earn the trust of employers. Marie-Hélène Gille, the social worker introduced at the end of chapter 2, told me in an interview:

> I think that if Gadjé who play jazz manouche have more gigs than Manouches, it's not for nothing. I think it's really for these reasons: punctuality, being sure that [the musicians] will be there. [Organizers are concerned about] the after-show, how that goes. [When Manouches say,] "I want to be paid under the table, I want to be paid in cash," that becomes hard for organizers. It's true, but there are those [Manouche musicians] who are very professional, and then there are those who will always privilege family or family events first. [They'll say,] "I have a gig then, but [that day is] the wedding of my niece or my daughter or whatever, so I'm going with my family."

Marie-Hélène went on to describe how the Manouches she has worked with conceive of time and planning for the future differently than Gadjé, adding that Manouches who can prove that they know how to plan ahead are the ones more able to secure gigs. Yet no matter how hard these musicians try to establish themselves as reliable and professional, the stigma of being Manouche persists. In the eyes of employers, Manouche ethnorace is, in itself, a liability.

Selectively downplaying one's Manouche background is a way for musicians to mitigate unwanted stereotyping. They promote their music as "jazz," "French jazz," "jazz in Django's style," and other terms that do not explicitly invoke their ethnorace. Meanwhile, Manouche musicians who wish *both* to assert their Manouche backgrounds *and* to be treated as professionals must contend with the burdens of stereotypes beyond their control. Musicians may adopt any of these approaches at different points in their careers, depending on which risks they are willing to take. Each of these choices reflects the awareness Manouche musicians have of how Gadjé ethnoracialize them, as well as musicians' tactics for navigating social and professional circumstances not of their own choosing.

Striving for Inclusion

In a spirit of collaboration across social boundaries, a number of my interlocutors have critiqued the term *jazz manouche* because it suggests a degree of ethnoracial sectarianism. The term may imply that only Manouches have the right to perform the music, or that jazz manouche is the only music appropriate for Manouches to perform. This is a stance that many musicians reject, in part by avoiding the term *jazz manouche* and referring to it as "this" or "that" music, as Biréli did in our interview:

> I know guitar players, Gypsies that I wouldn't mention, [who are] very closed to other guitar players who are *non*-Gypsies and who played that music. So if you're not a Gypsy, you *almost* are not allowed to play this kind of music. Like, it doesn't belong to you. And I think it's a terrible mistake, because you know, you can be Hindu, I don't know, Japanese, and play classical music, or jazz or whatever. I mean, to me, it doesn't matter where [you are from]. You can play whatever kind of music you like.

Manouche guitarist Cédric Loeffler similarly decried the divisive effects of using the "jazz manouche" label in an interview with me. Cédric earns his living primarily by playing rhythm guitar with his father, Marcel Loeffler, one of the most sought-after accordionists in France (in both jazz manouche and jazz more broadly). Musicians I've spoken with praise Cédric for his skill and nuance in the jazz manouche rhythmic style, though he takes issue with being labeled as a jazz manouche musician, telling me,

> When people say [jazz manouche], it forces us [Manouche musicians] into a box. It's almost like a sect when people do that. They have to understand that [the music] shouldn't be [labeled] like that, that things don't happen like that, that they stop modeling this music in that way, because they're in the process of spoiling it.

For Cédric, "jazz manouche" simultaneously produces unwanted aesthetic effects (it "spoils" the music) and social ones ("it's almost like a sect"). He bristles at how "jazz manouche" distills Manouche musicality into a single genre and reifies the idea that Manouches are unequivocally *different*. Christophe Astolfi, a Paris-based lead guitarist who has a long history of collaboration with musicians in the jazz manouche scene, echoed these concerns in an interview with me:

> For me, jazz manouche is a fiction, and the consequences of that are that it separates people. It creates antagonisms between people, and it creates a kind of folklore around the music. This folklore, it fixes, it limits the music. It prevents it from breathing, from advancing healthily, from evolving.

Here again, the label inhibits both social and aesthetic ideals in that it "separates people" and "limits the music," respectively. By using organic metaphors, Christophe suggests that music (like people) should develop naturally and independently of preordained, restrictive cultural categories. He continued to deride the stereotypes entailed in the "jazz manouche" label, focusing on the "grotesque" social consequences of its application:

> I've had people ask me where I park my caravan. And when [jazz manouche] started becoming trendy, I saw guys who were lawyers, insurance agents, who had boring lives, to put it bluntly. All of a sudden, they listened to so-called jazz manouche and they bought caravans to leave for the weekend with their wives. It seemed grotesque. These are things I don't participate in, and that are linked in part to this label of jazz manouche.

Christophe considers not only the attribution of stereotypes—that Manouches all live in caravans and roam whenever and wherever they please—but also the casual appropriation of such stereotypes by Gadjé to constitute a mockery both of Manouche populations and of the music labeled "jazz manouche." His critique is leveled less at the term itself and more at French men in white-collar jobs who see its ethnoracial implications as a fun antidote to their otherwise "boring lives." As a Gadjo himself, he makes an effort to distance himself from these Gadjé who unselfconsciously reproduce Manouche stereotypes.

Christophe further suggested that the "jazz manouche" label elides the diversity of the genre's participants, saying that although "it's true that Manouches have carried the torch, between Django's death and today," the label "reduces the [role of] the actors in this music, of which there are many." He concluded by saying that, in light of the reductive and inappropriate implications of the genre label, "when someone asks me, I say I play guitar in the tradition of Django Reinhardt, or Parisian jazz." Musicians like Christophe use the substitution of a geographic region for *manouche* in the genre label to simultaneously counter ethnoracially essentializing assumptions and assert the music's cross-cultural appeal. By calling the music Parisian—or, more generally, French—speakers acknowledge that a diverse array of people produces this music, not just Manouches.

From a Manouche perspective, calling the genre "French jazz" performs a claim to cultural citizenship. If the genre is already tightly associated with Manouche individuals and communities, recasting it as French jazz suggests that Manouche cultural production must also be considered an integral part of French cultural production. This synonym allows Manouches to claim that *they* have made significant contributions to French culture and should thus be afforded a greater degree of cultural citizenship. At the same time, it mitigates the idea that Manouches are incompatible with French culture and values, for if jazz manouche has been French jazz all along, perhaps Manouches might also be more French than many seem to believe.

Recall Dino Mehrstein insisting that, in addition to other cultural and gastronomical products, Django was also "part of *French* heritage!" Later in our interview, he told me that he prefers to call his music "French swing," saying that when it is called "jazz manouche,"

> There are divisions. When there are divisions, *whoa,* I don't like that. As soon as there are divisions, there are tensions. It's not about competition. I'll say that people attribute so many things to France, music included. Except that swing had its representative, and he was Manouche, okay. I want to reaffirm that [the music] is not uniquely Manouche, but it's rather part of swing. And it's in France that it was created. A swing purely, aesthetically French. That means that it has a certain connotation, that it is certainly not American.

With or without the elision of the *manouche* part of the label, Manouches may claim this genre to be part of a national or regional heritage in the interest of their own cultural citizenship. Gigi phrases his conception of the genre as especially Alsatian by saying that "Alsace has a *jazz,*" sometimes referring to this music as "jazz manouche" and other times as "Django-style jazz." He frames the genre as an untapped resource that French leaders should exploit, telling me at one point that "a country can be rich, whether in oil, in fruit, or in jazz." By construing his music as "jazz" above all, by indexing its practice to his Manouche family, and by emphasizing its connection to Alsace, Gigi attempts to carve out a place for Manouches in Alsatian heritage.

Gigi has even attempted, numerous times, to insert himself into local and regional politics by meeting with officials and proposing jazz manouche cultural projects. One day he expressed to me, in a strikingly poetic manner, how he manages what he perceives to be the implicit racism of political gatekeepers in these meetings, using quoted speech to describe a hypothetical, caricatured encounter. When speaking as himself, he looked up animatedly and used wide hand gestures with a relatively high-pitched, straining tone of voice; in the role of the politicians, he turned his head down and side to side with a stern facial expression, mumbling utterances tersely, except for the final line. Below, I put Gigi speaking in his own voice in bold and the imaginary, nameless politicians in italics:

Oh no, I'm Manouche!
[to each other] *Oh yes, a Manouche.*
So he [can] speak?
Yes, a Manouche!
Oh no, he's not just a Manouche.
He doesn't give a damn.
That's what a Manouche is.
Jazz intellectuals and the major conservatories and everything: open your doors! Yes, there is a jazz!
[to Gigi] *Oh Lord, stop!*
I'm French. Oh no—I'm Manouche. But French, yes.
Ah, you have a jazz!

Gesturally and prosodically, Gigi's soliloquy encapsulates the dismissive biases he imagines these gatekeepers must hold against him as a Manouche. It also reveals his internal struggle to reconcile his Manouche ethnorace with his French identity, as well as his conviction that jazz is the most feasible means by which to earn recognition from, and entry into, local and regional institutions. Gigi insists that by framing jazz manouche as Alsatian jazz, he can secure a place for himself and for other Manouche musicians within structures of institutional power. At the same time, he does not reject the "jazz manouche" label, but rather seeks to recontextualize it as simultaneously ethnoracial, regional, national, and even universal. In this imagined endeavor, Gigi articulates the contradictions of hearing himself, and being heard, as both French and Manouche, and of hearing jazz manouche as spanning scales of inclusion.

Redefining Manouche Freedom

If one of the most frequent complaints about the "jazz manouche" label is that Django would have abhorred or not recognized it, this is partly because many musicians idolize him primarily for his artistic ideals. Given that jazz manouche is grounded in the reproduction of his work, some consider the genre a contradiction to Django's own musical values. Musicians ask: Should players who want to emulate Django focus on how he executed his creative vision, or on that vision itself? For them, to follow in Django's footsteps is first to imitate his techniques, then to innovate *new* styles. As guitarist Sébastien Giniaux put it to me in an interview, "I'm kind of tired of this 'jazz manouche.' Okay, I'm not tired of it, because it's great, but I have too many other things to do. I don't want to turn sixty years old and look back on my life and say, 'Oh, I played Django.'"

To discursively situate themselves as creative musicians in what they believe to be the "spirit of Django," a number of musicians refuse to be categorized only, or at all, as jazz manouche. Their artistic choices reflect a desire to transcend a dichotomy, especially prevalent in discourse on jazz education in the United States, in which "creativity has come to index modernity whereas imitation has come to connote tradition" (Wilf 2012, 32). These musicians prefer to align themselves with the modern and innovative values of jazz—or of other musics, for that matter—rather than with the conservatism of jazz manouche alone, exercising the "active musical self-fashioning" that Monson calls "aesthetic agency" (2007, 73).

One such musician is Railo Helmstetter, whom I introduced briefly in the last chapter. Railo, a guitarist now in his thirties, was raised in a Manouche family, from whom he learned to play jazz manouche. However, as he told me in an interview, he knew from a young age that he wanted to branch out from his family's tradition. As a teenager, he started listening to "American jazz, then jazz fusion, jazz-rock-fusion, and funk," and by the time of our interview in 2013, he was preparing to visit Morocco to collaborate with local musicians there. Railo told me that in contrast to many other Manouche musicians,

> I don't ever want to put myself in a precise style. I really want to be able to distance myself from the Manouche [style], like through fusion, playing with distortion, you see? It's a choice, after all.

Musicians like Railo do not always view such self-distancing from jazz manouche as a *rejection* of the genre per se, but as a productive opening to other musical influences. They point to Biréli Lagrène as an example of a musician who has succeeded at crossing generic boundaries, sometimes integrating jazz manouche, and sometimes straying from it completely. Biréli is an especially important example for Manouche musicians who publicly identify as Manouche but who must make concerted efforts to avoid being pigeonholed as only interested in jazz manouche by virtue of their ethnorace. Such musicians are mainly concerned with how the generic label affects their audience reception and their opportunities for collaboration with a wide array of musicians.

Within certain Manouche communities, the rejection of jazz manouche (both as a label and as a set of stylistic parameters) can stir up conflict, though this has become less of an issue in recent years. Through their community-building work with Alsatian Manouche communities, Marcel Daval and Pierre Hauger (1989) concluded that in the 1980s, musicians who displayed too much individualism (by drawing on musical influences unfamiliar to the group, and/or by excessively showing off their improvisational skills) would be considered a threat to group solidarity. Since musical practice was considered central "to their internal cohesion, and to the regulation of their relations with the exterior" (487), such an expression of individual differentiation would be perceived as "an act of sectarianism and intolerance" (480), potentially alienating both fellow players and audience members. In an interview, Hauger told me that among the Manouches he worked with in the 1980s, a "division" along the lines of music would "have consequences well beyond the music. . . . There was not one person who would suddenly [proclaim] somewhat marginal tastes, because he would have been excluded from his milieu."[15]

Technological advances over the past several decades have increased the accessibility of various musical genres, including hip hop and other types of popular music, which allows for a more diverse musical landscape within Manouche communities. Today, without a clearly delineated scope of what constitutes "good" or appropriate music within and across these communities, individuals are far less likely to be sanctioned for performing or consuming newer styles of music. Still, judgments about what constitutes proper Manouche musical taste and genres of performance endure among certain people.

In my experience, these judgments may reveal other related concerns. One Manouche musician, Léo, once complained to me that he thought it was ridiculous that another Manouche musician, Oscar, was always asked to perform at Romani-themed events.[16] When I asked why, he said that Oscar was not representative of Alsatian Manouches because he played "klezmer." Oscar's influences include, among others, Eastern European Romani musics, which Léo erroneously labels "klezmer" in order to portray them as definitively non-Manouche (despite the Manouche history of performing "Hungarian" musics; see chapter 1).[17] While Léo's assessment is, on the surface, about accurate representation of his community's musical practices, it betrays an immediate concern with his own professional reputation and income as a musician who plays jazz manouche more exclusively than Oscar does. His complaint points to the economic incentivization of, and competing professional interests within, a field of ethnoracial representation. Much is at stake for both musicians in how they market themselves as Manouche: as faithful bearers of a jazz manouche tradition, or as musical polymaths uninhibited by this tradition.

Léo's complaint also points to an apparent paradox in certain conceptions of Manouche identity. A number of my interlocutors insist that jazz manouche is "real Manouche music," while also espousing the notion that Manouches are defined by their "freedom." They overwhelmingly describe themselves as "free" compared to Gadjé. For example, one Manouche musician told me in an interview that a Manouche

> is not someone who gets worked up about daily life. It's someone who is going to live day to day without really thinking about the next day. It's not someone who is going to worry about always calculating, about always lining things up in life. No, it's someone who has a very free mindset. Very, very free. And I think Gadjé envy us for that. They really envy us for having such a simple state of mind, and for not always taking things so seriously.

In countless other conversations, Manouches have made similar claims to me about their sense of freedom. But, as it became clear to me over time, this conception applies only to specific realms (and always with exceptions): freedom to enjoy the outdoors; freedom for children to do as they please; freedom from schedules, bureaucracy, and other demands the Gadjo world places on them. A general sense of "freedom" is also a commonly held stereotype about Romani cultures more broadly, one that is used both to romanticize Romanies and to disparage them as primitive and marginal to civil society. However, many Manouches cast this stereotype in a positive light, taking pride in what they consider to be a form of resistance to the barbarism of normative Gadjo society.

Within conservative Manouche communities, freedoms coexist with constraints, including restrictive gender roles, especially for women; ostracization for consorting too much with Gadjé or for pursuing higher education; and, sometimes, consensus on the proper limits of musical taste. Opinions vary as to what makes a person a "real" Manouche, whether blood, values, language, behaviors, or a combination thereof. Some insist that an itinerant lifestyle affirms their ethnoracial authenticity, while others claim the exact opposite. Individuals of mixed Manouche and non-Manouche parentage face extra scrutiny in these discussions.

In terms of its consumption and production, music is one of the realms in which some Manouches frequently pass judgment about ethnoracial fidelity. A person may call themself a "real" Manouche for espousing ideals of freedom in musical taste, while another may critique this same person as being a "fake" Manouche for straying from jazz manouche. The decision by someone like Railo to pursue different genres of music becomes simultaneously an affirmation of particular Manouche values and a disavowal of others. Musicians like these declare their sense of ethnoracial belonging by selectively challenging the very grounds on which others define their identities. In other words, these musicians embrace a degree of musical liberty that they perceive to be in line with a broader discourse of Romani freedom.

To prove this point, Biréli lamented to me, "I see so many Gypsy players who decided to just play the same solos as Django. . . . I used to do it too. And this doesn't bring this music any further. . . . I brought something else into it, something to give to the people, and to say to the audience, 'here, this is what we can do also, with this kind of music.' With great respect!" In an interview, Cédric Loeffler praised Biréli and his own father Marcel for being the only Manouches he knows to have an "unlimited open-mindedness" when it comes to music, adding that "it's really too bad that among us [Manouches], [there is no] evolution. That's what kind of closes the doors." When I asked why this is the case, he said that "it's because they might be scared. They're scared to commit an infidelity. You know how it is with us Manouches. It's kind of a closed-off thing. If someone wants to go toward other musical horizons, [other Manouches] won't always understand." Cédric characterizes this fear as a "misplaced [form of] respect," underscoring his belief that respect—both for Django and for one's own community—should manifest not through fealty to a rigid musical tradition, but through creative evolution and openness. He believes that the Manouche rhetoric of freedom should extend to musical practice and that respect for musical freedom epitomizes the cultural values *he* prioritizes as a Manouche person.

Musical freedom in this sense does not necessarily mean a renunciation of jazz manouche. For example, in their publicity materials, Manouche musicians such as Marcel Loeffler and Engé Helmstetter choose to highlight the fact that they perform other genres in addition to jazz manouche. The banner of Engé's website states: "Engé: jazz manouche and more . . . ," while the first lines of the website's text read:

> [A] pluralist guitarist, Engé Helmstetter traces a route between jazz and world musics. His repertoire privileges the guitar and [other] string [instruments,] and if the figure of Django Reinhardt always lingers with tenderness in the curve of a phrase, other musical influences complete the musical voyage he offers to us [with] bossa nova [and] Tsigane repertoire. Liberating himself from stylistic rigidities, he draws from his Manouche roots

> the ferments of a creative freedom expressed through composition, [with] his works well-received by the public and by critics. ("Engé" n.d.)

The English version of Marcel's landing page similarly states:

> Immersed in manouche music and jazz since [he was] a child, Marcel Loeffler marries tradition and new forms of expression with marvelous talent. His amazing ability to adapt to widely varying music genres allows him to improvise "with mastery and a harmoniously rhythmic subtlety on par with American specialists" (*Jazz Magazine*). From bebop to modern jazz, from tango to softer ambiances, Marcel lets his multiple talents bellow out from his instrument. A solid composer who never forgets the melody, he is an improviser with a lot of brio, and a clear song line. ("Marcel Loeffler, accordéoniste de jazz")

Engé and Marcel use adjectives like "pluralist" and "multiple" to describe how their musical styles reconcile their Manouche "tradition" and "roots" with "world musics," "creative freedom," and "widely varying music genres." Engé names the "stylistic rigidities" from which he "liberat[es] himself" without repudiating his Manouche roots. These roots give rise to "ferments of a creative freedom," suggesting that a plurality of musical influences is actually a welcome result of his ethnoracial background. Recent concert programs reflect these capacious approaches: Marcel's most prominent concert of 2019 was billed as "a meeting between jazz manouche and American gospel,"[18] while an evening titled "Tziganes en Liberté" featured Marcel, Cédric, Engé, and Biréli alongside several musicians who specialize in Romanian Romani musics. Engé's Facebook announcement of the latter concert describes it as "interspersing connections [between Romanian Romani musics and] jazz and Manouche swing." Engé's latest project, the Ytré Quartet with his brother violinist Tchatcho Helmstetter, violinist Yardani Torres Maiani, and Ralio, also prides itself on its generic eclecticism.

By explicitly defining their musicality in terms other than, or in addition to, jazz manouche, Engé's and Marcel's promotional strategies suggest alternative conceptions of Manouche authenticity. Descriptions of musical style offer possibilities for challenging both emic and etic notions of what it means to play like a Manouche, and by extension, what it means to be Manouche. Generic diversity may be used to challenge prevailing definitions of one's ethnorace, or simply to proclaim their privileging of artistic creativity over the preservation of tradition. In both cases, the refusal to adhere to the parameters of jazz manouche and to be categorized as a musician in the genre is simultaneously an aesthetic and a political choice. If Manouches and Gadjé alike have, for years, associated notions of Manouche identity with jazz manouche, firmly entangling ethnoracial ontology with stylistic parameters, the explicit adoption of musical practices outside this paradigm seeks to *un*tangle reductive assumptions linking ethnorace with aesthetics.

Navigating Ambivalence

To refuse strict musical categorization is also to refuse, or to realign, social categorization. It is a way to assert that an individual's ethnorace and nationality should not determine their social, political, and cultural allegiances, but that one can choose among such allegiances. Though the stakes are different, and likely higher, for Manouches to depart from jazz manouche in favor of stylistic plurality, the same can be said of Gadjé and of other musicians who deliberately situate themselves outside conventional genre boundaries.

In closing this chapter, I'd like to return to where it began, with Billy's response to the question "What is jazz manouche?" About a month after our initial interview, I had the opportunity to sit down with him and Yorgui. This time, I asked Billy a different question along similar lines:

SL: If someone asks you what kind of music you play, what do you say?

BW: [*laughs*] In my opinion, I don't know what I do! I play, I improvise. Well, you can say that Django, he gave us everything. . . . I'd say that [he changed] all of Manouche culture. It's enormous. But me, [*laughs*] I don't know what I do. Yorgui too, I don't know what he does when he plays!

In this response, Billy's strategy is to avoid generic categorization altogether, emphasizing the uniqueness of his music by claiming not to know how to describe it. Still, he cites Django as a major influence on Manouche culture, suggesting that although he himself was inspired by Django, his own music departs from what might typically be characterized as Manouche. He gave Yorgui the same treatment, to which Yorgui responded, half-jokingly,

You don't know, [but] me, I know what I do. [*Billy laughs*] You don't know; me, I know what I do! [*Yorgui laughs*] Yes, I do jazz manouche. That's clear, of course. Jazz, jazz manouche. With other musical influences, I try to do a lot of compositions. Not taking up too many tunes that have been—well, [not] copy-pasting. In fact, it's that. It's trying to progress in a musical style.

Rather than eliding musical description and equating ineffability with singularity, Yorgui is straightforward. He acknowledges that he plays jazz manouche, adding that by incorporating "other musical influences," he tries to push the boundaries of the genre he most closely identifies with. By prioritizing creative work such as composition and by avoiding imitation, his goal is "to progress" personally within this idiom. Yorgui both embraces and looks beyond jazz manouche, an approach that is crucial to the professional success he has earned.

Yorgui's self-assuredness in how he relates to jazz manouche is perhaps rare among professional musicians in the genre. For others, defining the genre and one's relation to it is a task at times agonizing, at times exciting, and seldom simple. It is the labor of ambivalent essentialism. As I've shown in this chapter, the discursive positioning of jazz manouche highlights temporally contingent, ideological contentions about ethnorace and citizenship that suffuse the genre's contexts and aesthetics. Statements about the ontology of jazz manouche convey opinions about why ethnorace matters (or does not), how ethnorace should be defined (or should not), who belongs to a particular community (and who does not), and the kinds of social and political ideals the genre's participants aspire to.

Discourse about jazz manouche also speaks to the heterogeneity of populations defined in relation to ethnorace. Interlocutors reveal both homogenizing and plural notions about what constitutes Manouche and Gadjo identities. Genre discourses may reinforce or challenge such social divisions, often throwing into relief how they can be arbitrary yet deeply rooted. In these ways, genre "is one of the arenas in which the patterns and contradictions of ideology become visible" (Brackett 2016, 26). Sometimes these (semiotic) ideologies are barely visible, obscured between the lines of discourse on jazz manouche, while at other times, discourse lays them bare. Just as the genre is multifaceted and contestable, so are the ideological stances articulated.

In the absence of any explicit political platform or agenda concerning Manouche rights, the debate over jazz manouche is a way for Manouches to express the degree to which they enjoy—or hope to enjoy—a sense of cultural citizenship in France. It indexes the complicated relationships musicians have both to their ethnoracial identity and to ideas about national belonging. It especially underscores the ambivalence they navigate with respect to cultural citizenship, for being simultaneously French and Manouche entails an unresolvable tension. Refusing jazz manouche is one way to address this tension: to have it subsumed by the supposedly universal nature of jazz, or to assert aspirations to republican ideals. In both cases, the repudiation of the "Manouche" label is meant as a liberating move. It need not entail a disavowal of musicians' own self-identifications *as Manouches*; rather, it realigns what it means to be minoritized in a French context.

FOUR

The Sound of Feeling

In the previous chapter, I explored the difficulties of defining a genre's contours as well as the generative spaces such difficulties open up. When I asked Billy how he would describe the music he plays, his immediate reaction was to laugh and say, "I don't know what I do!" This is not an uncommon response from musicians. Putting one's musical style, or even a particular sound, into words is often an onerous task. But while some people say they don't know how to describe musical sounds in terms of genre, timbre, or other technical aspects, they often have no problem explaining how these sounds make them *feel*.

Consider, for example, one listener's enthusiasm for Manouche guitarist Tchavolo Schmitt (known colloquially, like some others in the jazz manouche scene, by his first name only). Sitting with me outside a café near our apartments in Strasbourg one afternoon, guitarist Cédric Loeffler said that there are some fine guitarists in Paris, but few have a "really Manouche thing." He then started praising an Alsatian musician who he said sounded like Tchavolo "back in the day." Quickly, Cédric grew animated, his voice grittier with emphasis, as he exclaimed:

> You hear [Tchavolo], and he's *the Manouche* at two hundred percent! When you hear him, there are *flames* everywhere. In one blow he will *tear you apart*, you see. He and Django are the ones who *really* [gave me this] feeling in my stomach and made me want to [play this music].

Indeed, Tchavolo is known for an especially freewheeling, exuberant approach to soloing. This can be heard in a live version of the tune "Mire pral" in which he displays a strong right-hand attack, rapid fluctuations in dynamics, and some muffled notes alongside heavily accented ones.[1] For Cédric, a performance by Tchavolo is most striking in its sheer visceral force: one that generates sonic "flames," figuratively poses a physical threat to its listeners, and aligns with Tchavolo's ethnoracial identity. Tchavolo is, by Cédric's estimation, sonically Manouche beyond comparison. The gut feeling Cédric first experienced from this sound helped motivate him to join his Manouche family members in pursuing a career in music.

To many of my interlocutors, particular signs are understood to authentically represent Manouche identity, such as the use of the Manouche language, places of residence, taste in various forms of media, and for some, the way a person plays the guitar. The strategies used to describe such guitar sounds frequently entail the use of sensuous metaphors with regard to *force*: a sound can be powerful, feelingful, loud, fiery, raw; it can deliver a "punch" and even be laden with "testosterone." In talk about jazz manouche guitar, these powerful sensations are often associated with people of Manouche background, especially Alsatian Manouche men. Manouche identity even takes shape as a perceivable, yet ineffable, sensory characteristic in and of itself.

This chapter explores how listeners hear and make sense of ethnoracialized sound. I show that a raciosemiotic approach can reveal continuities between individual sonic perceptions of ethnorace and broader semiotic ideologies about ethnorace. By paying attention to how particular timbral and articulatory characteristics in guitar technique are perceived as "Manouche," we can better understand how "listening subjects" (Inoue 2006) naturalize ethnorace and link it to notions of place, history, gender, and other social domains. Furthermore, in delineating a unique sense of the Manouche, those who engage with these semiotic processes also delineate the normative Gadjo with whom the Manouche is contrasted.

Notably, many of the speakers I identify in chapter 3 who refuse the "jazz manouche" label also claim that there still exists a uniquely Manouche guitar sound. This kind of sonic ethnoracial difference can be promoted as something exclusive to Manouches, part of a branding strategy that establishes Manouche musical production as superior to that of Gadjé. The ability to produce and recognize these sounds can bolster a sense of Manouche pride and belonging while also being economically and politically advantageous. Yet such claims can reproduce stereotypes that posit musical style and talent as innate to Manouches. Ambivalence often arises from one's awareness of all these possible implications. In the pages that follow, I show how Manouches contend with being marked as inherently or culturally "different" and how they may attempt to manipulate these putative differences for their own gain.

Considering the widespread ethos of "racial avoidance" (Fleming 2017) in France, talk about ethnoracialized music can be an important means for listeners to express their positions on ethnorace. Such talk offers a window into how ethnoracial identities become discursively naturalized. In this chapter, I explore how those in the jazz manouche scene articulate what Manouche guitar techniques sound like, focusing on the affective dimensions of listening for "sono-racial difference" (Roberts 2016, 16).[2] In doing so, speakers give shape to their ideas about the ontology of ethnorace and how it should be valued and instilled. Often, they valorize gendered qualities that might otherwise be denigrating—such as rawness and loudness—as important aspects of their ethnoracial identity that must be learned, not necessarily inherited.[3] This helps Manouches define ethnoracial belonging on their own terms and refashion ethnoracializing discourses to their advantage.

The idea of a unique Manouche sound also reflects deeply rooted anxieties about the loss of tradition and exploitation by Gadjé, as well as uncertainties about the very constitution of Manouche ethnoracial identity. Construing a sound as ineffable—as impossible to capture in words—is a way to manage uncertainty about sonic and ethnoracial ontologies. Like Ronald Radano, who discusses the "seeming supradiscursivity" of "Black music's power" (2003, 21), I argue that a sound's indescribability can be considered proof of that sound's affective power. By attending to the strategies people use to describe sonic experience—how a sound makes a person *feel*—I show how, in turn, people comprehend ontologies of sound.

To be clear, I do not seek to objectively define a Manouche sound. Rather, I assess how listening subjects apperceive ethnoracialized sound.[4] While it may seem that, in doing so, I aim to debunk the very notion of a uniquely Manouche sound, this is not quite my intention. Instead, I am more interested in what attention to *how* people interpret such sounds can reveal about *why* they might ethnoracialize what they hear. What does belief in (or disavowal of) a Manouche sound accomplish for listeners, musicians included? What does this disclose about how listeners understand both the nature of sound and the nature of ethnorace? Claiming that sound is ineffable is an important part of this process, serving at times as a way to deal with the ambivalence that underlies the supposed audibility of ethnorace.

Raciosemiotic Ideologies of Sound

As explained in this book's introduction, a raciosemiotic approach accounts for how various semiotic modalities operate together in the generation of semiotic ideologies about (ethno)race. The semiotic theory of Charles S. Peirce forms the basis for such an approach, especially in that it accounts for fluidity between language and other semiotic modalities and between sensory experience and cognition. Peirce's broad conception of the sign—as "something which stands to somebody for something" and that "creates in the mind of that person an equivalent sign, or perhaps a more developed sign" (1955, 99)—means that any sound can become a sign through its apperception as a meaningful event.[5] Because this approach does not construct hard boundaries between semiotic modalities, such as language and music, it allows us to understand how different means of expression and interpretation operate together (Faudree 2012).

Peirce accounts for the semiosis of sensory experience through his concept of *qualia*, notably developed by several linguistic anthropologists inspired by Nancy Munn's (1986) work on the transformation of value.[6] As understood by these scholars, qualia can be defined as "sign vehicles reflexively taken to be sensuous instances of abstract qualities (stink, warmth, hardness, straightness, etc.)" (Harkness 2015, 574) and as "qualities instantiated or embodied in entities or events" (Chumley and Harkness 2013, 5; see also Harkness 2021). In other words, qualia are materializations of potential sensory qualities; so, for example, one can't conceive of "stink" without experiencing it through something stinky. *Qualisigns*, in turn, arise when qualities become signs in themselves. As Lily Chumley and Nicholas Harkness put it, "Properties like greenness and hotness only appear to us in the form of things like leaves and fire, and yet we get the sense that these properties can be abstracted 'hypostatically' for any particular object" (2013, 6)—in other words, that "greenness" can be abstracted from "green."[7] Thus, "in the qualisign, it is this abstracted property itself—greenness, hotness—that signifies, not just the leaf or the fire" (6). In cases where this abstracted property (quality) is interpreted as meaningful in itself, it can then be called a qualisign.

What Harkness calls "qualic transitivity" (2013, 26) occurs when the same qualia are perceived as linked across domains.[8] For example, the hotness of a fire can also be linked to the hotness of a pepper or of a mood. Qualic transitivity is important to understanding how the qualia of particular *sounds* become the qualia of *cultural attributes*. For some of my interlocutors, a sound perceived as fiery or raw will also index the supposed fieriness or rawness of Manouche culture. Attention to qualia and qualic transitivity can help describe how continuities emerge between semiotic modalities such as music and language. Thinking in these terms allows us to recognize how a musical sound can be perceived as *indexical* of an ethnoracial category, in that the sound points to or is contiguous with the presence of a specific ethnoracialized body or a general type of ethnorace. Sound can also be perceived as *iconic* of the ethnoracialized body assumed to be producing it, in that the sound and the body are perceived to share some kind of formal similarity (see Peirce 1998, 4–26; Parmentier 1994, 3–22). Importantly, the qualia of ethnorace can only be defined intersubjectively. The conventionalization of qualisigns allows "social actors to recognize particular people (and particular things) as having particular 'qualities'" (Chumley and Harkness 2013, 6), accounting for the social dimensions of sensory experience.[9]

The apperception of timbre is especially apt to involve processes of qualic transitivity. Timbre allows us to know—or to *think* we know—who or what is making a sound. Because timbre is "a slippery concept and a slippery percept, perceptually malleable and difficult to define in precisely arranged units" (Fales 2002, 58), speakers must rely on various linguistic strategies both to interpret and to convey their perceptions of timbre (see also Porcello 2002; Olwage 2004). Qualia are frequently invoked in these strategies because they can linguistically construct links between prior, intersubjectively shared sensory experiences. As metaphors that are understood to remedy the ineffability of timbre, qualia allow speakers to make sense of what they hear. And as they facilitate the communication of sensory experience, qualia can be taken to represent not only the sound itself, but also the source of the sound: in describing a sound as rough, a speaker might characterize the body producing that sound as rough, too.

Timbre plays an important role in how social identities such as ethnorace and gender are constructed and perceived. Identity categories are not just constituted through the realm of words but are produced at intersections between semiotic modalities such as sound, image, and bodily movement.[10] Studies of race and voice in particular tell us that voices are often heard as reliable indicators of racial identities. Voices heard as human are thought to emanate from bodies, like extensions of bodies themselves.[11] Nina Sun Eidsheim writes that when we hear a voice as racialized, we hear a "thick event" (2019, 10) that is actually "a composite of visual, textural, discursive, and other kinds of information.

In other words, the multisensory context surrounding a voice forms a filter, a 'suggestion' through which we listen" (Eidsheim 2012, 10). Various semiotic modalities comprise the thick event, but they are distilled in the act of perception. Listeners don't always consciously recognize this contextual complexity. A Peircean approach to qualia—one that emphasizes the *interpretation* of various sensory inputs—allows us to recognize the many elements of the thick event and to further develop the idea that ethnorace "is not the resonance of a particular type of body; instead *it resonates in the listener's ear*" (Eidsheim 2011, 646; emphasis in original).

The remainder of this chapter builds on the aforementioned approach to voice and race, but instead treats instrumental sound as perceived extensions of ethnoracialized and gendered bodies.[12] In talk about the sensory impressions made by guitar sounds, a certain guitar stroke is not only powerful, raw, feelingful, and so on; it is these things because *both* the (male) guitarist *and the sound itself* are heard—and felt—as palpably Manouche. Similar to "iconicity of feeling," in which Apache identity is considered a consistent "feeling" across temporalities and expressive forms (Samuels 2004, 11 and 54), speakers invoke qualia and qualic transitivity to explain that one can just *feel* when a Manouche person is producing certain sounds. In doing so, they render a masculinized notion of Manouche identity into a perceptible sensation and therefore a quality in and of itself, like the composite qualities used to describe it.

Borrowing from Ruth Frankenberg's (1993) concept of "racialness," I propose naming the feeling of ethnoracial identity *ethnoracialness*.[13] Ethnoracialness is both a quality—a potential sensation—and a qualisign—a potential sensation rendered meaningful.[14] The *-ness* of *ethnoracialness* emphasizes its sensorial dimensions as well as its often ineffable character, as when speakers name other qualia in order to convey the feeling of ethnoracial identity.[15] Ethnoracialness also suggests the ambiguity of ethnoracial differences as inherited and/or enculturated. In the way that *ethnorace* draws attention to the blurry lines between ethnicity and race, *ethnoracialness* underscores how differences are both naturalized and socially reproduced. It is worth reiterating here that just as race and ethnicity are social constructions with real effects, ethnoracialness exists not as a material fact but in the minds of its perceivers.

By classifying a series of qualia as inherently "Manouche," and by recognizing causal relationships between gendered ethnorace and qualia, interlocutors "rhematize" (Gal 2005, 35) Manouche identity from a social category into the embodied qualisign of ethnoracialness. Judith T. Irvine and Susan Gal originally named rhematization "iconization" and described the latter as when "linguistic features that index social groups or activities appear to be iconic representations of them, as if a linguistic feature somewhere depicted or displayed a social group's inherent nature or essence" (2000, 37; see also Gal 2013). Expanding "linguistic features" to include all possible semiotic modalities, and thus musical (and more broadly, sonic) semiosis, discourse linking sound to ethnorace can render *musical* features into icons of Manouche ethnoracialness.[16]

Ethnoracialness can be invoked as a sonically mediated qualisign when listeners articulate their affective responses to musical performance, especially jazz manouche. As I showed earlier, Cédric describes hearing Tchavolo as "*the Manouche* at two hundred percent!" before offering other qualia to further illustrate his own experience of Tchavolo's sound. By insisting upon the sensory perceptibility of Manouche identity, interlocutors naturalize this identity from an abstract social category into a qualisign of ethnoracialness they claim to perceive in sound. In many instances, they also render normative a specifically masculine conception of this ethnoracialness. The ability to produce (and to hear) such an ethnoracialized sound is attributed primarily to long-term immersion in regionally specific Manouche culture. It is reflective of Manouche ideals, inscribed in bodies but not determined by genetics. Listening subjects conventionalize instrumental sound as not only representative of ethnoracial attributes and social values, but as actual, palpable instantiations of these attributes and values.

The Poetics of Ineffability and "Feeling"

As chapters 1 and 3 explained, the existence (real or imagined) of Manouche qualities in jazz manouche are often retrofitted onto Django's recordings (Givan 2014; Williams 2015). Patrick Williams writes that if we (an audience) hear a Manouche influence in his music, it is because "we have learned to do so with all his disciples and followers" (2000, 411). But others, including certain musicians and critics from the swing era to the present day, have assumed the contrary (e.g., Dregni 2008, 144). In an interview with me, Manouche accordionist Marcel Loeffler linked the affective force of Django's recordings to his presumed influence from Romani music: "Django was able to create the same emotion in his music because he was really inspired by [Eastern European Romani] music. For example, he did a version of a tune called '[Waves of] the Danube,' and there, you hear very well that he was really inspired by this culture." Having grown up in a family of professional Manouche musicians in which Eastern European Romani tunes were prevalent, Marcel projects his own frame of reference onto Django's experience. He connects his perception of Django's Romani expressivity to the guitarist's choice of repertoire, "Waves of the Danube," a nineteenth-century Romanian piece composed by Ion Ivanovici (though Django recorded it under the title "Anniversary Song," arranged by Al Jolson and Saul Chaplin and published as such in 1946). Although Marcel's stated evidence for Django's Romani influence is tenuous, he draws on his own deep experience with Romani music to justify his claim that such influence is audible.

Marcel also told me that "when Django plays a ballad, it's almost as—I don't know how to say it. It's as if a violinist played a piece that made you cry like that." Here, he qualifies his lack of words by describing a hypothetical emotional response to the sound he is attempting to describe. As stated at the beginning of this chapter, asserting that a sound is ineffable does not always indicate a failure, but possibly a strategy: claims to ineffability can actually convey more affective force than emotional descriptors themselves. In other words, as Michael Gallope argues, "Vagueness can nonetheless be explanatory in its own right" (2017, 9). These claims can also work in tandem with descriptive language (e.g., "*I can't even tell you* how intense it was!"). As such, speakers enact a poetics of ineffability in which they convey affective intensity by suggesting that they lack the words for a felt phenomenon. The effectiveness of ineffability is reinforced by using affective descriptors simultaneously.

Later in our interview, Marcel elaborated on this sense of expressivity, saying that there is "not really a theoretical explanation to give about it" and that

> when a Manouche plays this music, you hear the soul. [You hear] the soul of this music, which was invented by Django, who himself was Manouche. So when we play it today, we try to reproduce it, as best as possible, the way Django composed it. But not everyone has this soul that we Manouches have.

Likewise, Engé Helmstetter told me in an interview that he hears Django as a "real human being" and a "real Manouche," one who "has a sincerity in his musical discourse that corresponds to his personality."[17] My interlocutors often gloss these apparently ineffable, yet immediately recognizable, characteristics of "soul" and "sincerity" as *feeling*. *Feeling*, as an English loanword, is defined by the *Dictionnaire de français Larousse* as "[a] quality of emotion and of sensitivity manifested by a performer, in particular in jazz, blues and rock" ("Définitions: feeling"; my translation).

In his work on country music among working-class Texans, Aaron Fox describes *feeling* as "a powerful cultural/verbal master trope for emotional depth, rightness, and intensity" (2004, 152). Similarly, David Samuels writes that *feelingful* (as an adjective) evokes "a wide variety of noncognitive responses to cultural expression" (2004, 11). Feeling in the French context aligns closely with these representations of the term. As expressed and perceived through musical performance, feeling confirms the emotional sincerity of the person performing. It recalls the "honest[y]" Alessandro Duranti and Kenny Burrell point to when they say that "for jazz musicians, the search for a unique type of sound indexes the search for a unique type of person, with particular moral values, including the quality of being 'honest' in what one chooses to play" (2004, 71–72). For some musicians, when a listener describes a performance as full of feeling, it is one of the highest compliments they may offer.[18]

Feeling is noted when a player incorporates particular kinds of tension into an improvised solo. Examples of this tension include the use of rubato, slides, pitch bends, ghost notes, and varying intensities of vibrato; dynamic contouring, especially to create a sense of swelling and deflation; playing slightly behind the beat; brief passages of polyrhythm; and the artful use of silence. An example of a performance often deemed particularly feelingful is Django's solo on a 1940 recording of his own composition "Nuages."[19] The solo opens with a series of understated harmonics, then delves into runs and arpeggiations, punctuated by a number of mordents and turns that have been hailed as some of his signature ornamentations.[20] At various points in the solo, Django plays somewhat behind the beat, briefly stretches the beat, experiments with syncopation and triplets, and makes frequent use of silence. Intentionally or not, some notes are slightly clipped, as if to evoke stuttering. He also deftly manipulates a relatively soft dynamic range (enabled by the electric amplification of his acoustic guitar), which he maintains throughout the solo.

For many of my interlocutors, Django's ethnorace plays an important role in his capacity for feeling. The use of "feeling" is not unique to descriptions of sounds produced by Manouches as opposed to the rest of the French population, nor is it applied only to jazz manouche. Yet certain Manouche interlocutors believe they have a particular capacity for both the expression and the perception of such a quality in jazz manouche specifically. By insisting that what makes Manouche performance superior to that of Gadjé is visceral and cannot be captured in words, these speakers mystify and valorize this property. Doing so not only secures economic advantages (a boon considering the discrimination many Manouches face when seeking employment), but also reinforces a sense of cultural pride. As Manouche guitarist Albert Weiss told me, "If you want to hear good music, you have to go to a Manouche. And I think that [*laughs*] most Gadjé want that. Real Manouches. . . . If you want jazz manouche, what do you look for? You *won't* go to the Gadjé!"

Descriptions of Manouche feeling tend to connote a thoroughly corporeal, even anti-intellectual musical orientation. This is frequently contrasted to more "theoretical" approaches, which are typified as "French" or "Gadjo," to musical study and performance. Such contrasts suggest Michael Herzfeld's notion of *cultural intimacy*, which he defines as "the recognition of those aspects of an officially shared identity that are considered a source of external embarrassment but that nevertheless provide insiders with their assurance of common sociality" and that "may erupt into public life and collective self-representation" ([1997] 2016, 7; see also Stokes 2010). As with the sense of "freedom" described in chapter 3, the attribution of feeling to Manouche performance can reinforce primitivist stereotypes while, at the same time, valorizing an exclusive capacity for affectively potent expression.

Within this paradigm, a musician's virtuosity is valued to a certain extent, but if it is perceived to override feeling, listeners may evaluate the performance negatively.[21] Musicians who play dizzying sequences of notes at breakneck speeds are disparaged as show-offs and thought to be missing the point of musical expression. My interlocutors associate this tendency much more frequently with Gadjé than with Manouches, and with amateurs as opposed to professionals. Too *much* precision can even indicate a *lack* of feeling, while certain "participatory discrepancies" (Keil 1987), such as slight inconsistencies in rhythm and intonation, may be considered a good thing. As one Manouche musician put it to me,

> There are some people who are not Manouche who play [jazz manouche] very well, [in terms of] technique and all that. But I'll say that at the level of *feeling*, I think that it's necessary to listen to it when it's played by Manouches. That's my opinion . . . and my perception. You see, one can really feel that there is a lot more sensitivity here, with Manouches, than with others.

In an interview with me, Albert similarly drew an analogy between jazz manouche played by Manouches and flamenco played by Spanish Gitanos: "When [Gitanos] play [flamenco], it comes from the heart. It's *them*, it's their music. And for us, it's the same. When we do jazz manouche, it's ours. And I think people understand that, they know that. They've understood that that's the way it is. That it's not otherwise. That it can't be otherwise."

As these quotations suggest, the ability to recognize feeling involves an "understand[ing]" of where feeling comes from. This understanding, in a way, is meant to be precognitive. In addition to being inherently intersubjective—the production of feeling through musical performance entails affective, feelingful responses from listeners—it is a form of visceral knowledge. Feeling, like ethnoracialness, is so widely understood as palpable that it is interpreted as a quality in itself.

The Manouche Blues

Baro Syntax is a Manouche rapper who advocates for the rights of Manouches and Gens du voyage through his music and social media. He incorporates jazz manouche influences into some of his recordings, but his performance of rap has stirred some controversy among those who do not regard the genre as appropriate for "real" Manouches to adopt. As he told me during our interview:

> One day, I met a guy like that, really closed[-minded], you see. And me, I do rap, with [other] musics, guitar, everything. I made him *crazy*! I made him crazy. And he says to me, "Yeah, you're not ashamed?" And he said, "You make *Black* music." And I say to him, "What do you think jazz is? Django's music, what is it? Jazz, what is it? Who [first] sang jazz? Was it the Swedish?!" And he was like this [*Baro imitates a shocked facial expression*]. You see?

Baro then added that, as part of his challenge to this man's racism, he tried to impress upon him that "all musics come from Blacks. Anyone can do what they want, but musics that have heart, they come from Blacks."

Although *négrophilie* is now broadly understood as part of a fetishizing early twentieth-century French racial imaginary (Sweeney 2001), in France there still exists a relatively unproblematized fascination with and desire for a presumed sense of heightened feeling embodied in African American music.[22] Jazz, gospel, and blues are widely consumed genres often said to manifest this racialized feeling. Upon realizing that I am from the United States, various people I've encountered in France have exclaimed how much they love African American music, describing it using visceral language similar to what I've outlined with regard to Manouche feeling.

In addition to equating the Manouche predisposition for feeling in jazz manouche to that of Gitanos in flamenco, as Albert Weiss does in the previous section of this chapter, listeners sometimes draw parallels between senses of feeling among Manouches and African Americans. Echoing mid-century comparisons made between Django and Black musicians (see chapter 1), some jazz manouche listeners valorize a unique sense of Manouche feeling as analogous to that of African American jazz performers, sometimes calling this the Manouche "blues." For example, in a 1997 interview, Django's son Babik Reinhardt was asked by the interviewer what he thought of the idea that "jazz manouche, just like the blues, is above all a feeling." In response to this rather leading question, he affirmed, "Yes, exactly. It's like [that] for all the little tribes, people of Latin origin, slaves also, where we find this melancholic aspect" (Reinhardt and Maestracci 1997, 38).

Similarly, Michel Lefort writes that jazz manouche, as performed by Manouches, "participates in a 'blues' spirit" (1991, 116) that is identifiable "not, of course, from a technical point of view, but as an 'expressive medium'" (115). He argues,

> As with the Blacks of America, the music of Tsiganes possesses a dimension of revelation, of proclamation—to oneself, to others—of personal and collective identity. Its character of *subversion* . . . also evokes the profound aspiration of Tsiganes to remain themselves, among and with others. (115–16; emphasis in original)[23]

This "character of subversion," whose definition remains unclear, is often attributed to experiences of discrimination and suffering to which both Romanies and African Americans have been subjected. Each population's histories of oppression are, of course, very distinct from one another, and arguably incomparable (cf. Chang and Rucker-Chang 2020). But some interlocutors suggest that the general contours of these experiences are similar enough to warrant analogous senses of musical feeling.[24] Such suggestions recall what Jon Cruz calls "ethnosympathetic interest" (1999, 4) in Black music, which he argues grew among abolitionists who "sought out the inner world that was presumably reflected in the expressions of slaves" (3). For example, Eric Faure (introduced in chapter 2) told me in an interview that Romanies have been able to cope with these circumstances thanks to their optimism. This optimism, as conveyed through jazz manouche, "allows them to live, to continue to live despite everything that happens to them, despite the hatred [from other] people. And it's really very revelatory. So it's another way to endure with respect to what Black Americans, for example, have been able to transmit through the blues."[25]

These analogies are ways for speakers to convey and justify their perceptions of sonic ethnoracialness in jazz manouche, similar to the appeals made by some Russian Romanies to ideas about US Blackness (Lemon 2000, 75–76). To be clear, I am not endorsing the argument that African Americans and Romanies share experiences similar enough that they would produce the capacity for heightened expressive feeling or even similar contours of feeling itself. As Radano points out, "the legacies of oppression and segregation that undoubtedly contributed to black music's distinctiveness are not enough to sustain arguments of an unyielding black essence" (2003, 5), and a similar claim can be made about Romani musics. But explaining Manouche feeling in terms of a more broadly acknowledged discourse about African American expressivity allows speakers to use an existing frame of reference—the notion of a uniquely Black "essence"—to communicate their convictions about the feeling of Manouche ethnoracialness. Analogies between Manouche and African American experiences of oppression are thought to further legitimize similarities between these senses of feeling as authentically produced through particular life experiences and collective memory to which only members of specific ethnoracial groups have access.

In the Right Hand

While many articulate their understanding of Manouche ethnoracialness with regard to the perceived total sound of jazz manouche, using whatever descriptors they deem appropriate, others (usually musicians) may locate ethnoracialness in specific performance techniques. Most commonly, they identify a Manouche sound in right-hand guitar technique, zeroing in on how a guitarist executes an "attack." Here, too, it may be difficult for speakers to find the appropriate words to describe this, in which case they draw on various qualia to capture the sensation of a certain guitar stroke. These qualia, in turn, become the descriptive building blocks of Manouche ethnoracialness.

Take, for example, *la pompe* ("the pump"). La pompe is the primary rhythmic technique that sets jazz manouche apart from other jazz subgenres. This entails a forceful and brisk right-hand downstroke, often accompanied by an upstroke, in a quick-paced swing rhythm. Williams writes that la pompe has become "the Manouche emblem par excellence" (1994, 29). The pompe may have precursors in similarly percussive techniques used on the banjo and guitar in pre-swing-era jazz. With its bass note on the 1 and 3 beats preceding full chords on the 2 and 4, it resembles stride piano technique (Williams 2000, 411). Use of la pompe is a practical way to amplify an acoustic guitar without electricity, a strategy that Django likely transferred from his initial training on the banjo-guitar to the guitar (411).[26]

Lefort argues that, contrary to popular belief, la pompe was developed primarily by Django's accompanists rather than by Django himself, noting that it is "firm and supple while full and colored, [a] veritable 'motor of swing'" (1991, 105). This description reflects the variety of sensations la pompe can evoke in a listener, especially its percussive dimensions. Also characteristic of jazz manouche technique is the rest-stroke (*le jeu en butée*), a downstroke in which the pick follows through to rest immediately on the next string (as with *apoyando* picking on classical guitar). Mitch Mercier told me that he likens the sound produced by the rest-stroke to that of a "cymbalom," distinguishing it as a "pinched sound, very nasal." Here, Mitch attributes a vocal characteristic to the stroke, illustrating a correspondence between its timbre and the physiological sensation of nasality.

While jazz manouche musicians acknowledge that it is possible for anyone, regardless of their ethnoracial background, to learn to perform the guitar techniques essential to the genre, for many, there is always a hard-to-define quality of right-hand technique unique to Manouche performers. When I asked guitarist Railo Helmstetter whether it is possible to distinguish aurally between Manouche and Gadjo ways of playing, he told me:

RH: I sense it right away. I hear it right away. I don't mean to create a difference, but I mean, [I hear it] even if I'm listening to a recording.

SL: But what are the differences?

RH: I think it's a lot of right hand, a question of attack. It's a complex question because I'm so used to feeling the music that [it's hard] to put it into words. . . . [With a Gadjo,] there isn't the same touch, there isn't the same attack. A musician like Adrien Moignard, he plays at such a high level! But he doesn't have the Manouche touch. You see? It's not a critique at all. I mean, if I get the chance to play with him, that will be great. But [he doesn't have] the attack, whereas when you listen to Tchavolo [Schmitt], there you feel it. Even if there isn't the same virtuosity, you still feel the difference right away.

Though Moignard is certainly not the only well-known Gadjo in jazz manouche, in the majority of my conversations about Gadjo jazz manouche players, speakers consistently refer to him as the epitome of a professional "Gadjo" style due in large part to his impressive technical prowess. In contrast, Tchavolo Schmitt's technique, praised earlier in this chapter by Cédric Loeffler as generating sonic "flames," exemplifies for my interlocutors a possibly less virtuosic but more feelingful sound.

Importantly, to articulate the differences between Manouche and Gadjo sounds, Railo repeatedly uses words evoking tactility: "there isn't the same touch," "the Manouche touch," he is "used to feeling the music," "you feel it," "you feel the difference." In our interview, Railo added that this "difference" is best felt in the way one plays the pompe. He suggested that the Manouche attack is something learned and embodied, saying it is possible for Gadjé to play it, but "there are very few Gadjé who really do it the Manouche way. Everything is in the right hand."

Provincializing Ethnoracialness

In addition to identifying differences between Manouche and Gadjo guitar sounds broadly, speakers will often distinguish between regional styles. Among my interlocutors, a uniquely Alsatian Manouche sound is frequently understood to be the quintessential expression of Manouche ethnoracialness. Alsace is popularly known as the "cradle" of jazz manouche, a claim that grounds the music in a specific place and authenticates the region's Manouche musicians as the rightful heirs to the tradition. The region is advertised as a bucolic destination proud of its hearty cuisine, wholesome agricultural products, quaint Christmas markets, and rustic Germanic architecture. Despite the fact that Strasbourg, the capital of Alsace, is one of France's most important *urban* centers, and one in which the majority of notable Alsatian Manouche musicians reside, the *rural* character of the region is discursively linked to an Alsatian approach to feeling in jazz manouche performance. This involves speech that both invokes and bundles together qualia such as vigor, roughness, and energy.[27] In turn, these qualia are associated both with broadly held notions of masculinity (not limited to Manouche identity) and with conceptions of regionally specific authenticity and honesty.

Alsatian jazz manouche guitar technique is most frequently contrasted with Parisian technique, with each location serving as a metonym for rural or urban life, respectively.[28] For my interlocutors in both locations, the Parisian style represents refinement, whereas the Alsatian style is raw; or, from an especially Alsatian perspective, the Parisian style is pretentious and delicate, while the Alsatian style is powerful and characteristically Manouche. Among those who favor the Alsatian sound, it is described as more feelingful, more visceral, and more sincere than its urban counterpart, like the vocal attributes valued by the working-class country musicians and listeners Fox (2004) documents. An important distinction to note is that within these characterizations, "Alsatian" is a gloss for Alsatian *Manouche*, while "Parisian" does not always carry such ethnoracially specific connotations.

Not everyone frames these differences in such expressly antagonistic ways, but descriptions of this dichotomy reveal a broadly held center-periphery notion in which Paris is the cosmopolitan locus of upper-class cultural sophistication and the other regions of the country are relegated to provincial status. Christophe Astolfi, who is based in Paris, explained these differences to me as such:

> [Alsatians] push all the time. [Their music] pushes, it pushes, it pushes. It's very energetic, in fact. A *very* energetic music. In Paris, it's different. It pushes a little, but not in the same way. It's more gradual. . . . The tempo remains stable. And me, I feel more at ease in this aesthetic. . . . I really like to take the time to play notes. For [my] style, it's true that I prefer the rhythm that one can call quote-unquote "Parisian," which is generally lighter.

Alsatians are said to be primarily concerned with speed and with what he calls "acrobatic prowess," which, especially by repeating the phrase "it pushes," Christophe suggests can be *too* "energetic." To the contrary, the style that suits him better is one whose tempo changes are less capricious, more controlled, and more "gradual"—in other words, more refined, or perhaps just "stable" as opposed to volatile. Here, Christophe's contrastive adjectives convey hierarchical judgments between Alsatian and Parisian styles in terms of felt intensity.[29]

From the perspective of an Alsatian Manouche musician, the same characteristics Astolfi identifies are valued differently. Marcel Loeffler told me:

> When you hear a guitarist who does the *pompe*, the rhythm, in Paris, and when you hear a guy who does rhythm here [in Alsace], they are totally different. Because the Parisian, he plays rhythm and he doesn't have a lot of energy. He doesn't have this this *punch* [here, Marcel used the English word "punch"], whereas here, if you hear a rhythm player, if you hear [Manouche guitarist] Hono [Winterstein] play, well, it's simply amazing.

Musicians I have spoken with broadly acknowledge that Alsatian rhythm guitar technique packs a "punch" relative to its Parisian counterpart, with musicians like Hono Winterstein exemplifying a particularly heightened "energy."[30] Such energy can also be attributed to, for example, Mandino and Sony Reinhardt's comping techniques in the previously described recording of "Mire pral" with Tchavolo Schmitt; both guitarists are Alsatian Manouches, and Mandino has played a significant role in shaping the Alsatian Manouche sound since the 1970s.

One Parisian musician told me that the Parisian rhythmic technique is "more swing" and uses more electric guitar, while the Alsatian style is "more compact," demonstrating this phonetically with a brisk "*chk chk chk chk chk*." An Alsatian musician said that the key difference between the regions can be heard in the way the pompe is played: whereas it is "finer, softer in Paris," in Alsace, "there is more testosterone in it, [it's] a little sturdier. It's more emphatic, often played more loudly." Another Alsatian told me that right-hand technique in his region has more "drive." In another sexualized metaphor, one Alsatian said critically of Parisian musicians, "I always get the impression that they're trying to hit on [someone], to play with the sound to make it kind of smooth." Gendered evaluations such as these are common, linking musical sound to idealized notions of Manouche masculinity—ones associated with power and testosterone as opposed to futile attempts to woo potential sexual partners.

Marcel also told me that he attributes such stylistic difference to *cultural* differences: "Personally, I have trouble playing with Parisian guitarists, because they don't have the same culture as us. . . . You can hear it [in their playing]." Dino Mehrstein, who is also Alsatian Manouche, expressed a related sentiment to me:

DM: [Parisians are] more into detail. In Alsace, it's more rustic. And more about the essential. I'm sorry, but you can hear it in the music.

SL: Do you prefer Alsatian music?

DM: *Bah oui!* It's a lot simpler, and a lot easier to communicate [with].

Dino aligns rusticity and simplicity with "the essential," saying the Alsatian style lends itself more to "communicat[ion]." Both he and Marcel identify and value certain cultural characteristics that are "in" the music, as evidenced by how easily they can communicate musically with other men from their region. These characteristics are contiguous both with musicians and with the music they perform, exhibiting a degree of qualic transitivity: energy, simplicity, rusticity, and so on are perceived both as sonic features on their own and as characteristics of Alsatian Manouche men.

In an interview with me, Francky Reinhardt (another Alsatian Manouche guitarist) drew similar parallels between cultural and aesthetic characteristics:

SL: On the subject of Parisians, I heard that there is a difference—

FR:—*Bah*, exactly. I'm not criticizing [them], I'm not, but the Parisians' style: you hear one soloist, you could hear ten. That's to say, they all sound like each other. That's the concern.

SL: Whereas in Alsace—

FR:—Alsace! *Bah*, Alsace has its sound. Alsace was the core. [In] Alsace, you have the biggest guitarists. . . . Everything begins from the core, [and] that was in Strasbourg. [Manouche guitarist] Mito Loeffler, who died, he was also a very, very good guitarist, in the old style! You can't find that in Paris.

By contrasting the Alsatian style to the allegedly homogeneous Parisian style, Francky makes a case for the creative and stylistic superiority of Alsatian musicians. The "old style" he identifies dates to the transitional phase Alsatian Manouches underwent in the 1970s between traditional "Hungarian" music and a more jazz-focused practice, ushered in partly by Musik Deutscher Zigeuner (as described in chapter 1). Today, the Alsatian Manouche sound of jazz manouche exhibits a sense of rhythmic vigor—what Railo described as a special right-hand "attack"—that may be interpreted as a vestige of the *oom-pah* rhythm of the csárdás. It represents the historical continuity of a particular Manouche sonic identity and is portrayed as a sign of enduring, place-oriented Manouche authenticity. The glorified "old style" Francky points out, as well as his references to Alsace as the origin of good jazz manouche, suggest that the specific history of Alsatian jazz manouche accounts for this superiority.

The historically grounded, vigorous character of Alsatian jazz manouche is an important aspect of the semiotic bundling involved in defining Manouche authenticity. For Alsatian Manouches, emphatically valorizing particular qualia—such as rawness, energy, rusticity, simplicity, and so on—is a means of reclaiming attributes that may otherwise be used to denigrate their communities. Instead of pushing back against these attributions, many Alsatian Manouches embrace the qualia with which they and their music are associated. These qualia are construed as artistic advantages and as inherent to a gendered sense of Manouche ethnoracial identity.

Ethnoracial Immersion

Variations between Manouche playing styles may be perceived in terms of regional distinctiveness, sometimes down to the level of particular families. In an interview, one musician's wife insisted to me that she could discern the familial origins of a number of Manouche musicians, saying that "each has their own style, and it's not that they're all the same. But you can understand when it comes to speed, how they use their picks, these little nuances, that they really come from the same source."

Among those who speak of a Manouche sound, regardless of which family it is associated with, some say it can only be acquired by growing up in a Manouche milieu. Gadjo guitarist David Gastine offered me an illustrative metaphor: "if you hear a Marseillais speaking, he's going to have [*imitates a Marseillais accent*] an accent from Marseille-uh. [*Returning to his own Parisian accent*] The Manouche, he has an accent on the guitar. You hear that he has a style, but it's a musical style on the guitar." People are socialized into accents through long-term immersion in communities of speakers, so Gastine argues that a parallel process occurs when one is immersed in a specific musical "accent." A person's performance style will necessarily reflect the influences they developed in musical conversation with others who speak the same musical "language."

Such immersion is understood not only in terms of musical exposure, but as the totality of life experiences a Manouche upbringing involves. This is contrasted with a Gadjo upbringing that necessarily lacks these experiences. Growing up Manouche often means living in a physically demarcated Manouche community space, such as the one guitarist Fléco Lafertin is part of. One summer afternoon, I joined him outside his mother's mobile home, one of several residences in the Zillisheim Manouche settlement that range from trailers to multi-room houses. The array of permanent and semipermanent residences on the settlement reflects the community's varying and historically contingent degrees of mobility. The daily life of this community unfolds both in and outside homes, oftentimes in front of and in the paths between them. As Fléco and I sat in lawn chairs on the grass, he told me that Manouches have an approach to music that differs from that of Gadjé

> thanks to traveling. That's why Manouches play differently. Traveling, freedom—they're outdoors. [*laughs*] That's why they have another life, and why they play differently from Gadjé. . . . My father [guitarist Mito Loeffler] also traveled a lot, so that's why he played

like that. When you travel, you learn a lot of things. You express yourself better when you travel. Ah yes. You see other things, and then that gets played on the guitar, too.

By "traveling," Fléco means the Manouche tradition of traveling across regions (and sometimes around the country) in a caravan, usually along with family members and other caravans. Historically, this was a way of life for many French Manouches, but in recent decades such traveling has become more restricted to summertime excursions and religious events. While traveling in and of itself is obviously not a uniquely Manouche practice, Fléco insists that the specifically Manouche experience of traveling sets them apart from "sedentary" Gadjé. It exemplifies the sense of freedom described earlier as concurrent with Manouche feeling.

In addition to traveling, Manouche social life is said to be an important factor in the development of a Manouche sound. For example, Fabrice Steinberger (mentioned briefly in chapter 2), of Manouche background himself and the manager of several Manouche performers, told me in an interview about the formative experiences of participating in Manouche social events as a child. He remembers convivial evenings spent listening to Manouche musicians whom his father, APPONA co-founder Rigo Steinberger, would invite to their house, and witnessing a young Tchavolo Schmitt playing with famous German Sinti musicians such as Schnuckenack Reinhardt and Schmitto Kling. He attributes much of Tchavolo's artistry to this kind of environment, saying "they shared [with each other] like a family, meaning that he went to their homes, they lived together." Furthermore, he told me, it is not just exchanges like this, but an entire Manouche "life history" that determines a specifically Manouche sound:

If a French person [i.e., a Gadjo] discovers this music, however good a musician he may be, when he plays this music, he needs to immerse himself in the culture. And for that, you can't just do it in a few years. It requires a life history. So if you take some musicians [*he lists several Manouche musicians*]—these are musicians who are on a fertile familial ground. [They're] anchored in a culture. That's to say that the tunes, they are played, played, played, played, replayed an incalculable number of times with musicians, with parents, with family, and at special family occasions: family parties, meetings, birthdays, marriages. That makes it so that this tune, it is *full* of history. . . . [This includes] a certain idea about life, which is living in the moment, and not the life of tomorrow, [worrying about] what you're going to do tomorrow. The relationship to time in Manouche culture . . . is completely different from the relationship to time in the dominant [French] culture. So inevitably, if you take all these phenomena, all the factors are completely different. That explains why I agree with those who say [that the

Manouche sound is distinctive]. Manouche music played by a Manouche is different from music played by a non-Manouche. [The latter] doesn't evoke any of their [i.e., Manouches'] qualities.

Likewise, Gadjo guitarist Pierre Vigneron told me that it is the entire Manouche "way of life" that shapes one's playing style. Pierre began learning jazz manouche as a teenager by taking guitar classes with Mandino Reinhardt, then went on to earn the French equivalent of a bachelor's degree in musicology. After a few years learning other styles of music at the Conservatoire de Strasbourg, he came back to jazz manouche performance in part because the conservatory's approach involved "too much theory" for his taste. Eventually, he married into a rural Manouche family. At the time of our interview, he had been living with his in-laws for three years. Pierre's perspective is somewhat unusual, as it is not common for middle-class Gadjé to incorporate themselves so deeply into rural Manouche communities. Thanks to this immersion, he insists confidently that extramusical experiences within a Manouche milieu are crucial to a musician's stylistic development:

I think, and this is really important, that what makes it so that the music Gadjé make will never be the same [as that made by Manouches] is that it's a way of life. When you drink, when you eat. I don't know quite how that has an impact, but it enormously influences your way of playing music. And [a Manouche like] Yorgui [Loeffler] surely has a way of living that's totally different from [a Gadjo like] Adrien Moignard.[31]

Whether Yorgui *actually* lives his life in ways that are qualitatively different ways from those of Gadjo musicians is somewhat beside the point here. To Fléco, Fabrice, Pierre, and others I have spoken with, even aspects of life experience not explicitly linked to music are transformed into musical technique: the way one travels, eats, drinks, conceives of "time" in a broad sense, and relates to family members. Music is one of many elements of Manouche ethnoracial identity, and its relation to these other elements is said to determine the character of Manouche sound. If one moves freely, eats heartily, drinks with gusto, thinks only in the moment, and participates in a robust family life, the qualities associated with these practices (energy, rawness, warmth, etc.) will be audible in one's music.[32] In certain ways, this resembles what Travis Jackson learned from his interlocutors in the New York City jazz scene: they believed that "understanding of or embeddedness within African American culture" was a prerequisite for understanding a "blues aesthetic" (2012, 127), and that this must be "learned through the engagement of individuals with those musics and cultures" (126). Similarly, though in a very different racial context than African American communities, listeners might insist that only the totality of Manouche "life history" can lead to a person's ability to produce (and, sometimes, to perceive) a Manouche sound.

An important aspect of community life that impacts a musician's sound is, of course, their musical training within that community. As opposed to "official" pedagogies, namely the standardized, music-literate curricula upheld by French cultural institutions, Manouche communities generally espouse a far less systematic approach to musical learning. Some of my Manouche interlocutors insist that musical skill must not be inculcated through externally imposed discipline, but should be acquired spontaneously, when the learner "feels like" doing it. More important than formal instruction is that children observe and imitate their elders, who guide and correct them as needed. Music is learned exclusively by ear, without the use of notation, and sometimes without much, if anything, in the way of formal music theory. In this process, freedom from formal pedagogical structures, from written music, and from coercion to learn is considered the best means to develop feelingful musical skill among learners.

It is this immersive, aural, and kinesthetic learning process that listeners understand to be key to the development of a perceptibly and properly Manouche sound. This, the logic goes, would not be possible if they undertook a more formalized, literate approach to pedagogy, for doing so would alienate them from their direct connection to sound itself. Pierre told me that a Gadjo who learns from a theoretical perspective "will learn the rhythm and the notes well, but he lacks a little something." This "little something" is the sonic excess that cannot be accounted for in music-theoretical (and sometimes even linguistic) terms: its feeling, its morally vested Manouche ethnoracialness. Through social immersion and aural pedagogy, individuals are thought to absorb not only certain behaviors and performance skills, but also Manouche cultural attributes and values perceptible in one's musical sound.

"In Our Blood"

A minority of interlocutors who recognize a Manouche sound say this also involves a hereditary component. Genetic claims to musical sovereignty usually involve a combination of constructionist and primordialist understandings, reflecting what Marilyn Strathern calls "seem[ingly] contradictory appeals to choice and to genes" (1996, 38). It is a nebulous conception of ethnorace that inhabits "two registers: as genetic endowment *and* the object of voluntary self-construction, as essence and interest, as nature and choice" (Comaroff and Comaroff 2009, 59; emphasis in original). One well-known Manouche musician told me, "Either you have [the music] in your blood, or you don't," but he then proceeded to draw analogies between music, language, literacy, and religion, collapsing all these practices together as both inherited and socialized. His understanding of music being "in your blood" or not reveals "blood" to be the site of both immutable genetic difference *and* learned culture.[33] For him, musical style is the most reliable indicator of one's roots, be they natural, nurtured, or a combination thereof.

For most of my interlocutors, however, saying that musical talent and style are in one's "blood" or have an otherwise genetic component is not a literal endorsement of a primordialist viewpoint, but a convenient way of articulating how deeply immersed in Manouche culture one must be in order to produce a characteristically Manouche sound. For example, in my field notes I recorded an exchange between a social worker and a Manouche musician who debated the degree to which jazz manouche should play a role in contemporary Manouche performance. While the musician insisted that the genre need not have such a strong influence on his own playing style, the social worker responded, smiling widely, "But [jazz manouche] is practically in your genetic heritage!" The social worker laughed, while the musician sarcastically rolled his eyes. This comment was intended to be tongue-in-cheek, a humorous provocation by the social worker that indexed just how tightly ideas about Manouche musicality are bound to jazz manouche.

Another instance of the metaphorical use of "blood" came up during an interview with a different Manouche musician. I asked him why jazz manouche is known as "jazz *manouche*," to which he responded:

> Well, it means—if you say jazz manouche now, you could believe that it belongs to us and only to us, [as if] it belongs not to the French, only to Manouches. But in fact, that's not really true, because anyone can play this music. Except that when you hear musicians who aren't Manouche, you still hear a difference. [This is] because we have this culture that is in our blood, and the others—

Here he paused for a moment to clarify what he meant, probably recognizing what a literal interpretation of "blood" might imply. He then continued:

> —we were raised with this music, but the others, they haven't been steeped in it like us. They came later. There are a few who have been steeped in it, too, but they're

still—there are fewer—when a Manouche plays this music, there is still a difference in relation to Gadjé. You see what I mean.

To this musician, locating culture in "blood" means that through prolonged, immersive exposure to Manouche music—being "steeped in it"—one can acquire Manouche culture permanently and palpably.

Using physiological metaphors like this allows speakers to articulate how Manouche culture is, to them, both enduringly embodied and sonically perceptible. In these cases, "blood" means habitus, not necessarily heredity. The capacity to produce a Manouche sound is understood to be inscribed within Manouche bodies, the result of an array of life experiences inaccessible outside a Manouche social milieu. The sound one hears is perceived as a distillation of all these experiences, rendered palpable as the qualia of ethnoracialness.

Ambivalent Apperception

Mendi Obadike writes of racial "sonic stereotypes" as phenomena that "haunt" and "lurk in the shadows of the threads of narratives we can easily see and dissect."[34] Like phantoms, these stereotypes point to "an ever-elusive object," in that "from a distance we may feel their presence, but when we 'approach' these stereotypes, they disappear." Thus, "like a ghost in the attic, [Blackness] is 'there' when it haunts us and 'not there' when we try to exorcise it" (2005, 125–26). Similarly, as some of my interlocutors do, one may write off the perception of ethnoracialness in sound as the projection of an ethnoracialist fantasy. But ethnoracialness continues to haunt—or, one might say, animate—talk about musical sound. It should not be dismissed as delusion, but rather assessed as a component of a discourse that has real material effects. Listeners summon ethnoracialness into being by sensing sound and making sense of that sound. In bringing semiotic ideologies about ethnorace to bear upon their sensorial perceptions of the world, they render ethnoracialness *real to them*.

Semiotic ideologies about Manouche ethnoracialness are not about Manouche identity alone. Ideas linking Manouche ethnorace and musical sound index binary notions about Manouches and Gadjé, revealing the marked status of the former and the unmarked status of the latter. This is especially the case when a Manouche musical sound is framed in opposition to the *lack* of such a sound among Gadjo performers. If Gadjé are both praised and derided for their supposed privileging of technical precision above feeling, then to claim that a Manouche sound is better than a Gadjo sound is to deprioritize such precision in favor of feeling to Manouches' advantage. This challenges dominant standards of musical quality, placing a distinctively Manouche sensitivity to sound—measured in terms of qualia, and articulated and perceived across semiotic modalities—as superior to supposedly Gadjo musical tendencies.

For Manouches facing widespread discrimination, ethnoracial distinctions become important resources in the struggle for recognition and material benefits. Manouche ethnoracialness, as something available *only* to Manouches, is an asset in the music industry, one of the few economic domains run by Gadjé in which there is a demand for specifically Manouche labor (see Marković 2015). Although appeals to Manouche singularity in the musical realm cannot transform the political-economic structures and ideologies that entrap Manouches in subordinate positions, these appeals are tactics meant to improve their material conditions at least marginally and to increase their public audibility. The harnessing of particular qualia is one important component of these tactics.

At the same time, such essentialization necessarily underpins the ethnoracial discrimination so pervasive in French society, and some interlocutors are keenly aware of this. A Manouche musician once recounted to me how another musician had boasted about his ability to tell the difference between a Gadjo and a Manouche based on guitar sound alone (cf. Reyes 2017b on the discernment of "unfakeable qualia"). The musician telling me this said that such words infuriated him, not because he did not believe the claim—in fact, he did not deny that this was possible—but because he felt the act of making such a statement was unnecessarily divisive. Even if a sonic difference does exist, he suggested, it is not worth putting into words, adding that "no real Manouche" would behave like this.

What's more, while sonic perception is often considered a privileged means through which to affirm the existence of ethnoracial differences, its interpretation can also reveal profound uncertainties about the very constitution of these differences. When I asked Pierre Vigneron about the possibility of any palpable distinction between Manouche and Gadjo musical sounds, he responded:

> I'm skeptical when [Manouches] say this kind of thing. They also say that they could pick out, out of a thousand people—this [is said] pretty often—[who is] a Gadjo or not. I've noticed that this is not the case. Sometimes, they think that I'm really Manouche. Gadjé [do], too. I think you have to take that with a grain of salt. But there is certainly some truth [to the notion of musical difference], because even I can hear some differences.

The ambivalence Pierre expresses here is, I would argue, less about whether a uniquely Manouche sound actually exists and more about the conviction with which, he says, people believe they can perceive it.

Pierre is by no means the only person, Manouche or Gadjo, to express skepticism about the ability to hear a player's Manouche background. Ambivalence about this ability points to the inevitable untenability of the Manouche-Gadjo binary. For all the categorical statements speakers make about what is and is not Manouche, there remains the underlying, perennial question about what Manouche ethnoracialness actually *is*. Sometimes this uncertainty is reflected in Manouche antagonism toward Gadjé, from assertions that a Gadjo sound is inferior to accusations against Gadjé of shoddy imitation or cultural appropriation. Such antagonism is, of course, fundamentally linked to the subordination Romanies have endured for centuries. Uncertainty also arises with the question of how to assess sounds produced by people of mixed Manouche and Gadjo backgrounds. These concerns draw attention to the instability of Manouche ethnoracialness, and of ethnoracial identity more broadly. To say that a quality is ineffable can be a way to manage ambivalence about the claim one wishes to make.

Attention to what is said and what is not said in context—to talk and its (meta)pragmatics—helps us understand how and why listening subjects generate semiotic ideologies of social difference. Speech about musical sound is a vector for articulating ideas about race, ethnicity, and slippage between the two categories. It also sutures notions of place, history, and gender to ethnoracial identities. Talk about ethnorace and music can be especially important in an environment where public discussions about race are avoided or constrained. In the case of jazz manouche, speakers imagine ethnoracial identity as materialized into bodies and into sound waves. The transitive distribution of qualia across sounds, concepts, and subjects reinforces these semiotic ideologies, hardening lines of ethnoracial difference in compelling (though unstable) ways.

As Webb Keane notes, "The social power of naturalization comes from . . . the misconstruing of the possible entailments of indexicals—their effects and possibilities—as if they were merely expressing something (such as character) that already exists" (2003, 417). The naturalization of particular musical sounds as inherently ethnoracial, and perceived as such through their constituent qualia, expresses ideas about ethnoracialness as a qualisign that "already exists"—even though, like all social identities, ethnoracialness is continually constructed through the dynamic interplay between language, sound, and other semiotic modalities.

FIVE

Heritage Stories

In the Angers metropolitan area, nestled in the Loire Valley to the southwest of Paris, the Festival Gipsy Swing took place nearly every year between 1993 and 2014. This festival was established following a long series of concerts organized by Michel Lefort, then the president of Angers' Gens du voyage assistance agency. A municipally funded program, the Service d'Accueil des Gens du Voyage—the "welcoming service" for Gens du voyage—provided logistical and social support in addition to raising public awareness about Gens du voyage communities.[1] Working with a volunteer-based nonprofit organization created specifically for the festival, L'Association Gipsy Swing, the agency produced one of the most acclaimed jazz manouche festivals in France.

An aerial photo of the city of Angers provides the backdrop for a postcard (figure 2), designed to promote the 2004 festival. In the center of the image, a Selmer-style guitar is superimposed onto the eastern bank of the Loire River. The guitar's curves articulate smoothly with the highway that also lines the bank. Its neck and strings suggest a parallel transportation infrastructure, and its headstock juts into the city's famed ninth-century castle. The guitar's body, flush with the terrain, is scattered with caravans and Gens du voyage going about their daily business. In the foreground, more caravans dot the countryside just beyond the city limits. Above the horizon, a swath of vibrant fabric blends into the sky, seeming to move with the skirt of a flamenco dancer (not shown in this version of the postcard). The logo's motto reads "radiating, enterprising, natural,

Figure 2 Postcard for 2004 Festival Gipsy Swing. Image designed by Jean-François Orillon for the Service d'Accueil des Gens du Voyage "Les Perrins."

united"—adjectives arguably reflected in the postcard's depiction of Gens du voyage.[2] Together, these images convey an imagined ideal for the Service d'Accueil and its clients. The insertion of this kind of guitar, specific to jazz manouche, into the Angevin landscape suggests that this music is also embedded into Angevin identity. This guitar, intertwined with the city's roadways, serves as a point of connection for Gens du voyage between the outskirts of the city and its interior. In contrast to popular assumptions that Gens du voyage are perpetual wanderers with nowhere to call home, the postcard presents them as an integral part of Angevin territory.

Juxtaposing visual indexes of jazz manouche with those of flamenco, and in conjunction with the title of the festival, the postcard also suggests that the Gens du voyage depicted are Romani. Although not all Gens du voyage are actually Romani, Lefort told me in an interview that many of those in the municipality identify as Manouche and strongly insisted to him that of all genres, jazz manouche best represented them. For Lefort, "the aim of the festival is to give voice to Tsiganes." He sought to promote the reputations of Romanies as talented musicians—what he called the "wonderful side" of the word *Tsigane* to the general public. At the same time, he said, the press often represents the "other side" of the ethnonym as "'delinquent Tsiganes,' or more simply, 'Tsiganes who bother us, with their caravans everywhere.'" The festival's central mission was to mitigate these biases by both celebrating Romani musical traditions and reshaping dominant ideas about Gens du voyage. As Lefort told me, "In a sort of utopian way, [the festival] aims to raise awareness about how Gens du voyage should be better welcomed, in flesh and bone, whether or not they are musicians, but who move around in caravans on the [local] territory." In other words, "It's their way to say, 'We exist.'"

In this chapter, I explore how jazz manouche festivals enact emplaced narratives of belonging and exclusion. These festivals typically draw on extant connections between their locations and Django Reinhardt's biography and/or Manouche communities to promote their own conceptions of local heritage. In doing so, they instrumentalize jazz manouche to serve a variety of political and economic agendas. From those that seek to meaningfully engage Manouche communities and to combat prejudice, to those that function primarily as drivers of the tourism industry, festivals use jazz manouche's ethnoracial associations and historical significance to shape public perceptions about place-centered identities. As frames for performing stories about who should belong to a place and who should not, festivals materialize these localized social imaginaries.

I formulate such narrative work in terms of *chronotopes*, a concept developed by the literary theorist Mikhail Bakhtin (1981). Bakhtin used this term to refer to configurations of time and space in the novel, or more specifically, "the intrinsic connectedness of temporal and spatial relationships" (84). In the past several decades, anthropologists have expanded its scope to account for how social narratives take shape in the real world. Asif Agha writes that a chronotope is a "representation of time and place peopled by certain social types" (2007b, 321); similarly, Jan Blommaert defines *chronotopes* as "elaborate frames in which time, space, and patterns of agency coincide, create meaning and value, and can be set off against other chronotopes" (2015, 110).[3] By invoking strategically crafted histories and grounding them spatially, festivals develop the chronotopes that sustain the various, sometimes conflicting agendas of different communities, institutions, and individuals.

Any heritage-making activity draws on and develops chronotopes by telling stories about the past and linking them to specific places (see, e.g., Jaffe 2019). To cite some examples relevant to the present context, various cultural centers and place markers in Paris and elsewhere are named for Django. Doing so invokes extant chronotopes—situated narratives of Django's life—to generate new chronotopes linking these narratives to particular sites and associated people. These chronotopes, old and new, are thus "calibrated" (Silverstein 1993; Wirtz 2016) with each other. The naming of Strasbourg's Espace culturel Django Reinhardt both recognizes the local Manouche community's jazz manouche tradition and suggests that the center currently plays a role in sustaining national heritage. Streets and squares named after Django are also meant to infuse these otherwise unremarkable sites with historical and cultural significance.[4]

As opposed to these physically permanent acts of heritage-making, festivals are processes that unfold within relatively stable, ritualized frames, allowing for long-term comparative analyses of the many factors that change and/or remain the same over time. Festivals craft representations of the past while situating them in the context of each festival's actual occurrence and projecting a vision of the future. Each festival calibrates these chronotopes across scales—between past, present, and future; from the venue to the municipality and from the region to the globe—resulting in narratives that invest it with broader significance. While any festival is necessarily temporary, these enduring narratives allow its impacts to extend well beyond the time-space of the event itself.[5]

The Festival Gipsy Swing postcard is an example of one such narrative. The embedding of the guitar into the landscape suggests both the local importance of jazz manouche—its emplacement as a physical part of Angers—and the genre's historical relevance to the municipality. The scattering of parked caravans on and around the guitar also suggests that Gens du voyage are, or should be considered, part of the municipality as well. These depictions all generate semiotically intermodal chronotopes linking space, time, music, imagery, and people. Many aspects of the festival contributed to these chronotopic constructions, including media (websites, recordings, photos, etc.) and musical performances, which would take place over several days in central Angers venues. Although the festival only occurred during this short period within specific locations, publicity materials and documentation of performances have ensured that the festival lives beyond this time-space and is broadcast to a wider public. This media links histories of Romani migration and settlement to histories of French heritage, all while envisioning utopian futures of Romani inclusion.

The Festival Gipsy Swing of Angers was somewhat exceptional among jazz manouche festivals for its concerted advocacy efforts. Many of these festivals take place annually across France and internationally with diverse approaches to Manouche involvement and representation.[6] Some draw on local connections to Django, such as the Festival Swing 41 in Salbris, the village where Django married his second wife, or the Django à Liberchies festival in the Belgian village where he was born. Some promote their proximity—spatial, historical, and/or political—to Manouche communities. To varying extents, most festivals engage in ethnoracial branding. While a handful do this self-consciously in the service of pro-Manouche activist endeavors, a majority of festivals do not espouse such overtly political objectives.[7]

In the following pages, I explore three jazz manouche festivals that represent the variety of agendas I allude to above. First, I outline APPONA's Festival International Tzigane, which took place nearly annually in the 1990s. Like the Festival Gipsy Swing, but on a larger scale, the goals of APPONA's festival were primarily oriented toward pro-Romani political advocacy and involved a high degree of engagement with local Manouche communities. Next, I examine the Festival Django Reinhardt, the most well-known jazz manouche festival in France, whose focus on the spectator experience reflects its problematic approach to involving Manouche communities. Finally, I describe my experience with the Festival Jazz Manouche de Zillisheim, a relatively new festival in which the local Manouche community and festival organizers have struggled with each other to convey divergent, materially consequential narratives. Each festival seeks to transform public conceptions of time-space (for example, by constructing narratives in which Manouches have long been an important part of French heritage or of a given locality) and/or to reinforce dominant narratives about place and history. In this chapter, I ask: How do festivals instrumentalize chronotopes? How does the mobilization of specific chronotopes challenge or reify ideas about ethnorace and their material implications? How do a festival's strategies in the present enact its vision for the future? Such orientations to the future may seek to preserve cultural and socioeconomic hierarchies as they are—or, more boldly, to imagine a French society in which the terms of cultural citizenship are transformed.

APPONA's Festival International Tzigane

In chapter 2, I introduced festivals as one of the most important musical activities APPONA undertook to raise awareness about Manouche communities, to promote interethnic solidarity, and to professionalize Manouche musicians. In the 1970s and 1980s, APPONA organized several one-off festivals in addition to smaller-scale musical events, gradually moving from a focus on local Manouche musicians to a more international scope. In 1991, APPONA inaugurated its largest event yet, the Festival International Tzigane, which was subsequently held almost every year until 2003 and attracted over 10,000 attendees to each of its later editions. The Festival International Tzigane is remembered by organizers, musicians, and audiences as one of APPONA's most enduring legacies.

Most editions of the festival took place in the Parc de la Citadelle, a large, well-frequented public park near downtown Strasbourg. Patrick Andresz, who was present at many of these editions, told me that never before had Manouches congregated in such large numbers so close to the heart of Strasbourg. He called this "a spectacle in itself," not only because "they dared to show themselves" in public. Rather, the main "spectacle" was that Manouches—especially those living on Strasbourg's margins—demonstrated that they too had the right to inhabit centrally located public space and to be represented within the city.[8]

Patrick's observation reflects how the Festival International Tzigane was an important aspect of APPONA's efforts to increase Manouche visibility and, ultimately, to foster a greater sense of Manouche cultural citizenship. For a few days to a whole week, APPONA would take over an important public space, as well as other urban spaces around Alsace, to welcome thousands of attendees. As its title suggests, the festival invited

Romani ensembles from all over Europe, representing various genres, to complement a robust array of local musicians who mainly performed jazz manouche. It also featured roundtables, exhibitions, public talks, children's activities, and other events that provided important cultural and historical context for the performances. These events, in addition to media about the festival, helped connect musical performance to APPONA's larger mission and strengthened the organization's relationships with local and international governmental bodies.

Through its activities and press coverage, the festival calibrated multiple chronotopes to make claims about Romani belonging in Alsace, France, and Europe. One chronotope, represented by performers from a variety of countries, accounted for the history of Romani migration from India to Europe over the course of a millennium. Invoking this long-term presence in Europe was a way to legitimize Romanies' right to inhabit the continent while drawing attention to the rootedness of distinctive Romani subgroups in particular countries. It also reinforced "the now-common marketing tactic that unites all 'Roma' and/or all 'Gypsies' through the trope of historical nomadism" (Helbig 2009, 178). Another chronotope centered on the more recent coalescence of an aspirationally borderless, "European" identity, manifested as of 1993 in the establishment of the European Union. In line with other pro-Romani organizations, APPONA put forth a multicultural ethos of unity-in-diversity that mirrored ideals of European interconnectedness while suggesting that Romanies were cosmopolitan European citizens par excellence.[9] As such, Romanies were depicted as essential to Europe's future. In turn, musical performances and other cultural productions by Alsatian Manouches, in conjunction with the promotion of APPONA's other pro-Romani projects, represented more localized chronotopes of long-term Romani presence in France and Alsace. Finally, the festival's recurrent present—its actual occurrence over several days each summer in central Strasbourg—constituted a ritualized chronotope in which Romanies made claims to public space, however temporarily. The calibration of these chronotopes across widely varying scales helped make a case for Romani inclusion at multiple levels while solidifying APPONA's status as a locally and transnationally influential organization. APPONA invoked the long history of Romani presence in Europe, as well as the importance of Romanies to Europe's future, to underscore the value and importance of its own constituents to Alsatian society, transposing large-scale chronotopes onto more localized ones.

This cross-scale calibration was facilitated by the festival's participation within larger activist and governmental networks. By the late 1990s, the majority of the festival's funding came from public sources ranging from local to international.[10] Since the early 1980s, the French Ministry of Culture had encouraged cultural institutions to promote diverse cultural heritages within the nation's borders.[11] This was a commitment that looked toward the eventual European Union's cultural mission to "contribute to the flowering of the cultures of the Member States, while respecting their national and regional diversity and at the same time bringing the common cultural heritage to the fore."[12] Supporting events such as the Festival International Tzigane was one way for the EU to project its endorsement of "respect for and protection of minorities," even if this standard was not actually achieved in practice.[13] Participants in festival-organized roundtables and conferences, which took place at venues such as the Council of Europe, included spokespeople from French and European governmental and nongovernmental organizations, as well as local representatives. Media coverage of the festival described its entertainment portions while emphasizing the broader activist goals that APPONA sought to promote. APPONA was thus able to implicate itself in the cultural and sociopolitical agendas of larger institutions—or, at least, the public-facing aspects of such agendas—by advocating for the importance of Romani cultural production to the harmony and vitality of local, national, and transnational economies and communities.

The first Festival International Tzigane took place in 1991 over the course of ten days at various locations throughout Alsace, culminating in a "Tzigane Night" at the Parc de la Citadelle on the eve of Bastille Day. APPONA's secretary at the time, Stella Funaro, told me that by including a wide variety of Romani musical acts, it sought to cultivate pan-Romani cultural consciousness: the festival "wasn't simply [about] valorizing Manouche culture and Manouche music, but [about] integrating a larger dimension of Tsigane music in general." The festival lineup thus included a total of 250 artists from the Netherlands, Czechoslovakia, Spain, Italy, Yugoslavia, Romania, the United Kingdom, Germany, Hungary, Poland, the Soviet Union,[14] and France, including a number of Alsatian musicians who already collaborated with APPONA. This array of nationally and regionally identified performers evoked narratives of the long Romani migration, late twentieth-century European unification, and Romani history in France and Alsace, all within the lived present of the festival's duration.

One of the most well-publicized events of the first festival was a three-day conference hosted at the European Parliament and the Council of Europe titled "Tziganes and Europe: Transmission of Tradition in a Transforming Europe." Romani constituents from twelve countries, along with representatives from governmental institutions and nongovernmental organizations, were invited to publicly discuss issues such as socioeconomic conditions for Romanies across Europe (especially following the dissolution of the Soviet Union), anti-Romani racism, governmental responsibilities for protecting the rights of minoritized groups, and definitions of "Romani identity." The APPONA President's Report of 1991 states that the goals of the conference were "to give Tziganes the chance to express that they belong to a people of European dimensions, to make their voice heard in European institutions, [and] to raise awareness about their culture to the largest public possible."[15] As a result, delegates conveyed "the importance of Tzigane culture as a unique and indispensable contribution [to] European space."[16] The conference presented Romani inclusion within Europe not only as a question of the rights of minoritized groups, but as a valuable asset for European society. By leading the organization of this event at prestigious European governing institutions, for an audience of both governmental leaders and the general public, APPONA scaled up the necessity of its work in Alsace. It localized transnational concerns for Romani rights and suggested that, as an asset for European society broadly defined, Romanies also had much to contribute to Alsatian society.

Subsequent editions of the Festival International Tzigane reiterated the historical and spatial scope of the Romani presence in Europe, with most editions appending thematic titles that reflected the festival's broader-scale chronotopic dimensions. For example, the theme of the second edition in 1994, "Baro Drom," built on the success of Tony Gatlif's widely acclaimed film *Latcho Drom*, released the year prior. The film, whose Romani title literally means "Good Road" (though it has been translated as "Safe Journey" for Anglophone audiences [Silverman 2000]), is a music-centered fictional account of Romani migration from India to Spain. "Baro Drom" similarly means "Long Road," and the festival's subtitle—"La Longue Route de L'Inde à L'Espagne"—spells out the story of Romani migration depicted in the film. The titles of the film and the festival are simultaneously spatial and temporal, indexing Romanies' vast geographic dispersal as well as their continuity of movement across centuries.[17]

As a figure of speech, the "long road" also refers to the protracted struggles for acceptance that Romanies continue to face despite having inhabited the European continent for so long, and to APPONA's own work, as stated in the festival's program notes: "A long road, the twenty years of APPONA['s work] for the recognition of a people. [We strive] to create and recreate connections incessantly, to retie the threads broken by a painful and tormented history." In addition to fifteen local jazz manouche ensembles, performers included Rajasthani musicians and dancers (described as "those who would become . . . Tsiganes!") as well as ensembles from Albania, Russia, Macedonia, Turkey, Spain, Romania, and elsewhere in France, assembled to spread the message that "music erases frontiers [and] overcomes barriers."[18] The 1994 President's Report states that the festival represented "an encouragement in the daily work of our organization for the recognition of the values of the Tzigane people and for a better understanding between Tziganes and non-Tziganes," reiterating how one of the festival's core missions was to strengthen relationships between Romanies and Gadjé.[19]

The 1996 festival, "Nevo Drom" ("New Road"), focused on Romani youth. Its brochure argues for the importance of Romanies in constructing a new Europe, emphasizing that they "know what it means" to take a "new road" both literally and figuratively. Strasbourg, the text states, is an "age-old crossroads" conducive to "encounters between diverse cultures in the past" and, as the "seat of European institutions, represents the ideal place for such a festival" to proclaim Romanies' contributions to European culture. At the same time that it promoted Strasbourg as the nexus of European cultures, satisfying the interests of local and regional institutional supporters, this festival also depicted Romanies as a model of innovation and adaptability. These were qualities endorsed by a European Community that was beginning to integrate formerly socialist countries into a neoliberal order. The road metaphor, as before, represented continuities between past, present, and future, this time speaking not just to a Romani-specific timeline, but to that of Europe as a whole.

In 1996, despite its textual focus on Europe, the festival could only afford to host one foreign group, a troupe of musicians and dancers from Rajasthan; the rest of the program was filled by local Manouche musicians. The 1997 edition of the festival, "Autour de la Méditerranée" ("Around the Mediterranean"), resuscitated the program's international scope in terms of countries represented (France, Italy, Macedonia, Greece, Germany, and Egypt). Budgetary constraints reduced the length of the festival to seven days and required cuts to some of its programming and to musicians' salaries. Even with these cuts, APPONA deemed the festival an overall success and was inspired to create a new music professionalization program for its musician constituents (see chapter 2). This initiative presaged increased Manouche involvement in the organization of the festival while furthering APPONA's endeavors to develop economic self-sustainability among Manouche entrepreneurs.

Several months after the 1998 festival,[20] Engé Helmstetter (then only twenty-three years old) took over as its principal organizer, fulfilling the youth-oriented directive of the 1996 festival and heralding a new era of Manouche leadership within APPONA. Following a truncated festival in 1999 ("Choukar Drom," or "Beautiful Road"), in 2000, "Tsiganes, peuple européen" ("Tsiganes, [a] European people") revived some of the rhetorical grandeur of previous editions. As stated in the festival press kit, the year 2000 "marks a thousand years of Tzigane history" from India to Europe, and thus,

> Conscious of its regional and national affiliations, [the Romani] community also traverses borders. Despite the political rifts of the countries in which they find themselves, despite a diversity of religious affiliations, Manouches, Gitans and Roms have a real spirit of solidarity toward others that goes beyond the concept of nationality, in a spirit of "transnationality."[21]

In other words, the Romani people were "a European people" before the notion of European identity coalesced, and they could serve as a model of unity-in-diversity for European institutions. The text argues that Romanies' status as "a true European people" must be recognized not only by governmental bodies and "majority society," but also "by Tsiganes themselves, in their own way, so they can become real agents of their own history and of the construction of Europe."[22] To this latter end, one of the objectives of this edition was to engage Alsatian Romani youth even more than before, involving them in various aspects of festival planning and implementation.[23]

One way the festival fulfilled this objective was through a musical theater production, *Maré Sinté* ("Our Sinté"), which Engé conceived and co-produced. I met with Engé one afternoon in 2014 to watch a home video of the musical that his uncle Tchavo had filmed at the festival in 2000. During the car ride to Tchavo's house, Engé told me that he had been inspired to produce something that went beyond music alone to "tell a story." He envisioned a collaboration between Manouches and Gadjé in which Manouches ultimately called the shots. Since the musical was meant to be primarily by and for his own people, he insisted that it be as thematically and musically accessible as possible to them—in his words, "not elitist." Hence, it employed a simple, humorous storyline that followed a young Gadjo as he journeyed with a family of Manouche musicians and dancers. The music, which combined 1960s and 1970s Musik Deutscher Zigeuner songs with more standard jazz manouche tunes and original compositions, would have been familiar to

Manouche audience members, evoking connections between past and present Manouche musical traditions.

Once Engé and I arrived at the house, the three of us gathered around a computer monitor to which Tchavo had connected his VHS camcorder. Tchavo rolled the tape while I divided my attention between the action on screen and the two men's reactions to it. As we watched an opening scene in which a clownish character, Batchi, acted out slapstick humor reminiscent of the Three Stooges, the audio was flooded with screams and roars of laughter. Engé said that the front rows of the audience were filled with Manouches who were dazzled by the musical, especially in these comedic moments. As for the Gadjé in the audience, he said their feedback was encouraging overall, though some later told him that "theater isn't necessary" for Manouches (a suggestion that Manouches are not as talented in acting as in music). Although Engé would have appreciated a more unanimously positive response, one of his main objectives was to make the production *for* Manouches. In this way, *Maré Sinté* represented a new direction of public Manouche cultural production: one in which the success of a project might be predicated less on its legitimation by Gadjé and more on validating the tastes of Manouche audiences.

Engé had thought that certain images and themes would resonate particularly well with Manouches, sometimes playing on or challenging stereotypes and other times, arguably, reinforcing them. Nature and travel were among these, with the apparently itinerant Manouche family scuttling around in their caravans through the Alsatian countryside (images of which were projected behind the action). While some might interpret these chronotopic frames to essentialize Romanies as timeless wandering nomads or even noble savages, Engé envisioned this as part of a Manouche cultural heritage that values tropes of nature and travel. Playing on another Romani stereotype, in an opening scene, Batchi steals an apple from the Gadjo character, returning it at the end of the musical as an act of reconciliation. In the penultimate scene, the Manouche troupe is hired to perform at a restaurant and a concert ensues within the frame of the musical. As we watched this scene together, Engé laughed at how the Manouche characters separated themselves by gender on opposite sides of the stage, telling me he hadn't realized how this reflected a typically patriarchal model of Manouche gender relations. After the restaurant kicks out the musicians for raising a ruckus, an image of a campfire appears behind the actors, signaling their rejection from Gadjo society and their return to life in the open air.

After we finished the tape, Engé recalled that two of *Maré Sinté*'s musician-actors were not so enthusiastic about the "traditional" aspects of the music (i.e., the interpretations of "Hungarian" songs from Musik Deutscher Zigeuner) and that they wished it would emphasize jazz more. Engé, a jazz musician himself, understood this concern, but he felt it was important to represent his community's musical links to the past. By depicting the aesthetic continuity between "traditional" and "modern" styles in a single production—between the past and the present—he sought to strengthen an ethos of intergenerational solidarity. This, in turn, fed into the festival's overarching themes of historical continuity and Manouche self-empowerment.

Furthering the festival theme of intercultural alliance-building, Engé stressed that *Maré Sinté* marked a new generation of Manouche-Gadjo collaboration. Through the production process, he told me, Manouches and Gadjé "learned a lot about themselves, and about each other." If, according to the festival's press kit, Romanies should understand themselves as a "true European people" so that they "can become real agents of their own history and of the construction of Europe," *Maré Sinté* signaled a step toward these objectives. More broadly, if a cornerstone of APPONA's mission was to reshape dominant conceptions of cultural citizenship in France, the kind of intercultural exchange and promotion of Manouche-oriented cultural production that *Maré Sinté* embraced also contributed to this desired dialogue. Its generally positive reception at the festival suggested that Manouches might also play a role in setting the terms of their cultural citizenship.

Maré Sinté generated enough laudatory press that it was produced again in other cities and a CD of its musical repertoire was released. For the 2001 festival, Engé co-produced another musical, *Ta Vées Bartalo* (a Romani greeting that translates as "good luck" or "may you be happy"). This complemented the festival's headlining event: an extravaganza to celebrate the eightieth birthday of Schnuckenack Reinhardt, the musician who inspired Alsatian Manouches to take up Django Reinhardt's music three decades prior. Although this festival ended on a high note, with the largest attendance the festival had yet seen, it took place amidst mounting financial problems. APPONA produced its last festival in 2002, the year of the organization's dissolution. In 2003, a nonprofit organization called Union Tzigane Des Initiatives Locales et Européennes took over the festival to run its very last edition.

Over the course of twelve years, the Festival International Tzigane facilitated support for APPONA's long-term goals. One important legacy of the festival was its narrative linking the broader history of Romani migration in Europe to more contemporary concerns about European identity. The calibration of multiple chronotopes in the festival's musical programming, publicity, conferences, and related events conveyed the message that Romanies have long represented a cultural ideal of European transnationalism. This message, in turn, buttressed APPONA's mission to promote Manouches as integral to the vitality of Alsatian society and to its standing as a hub of European culture. Furthermore, by holding large-scale performances in central locations, the festival enabled Alsatian Manouches to exercise their rights to public space (albeit temporarily) in contrast to the marginal locations they normally occupied. Finally, those who were formerly involved in the organization (like Engé) invoke extant chronotopes and create new ones through their narratives of the festival's significance (see chapter 2 on how APPONA "lives on" through the work of former members). Through its conjoining of multiple temporal and spatial scales, the Festival International Tzigane became one of the most effective ways in which APPONA asserted its relevance, secured institutional support, and amplified its broader goal of dialectically transforming and denaturalizing "majority society."

The Festival Django Reinhardt

The Festival Django Reinhardt is the longest-running, most well-publicized jazz manouche festival in existence. For decades, it was based in the quiet village of Samois-sur-Seine, also known as "Samois," about seventy kilometers southeast of Paris. Django lived here from late 1951 until his death, spending his days fishing by the Seine and playing billiards. The festival's first iteration was organized in 1968 by the association "Les Amis de Samois" to commemorate the fifteenth anniversary of Django's death. Following this event, local government and businesses continued to capitalize on Django's connection with Samois, expanding the festival into a lucrative annual event. Today, the festival normally spans several days in late June and early July and attracts thousands of people from around the world. Since 2016, it has taken place in the larger, neighboring town of Fontainebleau, where more spectators can be accommodated.[24]

Much of the festival's fame has to do with the range of chronotopes it has effectively constructed and exploited. Most obviously, the fact that Django resided in Samois for the last year and a half of his life was the basis for the festival's establishment. Festival publicity claims that Django loved Samois for its tranquility and proximity to nature and invites spectators to follow in his footsteps. According to one early member of Les Amis de Samois, the association considered Django to be

Figure 3 Ceremony at the grave of Django Reinhardt, Samois-sur-Seine, 1 July 2012. Photo by Siv B. Lie.

Samois's "illustrious adopted fellow citizen" (Bechtold n.d.). Django's memory has been cemented in Samois through commemorative acts such as a plaque on the house in which he lived (inaugurated during the 1968 festival), the installation of a bronze statue in 2010, and most significantly, his grave. A few days after his death on 16 May 1953, hundreds of Manouches, musicians, and others gathered for his burial in the village cemetery. Now, each Sunday of the festival, dozens of spectators recreate his memorial service by first attending a mass in his honor at the local church. A procession follows from the church to the cemetery, where the mayor and musicians lead a ceremony at the grave of Django and his immediate family members.[25]

In addition to Django's biography, the festival reflexively draws on its own history to legitimize its continuation in the present. This was especially the case in 2018, the festival's fiftieth anniversary. That year, Jean-François Robinet, longtime former organizer of the festival and former mayor of Samois, published a book detailing the festival's history. The book combines Robinet's own recollections with testimonies from festival organizers and musicians, biographies of musicians, and a large number of photographs and images of festival posters. It depicts how the Festival Django Reinhardt transformed from an intimate yet star-studded commemoration of Django's life in the 1960s and 1970s to a large-scale event with worldwide appeal. The festival's success is measured partly in terms of increasing recognition and support from the media, government officials, major jazz musicians, and other famous figures, as well as by gains in budgets and attendance. That it went from taking place every five years between 1968 and 1983 to every year from 1983 onward, and from one day to five days, is also considered proof of this success. Robinet's book is by no means the definitive account of the festival's history, but it is the "official" and perhaps the most comprehensive one publicly available.[26]

Some important components of this narrative are the festival's stylistic lineage and the evolution of its program. In earlier years, the program was dominated by French jazz musicians, especially those who had performed with Django. Although jazz manouche had not yet been codified as a genre in the festival's first two decades (see chapter 1), Robinet writes that the 2008 festival marked "40 years since the Île du Berceau resonated with the sounds of jazz manouche, all while progressively opening itself to more modern musics" (2018, 164). Starting in the 1980s, Django's son Babik Reinhardt became a regular performer, as did a number of non-French (primarily US) jazz musicians. Robinet writes that in the early 2000s, while "the Festival's original organizers wanted to conserve the swing manouche style and its fusion with original American jazz, thus making themselves appear a bit rigid and judged [to be] 'retro,' the younger people taking over wanted to be up-to-date" (2018, 154). A new festival director, Sébastien Vidal (head of TSF Jazz, a major jazz radio station), was put in charge of the 2006 festival and has steered it in a more eclectic direction ever since. This decision has long been a subject of controversy among some dedicated festivalgoers, resulting in petitions and negative public commentaries. As early as 1992, jazz manouche critic Francis Couvreux wrote that at Samois, "one sees fewer and fewer Manouches year after year, so much that this festival is becoming a festival like all the others" (1992, 54). Robinet's book maintains that although the festival's program has diversified, it retains a core lineage of jazz manouche artists, most importantly Django's direct descendants such as his grandson David Reinhardt and his great-grandson Lévis Adel-Reinhardt. Other famous Manouche musicians are vaunted as inheritors of Django's artistry and treated as guests of honor. Thus, the festival boasts the simultaneous maintenance of a Django-centered lineage *and* its inclusion of other jazz and jazz-related genres—its integration of ostensibly old and new musical threads as unique selling points.

Another important aspect of this narrative is its ritual transformation of local space. While permanent physical markers designate Samois as Django's final home (the plaque on his house, a statue, his grave), the cyclical occurrence of the festival has been the most important element of its Django-centered branding. Until very recently, Samois would metamorphize annually from a sleepy village into a thriving jazz manouche hub and back again. Most activities took place on Samois's Île du Berceau, a narrow island on the west bank of the Seine. The bucolic Île represented a liminal space both as an island—typically, spectators had to enter via one of several securitized footbridges from the mainland—and as the site of the festival itself. For the general public, the Île du Berceau *was* (and still *is*) the Festival Django Reinhardt, even if that was only the case for a few days each year, and even though it eventually moved to the neighboring commune of Fontainebleau. Robinet, too, insists that jazz manouche has a "permanent" place in Samois because "Django's descendants dropped [their] anchor there" (2018, 23), a nod to the festival's riparian roots.

A recurrent theme throughout this narrative is that "Django's descendants" have long called Samois home, literally or figuratively.[27] Emphasizing this succession allows festival organizers to fortify the continuity between Django's life, the history of the festival, and the festival's present-day perpetuation. That is, it calibrates chronotopes across temporal scales by asserting a common grounding among individuals in a specific location. These individuals are also linked together by their ethnorace, a fact that organizers selectively promote. The festival book and website, among other sources, point to how Django's extended Manouche family constituted a significant proportion of the festival's early contingent. But it is not made clear that, as the event grew into a more formalized, lucrative enterprise, organizers paid less attention to the participation of a wider Manouche community. This has not prevented the festival from advertising itself as a Manouche-centric event, one in which spectators can hope to witness a "big Manouche mass" (Bechtold n.d.).

What this narrative also elides is that the promised hordes of Manouches are meant to be specific *kinds* of Manouches—ones who are musically talented and who are not Gens du voyage, who respect the rules the village sets and don't cause trouble. As I observed at several editions of the festival, and as I gleaned through informal conversations, the Manouches who are welcomed to the festival grounds are those who entertain, and perhaps some in the entertainers' entourage, but not the ones who park their caravans on *terrains* specially designated for paying spectators during the festival period.[28] An interview I conducted with Robinet at the 2012 edition, when he was still a main organizer and the mayor of Samois, corroborated this observation. He told me that during the festival, Gens du voyage are

> a huge problem. It's not that we don't like them, but for one thing, there isn't much space. . . . We have a big problem with the Gens du voyage who come. Many come not for the festival, but they take advantage of it anyway. There are others who come [regardless of the festival], but I can't choose [among them]. There are some people in the village, even in the municipal council, who tell me, "The festival, it's all well and good, but without Manouches." Or even, "You have to choose the good ones. Those who play music, but not the others." I don't want segregation. It's forbidden, for one thing. So I'm not going to say, "You, you don't have a guitar, get out of here!" Because he's not going to leave, and it's impossible! Once they're there, we can't do anything. So we have to negotiate for hours and hours with them to make them move. There were some [Gens du voyage] who arrived in the middle of a *terrain* that we had reserved for spectators. . . . I told them, "You have to leave. Yes, move." [But a woman responded,] "We can't, my husband is at work!" [*Robinet laughs*] . . . And then, after three hours, when he came back, he conceded to moving, but it was very difficult.

Gens du voyage are in fact "a huge problem" for members of a village who value them only as entertainers. Robinet's repeated qualifications that "it's not that we don't like them" or "I don't want segregation" are preambles to the racist attitudes and actions he attributes to townspeople and local government, but with whom he also sympathizes. There is no actual lack of space, only disagreements about how and by whom that space should be used. The festival marks a period when tensions over the very presence of Gens du voyage within village limits, tensions that endure year-round, come to a head. Robinet laughs off his dispute with a working family of Gens du voyage, treating the festival's predicament here as "difficult" with little regard for the difficulties imposed on a few inconvenient inhabitants.

At certain sites, though, it is a different story. Two permanent campsites (*campings*) are located short distances from the festival grounds and are open to all paying occupants, Gens du voyage or not.[29] They are popular with ardent Gadjo jazz manouche fans from various parts of the world, who may spend a week or three around festival time camping and jamming, and with some of the better-known jazz manouche–playing Manouche and Sinti families from France, Germany, and the Netherlands who gather for annual reunions.[30] Especially in the hours after the official festival concerts, flocks of spectators converge at these sites to witness all-night jam sessions. As a camper there for several years, I observed that many are drawn to the promise of authentic Manouche and Sinti musicians in a setting less commercialized than the festival itself. Festival organizers are happy to encourage this; it's good business to have an unofficial afterparty that attracts festival attendees and for which the festival itself is not at all responsible. It also placates those who lament that the festival has become "less Manouche" in its programming. Robinet told me he gladly welcomes these gatherings at the campsites, repeatedly noting how wealthy many of the campers are. Indeed, a number of them—Manouches and Sinti included—appear to be relatively well off (at least, according to Robinet, judging by the expensive vehicles they drive). Along with the musical talents these temporary inhabitants provide, signs of wealth help render them a boon, not a problem, for the festival.

During my interview with Robinet, I mentioned the Festival Gipsy Swing in Angers with its pro-Manouche advocacy work and asked whether the Festival Django Reinhardt aimed to highlight Manouche performers as well. Robinet told me that "the Samois festival has a great reputation for being a large Manouche festival because it's one of the most important in the [*région* of] Île de France . . . It happens that [the festival] is Manouche, but that's not at all the question to ask. What's more, we don't seek to help [them]. Manouches: make do yourselves. That's not our problem."

Robinet's unambiguous admission that the festival "happens" to be Manouche (this is no coincidence) but that Manouches are "not our problem" (despite Gens du voyage posing a very particular kind of "problem") encapsulates the racist dimensions of ethnoracial branding and their unfolding in the context of color-blind French republicanism. Like the perceptions of "wonderful Tsiganes" and "delinquent Tsiganes" Michel Lefort describes in Angers, in Samois, there are "good" and "bad" types of Manouches. These types correspond, respectively, to Manouches who do the *right* things in the *right* places at the *right* times and those who do the *wrong* things in the *wrong* places at the *wrong* times. The chronotopes the Festival Django Reinhardt mobilizes—Django's biography, the festival's history, the festival present—are used all together to reinforce and publicly legitimize such racist attitudes, despite the hypocrisy of ethnoracial branding in this context. They function in tandem with French legislation that discriminates against Gens du voyage, and with broader ideologies about ethnorace, to determine a Manouche individual's right to belong in Samois.

The Festival Jazz Manouche de Zillisheim

Like many other Alsatian towns, Zillisheim is home to a Manouche community paradoxically designated as *Gens du voyage sédentarisés*, or "sedentarized travelers." Next to a narrow stretch of river, at least sixty Manouche people live in mobile homes and small, simple houses. The community is composed of four distinct families who, prior to World War II, traveled the region regularly, but since 1968 have been permanently settled on this *terrain* (to which local Gadjé refer pejoratively as a *camp*).[31] Until recently, the local government denied them services such as electricity, mail delivery, and basic plumbing infrastructure.[32] Members of the community say they are often treated with contempt by many of the town's other residents and elected officials. That is, with the exception of one Manouche, Mito Loeffler, who became a minor celebrity in the region thanks to his musical talent and his notoriously generous character.

In late 2011, Mito died suddenly of a heart attack. Among those who attended his funeral was Pierre Heyd, a successful businessperson who went to primary school with Mito. Along with several other Gadjé who were present at the funeral, he decided to create a festival in honor of Mito to take place in June 2012.[33] They reached an agreement with the town hall to hold it at the municipally owned recreational center immediately adjacent to the Manouche settlement. Over two days, musicians from around Alsace with close ties to Mito gathered to perform, including major figures such as Yorgui Loeffler and Marcel Loeffler.

Although I was unable to attend the inaugural festival, a few weeks after it, a volunteer from the nonprofit APPONA 68 brought me to Zillisheim to conduct an interview with Pierre.[34] Over lunch at a white-tablecloth restaurant, Pierre told me that one of the organizers' main objectives was for "the village residents, at least those who came [to the festival], to see that these are people who are capable of doing positive things, and not just people who are there to profit off the system." According to him, the festival was a huge success, not just in terms of ticket sales and reported good feelings, but in that it improved local Manouche-Gadjo relations. He said that although few residents of Zillisheim actually attended, the mayor, instead of "throwing a wrench in the works, now praises us. [He

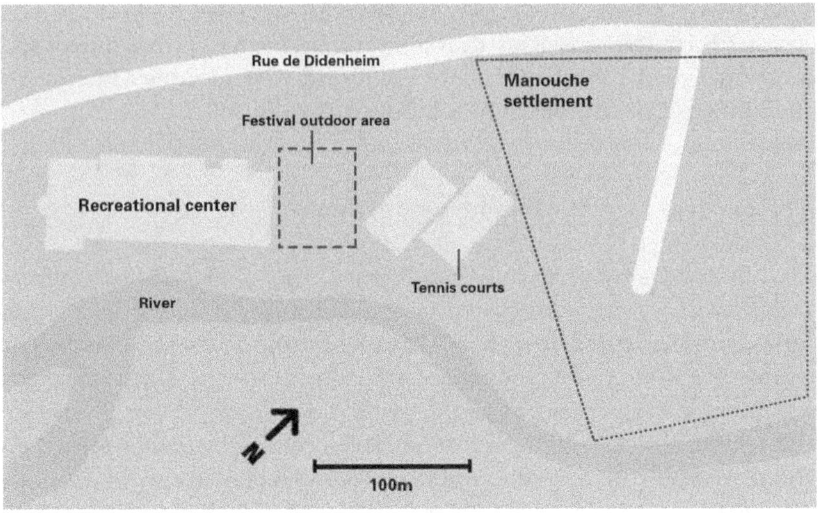

Figure 4 Map of the Festival Jazz Manouche de Zillisheim. Illustration by Siv B. Lie.

calls it] '*our*' festival!," adding that audience members—many of whom he characterized as "bourgeois" professionals—

> weren't *in* the camp, but next to it. And it [was] this Manouche spirit that people looked at. In other words, we don't do [the festival] in the camp because that would have been too voyeuristic, and that would have been badly received [by the community]. But we were *next* to it, at their home. . . . The caravans that are right next [to the festival], people see it—and that whole ambiance pleases people, both Manouches and the others.

Pierre then described how some local Manouches donated their time and labor to the festival, saying this was partly because "they especially didn't want [the festival] to give them a bad image. They were very attached to it. [They said,] 'This is going to be an homage to Mito. . . . [But] this has to go well because it's also *our* image that we want to defend, or that people are going to criticize if it goes badly.'" As we ended our interview, Pierre explained that the following year, he wanted to expand the festival considerably. In addition to inviting bigger-name musicians, he planned to incorporate other styles of Romani music, Romani dancers, an art exhibition, and one or two roulottes.

After my initial visit to Zillisheim, I remained in contact with Pierre and returned in 2013 to participate in the second edition of the festival.

Over the course of about six days, I got to know some of the musicians, organizers, and Manouche community members while observing the on-site logistics of the event from start to finish and participating as a volunteer.[35] That year, the festival was rebranded from the "Festival Hommage à Mito Loeffler" to the "Festival Jazz Manouche de Zillisheim," a name that has remained since.[36] In this and most future iterations of the festival, scheduled performances took place on Friday, Saturday, and Sunday evenings in the spacious gymnasium within the recreational center. Along the wall facing the bleachers, a stage was set up and flanked by two life-size portraits of Mito. On one evening, Mito's sons, Fléco and Zaïti, and his brother Dorno, all guitarists, were featured as performers of honor in addition to several jazz manouche luminaries. Just outside the recreational center, festivalgoers could purchase food and beverages at concession stands and relax at picnic tables. Like at other jazz manouche festivals, they could also ogle impromptu jam sessions at the luthiers' stands, which served as informal gathering points for musicians.[37]

Between the 2013 and 2014 editions of the festival, I followed the planning activities among the organizers (all Gadjé except for Gigi Loeffler, who, though not a resident of Zillisheim, served in a very limited capacity as an advisor), attended their meetings, and conducted interviews.[38] I also visited the Zillisheim Manouche community on several occasions and spent extensive time with the festival musicians. As I got to know all of these participants, I developed a better sense of the festival's internal dynamics, especially when it came to financial matters. In conversations with me, Pierre maintained that he had invested a great deal of his own time and resources into ensuring the festival stayed afloat, a position that other festival organizers corroborated. At the same time, some community members and musicians criticized him for being out of touch with their material needs. As a newcomer to the music business, he was unfamiliar with some of the concerns of musicians who perform for a living and sometimes suggested that musicians should be more appreciative of the exposure enabled by their inclusion.

Print publicity for the 2014 festival emphasized the tagline "100% Manouche," a perplexing phrase given that only a portion of the musicians identified as Manouche and that not all the styles of music performed would be considered specifically Manouche. The festival website's home page began using this phrase in 2017, stating that it was "the last French festival to offer a 100% Manouche program."[39] Pierre recruited some high-profile jazz manouche musicians to perform for the 2014 festival, assuming that the local community would appreciate having famous members of their ethnoracial group represented onstage. However, some members of the settlement did not consider these musicians to be part of their extended family in any meaningful sense and saw their presence as stealing momentum from local musicians who were there to honor Mito. While Pierre believed that the festival's publicity and expansion would be beneficial to all, the extensive branding of the festival as authentically "Manouche" was redolent of the essentialization that the Manouche community had come to expect.

Although there was no consensus within the community on how they should be publicly represented, they largely agreed that the festival could be used as leverage to petition the local government for basic necessities. One woman from the settlement told me that they hoped Pierre could assist them in convincing the mayor to install plumbing infrastructure for toilets, of which they had none on their property. They relied instead on having limited access to the neighboring recreational center for its toilets and showers. Another woman told me that she had been hired by the town to clean these showers. One day, she arrived to find that the locks had been changed without notice. She then learned that the mayor had ordered the placement of the locks and refused to give new keys to anyone in the community, leaving them without crucial facilities. To the community, the festival offered an opportunity to advance a dialogue with local government, not just in terms of negotiating their material needs, but also in order to achieve some sense of citizenship within the town.

In the lead-up to the 2014 festival, there were concerns that attendance would be subpar due to an increase in ticket prices. Despite a very full lineup that included internationally recognized jazz manouche stars, admissions did in fact take a hit. While organizers strove to ensure that the festival would remain financially solvent, conflicts emerged between them and some members of the Manouche settlement who thought that significant profits were being made. Tensions between organizers and community members persisted into the final day of the festival, during which Gigi and I were scheduled to give an informal presentation to attendees. For an audience of about two dozen, we each delivered short talks about jazz manouche and its significance to Manouche communities. We also invited several community members to speak for themselves; they elaborated on their reverence for Mito in the context of their own religious beliefs. Gigi then asked Pierre to say a few words. Pierre explained that he regretted not starting a festival while Mito was still alive, then began describing his own impressions of the community: "When I was a kid here, there wasn't a beautiful tennis court [like there is now]. There was what today one would politely call a garbage dump. . . . So it was really not very nice to live right there, but there weren't any other places [for this community]." He then spoke of a local teacher who led a charitable organization for Manouches; of Mito's widow, Colette, and the humility the couple demonstrated in the face of poverty; and of the general difficulties Manouches encounter, saying that they were "assisted," a reference to the social services and welfare payments that settlement members received. He closed by stating that the festival also struggled with financial hardship and was in need of support.

Pierre's speech seemed to be well received by the audience, but a few community members later told me they were dismayed to hear him speak publicly in such detail about the community's historical and ongoing conditions of poverty. They claimed that whereas the Manouches who spoke at the conference focused on praise of Mito and of the importance of jazz manouche in order to preserve a sense of dignity and pride, Pierre undermined their efforts by victimizing them and by lauding the charitable work Gadjé had done for them. Though Pierre expressed good intentions with his speech, he did not seem to understand how certain narratives prevented local Manouches from being considered citizens of the town.

Later Sunday night, after the final scheduled performances wrapped up, a number of people—largely musicians from the settlement and others, including extended family members, who had traveled to Zillisheim to hear the festival, to socialize, and to play—gathered for an unamplified jam session at the luthiers' stand, the traditional locus of jams at this and many other jazz manouche festivals. Normally, these jams go late into the evening and are one of the few opportunities musicians have to enjoy some time to play with each other away from the hordes of festival attendees. Participants often prefer the spontaneity and camaraderie of the jam over the presentational format of programmed concerts and consider jams to be a natural extension of "official" festival activities. However, the organizers had not accounted for this extension and, after a few tunes, the musicians were ordered to disperse. Even though jam participants did not seem to be constrained by any public ordinances to keep quiet, since the only community within earshot was the Manouche settlement itself (which had put up with a mass influx of people immediately next to their homes for three days straight), the organizers seemed to believe that the jam would compromise their own standing with the town. They considered the after-hours session both a liability and a nuisance rather than an integral part of the festival activities.

Despite the financial troubles resulting from the 2014 festival, it has continued unabated each year (except for 2020, due to the coronavirus pandemic). Funding increases from outside sources have allowed admission to be free to the public since 2016. I attended the festival again in 2018, this time volunteering mainly for food preparation instead of performing or lecturing.[40] Upon arrival, I caught up with a few members of the Manouche settlement and learned that several municipal construction projects had recently been completed nearby: the installation of *blocs sanitaires* (self-contained hygienic facilities with toilets, sinks, and showers), a new paved road leading from the recreational center to the local Catholic school, and fencing around the settlement. After years of petitioning, and with a great deal of help from APPONA 68, the installation of these blocs sanitaires was an important gain for the settlement. However, community members voiced complaints that although the town touted the paved road as another benefit to the settlement, all it did was create more traffic outside their homes, whereas the roads within the settlement remained unpaved. They also complained that the fencing was completely unnecessary, understanding it as an exclusionary gesture designed to further segregate them from the rest of the town.

The program and spatial layout of the festival that year were similar to the previous festivals I had attended. A few new additions included a public screening and discussion of the feature film *Django*, a biopic released the year prior; two Gadjo artists selling arts and crafts out of vintage caravans; and a series of tents sheltering other merchants and luthiers on the lawn near the tennis courts. But for the first time in the festival's short history, Mito's immediate family had not been included on the official festival program. One person from the settlement told me that since the last time I was there, the organizers had visited less frequently and that everyone was asking why they hadn't scheduled Mito's sons or brother as usual.[41]

In lieu of an onstage performance, that Friday afternoon a bassist and a rhythm guitarist joined Mito's son Fléco on lead guitar under one of the outlying tents for a very informal, electrically amplified set. On the edge of the small crowd gathered to hear them, I spotted and approached Mito's widow, Colette. Beaming warmly toward her son, then toward me, she reminisced about the annual trips Mito and their family used to make to Samois—"it was our pilgrimage!"—describing how countless jam sessions would materialize outside their caravan at all hours and how Mito would dash into the caravan in between sets to devour food she had prepared. Whenever they returned to Zillisheim, people would run after their caravan calling out his name. She told me that at one point, "I said to him, 'One day you're going to die, and you're going to become like Django Reinhardt.' He said, 'You think so?' And *voilà*, now we have this festival."

Later that evening, Fléco and his ensemble returned to perform under the tent. Meanwhile, speakers that had been installed on the exterior of the recreational building relayed the music being played on the interior stage; this allowed festivalgoers to continue purchasing food and beverages from the stalls outside without missing the sound of the scheduled acts. Fléco and his ensemble chose to ignore the clash of amplified sounds and continued their performance for several tunes. The next morning, one of the organizers approached me and a sound engineer to complain about this incident, blaming "those who aren't on the program" for causing trouble.

To me, both the literal dissonance that had occurred the previous evening and this organizer's reaction to it brought to mind clashes the Manouche community had long faced, clashes that went beyond the festival itself. As with the late-night jam session of 2014, Manouches were being accused of making unwanted noise—of using space in the wrong way, or at least at the wrong time. Simultaneously, the very presence of their bodies and their sounds challenged the organizers' terms of what constituted proper use of space in a given time frame. These incidents indexed the Manouche community's decades-long struggle with a local government that accused them of occupying space inappropriately and that took (in)actions to convey its contempt.

The sonic clash also represented divergent ideas about the chronotopic frames the festival was supposed to convey. For one thing, a number of Manouches complained that the festival had all but lost its original purpose of honoring Mito's life and his importance to local Manouches and Gadjé. Colette's premonition that in death Mito would "become like Django Reinhardt" did not pan out in the same enduring way as the Festival Django Reinhardt in Samois. In addition to the exclusion of Mito's immediate family from the program, over time, other gestures contributed to the erosion of his memory as part of the festival. After 2013, photos of him were no longer displayed onstage. The logo for the 2013 and 2014 festivals included his name, but in 2015 his name was removed. Whereas for years, the festival website had prominently displayed a photo of Mito on its landing page, by spring 2019, that photo had also been removed.[42]

When it comes to memorializing Mito, perhaps the most important aspect of the festival is the one with which organizers have nothing to do. Each Sunday morning of the festival, a mass is held in honor of Mito at the chapel of the nearby Catholic high school. Many of the attendees are members of the local Manouche community and others from across the region who have extant ties to it, but most festival organizers and volunteers typically do not attend the mass, remaining on the festival site to prepare for the final evening. At the masses I have attended, both the chaplain and religious leaders from within the Manouche community speak about Mito's character and the legacy he left, while Manouche musicians punctuate the service with jazz manouche standards and hymns adapted to guitar and violin.[43] These acts of remembering Mito are crucial in themselves for the local Manouche community, especially in that they help build a sense of intragroup solidarity. Many members of the community also believe that it is important to tell Mito's story to a broader public. Mito is consistently revered as a model citizen beloved by all who knew him, Manouches and Gadjé alike. By telling and retelling narratives of his life, with an emphasis on the fact that he belonged to *their* community, these members try to make a compelling case for their own inclusion in the town (and even the region or the nation). Their hope is that Mito's memorialization will render them publicly legible as citizens, and that the sense of dignity they already feel they deserve will also be recognized in the form of infrastructural necessities and spatial desegregation.

While telling Mito's story might be a source of leverage in negotiations with the town, it cannot guarantee this sort of hoped-for inclusion. Social workers who are part of the community's daily life play a necessary role as mediators in these endeavors. At the very end of the 2018 festival, I caught up with one such advocate who has worked with this community for many years. When I asked whether the festival had helped the Manouche settlement in any materially significant way, she responded, "No, not at all," and went on to describe the various actions the mayor has taken to limit Manouches' access to basic services and to punish the entire community for minor infractions made by individuals. She told me that, like many other mayors in the region, he considers the Manouches to be squatters and puts as much pressure as possible on them to relocate to a different municipality. At best, the festival allows the mayor to tolerate the Manouche presence temporarily, if only because it brings some business to the town. For this reason, his praise is directed toward the organizers, not toward the community itself.

Considering that, for decades, negotiations with the town have been minimally fruitful, it is understandable that the community would pin hopes for their future within the town on a high-profile festival. But as the festival has persisted and grown, these hopes have eroded along with the festival's investment in promoting Mito's life story. While some organizers thought that certain members of the community should have been more grateful toward them just for putting on the festival, Manouches experienced the festival within a much broader context of disenfranchisement at the hands of Gadjé. Ultimately, the charitable image of the festival only helped re-entrench a socioeconomic hierarchy in which a Manouche narrative of belonging could barely extend beyond the confines of the settlement.

Heritage Futures

As ritualized, place-oriented events, festivals provide windows into how heritage claims from the local to the international are made and remade. Ethnographic analyses of these contexts show that festivals offer performative frames for differently interested actors to strategically wield a variety of chronotopes. Jazz manouche festivals in particular rely on the commodification of Manouche identity, whether to advocate for the rights of Manouche communities or to exploit them under the guise of meaningful inclusion. It is understandable, then, that many Manouches are ambivalent about how their ethnoracial identity is essentialized and rendered expedient through events such as these.

More broadly, narratives enacted in these contexts reflect not only partial histories and ideas about the present, but also visions of possible futures. To return to this chapter's opening, the Festival Gipsy Swing's media reflected a mission to advocate for a fuller sense of cultural citizenship on behalf of Gens du voyage. It drew on the multiple heritages (local, national, and ethnoracial) to which jazz manouche belongs in order to produce forward-looking counternarratives. As Lefort put it, the festival imagined Romani inclusion "in a sort of utopian way." APPONA embarked on a similar mission, but with more explicit attention toward multiple geopolitical scales. While the advocacy-centered motivations of these festivals remained largely consistent over time, the same cannot be said about the Festival Django Reinhardt and the Festival Jazz Manouche de Zillisheim. These two festivals were never particularly invested in such efforts, though their public narratives have sometimes claimed differently. The futures they envision have more to do with building local economies and increasing the prestige of their municipalities for wide audiences. They selectively promote Manouches as part of their local identities only insofar as doing so contributes to these other goals.

A further contrast can be drawn between the long-term visions of these two sets of festivals. While the latter conceive of a future whose prosperity relies on a reiteration (one might say an exacerbation) of the status quo, the former imagined a future that would necessitate major reconfigurations of political-economic relations. Both festivals in Angers and Strasbourg offered transformative visions for how ethnoracial difference should be valued and negotiated within French and European societies. These more progressive ideals have not receded along with their associated festivals. Rather, as argued in previous chapters—and in this book's conclusion—they persist, if only in a "utopian way," in the memories and actions of individuals.

Conclusion

I sat in the passenger's seat of the car next to Gigi as he drove cautiously through the back roads of rural Alsace that he knew so well. The torrential downpour in which we found ourselves only heightened the intensity of this moment we were sharing together, reflecting on the events of the day. We had spent that bright July 2014 morning at a rose farm for the dedication ceremony of the new "Django Reinhardt rose." For months, Gigi had worked with local businesspeople to name this new variety and to nominate his brother Yorgui as its "godfather." In addition to playing a paid gig and getting a little publicity, he eagerly looked forward to giving a speech about the contributions of Manouches to Alsatian heritage. His strategy was to network with politicians and influential businesspeople and to leverage any opportunities these connections might afford. As long as he got his foot in the door and a spot on the stage, he thought, he could seize the chance to speak.

Upon our arrival, Gigi sensed that things would not pan out as he had planned. Once the ceremony got underway, he stood awkwardly onstage with Yorgui and their guitarist cousin Sébastien through lengthy oratories by businesspeople and elected officials. One speaker acknowledged that the Loefflers represented a jazz manouche tradition, noting that "we are always very happy to have them on our territory." After Yorgui and a politician unveiled a guitar-shaped rose arrangement for the cameras, the program passed directly to the musical entertainment portion. Gigi took a seat, picked up his guitar, and grinned through several tunes with Yorgui and Sébastien.

Once Yorgui wrapped up some post-performance photo ops, the four of us headed to a barbecue hosted by one of Gigi's guitar students. Gigi was livid, explaining to me that he felt used by wealthy Alsatians who only wanted to exploit Django's name for their own profit. I asked Yorgui whether he shared this sentiment. He agreed, saying he was turned off by the whole event, but that this was just part of working as a musician and doing business. He added that he had a meeting the next day with Pierre Heyd (the organizer of the Festival Jazz Manouche de Zillisheim) to discuss an opportunity for a collaboration with the pop star Thomas Dutronc.[1]

Noticing the darkened clouds overhead, Gigi and I left the barbecue hastily with the hope that we wouldn't be late for his next gig that day. As we drove through a strong rainstorm, listening to his cousins' latest jazz manouche album, he recounted how he had felt similarly insulted as part of the Zillisheim festival and wondered aloud whether all his efforts were for nothing. He lamented that Manouches had made no recent effort to coalesce a movement to demand better treatment, or at least to organize some kind of collective voice. He then skipped the CD to the song "Lass maro tschatschepen" and said, "*This* is what I think of when I think of all this stuff." The song, whose Romani title translates roughly to "Let's Take Our Rights," sparked controversy when the German Sinto guitarist Häns'che Weiss released it in 1977 as part of the Musik Deutscher Zigeuner series. As noted in chapter 1, the lyrics—which Weiss translated into German in the liner notes, to the dismay of a number of Sinti—exhort his fellow Sinti to speak out about the horrors they faced at the hands of Nazis during World War II and to demand recognition and reparations for their suffering. Pointing repeatedly at the CD player, Gigi translated each line of sung Romani into French so that I would be sure to understand its message.

This was neither the first nor the last time Gigi would share these kinds of grievances. He constantly voiced new ideas to promote the value of Manouche culture to Alsatian society. But most of the time, the pivotal moments he engineered to spark progress—moments in which he tried to shape others' understandings of what jazz manouche should *mean* and *do*—became letdowns. Gigi's chronic frustration reflected the fact that although the cultural activism propelled by APPONA lived on in the work of individuals, some of these individuals knew their own efforts were insufficient. The inclusive utopia Gigi envisioned could not be achieved only by valorizing a musical tradition and using it as a means to other ends. Those involved in collective cultural activist work have long known this, too: that much larger transformations are necessary in order to change the terms of inclusion for France's minoritized populations. While it is necessary to make do with the resources and access one has, there are serious limitations to working within a system that, by design, thwarts minority claims to cultural citizenship.[2]

As I have argued in this book, the success of jazz manouche as an industry and as a powerful expressive practice has largely to do with its polyvalence. This polyvalence is the condition for the apparent contradictions that the genre sustains: of being simultaneously Manouche and French, of its appeals to universality and to ethnoracial or national specificity, of its construal as both disinterested and expedient. It is the coexistence of incompatible essentialisms that makes jazz manouche work so well. Ambivalence is a symptom of these incompatibilities in practice, of the futility in reconciling the need for equal citizenship with the demands of French republicanism and late capitalism, as well as with one's own desires for recognition and cultural sovereignty. When Gigi finds himself frustrated, it is because he is reluctantly coming to terms with the contradictions between these needs, demands, and desires. And when Yorgui seems less bothered, it is because he is more willing to accept the contradictions, especially if they do not impede his professional advancement.

In France, denying the existence of race has only exacerbated the effects of racism. Although, in the absence of a well-developed public discourse of racialization, this process may appear to be covert, there is little covert about it from the perspective of a minoritized subject. As in many other places, such subjects must regularly contend with how the narratives they are given do or do not align with their lived experiences. Ambivalence surfaces when one is compelled to act in the service of these givens: here, the republican ideology in which race does not exist, the ideology that people are defined by ascribed cultural identities, and the ideology that laboring under capitalism will lead to equitable material and symbolic success. These ideologies entail an array of contradictions, both within themselves and between each other. But playing to different ideologies according to context, even in the face of these contradictions, is a fact of life for many people, especially those who are racially marked. They are frequently caught in the impossibility of these coexisting narratives and maneuver with the resources available to them. Under certain circumstances, they may also refuse any or all of these narratives.

Throughout this book, I have asked how people make sense of contradictory frameworks, in particular those concerning ethnorace. Sometimes Manouches look to broadly recognized narratives, such as those of

African Americans and Native Americans, to articulate their own experiences of discrimination. Sometimes they participate in cultural activism through jazz manouche to make claims about societal belonging, to voice specific political and socioeconomic concerns, and to broadcast pride and dignity in their heritage. They often use ethnoracial branding to their advantage, even if it tends to reinscribe stereotypes. They may argue for the value of an inimitable and irreducible Manouche sound, laying claim to it through a rhetoric of ineffability and feeling. Manouche musicians may also choose to position themselves as "jazz" artists and omit ethnorace from their public personae; they argue that the term *jazz manouche* is reductive and even racist. Above all, jazz manouche participants engage with any or all of these approaches in situationally dependent ways. They manage the ambivalence of self-essentialization (ethnoracial or otherwise) in recognizing that, even with its contradictions, essentialism has much to offer.

Taken together, these practices can operate as counternarratives to a dominant framework that denies racialization and its effects. They speak to the fact that ethnorace is produced not only in the realm of words, but through an array of interlinked semiotic processes. The raciosemiotic approach I have outlined shows that the maneuvers people use to articulate ethnorace across semiotic modalities are not merely circumlocutory strategies. They are creative acts that contribute to the very constitution, and to the challenging, of ethnorace. These semiotic processes work together to produce ideologies about ethnorace that merge with, chafe against, and transform one another. In particular, jazz manouche offers channels for voicing stances on ethnorace that are not so easily articulated otherwise. The semiotics of jazz manouche help people make sense of ethnorace, for better or for worse.

I'd like to make clear that the implications of this approach go well beyond French borders and Romani ethnorace. Globally, under capitalist regimes, people labor in contexts pervasively structured by adherence to a particular set of market values. They are told that this is the best and only way to make any life at all. The ways in which capitalism structures society are completely normalized, leaving few opportunities to work toward, let alone imagine, a different system that might not be predicated on the exploitation and abjection of entire classes of people. Given the normativity of capitalism—a system that also produced race as we know it today—anti-capitalist movements devise strategies that challenge this narrative. Many social movements for equal rights, the end of poverty, environmental justice, and other demands envision this kind of postcapitalist future as a condition for their success. In working to dismantle the structures that uphold capitalism as the only viable system, they strive to bring a new order into being.

Struggles over capitalism, in all its (neo)colonial forms, are necessarily tied to struggles over race and other forms of difference-making. They all involve imaginative labor across semiotic modalities that reframe hegemonic ideas about past, present, and future—about how things were, are, and should be. In the face of widely shared discourses that deny the lived experiences of marginalization, people often work creatively to render these realities legible to themselves and to others. They endeavor to shape the meanings of signs in ways prevailing discourses will not afford. We see this regularly in various musical practices, from Palestinian "resistance music" (McDonald 2013) to global hip hop (Rollefson 2017), among many other forms. People may also refuse to be rendered legible within normative frameworks (Simpson 2014). In both straightforward and subtle ways, they work imaginatively to realize different ways of seeing, hearing, relating to, and even constituting their communities that do not necessarily coincide with dominant narratives.

"Now *that's* Manouche!" In its pithiness and its ambiguity, this phrase captures more than I can account for. At the outset of this book, I described how Gigi's exclamation during a gig captured the polyvalence of "Manouche" as an identity marker. In the years since that performance, in ways that certainly exceed what Gigi meant in the moment, I've come to realize just how weighty these few words are. Contrary to its popular reputation as a "light" music best suited for gentle evenings out, jazz manouche reverberates with anxieties about exoticization, exploitation, sovereignty, and survival. Despite all the contradictions of essentialism and the ambivalence it inspires, Gigi uttered this phrase confidently—as anyone must do when their sense of self depends on such conviction.

In part because of its light and heavy sides, jazz manouche offers a revelatory lens through which to understand the stakes of ethnoracialization in France and beyond. Still, I don't want to forget what brought me and countless others to jazz manouche, and what keeps people like Gigi in the game: it is an immensely enjoyable and meaningful practice for those who make it so. The pleasure of jazz manouche affords some sense of certainty in the face of ambivalence. For all the weight it bears, "Now *that's* Manouche!" was, in that exact moment, an expression of genuine and irreducible *delight*.

Acknowledgments

I have saved the most difficult, least complete, yet best part of writing this book for last. Any inadvertent omissions are entirely my responsibility and my regret.

This project began in earnest at New York University. I am indebted to the people I worked with there, each of whom has shown me what it takes to be an exceptional scholar, colleague, and mentor. I may never understand how Michael Beckerman manages to bring such constructive incisiveness and excitement to all of our exchanges; his generosity is inexhaustible. In J. Martin Daughtry, I found a reassuring guide who never fails to motivate me with his curiosity and courageousness. Much of this book would be a mess without Maureen Mahon and her intellectual acuity, thoroughness, and compassion; she has helped immensely to develop my ideas. The seed of this project germinated in one of Bambi Schieffelin's enthralling seminars, and her continued attention and acumen have been pivotal to this work. In addition to lending her vast expertise in Romani studies, Carol Silverman has been a wonderful interlocutor and source of moral and scholarly support. And to my amazing advisor, David Samuels: you told me many times that it was better to get that project done than to make it good, yet you consistently pushed and inspired me to make it much more than good enough. You've taken my work seriously while bringing a truly humane approach to advising and an incredible eye for the important stuff. Every mentee should be so lucky.

From the earliest days of this project, Benjamin Givan's invaluable input, collaborative spirit, and abundant enthusiasm have meant a great deal to me. In our shared research and regular conversations, Shirley Brice Heath has been a model of intellectual curiosity, rigor, and care whom I admire tremendously. I thank Charles Lindholm, who has stuck with me since my undergraduate days at Boston University, for his dedicated mentorship and much-needed moments of levity. As a graduate student, I took fascinating courses with Aaron Fox, Faye Ginsburg, and Jane Sugarman, all of whom I thank for their continued guidance beyond my studies with them. I am grateful to Nina Eidsheim and Adriana Helbig for their insight and encouragement, and to Nicholas Harkness for providing crucial feedback. I would not have gotten involved with jazz manouche without my phenomenal violin and viola instructors, David Eure and Maciej Kaczmarek. Staff members in NYU's Department of Music deserve special recognition for all their help, patience, and kindness: Pauline Lum, Natasha Martinez, Freeman Williams, and Lawren Young.

I thank the many colleagues who have provided feedback, friendship, and relief over the years, among them Narges Bajoghli, Matthew Canfield, Ioanida Costache, Sonia Gaind Krishnan, Bradford Garvey, Claudia Huang, Joshua Hudelson, Yoon-Ji Lee, Irina Levin, Alexander Marković, Adam Mirza, Vijayanka Nair, You Nakai, Joseph Pfender, Catherine Provenazno, Alex Rodriguez, Kendra Salois, Benjamin Tausig, Nicholas Tochka, Aleysia Whitmore, Dave Wilson, and María Zuazu. I am especially grateful to Nadia Chana, Anaar Desai-Stephens, and Yun Emily Wang for their tireless encouragement and camaraderie.

I am very fortunate to be part of an exciting and supportive community at the University of Maryland. Sincere gratitude goes to all my colleagues in the Division of Musicology and Ethnomusicology: Barbara Haggh-Huglo, Olga Haldey, Richard King, Fernando Rios, William Robin, Patrick Warfield, and Larry Witzleben. I am especially grateful to Will for collaborating with me, to Pat for his professional guidance, and to Fernando for being an extraordinary mentor. In the College of Arts and Humanities, I am also grateful to Linda Aldoory and Amanda Dykema for helping me frame my project and develop grant proposals. To my advisees Meghan Creek, Heyni Solera, and Victoria Visceglia; my teaching assistants Victor Hernández-Sang, Benjamin Jackson, Julia Kuhlman, W. Donnie Scally, Victoria Visceglia, and Maxwell Yamane; and the students in my Roma in Europe, Music and Language, and Field Methods seminars: you are wonderful people to learn with. Thank you for keeping me on point and thinking in new ways.

Elizabeth Branch Dyson has been a fantastic editor, and I am grateful for her vision, her thoughtful feedback, and her belief in this project. I thank the editors of the Chicago Studies in Ethnomusicology series,

Philip V. Bohlman and Timothy Rommen, for their support of this book. I would also like to thank the two anonymous reviewers for engaging thoroughly with this work and providing constructive feedback; Mollie McFee for her assiduous editorial assistance; Marianne Tatom for her careful and enlightening copyediting; and Tamara Ghattas, Rian Lussier, and the rest of the team at the University of Chicago Press. Andrew Berish, Nomi Dave, Michael Heller, Morgan Luker, Douglas Shadle, and Nicholas Tochka provided enormously helpful guidance as I developed my book proposal and manuscript.

Portions of this book were developed through conference papers and invited colloquium presentations. For these invitations, I thank Aaron Fox at the Center for Ethnomusicology at Columbia University, Victor Stoichita at the Centre de Recherche en Ethnomusicologie at the Université Paris Nanterre, Ilsen About at the École des Hautes Études en Sciences Sociales in Paris, and Ethel Brooks at Rutgers University. A version of chapter 1 was published as "Genre, Ethnoracial Alterity, and the Genesis of *jazz manouche*" in the *Journal of the American Musicological Society* (2019, vol. 72, no. 3), reprinted here with permission from the American Musicological Society and University of California Press. A shortened version of chapter 4 was published as "Music That Tears You Apart: *Jazz manouche* and the Qualia of Ethnorace" in *Ethnomusicology* (2020, vol. 64, no. 3), reprinted here with permission from the Society for Ethnomusicology and University of Illinois Press. I thank the editors of these journals, Joy Calico and Frank Gunderson, for shepherding these articles to publication.

Funding for this research was provided by several sources: from New York University, a MacCracken Fellowship, an Andrew Sauter Fellowship for Predoctoral Students, a Torch Prize Fellowship, and a Mellon Dissertation Fellowship in the Humanities; from the French Ministry of Foreign Affairs, a Chateaubriand Fellowship in the Humanities and Social Sciences; from the Société des Professeurs Français et Francophones d'Amérique, a Jeanne Marandon Scholarship; from the University of Maryland, an Independent Scholarship, Research, and Creativity Award; and from the University of Maryland College of Arts and Humanities, a Faculty Seed Grant and a Special Purpose Innovation Grant.

In France, I have benefited greatly from scholarly dialogues with Ilsen About, Jean-Luc Poueyto, Adèle Sutre, and the late Patrick Williams. Special thanks go to Victor Stoichita and Estelle Amy de la Bretèque for their warm welcome, ongoing intellectual and musical exchanges, and guidance in the French academic sphere. Evelyne Pommerat at the Centre de Documentation of the Fédération Nationale des Associations

Solidaires d'Action avec les Tsiganes et les Gens du voyage provided generous research assistance and a rewarding internship opportunity. Several people were kind enough to give or lend me more archival materials than I knew what to do with, along with their invaluable insight and stories; among them are Patrick Andresz, the late Alain Antonietto, Francis Couvreux, Stella Funaro, Michel Lefort, and Scot Wise. I also thank the staff at the Archives de la Ville et de l'Eurométropole de Strasbourg and Jacques Provot for preserving the several decades' worth of documents that he donated to this institution.

I am deeply grateful to those who shared their time and knowledge through interviews for this project: Marie Amalfitano, Frank Anastasio, Patrick Andresz, the late Alain Antonietto, Christophe Astolfi, Kamlo Barré, Vincent Bessières, Denis Chang, Francis Couvreux, Samy Daussat, Eric Faure, Jean-Marie Fawer, Céline Flieg, Elisabeth Florentin, Stella Funaro, David Gastine, Sorin Gheraliu, Tony Gibier, Yan Gilg, Marie-Hélène Gille, Sébastien Giniaux, Marie-Reine Haug, Pierre Hauger, Engé Helmstetter, Railo Helmstetter, Pierre Heyd, Fléco Lafertin, Biréli Lagrène, Christophe Lartilleux, Michel Lefort, Natacha Lhenry, Tcha Limberger, Cédric Loeffler, Gigi Loeffler, Magalie Loeffler, Marcel Loeffler, the late Vindala Loeffler, Yorgui Loeffler, Patrick Maciejewski, Dino Mehrstein, Francko Mehrstein, Michel Mercier, Marc Mourer, Jean-Marie Pallen, the late Jean-François Pastor, Jacques Provot, Laetitia Quieti, David Reinhardt, Francky Reinhardt, Mandino Reinhardt, Jean-François Robinet, Bertrand Routhier-Faivre, Yves Schmitt, Fabrice Steinberger, Mickaël Stoll, Baro Syntax, Pierre Vigneron, Albert Weiss, Billy Weiss, Gaga Weiss, Matcho Winterstein, and Moreno and Marina Winterstein.

Some of my first and most consequential forays into the French jazz manouche scene happened through festivals. Stateside and on the Samoreau campgrounds, Juan Arenales, Titi Bamberger, Eve Seltzer, and Ben Wood have been wonderful friends and musical collaborators. In Zillisheim, Pierre Heyd and his family graciously hosted me during the Festival Jazz Manouche. I am also grateful to Colette Lafertin, Fléco Lafertin, Zaïti Lafertin, the late Dorno Loeffler, and the entire Lafertin, Loeffler, Meinhardt, and Winterstein families of Zillisheim for welcoming me to their homes. Luthiers are often the eyes and ears of these festivals, and I thank Philippe Moneret for his insight.

In early 2014, I was overjoyed to learn that the C(h)œur des Femmes at the École de musique du Centre social et culturel de Neuhof had accepted me as a member. I am grateful to its leaders Stella Funaro, Anne Huber, and Laetitia Quieti for this opportunity. My deep appreciation goes to all the choir members who welcomed me so readily, especially those with whom I developed lasting friendships: Eric Faure, Joelle Kempfer, and Ringo Weiss. I also thank the faculty members of the École de musique who have been generous with their time and expertise, including Natacha Lhenry, Francko Mehrstein, and Mandino Reinhardt.

My heartfelt thanks go to those who have gone above and beyond to help me along this journey. Monia Nei, my first host in Strasbourg, showed me the ropes and remains a friend and confidant. Early on, Gérard Gerber set up consequential meetings and continued to be a critical influence in my thinking. I've learned a lot from Tcha Limberger, who received me with open arms and an open mind. The boundless passion and knowledge of Alain Antonietto, may he rest in peace, have been key sources of motivation for me. Yorgui Loeffler, Tansa Kreutzer, and Sophie and Christian Weiss have, on many occasions and in many ways, made me feel right at home. I am eternally grateful to Marc Royer, Roselyne Derbre, Nils Graber, Elena Ussoltseva, and Giancarlo Tursi for taking care of me during extended stays in France and for coming along for the ride.

Several people have been especially central to this project and to my life in France. Engé Helmstetter took a sincere interest in my work and has kindly given me a great deal of insight over the years. Marcel Loeffler and Michèle Alix took me under their wings and have brought me much perspective and joy. Patrick Andresz became one of my most important and dedicated mentors. Many of my ideas would not have taken shape without his patient guidance, critical feedback, and sheer enthusiasm for my research. I cherish the monthly dinners in Strasbourg with Patrick, Marcel, and Michèle. I could not imagine completing this book without the generosity, dedication, and thorough input of Stella Funaro and Mandino Reinhardt. They brought me into the fold of APPONA's legacy and became more invested in my work than I could have wished for. To Gigi Loeffler, Laetitia Vincent, and Ambre Vincent: thank you from the bottom of my heart for bringing us into your lives. Your love and kindness know no bounds. *Kamau tumen.*

Finally, I would like to express my gratitude to other close friends and family. I am lucky to call Petra Gelbart a colleague, mentor, co-conspirator, role model, and dear friend; her influence on and support of me stretch well beyond this project. I am forever grateful to members of the Lie, Korey, Bamford, Royer, Salus, and Singh families for everything. Krystelle Bamford, Martine Bamford, Gail Levinson, Jane Korey, Ken Korey, Connor Lie-Spahn, Baldev Singh, Carolyn Singh, and Emilie Wyatt have been especially important supporters and sources of good humor. For their unconditional love and encouragement, I give special thanks to my mother, Ellen Korey-Lie, who never tires of cheerleading, and to

Cecelia Lie-Spahn, who is everything a sister and friend should be and more (not to mention a talented editor). My late father, Arne Brun Lie, to whom I dedicate this book, taught me what it truly means to persevere and live the fullest, most joyful life possible. His spirit continues to motivate all that I do. To my brilliant husband, Davindar Singh, whose eyes and ears have shaped this work immeasurably; with whom I have grown in so many ways; who inspires me every single day; whose utter devotion means the world to me; who has cared for, pushed, and lifted me through times of joy and agony: I love you, I thank you.

APPENDIX 1

Glossary

The nomenclature used for Romani groups can vary widely according to national, linguistic, and other contexts. The following glossary clarifies my use of several Romani-related terms that appear in this book. I have provided pronunciations in the International Phonetic Alphabet (IPA) using broad transcription in the language(s) indicated. For readers unfamiliar with the IPA, I suggest using a tool such as IPA Reader (http://ipa-reader.xyz/) to hear how these terms are pronounced. For more extensive definitions of these and other Romani-related terms, see "Council of Europe Descriptive Glossary of Terms Relating to Roma Issues," Council of Europe, 18 May 2012, https://rm.coe.in/CoERMPublicCommonSearchServices/DisplayDCTMContent?documentId=0900001680088eab.

caravane (French: /kaʁavan/). A mobile residence typically used by Gens du voyage and/or Romanies.

Gadjo (French: /gadʒo/; English: /ˈgad͡ʒo/). In the Manouche variety of Romani, the masculine singular for a non-Romani person. Other forms include *Gadji* (/gadʒi/; feminine singular), *Gadjé* (/gadʒe/; masculine plural), and *Gadjia* (/gadʒia/; feminine plural).

Gens du voyage (French: /ʒɑ̃ dy vwajaʒ/). A French administrative category used to designate populations who live (or once lived) in some type of mobile housing and/or earn income through mobility-dependent professions. Until 1969, Gens du voyage were classified as *nomades*. Although not all Gens du voyage identify as Romani, the two categories are often conflated in popular discourse.

Gitan(s) (French: /ʒitɑ̃/). Used either to refer to a specific subgroup of southwestern French and Spanish Romanies or to designate all Romanies colloquially. In my translations, I preserve *Gitan* in the former case and use *Gypsy* in the latter.

Gypsy (English: /ˈd͡ʒɪpsi/). Used to designate Romanies, often with pejorative connotations. While some Romanies self-identify as Gypsies, it is sometimes considered inappropriate for non-Romanies to use the term to refer to Romanies.

Manouche(s) (French: /manuʃ/ or /mɒnuʃ/). Sometimes spelled "Mānuš." A subgroup of Romanies who have resided primarily in France since at least the eighteenth century, who self-identify as such, and who may speak, with varying degrees of fluency, the Manouche variety of the Romani language. Manouches may also self-identify as Sinti, sometimes referring to themselves as "Manouche" in French-language contexts and as "Sinti" in Romani-language contexts.

Roma (English: /roma/). A major branch of Romanies.

Romanes (English: /romənes/). The Romani language. Also called *Romani*.

Romani (English: /roməni/). The adjectival form of *Romanies*. As a noun, the Romani language.

Romanies (English: /romәniz/). An ethnoracial group that traces its origins to northwestern India and that resides primarily in Europe. I use *Romanies* as a plural noun instead of the more commonly used *Roma* partly to avoid confusion with the French term *Roms*, which usually designates Romani people from Eastern Europe. I also use *Romanies* as a way of including Sinti as belonging to the same broadly defined ethnoracial group, since Sinti often regard themselves as related to, but separate from, Roma.

Sinti (English: /sɪnti/; French: /sinti/; masculine plural), also known as *Sinté* (French: /sinte/). A Western European Romani subgroup closely related to Manouches. Many Manouche groups (mainly those in northern and eastern France, as well as Belgium) consider themselves synonymous with Sinti, but most German and Dutch Sinti do not identify as Manouche.

terrain (French: /tɛʁɛ̃/). A plot of land designated for occupancy by Gens du voyage.

Tsigane(s) (French: /tsigan/). A French synonym for *Romani*. While in English *Gypsy* is often considered a pejorative term and *Romani* and its variants are generally more respectful and accurate, *Tsigane* is not directly translatable into either of these terms. Sometimes spelled "Tzigane."

Zigeuner (German: /siˈgɔʏːnər/). A German term for *Gypsy*. Though it was once widely used among German speakers, it is now considered an inappropriate label for Roma and Sinti, largely on account of its associations with Nazi racial policy.

APPENDIX 2

List of Formal Interviews

This list accounts for all audio-recorded interviews referenced in this book (thirty of the sixty-four I recorded as part of my research). All cities and towns are in France. All interviews were conducted in French unless otherwise noted.

Christophe Astolfi, Paris, 22 October 2013
Eric Faure, Strasbourg, 13 March 2014
Stella Funaro, Strasbourg, 10 February 2014
David Gastine, Paris, 21 August 2013
Marie-Hélène Gille, Strasbourg, 26 January 2014
Sébastien Giniaux, Paris, 6 August 2013
Pierre Hauger, Strasbourg, 21 May 2014
Engé Helmstetter, Barr, 27 July 2012
Railo Helmstetter, Strasbourg, 12 December 2013
Pierre Heyd, Zillisheim, 25 July 2012
Fléco Lafertin, Zillisheim, 14 June 2013
Biréli Lagrène, Strasbourg, 4 April 2014 (interview conducted in English)
Michel Lefort, telephone interview, 7 June 2012
Cédric Loeffler, Strasbourg, 11 July 2014
Marcel Loeffler, Strasbourg, 8 November 2013
Yorgui Loeffler and Billy Weiss, Strasbourg, 28 July 2012
Patrick Maciejewski, Schiltigheim, 8 January 2014
Dino Mehrstein, Strasbourg, 16 January 2014
Francko Mehrstein, Strasbourg, 21 November 2013
Michel Mercier, Paris, 17 December 2013 (interview conducted in English)
Jean-François Pastor, Strasbourg, 10 December 2013
Laetitia Quieti, Strasbourg, 2 July 2014
Francky Reinhardt, Strasbourg, 12 July 2014
Mandino Reinhardt, Strasbourg, 15 April 2014

Jean-François Robinet, Samois-sur-Seine, 1 July 2012
Bertrand Routhier-Faivre, Strasbourg, 28 January 2014
Fabrice Steinberger, Strasbourg, 3 April 2014
Baro Syntax, Vincennes, 30 November 2013
Pierre Vigneron, Wisches, 11 October 2013
Albert Weiss, Strasbourg, 2 July 2014
Billy Weiss and Gaga Weiss, Salbris, 3 June 2012

Notes

INTRODUCTION

1. Choucroute garnie is one of Alsace's "typical dishes," consisting of a large mound of sauerkraut on top of which various types of sausages and other smoked meat products are piled. The tarte flambée is also called *Flammekueche* in Alsatian and *Flammkuchen* in German and is consumed regularly in parts of Germany bordering Alsace. Both dishes are emblematic of the fact that Alsace is often considered the most Germanic of the French regions, and that it has changed hands between French and German rule several times in modern history.
2. Along with the department of Moselle, Alsace is the only place in France where the separation of church and state is officially not upheld. Additionally, the neofascist National Rally (*Rassemblement National,* formerly known as the National Front) party garners relatively high support there (though, in recent years, left-wing parties have also seen increased support in urban areas). In 2014, the French legislature passed territorial reforms that consolidated a number of regions. Alsace, Champagne-Ardenne, and Lorraine were combined into the new Grand Est administrative region, while Alsace was designated a "historical and cultural region" so as not to be confused with the administrative region. On Alsatian branding, see Burdick 2016.
3. In this book, I capitalize "White" to draw attention to how it is so frequently understood as an unmarked, normative category. As Eve L. Ewing puts it, "When we ignore the specificity and significance of Whiteness—the things that it is, the things that it does—we contribute to its seeming neutrality and thereby grant it power to maintain its invisibility" (2020).

4. Loïc is a pseudonym.
5. According to most scholars of Romani history, the ancestors of today's Romani populations migrated from northwest India beginning sometime around 1000 CE. As these groups moved westward over the course of centuries, arriving in present-day Western Europe by about 1400, they faced persecution from settled populations and took on a reputation as Europe's internal "Others" (Hancock 2002; Liégeois 2007). Romani groups are highly diverse in terms of cultural practices, religious beliefs, languages, and physical appearances. Contrary to the one Romani stereotype that never seems to fall out of fashion, the vast majority of today's Romanies worldwide are settled, not nomadic. On French Manouche history, see also Poueyto 2011; Vaux de Foletier 1970.
6. Such violence takes many forms; see, for example, Picker (2017) on Romani housing segregation and Sokolová (2005) on the forced sterilization of Romani women.
7. This figure was well below those for Muslims (61 percent), North Africans (72 percent), and "Blacks and Jews" ("les noirs et les juifs," 78 percent). See "Rapport sur la lutte contre le racisme, l'antisémitisme et la xénophobie: année 2017," Commission nationale consultative des droits de l'homme, République Française, accessed 19 October 2018, https://www.cncdh.fr/sites/default/files/essentiels_du_rapport_racisme_2017_-_pour_impression_ok_1.pdf, 8.
8. The title of a recent book by Aidan McGarry, *Romaphobia: The Last Acceptable Form of Racism* (2017), also reflects the banality of anti-Romani racism. On stereotyped representations of Romanies, see, for example, Piotrowska 2017; Saul and Tebbutt 2004; Silverman 2012, 2013; Trumpener 1992.
9. Details on the history and construction of the style of guitar typically used in jazz manouche, originally designed by Mario Maccaferri and produced by the Selmer company, are documented in Charle 1999.
10. *Musette*—more fully *bal-musette*—is a French popular dance music genre that originated in the nineteenth century and whose name derives from the musette bagpipe of the Auvergnat region. Musette remained popular through the mid-twentieth century and came to feature the accordion as its defining instrument.
11. For more on the contemporary stylistic parameters of jazz manouche, see Cruickshank 1994; Dregni, Antonietto, and Legrand 2006; Givan 2014; Lie and Givan 2019; Schaaser 2013; Tuzet 2007; Williams 2000, 2004. Jazz manouche draws primarily on Django's music from the mid-1930s through the mid-1940s, although he underwent several stylistic phases between the early 1930s and his death (Fargeton 2005; Givan 2010).
12. This apparent paradox of musical signification is nothing new: for example, various genres associated with and/or attributed to African Americans, from jazz to hip hop, are celebrated as both Black and US musics despite the persistent marginalization of African Americans in the United States

and fraught histories of racism in the music industry. On hip hop, see, for example, Keyes 2002; Rollefson 2017; Rose 1994. On the racial politics of jazz in the United States during the civil rights era and the need for scholars to attend to broader political and economic structures in Black music history, see Monson 2007.

13. Scholars have addressed the deliberate use of essentialism as "strategic essentialism" (Spivak 1985) and "autoexoticization" (Savigliano 1995), approaches that depend on essentialism's constitution as "a changing constellation of features and a changing weighing of them" (Stoler 1997, 200; see also Gupta and Ferguson 1992).
14. See chapter 4 for a more detailed explanation of the semiotic theory of Charles S. Peirce, which is generally espoused by linguistic anthropologists concerned with semiotics. This approach helps explain how and why, for example, racial categories take shape across expressive practices. Some ethnomusicological research has drawn on Peircean theory, with works by Thomas Turino (1999, 2008, 2014), David Samuels (2004), and Tony Perman (2010, 2020) among those that make particularly strong cases for the relevance of Peircean semiotics to ethnomusicology.
15. Keane's (2003) definition of semiotic ideologies builds on the linguistically centered notion of language ideologies (Kroskrity 2000; Schieffelin, Woolard, and Kroskrity 1998; Silverstein 1979).
16. On semiotic bundling, see Keane 2003. On the co-constitution of symbolic and material domains, see, for example, Bucholtz and Hall 2016; Keane 2003; Kockelman 2006; Cavanaugh and Shankar 2017; Williams 1977. Paja Faudree argues that an analysis of contingencies between music and language, "as variably constructed distinctions in a total semiotic field" (2012, 520), acknowledges the importance of simultaneously "attending to different signs—to nonlinguistic ones alongside linguistic ones, to signs in their material and sensual, relational totality" (2012, 530). See also Harkness 2013; Mendoza-Denton 2016.
17. Numerous scholars have explored relationships between musical sound and racial configurations; see, for example, Berish 2012; Braggs 2016; Eidsheim 2011, 2012, and 2019; Kajikawa 2015, 2019; Mahon 2004, 2020; Martin 2018; Orejuela and Shonekan 2018; Quintero 2018; Radano 2003 and 2013; Radano and Bohlman 2000; Roberts 2016; Stoever 2016.
18. The term *raciolinguistics* was initially developed by Nelson Flores and Jonathan Rosa (2015); see also Alim, Rickford, and Ball 2016; Rosa and Flores 2017, 2020. Most scholars who adopt this framework do account for a variety of semiotic modalities, and my use of *raciosemiotics* simply calls attention to the importance of these modalities together as "total semiotic facts" (Nakassis 2016), especially when musical sound plays an important role in processes of racialization. Some other works that have contributed to raciolinguistic study, with or without this heading, include Bucholtz 2010; Chun and Lo 2016; Hill 2008; Inoue 2006; Reyes and Lo 2009; Spears

1999. See especially the recent collection on race and language edited by H. Samy Alim, Angela Reyes, and Paul V. Kroskrity (2020).

19. For more on the political-economic construction of race and its malleability, see Fields and Fields 2012. A "colonial constitution of race thesis," as outlined by Barnor Hesse, holds that "race is not in the eye of the beholder or on the body of the objectified. Race is an inherited western, modern-colonial practice of violence, assemblage, superordination, exploitation and segregation. Race is constitutively and unequally relational, regulatory and governmental, demarcating the colonial rule of Europe over non-Europe" (2016, viii). Giovanni Picker (2017) argues that European Romanies have been subjected to racializing processes extremely similar to those developed under colonial administrations, such that Romani racialization can be considered of a piece with colonial (and, according to Geraldine Heng [2018], precolonial) racial logics broadly. On Romani racialization in the context of (post-)colonialism, see also Scheffel (2019, 204); Smith (2018, 188–89).

20. Ryan Powell and Huub van Baar (2019, 91) argue that "processes of neoliberalization and securitization" have shaped the "invisibilization" of Romani racialization in Europe. On how Romani racialization is downplayed or elided in official and popular discourses, see also Grill 2018; Picker 2017; Surdu 2016.

21. Numerous scholars have, from different angles, critiqued the premises of Western liberalism and the role of universalist ideologies in legitimizing white supremacist logics. For example, as Lisa Lowe argues, "the social inequalities of our time are a legacy of . . . processes through which 'the human' is 'freed' by liberal forms, while other subjects, practices, and geographies are placed at a distance from 'the human'" (2015, 3; see also Beliso-De Jesús and Pierre 2020; Fanon 1952; Feagin 2010; Lentin 2008). On the French government's policies against collecting ethnic, racial, and religious statistics, see Bleich 2000; Simon 2008. In 2012, presidential candidate François Hollande campaigned to remove the use of *race* in the French constitution (Faye 2012); following his election, in 2013, the National Assembly voted to remove the word *race* from all legislation. See http://www.assemblee-nationale.fr/14/ta/ta0139.asp. Article 1 of the legislation states, "The French Republic condemns racism, antisemitism, and xenophobia. It does not recognize the existence of any so-called race." On the "of foreign origin" designation, see Fassin [2006] 2009; Fernando 2014; Hargreaves [1995] 2007; Tissot 2011. On the construction and maintenance of white supremacy in France, see Beaman 2019; Dubois 2000; Escafré-Dublet 2019.

22. A robust body of work on color-blind racism in France has developed in the past several decades. Though this work has thoroughly shaped my understandings of race in France, I do not have the space to detail much of it in this book. In addition to sources cited in text, see, for example, Beaman and Petts 2020; Bleich 2003; Chapman and Frader 2004; Epstein 2011; Guillaumin 1972; Keaton 2010; Keaton, Sharpley-Whiting, and Stovall

2012; Knox 2016; Niang 2019; Peabody and Stovall 2003; Sabbagh and Peer 2008; Silverstein 2018; Wieviorka 1992.

23. On slippages between "race" and "culture," see also Abu-Lughod 1991; Bonilla-Silva and Mayorga 2011; Goldberg 2009; Lentin 2014; Stocking 1968, 265–66; Surdu 2016; Weiner 2012. Drawing on Michel-Rolph Trouillot, Jemima Pierre argues that anthropology's "ideological shift from race to culture" reflects, among some contemporary anthropologists, "a trained inability to acknowledge and/or examine the racial underpinnings of post-colonial societies" (2013, 199). In a similar vein, Adolph Reed Jr. writes that race is an "ideology of ascriptive difference"—often glossed as "culture"—that "help[s] to stabilize a social order by legitimizing its hierarchies of wealth, power, and privilege, including its social division of labor, as the natural order of things" (2013, 49).
24. On the plight of French Romanies during World War II, see Asséo 1994, 2005; Filhol 2007, 2013; Hubert 1997; Peschanski 2002; Sigot 2010.
25. On French intolerance of Islam, see Fernando 2014; Tissot 2011; Volpp 2007. Such debates about the use of religious emblems in public spaces are indicative of widespread Islamophobia in France, which was exacerbated following terrorist attacks in Paris in January and November 2015 (see, e.g., Kiwan 2016; Niang 2019; Silverstein 2018). See also Favell 1997 and Feldblum 1999 on the development of xenophobic discourse in French politics during the late twentieth century.
26. Since Romania and Bulgaria joined the European Union in 2007, the numbers of Romanies who migrate to Western Europe have increased. In 2010, President Sarkozy framed this migration as a national threat, conflated (im)-migrant Romanies with Gens du voyage (thus contradicting the republican "values" he claimed to uphold and making way for further slippage between administrative and racial categories; see Poueyto 2018; Sarkozy 2010), and implemented a racially targeted deportation policy that continued under the Hollande and Macron administrations. This situation has exacerbated xenophobia toward Romanies generally. Heightened tensions surrounding Romani (im)migrants have spilled over to French Romanies, including Manouches who claim that the public lumps all Romanies together under the same stigmatizing labels. In response to this perception, some Manouches strive to differentiate themselves ever more strictly from Eastern European Roma.
27. Until 2012, Gens du voyage faced voting restrictions inapplicable to any other class of French citizens, requiring a waiting period of three years from the date of their registration with a *commune de rattachement* (home commune) before their voting rights would become valid ("Droit de vote des Gens du voyage" 2012).
28. On the development of jazz worldwide, and the historiography thereof, see, for example, Atkins 2001, 2003; Bohlman and Plastino 2016; Feld 2012; Gebhardt 2012; Rodriguez 2018.

29. On jazz and racial imaginaries, see, for example, Berish 2012; Burke 2008; Horne 2019; Klotz 2016; Monson 2007.
30. See Lemon 1995; 2000, 62–79, on attributions of Blackness to Romanies within Russian racial imaginaries.
31. Pascal is a pseudonym.
32. For ethnomusicological perspectives on the generation and harnessing of plural meanings, see, for example, Quintero 2018; Samuels 2004.
33. On the rise of pro-Romani political organizations, see Acton and Mundy 1997; Hancock 2002; Liégeois 2007; Margalit and Matras 2013; Surdu 2016; Trehan and Sigona 2009; van Baar 2015; van Baar and Kóczé 2020; Vermeersch 2006. For further work on Romani music and identity, see, for example, Beissinger 2001; Hooker 2007; Lange 2003; Lemon 1996, 2000; Marković 2015; Silverman 2007; Stoichita 2008.
34. Similarly, Rogers Brubaker writes of "ethnopolitical entrepreneurs" as "specialists" who "may live 'off' as well as 'for' ethnicity," arguing that "by *invoking* groups, they seek to *evoke* them, summon them, call them into being. Their categories are *for doing*—designed to stir, summon, justify, mobilize, kindle, and energize" (2004, 10; emphasis in original).
35. These include, for example, sporting a pencil mustache and semiformal clothes made to look somewhat disheveled; using imagery of caravans and hedgehogs (emblems of Romani identity broadly); describing themselves as fiery, nomadic, bohemian, passionate, and other similar adjectives; and writing lyrics about things like the "Manouche lifestyle" and other clichéd ideas about Manouche people. These phenomena parallel similarly racialized notions of "hipness" as described by Monson (1995). For an especially blatant example, see the music video "T'as la Touche Manouche" ("You Have the Manouche Touch") by La Caravane Passe (https://www.youtube.com/watch?v=Wkkf-y9yYLA).
36. Scholars such as Andy Fry (2014), Jeffrey Jackson (2003), and Elizabeth Vihlen McGregor (2016), among others, address Django's legacy in the history of French jazz.
37. For further appeals to de-essentialize scholarly representations of Romanies, see, for example, Lee 2000; Matache 2016; Willems 1997. For overviews of anthropological scholarship on Romanies, see Olivera and Poueyto 2018; Stewart 2013.
38. My in-depth introduction both to the history of Django's music and to his ensemble's musical techniques came thanks to this teacher, David Eure.
39. In a way similar to *art world*, I use the term *scene* as defined by Bennett and Peterson: "the contexts in which clusters of producers, musicians, and fans collectively share their common musical tastes and collectively distinguish themselves from others" (2004, 1).
40. Because APPONA ceased to exist more than ten years before I began my field research, my work on the organization has been mostly informed by stories from former members and by a wealth of archival material. Much

of this material was provided to me by Stella Funaro in the form of audio recordings and a two-volume collection of APPONA festival programs and publicity, newspaper clippings, photos, and other documents. The official APPONA archives at the Archives de la Ville et de l'Eurométropole de Strasbourg were donated by a former president of the organization, Jacques Provot, and include thousands of pages of press materials, letters, memos, proposals, progress reports, financial statements, and other internal documents.

41. Justin worked under the supervision of Robert Ritter, who played a key role in developing Nazi plans for Romani genocide. Her research subjects were Romanies who had already been ordered to Auschwitz. Following the submission of her dissertation in 1943, in 1944 they were deported to and died in the camp (Gingrich 2005, 121–22). See also Ari Joskowicz's (2020) work on links between reticence among Romanies to testify about the Holocaust and concerns about contemporary surveillance.
42. Perhaps the most decisive event in this latter respect was the publication of anthropologist Marie-Paul Dollé's (1980) monograph on Alsatian Manouches, which included photographs of a funeral ceremony. Both the photographing of this ritual and the distribution of images violated the community's customs, and in turn destroyed their trust in Dollé, who had spent years living among them. Still a topic of conversation decades later, Dollé's actions only reinforced the apprehension among members of the community toward research conducted by outsiders.

CHAPTER ONE

1. The Quintette du Hot Club de France was the signature ensemble of the Hot Club de France, an organization founded in the early 1930s with the aim of promoting "hot" jazz throughout France. In 1934, Hot Club de France member Pierre Nourry enlisted Django, Django's brother Joseph and Roger Chaput on rhythm guitars, Stéphane Grappelli on violin, and Louis Vola on bass to form the first iteration of the Quintette (Delaunay 1968, 63–66).
2. Dregni has authored some of the most widely read English-language accounts of jazz manouche and Django's life (2004, 2008) in which he makes claims similar to those in the passage quoted here.
3. T. Roberts refers to this process as "sono-racialization," "the organization of sound into taxonomies based on racialized conception of bodies" (2016, 4). Similarly, Nina Sun Eidsheim explores how vocalization, as a necessarily "thick event," is routinely "reduced to socially and culturally categorized and evaluated vocal sounds, such as pitch and voice, as essential markers" of race (2019, 8–9).
4. My argument about the mutual constitution of ethnoracial and generic discourses dovetails with other scholars' work on the topic: for example,

Karl Hagstrom Miller (2010) on the "musical color line" in the Jim Crow South, Michael Birenbaum Quintero (2018) on the co-production of musical and social Blackness, and Ronald Radano (2003) on how the category "black music" took shape in the United States. This argument follows a logic similar to what H. Samy Alim calls "racing language" and "languaging race" (2016).

5. Andrew Berish observes that "writers on Reinhardt simply assert that he was everything all at once, regardless of any contradictions—'universal' but specifically European (or Manouche); a jazz musician steeped in tradition, but also unprecedented and original" (2009, 241). Several scholars have noted how Django's ethnoracial and national specificity as well as his universality were important factors in his ascension as a key figure in nationalist conceptions of French jazz (Braggs 2016; Fry 2014; Jackson 2003; Jordan 2010; McGregor 2016), despite the fact that some of his contemporaries did not consider him especially important at the time (Cugny 2013, 171–73).
6. Jean "Matelo" Ferret's brothers, Pierre "Baro" Ferret and Etienne "Sarane" Ferret, were frequent accompanists for Django. Of the three brothers, all of whom were French Gitans, Matelo was the youngest and went on to have the most illustrious career.
7. Django also struggled with literacy and therefore did not leave much of a written record, though Grappelli has said that he gave Django informal reading and writing lessons (Grappelli 1992, 91).
8. Antonietto and Billard (2004), Delaunay (1954), and Williams (1998) all provide much more detailed accounts of Django's life.
9. The banjo-guitar is a hybrid instrument, "less forceful" than a typical banjo but with "more harmonic and contrapuntal possibilities" (Roussin 1994, 136).
10. See note 10 in the introduction for a description of bal-musette.
11. Givan (2010, 200) points out that although numerous sources cite the date of the caravan fire as November 2, more recent documentation indicates otherwise.
12. Some of my interlocutors have hypothesized that contemporary jazz manouche left-hand technique developed as a retention of Django's adaptation to his disability. This technique involves the use of the left thumb to depress some notes on the low E string, which is unconventional for guitar technique generally. See Givan 2010 for analyses of how Django adapted his left-hand techniques to his injury. As Givan contends, many have tended to "exaggerat[e] his disability either because of misconceptions or for rhetorical effect" (2010, 8). Although the extent of his disability has often been overstated, he argues that Django's overcoming "this challenge attests not so much to the inconsequence of his affliction as to his extraordinary feat in transcending it" (24).
13. Antonietto and Billard recognize the developments in string-based "hot jazz" that were contemporaneous with the QHCF, developments that complicate the designation of a jazz manouche genre based almost entirely on

Django's work as part of an all-string swing group. See Antonietto and Billard 2004, 399–401.

14. For more on Django's postwar period, see Berish 2009; Cugny 2013; Fargeton 2005.
15. See McGregor 2016, 174–81; Goffin 1932.
16. André Cœuroy, a Nazi sympathizer, went so far as to proclaim in 1942 that jazz was truly and rightfully a white European form that had been misappropriated by African Americans, writing, "all these whites who play—[André] Ekyan, [Django] Reinhardt—play swing, a swing that's theirs, a white swing, a European swing, a 'classic' swing, close in spirit to the music of the same name" (1942, 220).
17. Such racializing descriptions were not limited to Django himself. Jean Cocteau (an acquaintance of Django) wrote in promotional materials for the Quintette du Hot Club de France: "The Django Reinhardt-Grappelly [*sic*] 'band' creates a 'hot' atmosphere like the one we know thanks to the Blacks from America. It brings us around the fire of a Bohemian camp and takes us away to our spiritual families . . . by the prodigy of a race that seems to arise from the beginning of time" (1937).
18. A *roulotte* is an old-fashioned, horse-drawn caravan, usually made of wood.
19. For further instances of this stereotyping, see Delaunay 1954, 13–16, 22–26, 34–35, 43–44. At one point, Delaunay refers to Django's Manouche cousins as mischievous "monkeys" (34).
20. See McGregor 2016, 167–74, for further evidence of racializing descriptions of Django by Delaunay and other jazz critics.
21. In a 1944 interview about a mass he had begun writing in dedication to Romanies, Django said that he was "loved by" other Romanies, but this is the only known statement Django made on record about any connection between his music and his sense of belonging to a Romani community. He never indicated whether the composition reflected any specifically Manouche influences (*Intégrale Django Reinhardt*, vol. 12, *1943–1945* [Frémeaux & Associés FA 312, 2002], compact disc; this interview appears on disc 1, track 20, at 1:38).
22. See, for example, Cascio 2010; de Fatto 1977; Gaspard 1963; Gatlif 2002; Jeremy 1989; Le Jean 2012; Lefort 1991; Pac 1979; Reinhardt and Maestracci 1997; Ténot 1988; Tuzet 2007.
23. See Abrams 1978; Blesh 1946, 270; Dregni 2004, 2008, 2018; Hajdu 2010; Hoefer 1966; MacDougald 1938; Schuller 1989, 566; Shipton 2007, 388–89; Simon 1957, 318; Ulanov 1953; Zwerin 2000.
24. To be sure, a number of critics have not essentialized Django in these ways; see, for example, the œuvres of Alain Antonietto, Benjamin Givan, and Patrick Williams, in addition to Berish 2009; Cugny 2013; and Fargeton 2005. Additionally, in his writings and interviews, Stéphane Grappelli did not seem to emphasize connections between Django's music, his character, and his ethnorace (see, for example, Grappelli 1992).

25. Neither Charles Delaunay's 1954 book, *Django Reinhardt: Souvenirs*, nor the revised version of this book (published in 1968 as *Django mon frère*) contains any instances of "jazz manouche," "jazz gitan," "swing manouche," or "swing gitan." A Google Books Ngram Viewer search conducted on 12 September 2016 shows the earliest use in French literature of "jazz manouche" as 1976, though this search is of course limited to the texts obtained by Google. The same search performed on "Gypsy jazz" in English literature reveals a review in the *Saturday Review* dating to 1959.
26. These continuers include Joseph Reinhardt, Eugène Vees, Sarane Ferret, René Mailhes, and Laro Sollero, among others. More than by their "language" (a word he uses as a metaphor for style) based on Django's work, the "continuers" of the school are defined by "the kind of sensitivity and the creative attitude that manifests itself through this language" (Jalard 1959, 60).
27. Within Manouche communities on the outskirts of Paris, musicians such as Joseph Reinhardt and Lousson Baumgartner continued to perform Django's repertoire and to develop jazz guitar performance through a limited degree of community practice. Other Romani guitarists, including René Mailhes, Spatzo Adel, Piton Reinhardt, and Laro Sollero, are frequently identified as part of Django's milieu, as "inheritors" of his style, or are otherwise associated with the period of Parisian jazz guitar playing in the years immediately following Django's death (Antonietto and Billard 2004, 410–11). Some critics and musicians consider these musicians to be tangential to, if not members of, the progenitors of jazz manouche.
28. In addition to his 1959 article, other references to Jalard's criticism appear in issues of the journal *Études tsiganes* in the late 1950s and early 1960s, suggesting that those in the pro-Romani activism community were also reading his work at this time.
29. Pilgrimages ("pèlerinages") were Catholic and conventions ("conventions") were evangelical. Manouche-oriented evangelical organizations emerged in the early 1950s, splitting many Manouche communities between evangelical and Catholic followers (Garo 2005).
30. An article in the same issue of *Études tsiganes* refers to the performances by Matelo Ferret, Boulou Ferret, Joseph Reinhardt, and Babik Reinhardt as *"jazz manouche et gitan,"* though only to identify the Romani subgroups to which the Ferrets and Reinhardts belonged, not to designate a new genre (Cullaz 1967, 35). See also Andresz 2015, 135–36.
31. Seven albums, numbered consecutively, were released with the title *Musik Deustcher Zigeuner* between 1969 and 1974; an eighth, a compilation of previously released recordings, was released on compact disc in 1995. Musicians in the MDZ collective also released other albums under different names.
32. According to historian Gilad Margalit and linguist Yaron Matras, "The Romani national revival of the late 1960s borrowed its methods from the civil

rights struggle of the American Indians and from the struggle of the 1968 student movements" (2013, 111).

33. Häns'che Weiss Quintett, *Fünf Jahre Musik Deutscher Zigeuner*, Intercord INT 160.088, 1977, LP.
34. An interview with an elder Manouche luthier and musician in 1968 corroborates this information ("Un Manouche musicien et luthier" 1968, 12).
35. Since at least the 1970s, Alsatian Manouche guitarists have far outnumbered Alsatian Manouche violinists. Among these violinists, techniques have tended to imitate Schnuckenack Reinhardt more than Grappelli or other jazz violinists (see Antonietto and Williams 1985; Williams 2000).
36. For French Manouches outside Alsace, the direct influence of MDZ was not nearly as strong. However, starting in the 1960s they still adopted Django's music through direct contact with other musicians familiar with his music, as well as through Django's recordings. See Williams 2000.
37. For an extended oral history with Mandino Reinhardt, see Lie 2018.
38. The Comité Mondiale Gitane had been established in 1959 in Paris to aid and unite Romani immigrants primarily from Yugoslavia, though some Manouches and members of other Romani subgroups participated as well. After its disbandment by the police in 1965 (apparently due in part to the fact that its leader was issuing Romani "passports"), it regrouped as the Comité Internationale Tsigane and became closely linked to the Romani evangelical movement that had gained momentum in France. At the Romani World Congress in 1971, the Comité Internationale Tsigane was redesignated the Comité Internationale Rom (Liégeois 1975, 300–303).
39. Archives de la Ville et de l'Eurométropole de Strasbourg, 168 Z, "Insertion par le travail: Formation pour bénéficiaires du RMI pratiquant un instrument de musique, stage également ouvert aux non bénéficiaires du RMI" (undated), 2.
40. Kautzmann, "Musique" (private APPONA archive), 1978.
41. Django was not "the founder" of the QHCF, but its most famous member.
42. "Variety music" here most likely means light music of the sort performed by pops orchestras, as well as mid-century French chansons. "Middle-jazz" is a French synonym for swing-era jazz. The authors do not distinguish which genres Manouches practiced and which they simply listened to. According to those among my interlocutors who can recall this era, these genres spanned both listening and performing practices to some extent. The authors do note that by 1989, the "nodal point" of Manouche performance practice was "the repertoire of Django Reinhardt" (Daval and Hauger 1989, 478).
43. As described in chapter 5, APPONA also frequently included Romani groups of non-French origin in their concert and festival programming. Performances by foreign Romani groups such as Ando Drom suggested that APPONA sought to cultivate a pan-Romani ethnoracial identity.

44. Archives de la Ville et de l'Eurométropole de Strasbourg, 168 Z, "Le Quartet Reinhardt" (undated).
45. Some standards of the contemporary jazz manouche repertoire include "Blue Bossa," "Mañha de Carnaval," and "Bossa Dorado." The other styles include, to greater or lesser extents depending on the jazz manouche musicians in question, waltzes, csárdás, and songs in Romani.
46. Archives de la Ville et de l'Eurométropole de Strasbourg, 168 Z, "Traditions manouches d'aujourd'hui: une présentation de l'APPONA aux rencontres internationales de folklore tsigane" (1987), 2–3.
47. Archives de la Ville, 168 Z, "Traditions manouches," 4.
48. Archives de la Ville, 168 Z, "Traditions manouches," 4.
49. Lorraine, home to famed Manouche guitarist Dorado Schmitt and his family, is also an important region in this respect, and APPONA's music promotion efforts often involved these musicians.
50. This interview was conducted in English, so Mercier would sometimes say "Gypsy jazz" instead of "jazz manouche."
51. FNAC (Fédération Nationale d'Achats des Cadres), pronounced in French as /fənæk/, is one of France's largest media and electronics retail chain stores.
52. Early in his career, Lagrène benefited from APPONA's support, though his rapid rise to fame meant that he did not depend on it for long.
53. Mitch clarifies that although the genre is now widely known as "jazz manouche," "fifteen years ago, everybody was saying jazz gitan, in magazines everywhere. So thanks to the trend, now people make the difference between Manouche and Gitan people."
54. Fremeaux.com, accessed 15 March 2017, https://www.fremeaux.com/index.php?option=com_virtuemart&page=shop.product_details&flypage=shop.flypage&product_id=503&Itemid=13.
55. Fremeaux.com, accessed 15 March 2017, https://www.fremeaux.com/index.php?page=shop.product_details&category_id=64&flypage=shop.flypage&product_id=944&option=com_virtuemart&Itemid=0.

CHAPTER TWO

1. In line with the choir's mission to provide a space for those marginalized both within and outside of Manouche communities, its leadership welcomed this Manouche man, Ringo Weiss, who has cerebral palsy. Ringo has been an outspoken local advocate for disability rights.
2. In the organization's name, the term *d'Origine Nomade*, "of nomadic origin," reflected the fact that many of the organization's constituents were semi- or fully sedentary. "Nomadic origin" implied Romani, and the vast majority of APPONA's constituents identified as Manouche, as another Romani subgroup, and/or as Gens du voyage. Among Gens du voyage, a small minority were Yéniche, a group generally considered separate from Romanies (see Meier 2008).

3. "Une Favella en Alsace." Unidentifiable newspaper dating from 1972, pp. 8–10. Archives de la Ville et de l'Eurométropole de Strasbourg, 168 Z.
4. One of APPONA's former presidents, Jacques Provot, recounted this incident in a draft of the President's Report of 1996. Early in 1974, several villagers, armed with rifles and dogs, chased a Manouche family from their dilapidated riverside encampment into the woods. Following this, the mayor of the village killed the cats and dogs that remained at the encampment, burned the family's belongings, and bulldozed the mess. The family was found two months later living under a tent in the junkyard of another village, the mayor of which ordered them to leave. Upon learning this, a "help committee" of members of local nonprofit organizations assembled to help the family find housing and put their children in school. The mayor of the village from which the family was expelled, Charles Arlen, described his actions as an effort to "clean" the territory (Meyer 1974). In 1983, he was found guilty of destroying others' property and fined, though he was not charged with any hate crime (Reinheimer 1983).
5. Archives de la Ville et de l'Eurométropole de Strasbourg, 168 Z. The summary of this 1974 meeting lists thirty-two members, of whom eight comprise the Administrative Council. By 2002, APPONA had thirty to forty dues-paying members, 120 "sympathetic" (presumably non-dues-paying) members, an Administrative Council of fifteen members, a director, an accountant, two secretaries, and twenty-four other salaried employees. Although the general APPONA membership showed no discernible gender imbalances, those at the highest levels of leadership were most often identified as men.
6. Once Manouches sedentarized, it became impossible to continue many of their traditional professions (carnivals and circuses, agricultural work, scrap metal collecting, and commerce at traveling markets, among other professions) because they required seasonal or year-round mobility. With the advent of cheaper mass manufacturing methods, the demand for artisanal industries on which many Manouches made a living (basketry, broom-making, carving, and luthiery, among other crafts) also began to disappear.
7. See Bleich 2003, 130–40. According to Bleich, "The French laws against racism made no provision for counting, protecting, or aiding groups defined by race or ethnicity," and the legislation almost passed without even including the word *race* (2000, 58).
8. See Liégeois 1975 on the First Romani World Congress. APPONA, too, faced racially motivated harassment. At one point in the organization's early years, an anonymous tract was distributed to residents of one village and sent to APPONA. It characterized "Gitans" (here, in the general sense of "Gypsies") as a "band of sloths," "vermin," "dogs," and "rats that maim our Alsace," and suggested that "the best solution would be to crush them with heavy tanks or to eliminate them with a shock troop. We might be

sorry that the Nazis didn't radically exterminate this band." It also criticized APPONA members as "lazy bureaucrats" and a "band of shitheads" who, because they support a "race [that] lives on welfare payments and social aid," "deserve to be beaten without mercy." This and other tracts similar in tone were distributed in late 1981, prompting APPONA to seek legal counsel and to file complaints with the village's mayor, a regional court, and the Ministry of National Solidarity (Archives de la Ville et de l'Eurométropole de Strasbourg, 168 Z).

9. For more on the "right to difference" and its political repercussions, see Bleich 2003; Favell 1997; Feldblum 1999; Hargreaves 2007.
10. Françoise Gaspard argues that since assimilation became a "taboo" word in French political discourse during the 1970s (1992, 14), insertion and integration became the preferred terms not only to "name the other[,] but to recognize, to accept the other as himself, [and] to incorporate him all the same" (15). In Gaspard's reading, the "other" pertains exclusively to the immigrant, whereas in other literature on this terminology, it may also include those with disabilities. Manouches were often considered "others" in both senses—as cultural "others" of foreign origin *and* as unfit to participate in the workforce.
11. The *Haut Conseil à l'intégration* (High Council for Integration), established in 1990 and active until 2012, included non-immigrants in its definition of integration (Barou 2014).
12. According to the Institut national de la statistique et des études économiques, the RMI's purpose was "to guarantee a minimum level of resources and to facilitate the insertion or the reinsertion of persons with poor revenues. The RMI is allocated to every person fulfilling the following conditions: living in France, being at least 25 years old (except for particular cases: pregnant women, etc.), having resources inferior to the RMI amount, and signing an insertion contract" involving obligations that may include seeking employment in some form (https://www.insee.fr/fr/metadonnees/definition/c1852). The RMI was replaced by the Revenu de solidarité active (RSA) in 2009.
13. Private APPONA archive, "La roulotte des tsiganes."
14. Archives de la Ville et de l'Eurométropole de Strasbourg, 168 Z, "Rapport moral 1991," 1.
15. Archives de la Ville et de l'Eurométropole de Strasbourg, 168 Z, "Rapport moral 1986," 3.
16. On the rise of neoliberalism in France, see Evans and Sewell 2013, 53; Howell 1992, 2018; Prasad 2005. Ryan Powell and Huub van Baar write that broad allegiance to neoliberal logics has cast anti-Romani racism as a problem Romanies bring unto themselves; in this view, "it is not the Roma who are confronted with the serious, large-scale violation of their rights, but it is the Roma themselves . . . who [are thought to] have violated rights and failed in their duties" (2019, 95–96).

17. I use *professionalization* here to encompass projects geared toward developing a wide variety of professional skills. My use of the term is somewhat different from that of some of my interlocutors, who employ it in a narrower sense to mean official professional procedures such as contracts and tax declarations.
18. Archives de la Ville et de l'Eurométropole de Strasbourg, 168 Z, "Rapport moral 1991," 8; emphasis added.
19. Archives de la Ville et de l'Eurométropole de Strasbourg, 168 Z, "Insertion par le travail: Formation pour bénéficiaires du RMI pratiquant un instrument de musique, stage également ouvert aux non bénéficiaires du RMI" (undated), 4.
20. Archives de la Ville et de l'Eurométropole de Strasbourg, 168 Z, "Une semaine pour la diffusion de la culture tzigane."
21. Previously, in 1986, APPONA began developing a film project, *Musique Tsigane en Alsace,* that highlighted local Manouche musical culture. The proposal for the film outlined several objectives: "to give a positive image to the Tsigane world . . . to provide a promotional tool for Tsigane musicians . . . [and] to leave a trace of the artistic dynamism that our action[s] wish to support, for ourselves and [for] all those who are invested in the promotion of the Tsigane world" (Archives de la Ville et de l'Eurométropole de Strasbourg, 168 Z, "Musique Tsigane en Alsace"). By insisting that Manouches have "control over the content of the film," this project emphasized the need to raise awareness about the realities of Manouche communities on terms set by Manouches themselves (implying that Gadjé otherwise guided APPONA's cultural programming). The proposal also explicitly linked this awareness-raising with the practical needs of musicians to promote themselves, bringing into focus the fact that social objectives were inseparable from economic ones. Film was considered an effective means to bring public exposure to Manouches in the service of these goals.
22. In addition to print media, APPONA organized occasional radio programming. The President's Report from 1995 states that a local Christian radio program, *Arc en ciel,* invited APPONA musicians, music students, and music teachers to perform for a special show about "the place of music in the Tsigane world." Reportedly, "the children present for this show were able to express through music all the sensitivity of the Manouche world." That same year, an unnamed musician from Mandino's ensemble Note Manouche spoke on a radio program during the "Festival of Ethnic Music" in Rennes about "the actions promoting Tsigane culture that our organization has led for twenty years."
23. Because most of my interlocutors familiar with APPONA's work were either deeply involved with the organization or had a stake in its cultural activism otherwise, I have not been able to acquire a comprehensive picture of how people across Manouche communities conceived of this ethnocidal threat at the time. Present-day opinions about the threat of ethnocide vary greatly among those who self-identify as Manouche.

24. Archives de la Ville et de l'Eurométropole de Strasbourg, 168 Z, "Insertion par le travail," 2.
25. Archives de la Ville, "Insertion par le travail," 2.
26. Archives de la Ville, "Insertion par le travail," 2.
27. Archives de la Ville et de l'Eurométropole de Strasbourg, 168 Z, "Insertion par le travail," 2. Although not clear in this passage, it is likely that the author uses "Tzigane" to refer to French Manouche populations, and possibly Alsatian Manouches in particular, as opposed to Romanies generally, considering that such claims to ethnoracial sovereignty and linguistic recognition had already been made in other parts of Europe by this point.
28. Archives de la Ville, "Insertion par le travail," 2.
29. Several documents in the APPONA files at the Strasbourg municipal archives reveal uncertainty about the date of the school's official creation. Documents commemorating the school's twentieth anniversary state that it was established in 1978, while memos from former APPONA president Jacques Provot state that the earliest it could have been established was 1981.
30. Archives de la Ville et de l'Eurométropole de Strasbourg, 168 Z, "Bilan de l'école de musique de l'APPONA 1978–1998," 2.
31. Archives de la Ville, "Bilan de l'école de musique," 2.
32. Archives de la Ville et de l'Eurométropole de Strasbourg, 168 Z, "APPONA 1985," 19.
33. Archives de la Ville, "APPONA 1985," 19.
34. Private APPONA archive, "Rigo Steinberger fait Officier des Arts et Lettres: 'La reconnaissance d'une culture.'" This appeared in the 3 June 1986 edition of *Dernières nouvelles d'Alsace*, but the page number and interviewer's name were not indicated on this clipping.
35. "Rigo Steinberger fait Officier des Arts et Lettres."
36. Archives de la Ville et de l'Eurométropole de Strasbourg, 168 Z, "Rapport d'activités & Rapport moral 1998," 12.
37. Archives de la Ville et de l'Eurométropole de Strasbourg, 168 Z, "Projet pour un stage d'insertion en milieu tsigane," 4.
38. Archives de la Ville et de l'Eurométropole de Strasbourg, 168 Z, "Rapport moral 1987," 9.
39. Archives de la Ville et de l'Eurométropole de Strasbourg, 168 Z, "Rapport moral 1998," 12.
40. Archives de la Ville et de l'Eurométropole de Strasbourg, 168 Z, "Rapport d'activités & Rapport moral 1997," 17.
41. Archives de la Ville et de l'Eurométropole de Strasbourg, 168 Z, "Convention entre l'APPONA et ATEMA Alsace."
42. Archives de la Ville et de l'Eurométropole de Strasbourg, 168 Z (untitled spreadsheet).
43. One category listed is that of the *intermittent du spectacle*, a person who works in the entertainment industry and who receives governmental

subsidies for fulfilling certain criteria (e.g., performing a certain number of shows for which they declare taxable income).

44. There appear to be weak correlations between any of these factors: some groups whose members receive RMI payments obtain a relatively high number of gigs, while others do not; some groups whose members do not receive RMI or disability payments obtain fewer gigs, while others perform frequently; whether or not a musician was trained through APPONA seems to have little to do with their financial situation or musical employability.
45. Archives de la Ville et de l'Eurométropole de Strasbourg, 168 Z, "Insertion par le travail," 2. Referencing an earlier but failed attempt in 1994 to train welfare recipients in music professionalization, the proposal states that the festival "brought to light some lacunae of a number of groups who did not possess professional quality[, an] indispensable condition for becoming recognized. The musicians concerned realized their deficiency and asked us to help them."
46. Archives de la Ville, "Insertion par le travail," 2.
47. Archives de la Ville, "Insertion par le travail," 4.
48. See http://www.appona68.fr/page4.html. At the time of my fieldwork, the Haut-Rhin was the less populous of Alsace's two departments. The departmental codes for the Haut-Rhin and the Bas-Rhin are 68 and 67, respectively, hence the offshoot organization's name. In 2016, Alsace was subsumed into a larger region, the Grand Est.
49. AVA works in the Haut-Rhin as well, but it is based just outside Strasbourg. The Association pour une Recherche Pédagogique Ouverte en Milieu Tzigane, or ARPOMT, as it is more commonly known, was active during my principal fieldwork in 2013–2014 but has since shut down. It was led by Dominique Steinberger, son of APPONA co-founder Rigo Steinberger and brother of Fabrice Steinberger.
50. Stella began this work just before the director Tony Gatlif began shooting in Neuhof for the film *Swing*, a coming-of-age story about a Gadjo boy and a Manouche girl. Stella said that she coordinated between Gatlif and members of the Manouche community so that everyone could participate as they wished, which included hiring them in various capacities and featuring them in small onscreen roles. Mandino collaborated with one of the film's lead actors, Tchavolo Schmitt, on the music, and also had a minor role as an antiques dealer (his real-life occupation in addition to music teaching and performance).
51. See http://lupovino.free.fr/?page_id=954.
52. Eric has also undertaken documentary and artistic work on the Polygone's history, culminating in the publication of two books aimed at raising awareness about the neighborhood: *Polygone en force* (2016) and *Le gosse du Polygone* (2018).
53. A documentary film centering on this ambivalence about the housing construction, *Tsiganes, un voyage infini* (dir. Jean-Marie Fawer), was released in 2014.

54. Director Jean-François Pastor told me that he drew a firm distinction between "world music" and "musiques du monde," designating the former as a primarily commercial practice with a tendency toward cultural appropriation, and the latter as a category that involves performers' "real cultural backgrounds" and "stories." I take this as a problematic distinction.
55. See http://www.espacedjango.eu for a complete account of the Espace Django's programming. In 2016, the City of Strasbourg signed a four-year contract with the organization BeCoze to manage the Espace Django's operations. This resulted in a turnover of Espace Django leadership. See http://www.becoze.fr/2015/12/09/la-ville-de-strasbourg-confie-lespace-culturel-django-reinhardt-a-lassociation-becoze/ for details on this partnership. One source told me that the Espace Django's programming has since shifted to cater more to the needs of the local community, as opposed to attracting audiences from the greater Strasbourg area.
56. Laetitia told me that in the years between APPONA's dissolution and the opening of the Neuhof Music School, there was such a demand for guitar lessons among Neuhof residents that Mandino and Francko gave them for free in whatever spaces they could find, including a defunct bakery.
57. In 2014, there were 16 music teachers employed by the Neuhof Music School with a total of 250 students, of which 42 were enrolled in private jazz manouche guitar lessons. As opposed to the Strasbourg Conservatory, which is geared toward developing music professionals, the various municipally funded music schools throughout Strasbourg are intended to serve the social and cultural needs of local communities.
58. As with other musicians, Francko's travel and performance opportunities were severely compromised by the outbreak of the coronavirus pandemic.
59. Shortly before her death, Pisla published a memoir in collaboration with Sophie Képès (Helmstetter and Képès 2012).
60. See https://www.youtube.com/watch?v=y08TASmwfJY for our performance of "Mer Djina."
61. In the lead-up to Saintes-Maries, two family members of some of the choir's Manouche women passed away. Traditionally, within Manouche communities, various restrictions are placed on activity during and after periods of mourning. For example, Patrick Williams observed in his fieldwork with Manouches in south-central France that community members were prohibited from speaking the names of their deceased relatives (Williams 2003; see also Poueyto 2018). Among the Alsatian Manouche communities I have worked with, these restrictions may include abstention from listening to or performing music. While many in the choir had hoped that this mourning phase would be over in time for Saintes-Maries, it continued on. This was a disappointment to those who believed that the women felt overly pressured to refrain from embarking on a journey that they deeply desired to make. After some debate among the remaining choir members about whether to make the trip without these women, we decided it would

be worth it, especially for Pisla's memorial, and that we could organize a special trip the following year for the absentees.

62. "Le C(h)oeur des Femmes du Neuhof aux Saintes Marie de la Mer—KissKissBankBank," accessed 2 June 2014 and 15 July 2019, https://www.kisskissbankbank.com/de/projects/le-c-h-oeur-des-femmes-du-neuhof-aux-saintes-marie-de-la-mer/tabs/description.
63. For an overview of the events and contexts of the 2005 riots that occurred across France, see Schneider 2008; Silverstein and Tetreault 2006. In 2009–2010, President Sarkozy called for a series of town hall meetings across the country to consider the definition of "French identity" ("Sarkozy justifie le débat sur l'identité nationale"). Winnie Lem writes that these gatherings "were often a venue for the expression of racist and xenophobic comments made by politicians and participants alike" (2013, 454). On the aftermath of the 2015 terrorist attacks at the *Charlie Hebdo* headquarters in Paris, see the articles in the special issue of *French Cultural Studies* (2016, vol. 27, no. 3). The death of George Floyd spurred renewed, highly visible protests in France against police brutality and racism; demonstrations had previously taken place in the name of Adama Traroé, who was killed by police in 2016 (Diallo 2020; Niang 2020).
64. See http://www.fnasat.asso.fr/carteasso.html for a partial listing of France's pro-Romani organizations.

CHAPTER THREE

1. These questions are shaped in part by linguistic anthropological approaches to the ethnography of communication, pioneered by Dell Hymes (1964; see also Kroskrity and Webster 2015) and developed by numerous scholars such as Richard Bauman and Joel Sherzer (1989). Such approaches have been productively used in other ethnographic studies exploring how jazz musicians talk about their practice (e.g., Berliner 1994; Black 2008; Duranti 2009; Duranti and Burrell 2004; Monson 1996; Wilf 2014).
2. On the anthropology of refusal, see also Ortner 1995; Simpson 2014; Weiss 2016.
3. Similarly, Margaret Beissinger argues that in Romania, "Through their discourse on ethnicity, class, culture, and politics, Romani musicians manipulate boundaries between themselves and others in order to associate themselves with the socially powerful, disassociate themselves from the powerless, and enhance their market niche and status" (2001, 26). See also Marković 2015; Silverman 2007, 2012, 2013.
4. Manouche musicians navigate various positions in ways similar to the Serbian Romani musicians Alexander Marković describes, musicians whose "value relies on the juxtaposition of two distinct but inter-related Gypsy stereotype complexes—an authenticity complex that characterises Roma as primitive, mystical and exotic, and a hybridity complex that constructs

their music and culture as inherently mixed, channelling and re-working elements combined from widely disparate sources" (2015, 263–64). Marković argues that "For non-Roma, the Gypsy authenticity and hybridity tropes are mutually reinforcing," and that "while non-Romani audiences and producers grant themselves access to Gypsy Otherness by conflating these stereotype complexes, Romani musicians counter by strategically playing them against each other" (264). See also Silverman 2012, 2013.

5. On dialogism, see Bakhtin 1981; see also Biehl and Locke 2010 on processes of "becoming" and Bucholtz and Hall 2004 on intersubjectivity in identity formation.
6. Lopes's (2002) study is primarily concerned with the legitimization of jazz in the United States; however, the rise of jazz to a "high art" status was also a transnational phenomenon, and jazz in France today occupies this status (as indexed by, for example, its inclusion in the curricula of top conservatories).
7. See Lewis 2016, xii–xv, for an overview of such critics. The embrace of the "jazz" label by jazz manouche musicians contrasts especially with the label's rejection, by a number of notable musicians, and its associations with "the abuse and exploitation of black musicians" (Roach 1972, 4), as well as the recognition that "the road to jazz's cultural legitimacy . . . has entailed the incorporation of the same institutional bases and markers that many individuals in the jazz world associate with the elitism and bigotry that were responsible for jazz's marginalization by gatekeepers for so long" (Wilf 2014, 64–65).
8. Jazz manouche players often recognize similarities across Django's improvisations and treat them as licks to draw upon in their own improvisations. Instructional materials typically identify these formulas as variations on arpeggiations and chromatic movement, usually providing specific examples of improvisations that employ such patterns. Many other aspects of Django's improvisational style, such as his use of ornamentation, his attention to dynamic contrast, and his relationship to musical time, are also explored and codified in these materials. By learning Django solos both in their entireties and as discrete formulaic units, players develop improvisational vocabularies readily recognizable as jazz manouche. This enables them to perform competently with other jazz manouche players, as it socializes them into the jazz manouche genre collectivity.
9. Michael Horowitz, a US jazz manouche performer and ethnomusicologist, writes in one of his instructional books that the genre's pompe rhythmic technique "is criticized for the very qualities that make it so popular with others: its repetitiveness, naive simplicity, and dependence on the guitar," adding that "such criticisms are usually leveled by jazz musicians and authors whose sense of musical aesthetics is informed by the bebop or post-bop era of jazz" (2007, ix).

10. Gal later reformulated "iconization" as "rhematization" (2005, 35n5); see pp. 133–34 for more on this semiotic process.
11. On connections between class distinction and taste, see Bourdieu 1984.
12. This interview was conducted in English. Biréli is fluent in English, thanks in part to having lived in the United States and having collaborated extensively with US bassist Jaco Pastorius.
13. See http://cie-memoires-vives.org/samudaripen/.
14. *Sinto* is the male singular of *Sinti*, a Romani group with which some Manouches also self-identify (see appendix 1: Glossary).
15. Hauger also told me that for these Manouches, it was "out of the question to listen to rap. It was a forbidden music. . . . I remember well the words they used. They thought it was raw, that it was *ialo* [a Romani word for 'raw' that also means 'crude' or 'uncivilized'], that it was a music without any dignity."
16. Léo and Oscar are pseudonyms.
17. Léo's misunderstanding here may reflect the emergence of a hybrid "New Old Europe Sound," which David Kaminsky defines as "an East European bricolage—Balkan, Romani and klezmer music, and, perhaps most significantly, the generic mixing of all three" (2015, 143). See also Marković 2015.
18. "Marcel Loeffler Invite Lisa Doby & Nishati Gospel Singers."

CHAPTER FOUR

1. "Mire pral" is an original composition by Tchavolo Schmitt and Mandino Reinhardt, first released as part of the film *Swing* (dir. Tony Gatlif, 2002). The title means "my brother" in Manouche Romani. The live version described in this article is available at https://www.youtube.com/watch?v=6TgBwVlmnB4. The musicians are, from left to right, Mandino Reinhardt, Tchavolo Schmitt, Gautier Laurent, and Sony Reinhardt; Tchavolo's solo begins at 1:21.
2. Roberts defines *sono-racialization* as "the organization of sound into taxonomies based on racialized conceptions of bodies," emphasizing that sonoracial categories constitute "discursive signifiers that can be deployed or consumed toward the production or maintenance of racial structures" (2016, 4). See also Stoever 2016. Contra certain leading figures in affect theory, Margaret Wetherell argues that if "the broad aim of affect theory is to deliver the tools required for lively, textured research on embodied social action and for productive insights into the entangled forms of assembling constituting social life moment to moment," then "fine-grain studies of discourse practice might offer ways of doing this at a point where attempts to construct nonrepresentational research seem to run into the sand" (2013, 351).
3. A thorough exploration of intersections between gender and ethnoracial identity is somewhat beyond this scope of this chapter; see works such as

Monson 1995; Tucker 2002; and Rustin-Paschal 2017 for analyses of masculinity in jazz.

4. There is an extensive anthropological and ethnomusicological body of research stemming largely from the work of Franz Boas and Edward Sapir that addresses how human-produced sounds are apperceived in relation to social types, including ethnoracial categories; see Harkness 2014, 11–21, for a review of this literature as it pertains especially to voice. Linguistic anthropologists refer to the process by which social types become stereotypically associated with specific communicative styles as *enregisterment* (see, e.g., Irvine 1990; Agha 2007a, 55; Gal and Irvine 2019). On how "voiceness" is perceived in instrumental sound, see Fales 2019. Grant Olwage has suggested that "instead of the colour of the voice, we might speak about the colour of the ear" (2004, 217).
5. It is worth noting that Peirce himself held racist beliefs (see, e.g., Peirce 1994, secs. 2.550, 2.702, 2.400, and 5.285).
6. This cohort took shape through a graduate seminar convened by Michael Silverstein in 2005; see Chumley and Harkness 2013, 7–8, as well as the special issues of *Anthropological Theory* (vol. 13, no. 1–2) and *Signs and Society* (vol. 5, no. S1). Philosophers have developed various conceptions of *qualia*, but I limit myself here to qualia as defined by semiotic anthropologists. For more detailed explanations of Peirce's trichotomies and sign classes, see Parmentier 1994; Peirce 1955; Perman 2010, 2020; Turino 1999.
7. Peirce refers to "hypostatic abstraction" as "that process whereby we regard a thought as a thing, [and] make an interpretant sign the object of a sign" (1998, 394). See also Parmentier 1994, 28–29.
8. Harkness defines qualic transitivity as a phenomenon in which "the properties or features that apply to one modality . . . also apply to the various other modalities to which the former is indexically linked" (2013, 26).
9. See Silverstein 2003 for the cultural construction of "indexical orders."
10. See, for example, Kristina Wirtz on the semiosis of Blackness in Cuba as "a configuration of signs" whose "co-occurrence . . . produces Blackness (just as 'race' more generally has never been just about phenotypic markers, never just about place of origin)" (2014, 14).
11. On semiotics and embodiment, see, for example, Bucholtz and Hall 2016; Violi 2013. On voice and embodiment specifically, see Connor 2000; Daughtry 2012; Kane 2014.
12. See Weidman on how, similarly, the violin may be considered a "ventriloquizer" of the voice because it possesses "a seemingly natural ability to reproduce the voice" (2009, 61–62).
13. Frankenberg discusses white racialness in terms of structure, vantage point, and "cultural practices" (1993, 1); my modification of "racialness" emphasizes the semiotic and affective dimensions of this schema.
14. One kind of ethnoracialness is "sonic blackness" (Obadike 2005), which, when manifested in the form of Black music, can "produc[e] a palpable

affect of human form so enduring that it is difficult to listen without also experiencing the fleshly sensation of blackness as such" (Radano 2013, 127). Much research on sound and race has focused on sound and Blackness, though I avoid equating understandings of Blackness with all forms of ethnoracialness.

15. For these reasons, and to draw the parallel with Frankenberg's "whiteness," I have chosen the derivational suffix "-ness" as opposed to "-ity" (which is used more often to indicate the hypostatic abstraction of adjectives ending in "-al"; e.g., "aurality").
16. This process renders Manouche ethnoracialness an "indexical icon," which Asif Agha defines as "a sign that reveals properties or qualities (the iconic part) of the one contextually linked to it (the indexical part)" (2007a, 257). Michael Silverstein writes that indexical iconicity involves "rationalizing, systematizing, indeed most importantly *naturalizing* schemata that 'explain' the indexical value of signs in terms of some order(s) of phenomena stipulatively presupposable by—hence, in context, autonomous of—the indexical phenomena to be understood. . . . Ideological construals/constructions of indexicality . . . turn the indexicals into seemingly natural indexical icons" (1992, 316; emphasis in original). With indexical iconicity, "iconic logics of metaphor are linked to indexical logics of causation" (Chumley and Harkness 2013, 7).
17. Another interlocutor once told me that there is a distinctive "Manouche mood" apparent in Django's improvisations. This echoes Michel-Claude Jalard's claim that a recording by Django's brother Joseph evinces "a delicate nuance of typically 'Manouche' melancholy" (1959, 62).
18. For more on the concept of "feeling" in jazz specifically, see Jackson 2012; Monson 1996; Porter 2002.
19. Swing SW 88 (OSW 146); also available on *Django Reinhardt—Intégrale Volume 10: Nuages 1940* (Frémeaux et Associés FA310, 1998, disc 2).
20. On the guitar, harmonics are pitches produced by lightly placing a finger on a string at a particular interval (rather than pressing down on the string); the sound produced typically has an ethereal quality to it. A run is a fast sequence of notes played in order from low to high or high to low. An arpeggiation is a delineation of the individual notes in a chord, played one after another. A mordent is a quick alternation between two adjacent notes. A turn is similar to a mordent but involves alternation between the notes both above and below the given note. See Givan 2010 for a comprehensive overview of Django's most characteristic improvisational techniques.
21. See Jackson (2012, 109–35) for a similar case in which audiences and musicians negatively evaluate performances for their lack of "blues feeling."
22. See Smalls 2020 on the semiotics of Blackness. In France, African Americans are often referred to using the English term "Blacks," and African American music, *la musique black*. One interlocutor told me that she feels

more comfortable saying "Black" instead of "noir" due to the perceived racist connotations of "noir" in French.

23. Lefort further identifies a religious dimension of the "blues spirit" across Manouche and African American populations, arguing that "an example of this attitude is the integration of secular elements into the religious context. How can [one] not think, in listening to a 'swung' or 'waltzed' [jazz manouche] evangelical hymn, and picked up by the audience, of the spirit of gospel songs and Negro spirituals?" (1991, 116).
24. Recall from chapter 1, for example, APPONA leader Marcel Daval's musing that jazz, which grew out of "Negro spirituals, prayer, the shout of black slaves in America," was the medium through which Django would "[unleash] his own shout, around the 1930s, unsettling traditional Tsigane music, renewing the language of their ancestors, recounting in his way the long tragedy of his people across history" ("En Alsace avec Les Tsiganes," 6). Michael Dregni also writes that "from the beginning, Gypsy jazz was also a pariah's music. Just as the blues and jazz gave voice to African Americans, this bastardized string jazz allowed a dispossessed people to speak" (Dregni, Antonietto, and Legrand 2006, 7). Several of my interlocutors have echoed this sentiment to me.
25. See also van de Port 1999 on how Serbian Romani musicians are thought to bring out the "stranger within" when performing for Serbian Gadjé.
26. According to ethnomusicologist and jazz manouche performer Michael Horowitz, author of the instructional book *Gypsy Rhythm*, "What makes *la pompe* unique is that its accent patterns imitate those of a swing drummer. A typical ride cymbal or hi-hat pattern is imitated by inserting a subtle upstroke before beats one and three. Beats two and four are heavily accented to provide a back beat normally played on the snare drum. By using this method of accompaniment, Django was able to create the illusion of a full jazz-rhythm section with just one guitar" (2007, 3). Horowitz also writes that the "flat-four" style, a technique associated with early New Orleans jazz in which all four beats are typically accented evenly, "is rarely used by contemporary Gypsy jazz musicians despite the fact that Django used it for most of his career" (30).
27. See Keane 2003 for more on the "bundling" of qualisigns.
28. The regional differences identified within an ethnoracial category exhibit what Irvine and Gal call "fractal recursivity," which "involves the projection of an opposition, salient at some level of relationship, onto some other level" (2000, 38). These sets of oppositions can "provide actors with the discursive or cultural resources to claim and thus attempt to create shifting 'communities,' identities, selves, and roles, at different levels of contrast, within a cultural field" (38). See also Gal 2012.
29. Perceptions of qualia also entail perceptions of quantia, which Paul Kockelman describes as "change in the intensities . . . of various dimensions: more or less pain, heat, resistance, softness, illumination, noisiness, warmth, and so forth" (2016, 343).

30. Listen, for example, to a recording of "Them There Eyes" featuring Hono Winterstein on rhythm guitar, Brady Winterstein on lead guitar, and Gautier Laurent on bass (*Generation Django*, Dreyfus Jazz FDM 46050 369 432, 2009; also available at https://www.youtube.com/watch?v=tyGS_dH5M0s).
31. For another account of the development of a "Gypsy sound" from the perspective of a Gadjo who has learned within various Manouche/Sinti communities, see Chang n.d. Chang writes on his personal website, "Nowadays, there are books that talk about the Gypsy guitar right hand technique and many Gadje guitarists have adopted this technique. However, I still hear a clear difference. This is worthy of an entire chapter of its own but I will just say that it has to do with the Gypsy culture itself." He adds, "it was an obsession for me to understand the elusive Gypsy sound . . . now that I'm older and very familiar with their culture, I would say that, musically, I don't want to sound like a Gypsy. For one thing, I am obviously not a Gypsy and I have my own unique background."
32. To be clear, these practices are not shared by all Manouche people, but are part of generalizing discourses about Manouche identity. Immoderate consumption of food and alcohol is especially associated more with Manouche men than Manouche women.
33. His comments resemble those of Alaina Lemon's interlocutors in the former USSR, who argued that with regard to Romanies, "'talent,' especially in music or dancing, was said to lie 'in the blood,' passed along through the generations" (2000, 69). An inherited component of musicality might also be understood as talent, as Fabrice does when he says many Manouche musicians have a "gift." Yet, he clarified to me, "it's not *just* a gift. . . . These are people who work on their instruments every day, and not just half an hour per day, but hours and hours and hours, entire nights. . . . So effectively, a Gadjo could do this too, could work as much as [Manouche musicians]. But once again, he is not charged with this entire culture, this entire life history, you see?"
34. Here, Obadike draws on Frederick Douglass's phantasmal simile: "a long-standing prejudice . . . paints a hateful picture according to its own diseased imagination, and distorts the features of the fancied original to suit the portrait. As those who believe in the visibility of ghosts can easily see them, so it is always easy to see repulsive qualities in those we despise and hate" (1881, 567).

CHAPTER FIVE

1. French law requires that all municipalities with over 5,000 inhabitants must provide a designated area for Gens du voyage to station their vehicles temporarily or semipermanently (https://www.senat.fr/lc/lc145/lc1450.html). Larger municipalities, such as Angers, often have entire agencies devoted to managing Gens du voyage affairs. This service d'accueil still

exists in the Angers area, though the scope of its mission and activities has diminished in recent years.

2. The word *rayonnant[e]* literally means "radiating" or "beaming," but it is used metaphorically in branding to suggest a wide-ranging influence.
3. In recent years, a robust literature on chronotopes has developed in linguistic anthropology, among other fields; see, for example, Harkness 2014; Lemon 2009; Lempert and Perrino 2007; Silverstein 2005; Woolard 2013.
4. The Place Django Reinhardt in the Saint-Ouen district just north of Paris, also home to the jazz manouche club La Chope des Puces (which touts itself as the "temple of jazz manouche"), accomplishes this; there is also an Allée Django Reinhardt, inaugurated in 2007, in Paris's 13th arrondissement.
5. On chronotopes and scale, see Blommaert 2015; Carr and Lempert 2016.
6. For a partial listing of jazz manouche festivals worldwide, see http://www.ireneypenburgmusic.com/gypsyjazzfestiva.html.
7. Typically, a festival is organized through an *association* (a type of nonprofit organization) consisting largely of volunteers. A festival may rely primarily on public or private funding, or a combination of both, and may involve collaboration with local, regional, national, and/or international institutions.
8. APPONA organized other events in prestigious locations in and around Strasbourg throughout the 1980s and 1990s as well. Although these events did not usually draw such large contingents of Manouche attendees as the festivals did, they increased Manouche visibility within the city.
9. On the construction of the "Roma migrant" and transnational Romani identity within Europe, see Magazzini and Piemontese 2019; Simhandl 2006.
10. These included the City of Strasbourg, the Departmental Council of the Bas-Rhin, the Regional Council of Alsace, the Regional Directorate of Cultural Affairs of Alsace, and at certain points, the European Union and the European Social Fund.
11. Décret no. 82–394 du 10 mai 1982 (https://bbf.enssib.fr/consulter/bbf-1982-06-0353-002).
12. Maastricht Treaty, Title IX, Article 128, p. 48.
13. "Presidency Conclusions," 7.A.iii (http://www.europarl.europa.eu/enlargement_new/europeancouncil/pdf/cop_en.pdf). This document's endorsement of "respect for and protection of minorities" was understood to apply primarily to applicant countries in Central and Eastern Europe, since "Western EU Member States did not want to be held accountable for the condition of their indigenous Romani communities" (Sigona and Trehan 2009, 9).
14. Promotional materials for this festival refer to both "Russia" and the "Soviet Union." The Soviet Union was officially dissolved in December 1991.
15. Archives de la Ville et de l'Eurométropole de Strasbourg, 168 Z, "Rapport moral 1991," 5.
16. Archives de la Ville, "Rapport moral 1991," 6.

17. Helbig also notes the use of "road" in the names of several Ukrainian Romani NGOs (2009, 178).
18. Archives de la Ville et de l'Eurométropole de Strasbourg, 168 Z, " Festival International Tzigane: Baro Drom," 2.
19. Archives de la Ville et de l'Eurométropole de Strasbourg, 168 Z, "Rapport moral 1994," 3.
20. The 1998 festival had a long sequence of titles—"Festival International Tzigane: Flamme Tzigane: Romni: Havo Drom?" ("International Tzigane Festival: Tzigane Flame: Romani Woman: Which Road?")—to draw attention to Romani women, who were often underrepresented in French pro-Romani activism.
21. Archives de la Ville et de l'Eurométropole de Strasbourg, 168 Z, "Dossier de presse," 3.
22. Archives de la Ville, "Dossier de presse," 3.
23. Archives de la Ville, "Dossier de presse," 4.
24. According to the festival organizers, the festival was relocated because of severe flooding during the summer of 2016 and increased concerns about security. Due to the coronavirus pandemic, in 2020 a series of livestreamed performances was substituted for the in-person festival.
25. The mass I attended in 2012 featured an ensemble of jazz manouche musicians performing hymns and Django-composed tunes along with the choir. I have been told that few members of Django's extended family have participated in this service in recent years, possibly because a number of them converted to the evangelical movement Vie et Lumière (see Garo 2005). Following Manouche funerary traditions of the time, most of Django's belongings were burned, except for a guitar that his wife preserved and eventually donated to the Cité de la Musique in Paris.
26. The history of the Festival Django Reinhardt has been addressed more succinctly in other works on Django's legacy, such as in the documentary *Three Fingered Lightning* (dir. Christian Gascio, 2010) and in books such as Dregni, Antonietto, and Legrand 2006 and Tuzet 2007. The festival's official website has also been an important source for information about the festival's history, though more recent revisions of it have omitted this information.
27. Robinet writes that, generally, among musicians who have moved to Samois, the Gadjé live in buildings whereas the Manouches are "semi-sedentary," keeping their caravans "to be able to go on the road at any moment. Precious liberty!" (2018, 137). Statements like this reinforce racializing assumptions that conflate Manouche identity with specific residential patterns.
28. At the time of my fieldwork, there was a *terrain* used exclusively by Gens du voyage in Samois, though it was unclear to me whether this was designated formally in line with the *loi Besson* of 2000, legislation that mandated towns with populations above 5,000 to provide space and access to utilities for Gens du voyage. Giovanni Picker writes that this law "accommodated and at the same time domesticized, spatially and administratively, the

'travelling way of life.' Due to the deep-rooted racial stigma of vagrancy, the law ultimately contributed to constructing an image of 'travelling people' as threats to the typically fixed socio-spatial order" (2017, 89).

29. Whereas the word *camping* is used to designate a campsite generally used by vacationers who are otherwise settled, a *terrain* is a space for caravans normally designated for Gens du voyage.
30. At one of the campsites, Samoreau, certain groups of people tended to occupy the same spaces during the years I was there (2012–2014): Titi Bamberger, a charming German Sinto who has earned the title of "Godfather" of Samoreau, parks his Christmas-lighted caravan just behind the campsite's bar on the southwest corner of the grounds. Other Sinti and Manouche families park their caravans and cars in the same quadrant. A group of younger French and Dutch Gadjo players set up tents around an awning by the river, and those without reservations or connections to regulars squat on the fringes of the property, hoping to elude the watch of the campsite's groundskeeper.
31. The word *camp* is often considered to be derogatory because it recalls Nazi *camps de concentration*.
32. One social worker told me that the mayor at the time attributed this denial of services to the fact that the settlement is located in a flood zone, but this did not prevent him from approving other construction projects in the same zone.
33. The timing of the first edition of the festival conflicted with some of the mourning rituals the community was obligated to observe. As described in chapter 2, note 61, within some Manouche communities, those close to a recently deceased person are often prohibited from playing or listening to music, among other diversions, for a period of time. For this reason, Mito's widow, Colette, could not attend the first festival, while others were put in still more uncomfortable positions.
34. Early in my fieldwork, this volunteer, Gérard Gerber, generously set up several visits with important figures in Alsace's jazz manouche economy and provided valuable insight into dynamics between nonprofits and jazz manouche artists.
35. Prior to my arrival, Pierre touted my presence as a researcher from New York, and an article about me appeared in a local newspaper. My status was understood to help garner further publicity for the festival. I also joined Mito's sons and brother as well as a luthier, Philippe Moneret, to give a presentation on Django and jazz manouche to local schoolchildren the day before the festival began.
36. The name of the festival is indicated somewhat inconsistently on its website and in the press; I have seen it called the "Festival de Jazz Manouche de Zillisheim" and the "Festival de Jazz Manouche à Zillisheim," often with irregular capitalization of common nouns.
37. A sizable team of Gadjo volunteers, a small handful of whom already knew members of the Manouche community, sold and collected tickets, ran the

concession stands, prepared food, directed parking, tended to musicians, and did most of the setup and breakdown. Among the paid workers were several sound technicians for the concerts, a local Manouche woman who cleaned the bathrooms, and musicians.

38. For its first two editions in 2012 and 2013, the festival had been organized under the auspices of a Manouche outreach organization, "Association Education et Vie." For the 2014 edition of the festival, Pierre decided it would be more efficient to establish an official nonprofit organization ("Jazz à Zillis") dedicated solely to the festival. In 2013, the sponsoring partners were the local Rotary and Lions clubs, the Town of Zillisheim, the bank Crédit Mutuel, and the radio stations France Bleu Alsace and FIP; in 2014, partnerships grew to include the City of Mulhouse, the General Council of the Haut-Rhin, the Region of Alsace, Rossini France (Pierre's packaging company), and several other businesses.
39. In 2019 this was rephrased to "one of the rare French festivals to offer a 100% Manouche program." Over the years, a number of attendees have expressed to me that they prefer this festival because it programs more "pure" Manouche music than others.
40. This role provided me extra time with organizers, volunteers, and nonmusician workers. As with some of the organizational meetings I attended in 2013–2014, it was not unusual for participants to express some casually racist views in the absence of Manouches. For example, on a particularly sunny day, one of the sound engineers, a young woman from Mexico, reported to me that one of the (French) volunteers told her, "Be careful with the sun! If you don't, you'll get a tan and we'll confuse you with a Manouche!"—a statement that put the woman ill at ease for its racist overtones toward both Manouches and Mexicans.
41. Perhaps in response to these concerns, Mito's immediate family members were added back to the program in 2019 as part of the final day's large closing act, which included other musicians who had already performed during the festival.
42. The Internet Archive's Wayback Machine shows that while this photo was displayed on the landing page in every capture between April 2013 and December 2018, it was removed sometime between December 2018 and May 2019.
43. The service is led by the departmental "aumônier des Gens du voyage," a Gadjo chaplain who serves Gens du voyage as well as Manouches (since the Zillisheim community is settled).

CONCLUSION

1. Thomas Dutronc, son of the famed Jacques Dutronc and Françoise Hardy, is quite well known in his own right as a musician who produces pop music with jazz manouche inflections. His 2007 debut album, *Comme un manouche sans guitare*, was certified gold one month after its debut, and

its title track received the award for Original Song of the Year at the 2009 Victoires de la musique (the French equivalent of the Grammys).

2. In 2020, a Manouche community with which Gigi has close ties suffered increased municipal neglect following the outbreak of the coronavirus pandemic. As a result, he stepped in to help with food distribution and other volunteer work. Later that year, he partnered with local teachers to establish a nonprofit organization to continue these and other Manouche-centered outreach efforts. It has yet to be seen whether this organization, whose focus is more on the material and educational needs of a Manouche community than on its music, will have outcomes different from Gigi's prior endeavors.

References

"À la recherche de ses racines et de sa dignité: La jeune génération manouche au Festival de musique de Hongrie." 1985. *Dernières nouvelles d'Alsace*, August 17.

About, Ilsen. 2012. "Underclass Gypsies: An Historical Approach on Categorisation and Exclusion in France in the Nineteenth and the Twentieth Centuries." In *The Gypsy "Menace": Populism and the New Anti-Gypsy Politics*, edited by Michael Stewart, 95–114. London: Hurst.

Abrams, Max. 1978. "Django Reinhardt: The Jazz Gypsy." *Storyville*, no. 77 (July): 163–70.

Abu-Lughod, Lila. 1991. "Writing Against Culture." In *Recapturing Anthropology: Working in the Present*, edited by Richard G. Fox. Santa Fe, NM: School of American Research Press.

Acton, Thomas A., and Gary Mundy, eds. 1997. *Romani Culture and Gypsy Identity*. Hatfield, Hertfordshire: University of Hertfordshire Press.

Agha, Asif. 2007a. *Language and Social Relations*. Cambridge: Cambridge University Press.

———. 2007b. "Recombinant Selves in Mass Mediated Spacetime." *Language & Communication* 27 (3): 320–35.

Alim, H. Samy. 2016. "Introducing Raciolinguistics: Racing Language and Languaging Race in Hyperracial Times." In *Raciolinguistics: How Language Shapes Our Ideas about Race*, edited by H. Samy Alim, John R. Rickford, and Arnetha F. Ball, 1–32. New York: Oxford University Press.

Alim, H. Samy, Angela Reyes, and Paul V. Kroskrity, eds. 2020. *The Oxford Handbook of Language and Race*. New York: Oxford University Press.

Alim, H. Samy, John R. Rickford, and Arnetha F. Ball, eds. 2016. *Raciolinguistics: How Language Shapes Our Ideas about Race*. New York: Oxford University Press.

Andresz, Patrick. 2015. "La musique des Manouches sinti alsaciens: Le tournant des années 1970–1980." *Études tsiganes* 54–55 (2): 132–43.

Antonietto, Alain. 1984. "Django: De la virtuosité tsigane . . . innée ou acquise?" *Études tsiganes*, no. 4: 77–83.

Antonietto, Alain, and François Billard. 2004. *Django Reinhardt: Rythmes futurs*. Paris: Fayard.

Antonietto, Alain, and Patrick Williams. 1985. "50 ans de jazz gitan." *Jazz Hot*, no. 426: 22–34.

APPONA. 1979. "Essai pour la revalorisation d'une culture minoritaire." *Saisons d'Alsace* 67: 139–47.

Asséo, Henriette. 1994. *Les Tsiganes: Une destinée européenne*. Paris: Gallimard.

———. 2005. "L'avènement politique des Roms (Tsiganes) et le génocide: La construction mémorielle en Allemagne et en France." *Le temps des médias*, no. 2: 78–91.

Atkins, E. Taylor. 2001. *Blue Nippon: Authenticating Jazz in Japan*. Durham, NC: Duke University Press.

Atkins, E. Taylor, ed. 2003. *Jazz Planet*. Jackson: University Press of Mississippi.

Awosusi, Anita. 1996. *Die Musik der Sinti und Roma*. 1. Aufl. Vol. 2: Der Sinti Jazz. 5–7. Heidelberg: Dokumentations- und Kulturzentrum Deutscher Sinti und Roma.

Bakhtin, Mikhail Mikhaĭlovich. 1981. *The Dialogic Imagination: Four Essays*. Austin: University of Texas Press.

Balibar, Etienne. 1991. "Is There a 'Neo-Racism'?" In *Race, Nation, Class: Ambiguous Identities*, by Etienne Balibar and Immanuel Wallerstein, translated by Chris Turner, 17–28. New York: Verso.

Barou, Jacques. 2014. "Integration of Immigrants in France: A Historical Perspective." *Identities* 21 (6): 642–57.

Bauman, Richard, and Joel Sherzer, eds. 1989. *Explorations in the Ethnography of Speaking*. 2nd ed. New York: Cambridge University Press.

Bauman, Zygmunt. 1991. *Modernity and Ambivalence*. Oxford: Polity Press.

Beaman, Jean. 2017. *Citizen Outsider: Children of North African Immigrants in France*. Oakland: University of California Press.

———. 2019. "Are French People White? Towards an Understanding of Whiteness in Republican France." *Identities* 26 (5): 546–62.

Beaman, Jean, and Amy Petts. 2020. "Towards a Global Theory of Colorblindness: Comparing Colorblind Racial Ideology in France and the United States." *Sociology Compass* 14 (4): e12774.

Bechtold, Jean-Pierre. n.d. "Historique: Un fondateur raconte." *Festival Django Reinhardt* (blog), https://web.archive.org/web/20161029014901/http://www.festivaldjangoreinhardt.com/spip.php?rubrique26.

Becker, Howard Saul. 1982. *Art Worlds*. Berkeley: University of California Press.

Beissinger, Margaret H. 2001. "Occupation and Ethnicity: Constructing Identity among Professional Romani (Gypsy) Musicians in Romania." *Slavic Review* 60 (1): 24–49.

Beliso-De Jesús, Aisha M., and Jemima Pierre. 2020. "Special Section: Anthropology of White Supremacy." *American Anthropologist* 122 (1): 65–75.

Bennett, Andy, and Richard A. Peterson. 2004. *Music Scenes: Local, Translocal and Virtual*. Nashville: Vanderbilt University Press.

Berish, Andrew S. 2009. "Negotiating 'A Blues Riff': Listening for Django Reinhardt's Place in American Jazz." *Jazz Perspectives* 3 (3): 233–64.

———. 2012. *Lonesome Roads and Streets of Dreams: Place, Mobility, and Race in Jazz of the 1930s and '40s*. Chicago: University of Chicago Press.

Beriss, David. 2004. *Black Skins, French Voices: Caribbean Ethnicity and Activism in Urban France*. New York: Westview Press.

Berliner, Brett A. 2002. *Ambivalent Desire: The Exotic Black Other in Jazz-Age France*. Amherst: University of Massachusetts Press.

Berliner, Paul F. 1994. *Thinking in Jazz: The Infinite Art of Improvisation*. Chicago: University of Chicago Press.

Bertaux, Sandrine. 2016. "Towards the Unmaking of the French Mainstream: The Empirical Turn in Immigrant Assimilation and the Making of Frenchness." *Journal of Ethnic and Migration Studies* 42 (9): 1496–1512.

Biehl, João, and Peter Locke. 2010. "Deleuze and the Anthropology of Becoming." *Current Anthropology* 51 (3): 317–37.

Billard, François. 2011. "Manouche (jazz)." In *Le nouveau dictionnaire du jazz*, edited by Philippe Carles, André Clergeat, and Jean-Louis Comolli, 819–20. Paris: Robert Laffont.

Black, Steven P. 2008. "Creativity and Learning Jazz: The Practice of 'Listening.'" *Mind, Culture, and Activity* 15 (4): 279–95.

Blake, Felice, Paula Ioanide, and Alison Reed, eds. 2019. *Antiracism Inc.: Why the Way We Talk about Racial Justice Matters*. Earth, Milky Way: punctum books.

Bleich, Erik. 2000. "Antiracism without Races: Politics and Policy in a 'Color-Blind' State." *French Politics, Culture & Society* 18 (3): 48–74.

———. 2003. *Race Politics in Britain and France: Ideas and Policymaking since the 1960s*. Cambridge: Cambridge University Press.

Blesh, Rudi. 1946. *Shining Trumpets: A History of Jazz*. 2nd ed. New York: Alfred A. Knopf.

Blommaert, Jan. 2015. "Chronotopes, Scales, and Complexity in the Study of Language in Society." *Annual Review of Anthropology* 44: 105–16.

Bohlman, Philip V., and Goffredo Plastino, eds. 2016. *Jazz Worlds, World Jazz*. Chicago: University of Chicago Press.

Bonilla-Silva, Eduardo. [2006] 2014. *Racism without Racists: Color-Blind Racism and the Persistence of Racial Inequality in America*. 4th ed. Lanham, MD: Rowman & Littlefield.

Bonilla-Silva, Eduardo, and Sarah Mayorga. 2011. "On (Not) Belonging: Why Citizenship Does Not Remedy Racial Inequality." In *State of White Supremacy: Racism, Governance, and the United States*, edited by Moon-Kie Jung, João H. Costa Vargas, and Eduardo Bonilla-Silva, 77–92. Stanford, CA: Stanford University Press.

Bonneau, Pierre. 1945. "Notes biographiques sur Django Reinhardt." *Jazz Hot* 2 (November): 13–16.

Bourdieu, Pierre. 1984. *Distinction: A Social Critique of the Judgement of Taste*. Translated by Richard Nice. Cambridge, MA: Harvard University Press.

Brackett, David. 2016. *Categorizing Sound: Genre and Twentieth-Century Popular Music*. Oakland: University of California Press.

Braggs, Rashida K. 2016. *Jazz Diasporas: Race, Music, and Migration in Post–World War II Paris*. Oakland: University of California Press.

Brassart-Goerg, Marie. 1987. "Tsiganes en Alsace: Deux formations musicales invitées en Hongrie." *Dernières nouvelles d'Alsace*, September 3.

Briggs, Charles L., and Richard Bauman. 1992. "Genre, Intertextuality, and Social Power." *Journal of Linguistic Anthropology* 2 (2): 131–72.

Brooks, Ethel, and Jane Collins. 2017. "Scenography Matters: Performing Romani Identities as Strategy and Critique." In *Scenography Expanded: An Introduction to Contemporary Performance Design*, edited by Scott Palmer, Joslin McKinney, and Stephen A. Di Benedetto, 95–111. London: Bloomsbury.

Brubaker, Rogers. 2004. *Ethnicity Without Groups*. Cambridge, MA: Harvard University Press.

———. 2009. "Ethnicity, Race, and Nationalism." *Annual Review of Sociology* 35: 21–42.

Bucholtz, Mary. 2010. *White Kids: Language, Race, and Styles of Youth Identity*. New York: Cambridge University Press.

Bucholtz, Mary, and Kira Hall. 2004. "Language and Identity." In *A Companion to Linguistic Anthropology*, edited by Alessandro Duranti, 369–94. Malden, MA: Blackwell Publishing.

———. 2016. "Embodied Sociolinguistics." In *Sociolinguistics: Theoretical Debates*, edited by Nikolas Coupland, 173–98. Cambridge: Cambridge University Press.

Burdick, Christa. 2016. "Branding the Alsatian Oxymoron: The Production of Ambivalent Identity." *Signs and Society* 4 (S1): S163–87.

Burke, Patrick. 2008. *Come in and Hear the Truth: Jazz and Race on 52nd Street*. Chicago: University of Chicago Press.

"Cannes: Le festival de jazz." 1948. *Terre et ciel: Revue du personnel d'Air France*, no. 5: 9.

Canut, Cécile. 2019. "Tell Me That I Am Not a Ciganin, Damn Your Mother! The Social and Political Consequences of Enregisterment in Bulgaria." *Signs and Society* 7 (3): 398–426.

Carr, E. Summerson, and Michael Lempert. 2016. *Scale: Discourse and Dimensions of Social Life*. Oakland: University of California Press.

Cascio, Christian. 2010. *Trois doigts de génie*. Berlin: EuroArts Music International; Paris: Idéale Audience. DVD.

Cavanaugh, Jillian R., and Shalini Shankar, eds. 2017. *Language and Materiality: Ethnographic and Theoretical Explorations*. New York: Cambridge University Press.

Chang, Denis. n.d. "ABOUT." *Denis Chang* (blog), http://denischang.com/index.php/bio-2/.

Chang, Felix B., and Sunnie T. Rucker-Chang. 2020. *Roma Rights and Civil Rights: A Transatlantic Comparison*. New York: Cambridge University Press.

Chapman, Herrick, and Laura L. Frader. 2004. *Race in France: Interdisciplinary Perspectives on the Politics of Difference*. New York: Berghahn Books.

Charle, François. 1999. *L'histoire des guitares Selmer Maccaferri*. Paris: François Charle Publishing.

Chumley, Lily Hope, and Nicholas Harkness. 2013. "Introduction: Qualia." *Anthropological Theory* 13 (1–2): 3–11.

Chun, Elaine W. 2016. "The Meaning of Ching-Chong: Language, Racism, and Response in New Media." In *Raciolinguistics: How Language Shapes Our Ideas about Race*, edited by H. Samy Alim, John R. Rickford, and Arnetha F. Ball, 81–96. New York: Oxford University Press.

Chun, Elaine W., and Adrienne Lo. 2016. "Language and Racialization." Edited by Nancy Bonvillain. *The Routledge Handbook of Linguistic Anthropology*, 220–33. New York: Routledge.

Cocteau, Jean. 1937. "Django, fils de l'air." Program notes presented at a concert by the Quintette du Hot Club de France, Salle Giveau, Paris, October 20.

Cœuroy, André. 1942. *Histoire générale du jazz: Strette, hot, swing*. Paris: Editions Denoël.

Comaroff, John L., and Jean Comaroff. 2009. *Ethnicity, Inc.* Chicago: University of Chicago Press.

"Concert pour une symphonie tzigane." 1978. *Dernières nouvelles d'Alsace*, May 23.

Connor, Steven. 2000. "What I Say Goes." In *Dumbstruck: A Cultural History of Ventriloquism*, 3–43. New York: Oxford University Press.

Cossée, Claire. 2016. "Le statut 'Gens du voyage' comme institution de l'antitsiganisme en France." *Migrations Société* 153 (1): 75–90.

Courthiade, Marcel. 2013. "Le rromani et les autres langues en usage parmi les Rroms, Manouches et Gitans." In *Histoire sociale des langues de France*, edited by Georg Kremnitz, 567–80. Rennes: Presses Universitaires de Rennes.

Couvreux, Francis. 1992. "6e Festival Django Reinhardt Rijswijk (Hollande)." *Études tsiganes* 2: 53–55.

Cruickshank, Ian, ed. 1994. *Django's Gypsies: The Mystique of Django Reinhardt and His People*. Newcastle-upon-Tyne: Ashley Mark Publishing Company.

Cruz, Jon. 1999. *Culture on the Margins: The Black Spiritual and the Rise of American Cultural Interpretation*. Princeton, NJ: Princeton University Press.

Cugny, Laurent. 2013. "Django Reinhardt et 'Flèche d'or': Pourquoi ne l'a-t-on pas entendu?" In *La catastrophe apprivoisée: Regards sur le jazz en France*, edited by Vincent Cotro, Laurent Cugny, and Philippe Gumplowicz, 169–74. Paris: Outre Mesure.

Cullaz, Maurice. 1967. "Le jazz manouche et gitan au Cirque d'hiver." *Études tsiganes*, no. 1–2: 35–36.

Daughtry, J. Martin. 2012. "Afterword: From Voice to Violence and Back Again." In *Music, Politics, and Violence*, edited by Susan Fast and Kip Pegley, 243–63. Middletown, CT: Wesleyan University Press.

Daval, Marcel. 1974. "Un voyage en roulotte." *Monde Gitan*, no. 32: 13–14.

———. 1982. "En Alsace avec les Tsiganes." *Uss'm Follik*, no. 152: 6.

Daval, Marcel, and Pierre Hauger. 1989. "La singularité et le rôle de la musique dans l'affirmation de l'identité des Manouches d'Alsace." In *Tsiganes: Identité, évolution*, edited by Patrick Williams, 477–87. Paris: Études Tsiganes/Syros Alternatives.

de Fatto, Père Guy. 1977. "Florilège pour un anniversaire." *Monde Gitan*, no. 42: 4–5.

"Définitions: feeling." n.d. In *Dictionnaire de français Larousse*. https://www.larousse.fr/dictionnaires/francais/feeling/33160.

Delaunay, Charles. 1948. "L'histoire du Hot Club de France." *Jazz Hot* 2 (14): 12.

———. 1953. "Django Reinhardt." *Jazz Hot* 2 (19): 9–11.

———. 1954. *Django Reinhardt: Souvenirs*. Paris: Éditions Jazz-Hot.

———. 1968. *Django mon frère*. Paris: Le Terrain Vague.

Diallo, Rokhaya. 2020. "France Refuses to Talk about Race. New Protests Could Change That." *Washington Post*, June 18. https://www.washingtonpost.com/opinions/2020/06/18/france-refuses-talk-about-race-new-protests-could-change-that/.

Dick, Hilary Parsons, and Kristina Wirtz. 2011. "Racializing Discourses." *Journal of Linguistic Anthropology* 21 (S1): E2–E10.

Douglass, Frederick. 1881. "The Color Line." *North American Review* 132 (295): 567–77.

Dregni, Michael. 2004. *Django: The Life and Music of a Gypsy Legend*. New York: Oxford University Press.

———. 2008. *Gypsy Jazz: In Search of Django Reinhardt and the Soul of Gypsy Swing*. New York: Oxford University Press.

———. 2018. "Django Reinhardt and Jazz Manouche." In *The History of European Jazz: The Music, Musicians and Audience In Context*, 653–66. Sheffield, South Yorkshire, UK: Equinox Publishing.

Dregni, Michael, Alain Antonietto, and Anne Legrand. 2006. *Django Reinhardt and the Illustrated History of Gypsy Jazz*. Denver: Speck Press.

"Droit de vote des Gens du voyage." 2012. Sénat: Un site de service aux citoyens, September 20. https://www.senat.fr/questions/base/2012/qSEQ120901943.html.

Dubois, Laurent. 2000. "La République Métissée: Citizenship, Colonialism, and the Borders of French History." *Cultural Studies* 14 (1): 15–34.

Duranti, Alessandro. 2009. "L'oralité avec impertinence. Ambivalence par rapport à l'écrit chez les orateurs samoans et les musiciens de jazz américains." *L'Homme—Revue française d'anthropologie*, no. 189: 23–47.

Duranti, Alessandro, and Kenny Burrell. 2004. "Jazz Improvisation: A Search for Hidden Harmonies and a Unique Self." *Ricerche di psicologia* 27 (3): 71–102.

Eidsheim, Nina Sun. 2011. "Marian Anderson and 'Sonic Blackness' in American Opera." *American Quarterly* 63 (3): 641–71.

———. 2012. "Voice as Action: Toward a Model for Analyzing the Dynamic Construction of Racialized Voice." *Current Musicology* 93 (1): 9–33.

———. 2019. *The Race of Sound: Listening, Timbre, and Vocality in African American Music*. Durham, NC: Duke University Press.

"Engé." n.d. http://www.enge-music.com.

Epstein, Beth S. 2011. *Collective Terms: Race, Culture, and Community in a State-Planned City in France*. New York: Berghahn Books.

Escafré-Dublet, Angéline. 2019. "The Whiteness of Cultural Boundaries in France." *Identities* 26 (5): 563–78.

Evans, Peter B., and William H. Sewell Jr. 2013. "Neoliberalism: Policy Regimes, International Regimes, and Social Effects." In *Social Resilience in the Neoliberal Era*, edited by Peter A. Hall and Michèle Lamont, 35–68. Cambridge: Cambridge University Press.

Ewing, Eve L. 2020. "I'm a Black Scholar Who Studies Race. Here's Why I Capitalize 'White.'" *Medium*, July 2. https://zora.medium.com/im-a-black-scholar-who-studies-race-here-s-why-i-capitalize-white-f94883aa2dd3.

Fales, Cornelia. 2002. "The Paradox of Timbre." *Ethnomusicology* 46 (1): 56–95.

———. 2019. "Voiceness in Musical Instruments." In *The Oxford Handbook of Voice Studies*, edited by Nina Sun Eidsheim and Katherine Meizel, 237–68. New York: Oxford University Press.

Fanon, Frantz. 1952. *Peau noire, masques blancs*. Paris: Éditions du Seuil.

Fargeton, Pierre. 2005. *La modernité chez Django: L'influence du be-bop sur le langage de Django Reinhardt, entre 1947 et 1953*. Aubais: Mémoires d'Oc Éditions et Recherches.

Fassin, Didier. 2009. "Nommer, interpréter. Le sens commun de la question raciale." In *De la question sociale à la question raciale: Représenter la société française*, edited by Didier Fassin and Éric Fassin, 27–44. Paris: Éditions La Découverte.

Faudree, Paja. 2012. "Music, Language, and Texts: Sound and Semiotic Ethnography." *Annual Review of Anthropology* 41: 519–36.

Favell, Adrian. 1997. "Citizenship and Immigration: Pathologies of a Progressive Philosophy." *Journal of Ethnic and Migration Studies* 23 (2): 173–95.

Faye, Olivier. 2012. "François Hollande veut supprimer le mot 'race' de la Constitution." *La Croix*, March 11. https://www.la-croix.com/Actualite/France/Francois-Hollande-veut-supprimer-le-mot-race-de-la-Constitution-_EP_-2012-03-11-777139.

Feagin, Joe R. 2010. *The White Racial Frame: Centuries of Racial Framing and Counter-Framing*. New York: Routledge.

Feld, Steven. 2012. *Jazz Cosmopolitanism in Accra: Five Musical Years in Ghana*. Durham, NC: Duke University Press.

Feldblum, Miriam. 1999. *Reconstructing Citizenship: The Politics of Nationality Reform and Immigration in Contemporary France*. Albany: State University of New York Press.

Fellezs, Kevin. 2011. *Birds of Fire: Jazz, Rock, Funk, and the Creation of Fusion*. Durham, NC: Duke University Press.

Fernando, Mayanthi L. 2014. *The Republic Unsettled: Muslim French and the Contradictions of Secularism*. Durham, NC: Duke University Press.

Fields, Karen E., and Barbara Jeanne Fields. 2012. *Racecraft: The Soul of Inequality in American Life*. New York: Verso.

Filhol, Emmanuel. 2007. "L'indifférence collective au sort des tsiganes internés dans les camps français, 1940–1946." *Guerres mondiales et conflits contemporains*, no. 226: 69–82.

———. 2013. *Le contrôle des Tsiganes en France (1912–1969)*. Paris: Éditions Karthala.

Fleming, Crystal Marie. 2017. *Resurrecting Slavery: Racial Legacies and White Supremacy in France*. Philadelphia: Temple University Press.

Flores, Nelson, and Jonathan Rosa. 2015. "Undoing Appropriateness: Raciolinguistic Ideologies and Language Diversity in Education." *Harvard Educational Review* 85 (2): 149–71.

FNASAT–Gens du Voyage. 2010. "Le statut des 'Gens du voyage' et ses conséquences discriminatoires légales." FNASAT. http://www.fnasat.asso.fr/biblio%20virtuelle/Statut%20GV.pdf.

Foucault, Michel. 1977. *Discipline and Punish: The Birth of the Prison*. Translated by Alan Sheridan. New York: Vintage Books.

Fox, Aaron A. 2004. *Real Country: Music and Language in Working-Class Culture*. Durham, NC: Duke University Press.

Frankenberg, Ruth. 1993. *White Women, Race Matters: The Social Construction of Whiteness*. Minneapolis: University of Minnesota Press.

Fry, Andy. 2014. *Paris Blues: African American Music and French Popular Culture, 1920–1960*. Chicago: University of Chicago Press.

Gal, Susan. 2005. "Language Ideologies Compared: Metaphors of Public/Private." *Journal of Linguistic Anthropology* 15 (1): 23–37.

———. 2012. "Sociolinguistic Regimes and the Management of 'Diversity.'" In *Language in Late Capitalism: Pride and Profit*, edited by Alexandre Duchêne and Monica Heller, 22–42. New York: Routledge.

———. 2013. "Tastes of Talk: Qualia and the Moral Flavor of Signs." *Anthropological Theory* 13 (1–2): 31–48.

Gal, Susan, and Judith T. Irvine. 2019. *Signs of Difference: Language and Ideology in Social Life*. Cambridge: Cambridge University Press.

Gallope, Michael. 2017. *Deep Refrains: Music, Philosophy, and the Ineffable*. Chicago: University of Chicago Press.

Garo, Morgan. 2005. "Les Rroms et les organisations évangéliques: Entre culte religieux et stratégie 'politique'?" *Hérodote*, no. 4: 81–94.

Gaspard, Françoise. 1992. "Assimilation, insertion, intégration: Les mots pour 'devenir français." *Hommes & Migrations*, no. 1154: 14–23.

Gaspard, Jacques J. 1963. "Un blues gitan." *Jazz Hot*, no. 187 (May): 22–28.

Gatlif, Tony. 2002. *Swing*. Princes Films.

Gebhardt, Nicholas. 2012. "When Jazz Was Foreign: Rethinking Jazz History." *Jazzforschung/Jazz Research* 44: 185–97.

Gelbart, Petra. 2010. "Learning Music, Race and Nation in the Czech Republic." Ph.D. dissertation, Harvard University.

Giacobbi, François, and Marcel Descamps. 1950. "Ce gitan infirme est un des rois du Jazz." *Paris-Match*, no. 90.

Gilroy, Paul. 1993. *The Black Atlantic: Modernity and Double Consciousness*. Cambridge, MA: Harvard University Press.

Gingrich, Andre. 2005. "Ruptures, Schools, and Nontraditions: Reassessing the History of Sociocultural Anthropology in Germany." In *One Discipline, Four Ways: British, German, French, and American Anthropology*, edited by Fredrik Barth, Andre Gingrich, Robert Parkin, and Sydel Silverman, 59–153. Chicago: University of Chicago Press.

Ginsburg, Faye. 2004. "Foreword." In *Local Actions: Cultural Activism, Power, and Public Life in America*, edited by Melissa Checker and Maggie Fishman, ix–xvii. New York: Columbia University Press.

Givan, Benjamin. 2010. *The Music of Django Reinhardt*. Ann Arbor: University of Michigan Press.

———. 2014. "'Django's Tiger': From Jazz to Jazz Manouche." *Current Musicology* 98: 7–40.

Goffin, Robert. 1932. *Aux frontières du jazz*. Paris: Editions du Sagittaire.

Goldberg, David Theo. 1993. *Racist Culture*. Cambridge, MA: Blackwell Publishers.

———. 2002. *The Racial State*. Oxford: Blackwell.

———. 2009. *The Threat of Race: Reflections on Racial Neoliberalism*. Malden, MA: Blackwell Publishing.

"Grands événements—Association Lupovino." n.d. http://lupovino.free.fr/?page_id=353.

Grappelli, Stéphane. 1992. *Mon violon pour tout bagage: Mémoires*. Paris: Calmann-Lévy.

Grill, Jan. 2018. "'In England, They Don't Call You Black!': Migrating Racialisations and the Production of Roma Difference across Europe." *Journal of Ethnic and Migration Studies* 44 (7): 1136–55.

Guillaumin, Colette. 1972. *L'idéologie raciste: Genèse et langage actuel*. Paris: Mouton & Co.

Gupta, Akhil, and James Ferguson. 1992. "Beyond 'Culture': Space, Identity, and the Politics of Difference." *Cultural Anthropology* 7 (1): 6–23.

Hajdu, David. 2010. "Triumph of the Gypsies." *The New Republic*, May 20. https://newrepublic.com/article/74546/triumph-the-gypsies.

Hall, Stuart. 1995. "Fantasy, Identity, Politics." In *Cultural Remix: Theories and Politics of the Popular*, edited by Erica Carter, James Donald, and Judith Squires, 63–69. London: Lawrence & Wishart.

———. 2003. "'In but Not of Europe': Europe and Its Myths." *Soundings* 22: 57–69.

Hancock, Ian F. 2002. *We Are the Romani People*. Hatfield, UK: University of Hertfordshire Press.

Hargreaves, Alec G. 2007. *Multi-Ethnic France: Immigration, Politics, Culture and Society*. New York: Routledge.

Harkness, Nicholas. 2013. "Softer Soju in South Korea." *Anthropological Theory* 13 (1–2): 12–30.

———. 2014. *Songs of Seoul: An Ethnography of Voice and Voicing in Christian South Korea*. Berkeley: University of California Press.

———. 2015. "The Pragmatics of Qualia in Practice." *Annual Review of Anthropology* 44: 573–89.

———. 2021. "Qualia." In *The International Encyclopedia of Linguistic Anthropology*, edited by James Stanlaw, 1–5. New York: John Wiley & Sons. https://doi.org/10.1002/9781118786093.iela0330.

Hauger, Pierre, and Marcel Daval. 1983. "La révalorisation culturelle des jeunes Sinte: Un objectif d'association." *Monde Gitan* 65: 4–8.

Helbig, Adriana. 2005. "'Play for Me, Old Gypsy': Music as Political Resource in the Roma Rights Movement in Ukraine." Ph.D. dissertation, Columbia University.

———. 2009. "Representation and Intracultural Dynamics: Romani Musicians and Cultural Rights Discourse in Ukraine." In *Music and Cultural Rights*, edited by Andrew N. Weintraub and Bell Yung, 169–86. Urbana: University of Illinois Press.

Helmstetter, Engé. 2000. "L'école de musique de l'APPONA." *Feuilles de route*.

Helmstetter, Louise, and Sophie Képès. 2012. *Sur ces chemins où nos pas se sont effacés: Souvenirs d'une Tzigane d'Alsace*. Strasbourg: Éditions La Nuée Bleue.

Heng, Geraldine. 2018. *The Invention of Race in the European Middle Ages*. Cambridge: Cambridge University Press.

Herzfeld, Michael. [1997] 2016. *Cultural Intimacy: Social Poetics and the Real Life of States, Societies, and Institutions*. 3rd ed. New York: Routledge.

Hesse, Barnor. 2016. "Counter-Racial Formation Theory." In *Conceptual Aphasia in Black: Displacing Racial Formation*, edited by P. Khalil Saucier and Tryon P. Woods, vii–x. Lanham, MD: Lexington Books.

Hill, Jane H. 2008. *The Everyday Language of White Racism*. Malden, MA: Wiley-Blackwell.

Hodeir, André. 1962. *Toward Jazz*. Translated by Noel Burch. New York: Grove Press.

Hoefer, George. 1966. "The Magnificent Gypsy." *Down Beat* 33 (14): 21–25, 60–61.

Holt, Fabian. 2007. *Genre in Popular Music*. Chicago: University of Chicago Press.

Hooker, Lynn. 2007. "Controlling the Liminal Power of Performance: Hungarian Scholars and Romani Musicians in the Hungarian Folk Revival." *twentieth-century music* 3 (1): 51.

Horne, Gerald. 2019. *Jazz and Justice: Racism and the Political Economy of the Music*. New York: Monthly Review Press.

Horowitz, Michael. 2007. *Gypsy Rhythm, Volume 1: A Tutorial for Gypsy Jazz Rhythm Guitar*. Djangobooks.com.

Howell, Chris. 1992. *Regulating Labor: The State and Industrial Relations Reform in Postwar France*. Princeton, NJ: Princeton University Press.

———. 2018. "The French Road to Neoliberalism." *Catalyst* 2 (3): 83–121.

Hubert, Marie-Christine. 1997. "Les Tsiganes en France, 1939–1946: Assignation à résidence, internement, déportation." Ph.D. dissertation, Paris Nanterre University.

———. 2003. "Génocide et internement: Histoire gadjé et mémoires tsiganes: I. Du déni à la reconnaissance." In *L'histoire trouée: Négation et témoignage*, edited by Catherine Coquio, 475–88. Nantes, France: L'Atalante.

Hymes, Dell. 1964. "Introduction: Toward Ethnographies of Communication." *American Anthropologist* 66 (6, part 2): 1–34.

Inoue, Miyako. 2006. *Vicarious Language: Gender and Linguistic Modernity in Japan*. Berkeley: University of California Press.

Sept jours du monde. 1964. "Interview de l'épouse de Django." *Office national de radiodiffusion télévision française*. http://www.ina.fr/video/I12282117.

Irvine, Judith T. 1990. "Registering Affect: Heteroglossia in the Linguistic Expression of Emotion." In *Language and the Politics of Emotion*, edited by Lila Abu-Lughod and Catherine Lutz, 126–61. Cambridge: Cambridge University Press.

Irvine, Judith T., and Susan Gal. 2000. "Language Ideology and Linguistic Differentiation." In *Regimes of Language: Ideologies, Polities, and Identities*, edited by Paul V. Kroskrity, 35–83. School of American Research Advanced Seminar Series. Santa Fe, NM: School of American Research Press.

Jackson, Jeffrey H. 2003. *Making Jazz French: Music and Modern Life in Interwar Paris*. Durham, NC: Duke University Press.

Jackson, Travis A. 2012. *Blowin' the Blues Away: Performance and Meaning on the New York Jazz Scene*. Berkeley: University of California Press.

Jaffe, Alexandra. 2019. "Poeticizing the Economy: The Corsican Language in a Nexus of Pride and Profit." *Multilingua* 38 (1): 9–27.

Jalard, Michel-Claude. 1958. "'Django Reinhardt' de Paul Paviot." *La gazette de Lausanne*, April 19.

———. 1959. "Django et l'école tsigane du jazz." *Les cahiers du jazz* 1: 54–73.

Jeremy, John. 1989. *Django Legacy*. RDC Videos.

Jordan, Matthew F. 2010. *Le Jazz: Jazz and French Cultural Identity*. Urbana: University of Illinois Press.

Joskowicz, Ari. 2020. "The Age of the Witness and the Age of Surveillance: Romani Holocaust Testimony and the Perils of Digital Scholarship." *American Historical Review* 125 (4): 1205–31.

Kajikawa, Loren. 2015. *Sounding Race in Rap Songs*. Oakland: University of California Press.

———. 2019. "The Possessive Investment in Classical Music: Confronting Legacies of White Supremacy in US Schools and Departments of Music." In *Seeing Race Again: Countering Colorblindness across the Disciplines*, edited by Kimberlé Williams Crenshaw, Luke Charles Harris, Daniel Martinez HoSang, and George Lipsitz, 155–74. Oakland: University of California Press.

Kaminsky, David. 2015. "Introduction: The New Old Europe Sound." *Ethnomusicology Forum* 24 (2): 143–58.

Kane, Brian. 2014. *Sound Unseen: Acousmatic Sound in Theory and Practice*. New York: Oxford University Press.

Keane, Webb. 2003. "Semiotics and the Social Analysis of Material Things." *Language & Communication* 23 (3–4): 409–25.

———. 2018. "On Semiotic Ideology." *Signs and Society* 6 (1): 64–87.

Keaton, Trica Danielle. 2010. "The Politics of Race-Blindness: (Anti) Blackness and Category-Blindness in Contemporary France." *Du Bois Review: Social Science Research on Race* 7 (1): 103–31.

Keaton, Trica Danielle, T. Denean Sharpley-Whiting, and Tyler Stovall, eds. 2012. *Black France/France Noire: The History and Politics of Blackness*. Durham, NC: Duke University Press.

Keil, Charles. 1987. "Participatory Discrepancies and the Power of Music." *Cultural Anthropology* 2 (3): 275–83.

Kenrick, Donald. 1998. *Historical Dictionary of the Gypsies (Romanies)*. Lanham, MD: Scarecrow Press.

Keyes, Cheryl L. 2002. *Rap Music and Street Consciousness*. Urbana: University of Illinois Press.

Kiwan, Nadia. 2016. "Freedom of Thought in the Aftermath of the Charlie Hebdo Attacks." *French Cultural Studies* 27 (3): 233–44.

Klotz, Kelsey. 2016. "Racial Ideologies in 1950s Cool Jazz." Ph.D. dissertation, Washington University in St. Louis.

Knox, Katelyn E. 2016. *Race on Display in 20th- and 21st-Century France*. Liverpool: Liverpool University Press.

Kockelman, Paul. 2006. "A Semiotic Ontology of the Commodity." *Journal of Linguistic Anthropology* 16 (1): 76–102.

———. 2016. "Grading, Gradients, Degradation, Grace: Part 2: Phenomenology, Materiality, and Cosmology." *HAU: Journal of Ethnographic Theory* 6 (3): 337–65.

Kovalcsik, Katalin. 2010. "The Romani Musicians on the Stage of PluriCulturalism: The Case of the Kalyi Jag Group in Hungary." In *Multi-Disciplinary Approaches to Romany Studies*, edited by Márton Rövid and Michael Stewart, 55–70. Budapest: Central European University Press.

Krieg-Planque, Alice. 2005. "Le mot 'ethnie': Nommer autrui. Origine et fonctionnement du terme 'ethnie' dans l'univers discursif français." *Cahiers de lexicologie* 87: 141–61.

Kroskrity, Paul V. 2000. "Regimenting Languages: Language Ideological Perspectives." In *Regimes of Language: Ideologies, Polities, and Identities*, edited by Paul V. Kroskrity, 1–34. School of American Research Advanced Seminar Series. Santa Fe, NM: School of American Research Press.

Kroskrity, Paul V., and Anthony K. Webster, eds. 2015. *The Legacy of Dell Hymes: Ethnopoetics, Narrative Inequality, and Voice*. Bloomington and Indianapolis: Indiana University Press.

"La fête des Gitans ce soir au Polygone: Une rencontre, au-delà des séductions de l'exotisme." 1974. *Le nouvel Alsacien*, August 24.

Lange, Barbara Rose. 1997. "Hungarian Rom (Gypsy) Political Activism and the Development of Folklór Ensemble Music." *World of Music* 39 (3): 5–30.

———. 2003. *Holy Brotherhood: Romani Music in a Hungarian Pentecostal Church.* New York: Oxford University Press.

Le Jean, Bruno. 2012. *Les fils du vent.* Zelig Films Distribution.

Lee, Ken. 2000. "Orientalism and Gypsylorism." *Social Analysis: The International Journal of Social and Cultural Practice* 44 (2): 129–56.

Lefort, Michel. 1990. "Ce 'jazz tsigane' qui nous (re)vient . . . de loin." *Monde Gitan,* no. 75: 36–37.

———. 1991. "Le jazz des tsiganes." *Monde Gitan,* no. 81–82: 100–118.

———. 1994. "La musique des caravanes." *Études tsiganes,* no. 1: 10–19.

———. 1997. "Django for ever." *Jazz Hot* 500: 40–41.

Lefort, Michel, and Siegfried Maeker. 1997. "Musik Deutscher Zigeuner." *Jazz Hot,* no. 540 (May): 18–25.

Lem, Winnie. 2013. "Citizenship, Migration and Formations of Class in Urban France." *Dialectical Anthropology* 37 (3–4): 443–61.

Lemon, Alaina. 1995. "'What Are They Writing About Us Blacks?' Roma and 'Race' in Russia." *Anthropology of East Europe Review* 13 (2): 34–40.

———. 1996. "Hot Blood and Black Pearls: Socialism, Society, and Authenticity at the Moscow Teatr Romen." *Theatre Journal* 48 (4): 479–94.

———. 2000. *Between Two Fires: Gypsy Performance and Romani Memory from Pushkin to Post-Socialism.* Durham, NC: Duke University Press.

———. 2009. "Sympathy for the Weary State? Cold War Chronotopes and Moscow Others." *Comparative Studies in Society and History* 51 (4): 832–64.

Lempert, Michael, and Sabina Perrino. 2007. "Entextualization and the Ends of Temporality." *Language and Communication* 3 (27): 205–11.

Lena, Jennifer C. 2012. *Banding Together: How Communities Create Genres in Popular Music.* Princeton, NJ: Princeton University Press.

Lentin, Alana. 2008. "Europe and the Silence about Race." *European Journal of Social Theory* 11 (4): 487–503.

———. 2014. "Post-Race, Post Politics: The Paradoxical Rise of Culture after Multiculturalism." *Ethnic and Racial Studies* 37 (8): 1268–85.

"Les associations membres par Région." n.d. FNASAT–Gens du voyage. http://www.fnasat.asso.fr/carteasso.html.

Lewis, George E. 2016. "Foreword: What Is Jazz?" In *Jazz Worlds, World Jazz,* edited by Philip V. Bohlman and Goffredo Plastino, ix–xxiv. Chicago: University of Chicago Press.

Lie, Siv B. 2013. "'His Soul Was Wandering and Holy': Employing and Contesting Religious Terminology in Django Fandom." *Popular Music and Society* 36 (3): 380–96.

———. 2017. "The Politics of 'Understanding': Secrecy, Language, and Manouche Song." *Ethnic and Racial Studies* 40 (1): 96–113.

———. 2018. "Rich Theory: Mandino Reinhardt on Jazz Manouche in Alsace." *Jazz & Culture* 1: 104–21.

———. 2019. "Genre, Ethnoracial Alterity, and the Genesis of *jazz manouche*." *Journal of the American Musicological Society* 72 (3): 665–718.

———. 2020. "Music That Tears You Apart: Jazz Manouche and the Qualia of Ethnorace." *Ethnomusicology* 64 (3): 369–93.

Lie, Siv B., and Benjamin Givan. 2019. "Jazz Manouche." In *Grove Music Online*. https://doi.org/10.1093/omo/9781561592630.013.90000315373.

Liégeois, Jean-Pierre. 1975. "Naissance du pouvoir tsigane." *Revue française de sociologie* 16 (3): 295–316.

———. 2007. *Roma in Europe*. Strasbourg: Council of Europe.

Lipsitz, George. 1994. *Dangerous Crossroads: Popular Music, Postmodernism and the Poetics of Place*. New York: Verso.

Lopes, Paul Douglas. 2002. *The Rise of a Jazz Art World*. Cambridge: Cambridge University Press.

Loriol, Marc. 1999. "Qu'est-ce que l'insertion? Propositions pour la formalisation théorique d'une notion pratique." In *Qu'est-ce que l'insertion? Entre pratiques institutionnelles et représentations sociales*, edited by Marc Loriol, 7–32. Paris: L'Harmattan.

Lowe, Lisa. 2015. *The Intimacies of Four Continents*. Durham, NC: Duke University Press.

Luker, Morgan James. 2016. *The Tango Machine: Musical Culture in the Age of Expediency*. Chicago: University of Chicago Press.

MacDougald, Duncan. 1938. "Is This the Best Small Swing Group?" *Metronome* 54 (6): 12.

Maeker, Siegfried. 1969. "Dans la lignée de Django: L'orchestre Schnuckenack Reinhardt." *Monde Gitan*, no. 10: 13–15.

Magazzini, Tina, and Stefano Piemontese, eds. 2019. *Constructing Roma Migrants: European Narratives and Local Governance*. Springer International Publishing. https://doi.org/10.1007/978-3-030-11373-5.

Mahon, Maureen. 2000. "The Visible Evidence of Cultural Producers." *Annual Review of Anthropology* 29 (January): 467–92.

———. 2004. *Right to Rock: The Black Rock Coalition and the Cultural Politics of Race*. Durham, NC: Duke University Press.

———. 2020. *Black Diamond Queens: African American Women and Rock and Roll*. Durham, NC: Duke University Press.

"Marcel Loeffler, accordéoniste de jazz." n.d. Marcel Loeffler. http://www.marcel-loeffler.com/en/index.html.

"Marcel Loeffler Invite Lisa Doby & Nishati Gospel Singers." n.d. Le Printemps des Bretelles. http://www.printempsdesbretelles.com/groupe.php?concert=2.

Margalit, Gilad, and Yaron Matras. 2013. "Gypsies in Germany—German Gypsies? Identity and Politics of Sinti and Roma in Germany." In *The Roma: A Minority in Europe: Historical, Political and Social Perspectives*, edited by Roni Stauber and Raphael Vago, 103–16. Budapest: Central European University Press. http://books.openedition.org/ceup/1417.

Marković, Alexander. 2015. "'So That We Look More Gypsy': Strategic Performances and Ambivalent Discourses of Romani Brass for the World Music Scene." *Ethnomusicology Forum* 24 (2): 260–85.

Marmande, Francis. 1978. "Le troisième Carrefour Mondial de la Guitare en Martinique: Des accords dans la nuit tropicale." *Le Monde*, December 26. http://www.lemonde.fr/archives/article/1978/12/26/le-troisieme-carrefour-mondial-de-la-guitare-en-martinique-des-accords-dans-la-nuit-tropicale_3131011_1819218.html.

Martin, Alison. 2018. "Black Music Matters: Affirmation and Resilience in African American Musical Spaces in Washington, DC." In *Black Lives Matter & Music: Protest, Intervention, Reflection*, edited by Fernando Orejuela and Stephanie Shonekan, 70–85. Bloomington: Indiana University Press.

Matache, Margareta. 2016. "Word, Image and Thought: Creating the Romani Other." *FXB Center for Health & Human Rights | Harvard University* (blog), October 5. https://fxb.harvard.edu/2016/10/05/word-image-and-thought-creating-the-romani-other/.

Matras, Yaron. 2015. *The Romani Gypsies*. Cambridge, MA: Belknap Press of Harvard University Press.

McDonald, David A. 2013. *My Voice Is My Weapon: Music, Nationalism, and the Poetics of Palestinian Resistance*. Durham, NC: Duke University Press.

McGarry, Aidan. 2017. *Romaphobia: The Last Acceptable Form of Racism*. London: Zed Books.

McGranahan, Carole. 2016. "Theorizing Refusal: An Introduction." *Cultural Anthropology* 31 (3): 319–25.

McGregor, Elizabeth Vihlen. 2016. *Jazz and Postwar French Identity: Improvising the Nation*. Lanham, MD: Lexington Books.

Meier, Thomas. 2008. "The Fight against the Swiss Yenish and the 'Children of the Open Road' Campaign." *Romani Studies* 18 (2): 101–21.

Mendoza-Denton, Norma. 2016. "Norteño and Sureño Gangs, Hip Hop, and Ethnicity on YouTube: Localism in California through Spanish Accent Variation." In *Raciolinguistics: How Language Shapes Our Ideas about Race*, edited by H. Samy Alim, John R. Rickford, and Arnetha F. Ball, 135–50. New York: Oxford University Press.

Meyer, Claudine. 1974. "Hoerdt: Une vilaine affaire." *L'expression de l'Est*, April, n.p.

Miller, Karl Hagstrom. 2010. *Segregating Sound: Inventing Folk and Pop Music in the Age of Jim Crow*. Durham, NC: Duke University Press.

Mirga-Kruszelnicka, Anna. 2018. "Challenging Anti-Gypsyism in Academia: The Role of Romani Scholars." *Critical Romani Studies* 1 (1): 8–28.

Monson, Ingrid. 1995. "The Problem with White Hipness: Race, Gender, and Cultural Conceptions in Jazz Historical Discourse." *Journal of the American Musicological Society* 48 (3): 396–422.

———. 1996. *Saying Something: Jazz Improvisation and Interaction*. Chicago: University of Chicago Press.

———. 2007. *Freedom Sounds: Civil Rights Call out to Jazz and Africa*. New York: Oxford University Press.

Moog, Jean-Claude. 2003. "L'activité économique, moyen de lutte contre l'exclusion des Tziganes: Évaluer le projet d'ATEMA et l'améliorer." Master's thesis, L'École Nationale de la Santé Publique, Rennes.

Munn, Nancy D. 1986. *The Fame of Gawa: A Symbolic Study of Value Transformation in a Massim (Papua New Guinea) Society*. Cambridge: Cambridge University Press.

"Musique, films et artisanat pour faire connaître la culture tzigane." 1977. *Dernières nouvelles d'Alsace*, April 22.

Nakassis, Constantine V. 2016. "Linguistic Anthropology in 2015: Not the Study of Language." *American Anthropologist* 118 (2): 330–45.

———. 2018. "Indexicality's Ambivalent Ground." *Signs and Society* 6 (1): 281–304.

Negus, Keith. 1999. *Music Genres and Corporate Cultures*. New York: Routledge.

Niang, Mame-Fatou. 2019. *Identités françaises: Banlieues, féminités et universalisme*. Leiden: Brill Rodopi.

———. 2020. "France's Racial Spring." *Rosa Luxemburg Stiftung* (blog), August 26. https://www.rosalux.eu/en/article/1761.france-s-racial-spring.html.

Obadike, Mendi. 2005. "Low Fidelity: Stereotyped Blackness in the Field of Sound." Ph.D. dissertation, Duke University.

Olivera, Martin. 2011. "La fabrique experte de la 'question Rom': Multiculturalisme et néolibéralisme imbriqués." *Lignes* 34 (1): 104–18.

———. 2015. "Roma/Gypsies in France: The Extent of Diversities versus the Permanence of Public Policies." In *Virtual Citizenship? Roma Communities, ICTs and Inclusion Policies in Europe*, edited by Alfredo Alietti, Martin Olivera, and Veronica Riniolo, 37–54. Milan: McGraw-Hill.

Olivera, Martin, and Jean-Luc Poueyto. 2018. "Tsiganes et anthropologie: Héritages, enjeux et perspectives." *Ethnologie française* 172 (4): 581–600.

Olwage, Grant. 2004. "The Class and Colour of Tone: An Essay on the Social History of Vocal Timbre." *Ethnomusicology Forum* 13: 203–26.

Ong, Aihwa. 1996. "Cultural Citizenship as Subject-Making: Immigrants Negotiate Racial and Cultural Boundaries in the United States [and Comments and Reply]." *Current Anthropology* 37 (5): 737–51.

Orejuela, Fernando, and Stephanie Shonekan, eds. 2018. *Black Lives Matter & Music: Protest, Intervention, Reflection*. Bloomington: Indiana University Press.

Ortner, Sherry B. 1995. "Resistance and the Problem of Ethnographic Refusal." *Comparative Studies in Society and History* 37 (1): 173–93.

Pac, Robert. 1979. "Django." *Droit et Liberté*, no. 376 (January): 17.

Panassié, Hugues. 1942. *The Real Jazz*. Translated by A. S. Williams. New York: Smith and Durrell.

———. 1946. *La véritable musique de jazz*. Paris: Robert Laffont.

Panassié, Hugues, and Pierre Casalta. 1975. *Monsieur Jazz: entretiens avec Pierre Casalta*. Paris: Stock.

Parmentier, Richard J. 1994. *Signs in Society: Studies in Semiotic Anthropology*. Bloomington: Indiana University Press.

Paugam, Serge. 2003. "The Revenu Minimum d'Insertion (RMI) in France: The Limits of a Progressive Social Policy." In *Minimum Income Schemes in Europe*, edited by Guy Standing, 29–54. Geneva: International Labour Office.

Paviot, Paul. 1958. *Django Reinhardt*. DVD. Citel.

Peabody, Sue, and Tyler Stovall, eds. 2003. *The Color of Liberty: Histories of Race in France*. Durham, NC: Duke University Press.

Peirce, Charles Sanders. 1955. *Philosophical Writings of Peirce*. Edited by Justus Buchler. New York: Dover.

———. 1994. *The Collected Papers of Charles Sanders Peirce*. Edited by John Deely. Charlottesville, VA: InteLex Past Masters.

———. 1998. *The Essential Peirce: Selected Philosophical Writings*. Edited by the Peirce Edition Project. Vol. 2. Bloomington: Indiana University Press.

Perchard, Tom. 2015. *After Django: Making Jazz in Postwar France*. Ann Arbor: University of Michigan Press.

Perman, Tony. 2010. "Dancing in Opposition: Muchongoyo, Emotion, and the Politics of Performance in Southeastern Zimbabwe." *Ethnomusicology* 54 (3): 425–51.

———. 2020. *Signs of the Spirit: Music and the Experience of Meaning in Ndau Ceremonial Life*. Urbana: University of Illinois Press.

Peschanski, Denis. 2002. "The Gypsies in the Upheaval: The Situation in France, 1939–1946." In *Roma and Sinti: Understudied Victims of Nazism*, 49–58. Washington, DC: Center for Advanced Holocaust Studies, United States Holocaust Memorial Museum.

Picker, Giovanni. 2017. *Racial Cities: Governance and the Segregation of Romani People in Urban Europe*. New York: Routledge.

Pierre, Jemima. 2013. *The Predicament of Blackness: Postcolonial Ghana and the Politics of Race*. Chicago: University of Chicago Press.

Piotrowska, Anna G. 2017. "The Concept of Race in Musicological Thought: From General Remarks to a Case Study of So-Called Gypsy Music in European Culture." In *Ideas of "Race" in the History of the Humanities*, 215–34. New York: Palgrave Macmillan.

Porcello, Thomas. 2002. "Music Mediated as Live in Austin: Sound, Technology, and Recording Practice." *City & Society* 14 (1): 69–86.

Porter, Eric. 2002. *What Is This Thing Called Jazz? African American Musicians as Artists, Critics, and Activists*. Berkeley: University of California Press.

Potot, Swanie. 2018. *"Nous les Tsiganes, ou les Roms, comme vous dites, vous": Catégorisations ethniques et frontières sociales en Europe*. Rennes: Presses Universitaires de Rennes.

Poueyto, Jean-Luc. 2003. "Génocide et internement: Histoire gadjé et mémoires tsiganes: II. La mémoire de l'internement dans une communauté manouche en France." In *L'histoire trouée: Négation et témoignage*, edited by Catherine Coquio, 475–88. Nantes, France: L'Atalante.

———. 2011. *Manouches et mondes de l'écrit*. Paris: Éditions Karthala.

———. 2015. "Loin de Django, la musique des Manouches de Pau." *Gradhiva*, no. 21: 182–205.

———. 2018. "Être manouche: Une histoire de familles." *Ethnologie française* 172 (4): 601–12.

Powell, Ryan, and Huub van Baar. 2019. "The Invisibilization of Anti-Roma Racisms." In *The Securitization of the Roma in Europe*, edited by Huub van Baar, Ana Ivasiuc, and Regina Kreide, 91–113. New York: Palgrave Macmillan.

Prasad, Monica. 2005. "Why Is France So French? Culture, Institutions, and Neoliberalism, 1974–1981." *American Journal of Sociology* 111 (2): 357–407.

Quintero, Michael Birenbaum. 2018. *Rites, Rights and Rhythms: A Genealogy of Musical Meaning in Colombia's Black Pacific*. New York: Oxford University Press.

Radano, Ronald. 2003. *Lying Up a Nation: Race and Black Music*. Chicago: University of Chicago Press.

———. 2013. "The Sound of Racial Feeling." *Daedalus* 142 (4): 126–34.

Radano, Ronald, and Philip V. Bohlman. 2000. *Music and the Racial Imagination*. Chicago: University of Chicago Press.

Reed, Adolph Jr. 2013. "Marx, Race, and Neoliberalism." *New Labor Forum* 22 (1): 49–57.

———. 2016. "Revolution as 'National Liberation' and the Origins of Neoliberal Antiracism." *Socialist Register 2017: Rethinking Revolution* 53: 299–322.

Reinhardt, Babik. 1994. "Avant-propos." In *Django's Gypsies: The Mystique of Django Reinhardt and His People*, edited by Ian Cruickshank, 1. Newcastle-upon-Tyne, UK: Ashley Mark Publishing Company.

Reinhardt, Babik, and Michel Maestracci. 1997. "Au nom du fils." *Jazz Hot*, no. 541 (June): 38–39.

Reinheimer, Robert. 1979. "Nous ne voulons plus être comme des Indiens assistés. . . ." *Dernières nouvelles d'Alsace*, November 22.

———. 1983. "Les Weiss obtiennent gain de cause." *Dernières nouvelles d'Alsace*, April 22.

Reyes, Angela. 2017a. "Inventing Postcolonial Elites: Race, Language, Mix, Excess." *Journal of Linguistic Anthropology* 27 (2): 210–31.

———. 2017b. "Ontology of Fake: Discerning the Philippine Elite." *Signs and Society* 5 (S1): S100–S127.

Reyes, Angela, and Adrienne Lo, eds. 2009. *Beyond Yellow English: Toward a Linguistic Anthropology of Asian Pacific America*. New York: Oxford University Press.

Roach, Max. 1972. "What 'Jazz' Means to Me." *Black Scholar* 3 (10): 2–6.

Roberts, T. 2016. *Resounding Afro Asia: Interracial Music and the Politics of Collaboration*. New York: Oxford University Press.

Robinet, Jean-François. 2018. *50 ans de Festival Django Reinhardt*. Fontainebleau, France: Éditions AKFG.

Rodriguez, Alex Warner. 2018. "Making Jazz Space: Clubs and Creative Practice in California, Chile, and Siberia." Ph.D. dissertation, University of California, Los Angeles.

Rollefson, J. Griffith. 2017. *Flip the Script: European Hip Hop and the Politics of Postcoloniality*. Chicago: University of Chicago Press.

Rosa, Jonathan. 2019. *Looking like a Language, Sounding like a Race: Raciolinguistic Ideologies and the Learning of Latinidad*. New York: Oxford University Press.

Rosa, Jonathan, and Nelson Flores. 2017. "Unsettling Race and Language: Toward a Raciolinguistic Perspective." *Language in Society* 46 (5): 621–47.

———. 2020. "Reimagining Race and Language: From Raciolinguistic Ideologies to a Raciolinguistic Perspective." In *The Oxford Handbook of Language and Race*, edited by H. Samy Alim, Angela Reyes, and Paul V. Kroskrity, 90–107. New York: Oxford University Press.

Rosaldo, Renato. 1994. "Cultural Citizenship in San Jose, California." *PoLAR* 17 (2): 57–63.

Rose, Tricia. 1994. *Black Noise: Rap Music and Black Culture in Contemporary America*. Hanover, NH: University Press of New England.

Rosenhaft, Eve. 2008. "Exchanging Glances: Ambivalence in Twentieth-Century Photographs of German Sinti." *Third Text* 22 (3): 311–24.

Roussin, Didier. 1994. "Les Tsiganes, le musette, la guitare et le banjo." *Études tsiganes*, no. 1: 134–45.

Rustin-Paschal, Nichole. 2017. *The Kind of Man I Am: Jazzmasculinity and the World of Charles Mingus Jr.* Middletown, CT: Wesleyan University Press.

Sabbagh, Daniel, and Shanny Peer. 2008. "French Color Blindness in Perspective: The Controversy over 'Statistiques Ethniques.'" *French Politics, Culture & Society* 26 (1): 1–6.

Salgues, Yves. 1958. "La légende de Django Reinhardt IX." *Jazz Magazine*, no. 41 (October): 31–33.

Samuels, David William. 2004. *Putting a Song on Top of It: Expression and Identity on the San Carlos Apache Reservation*. Tucson: University of Arizona Press.

"Sarkozy justifie le débat sur l'identité nationale." 2009. *L'Express*, November 12. https://www.lexpress.fr/actualite/societe/sarkozy-justifie-le-debat-sur-l-identite-nationale_828004.html.

Sarkozy, Nicolas. 2010. "Prise de fonction du nouveau préfet." *Élysée*, August 4. Available at https://web.archive.org/web/20100804045813/http:/www.elysee.fr/president/les-actualites/discours/2010/prise-de-fonction-du-nouveau-prefet.9399.html.

Saul, Nicholas, and Susan Tebbutt, eds. 2004. *The Role of the Romanies: Images and Counter-Images of "Gypsies"/Romanies in European Cultures*. Liverpool: Liverpool University Press.

Savigliano, Marta. 1995. *Tango and the Political Economy of Passion*. Boulder, CO: Westview Press.

Schaaser, Marita. 2013. "'Sinti–Jazz–Manouche': Musik und Identität." M.Phil. thesis, University of Vienna.

Scheffel, David Z. 2019. "The Slovak 'Gypsy Fringe' as a Semi-Colonial Entity." In *Shifting Forms of Continental Colonialism: Unfinished Struggles and Tensions*, edited by Dittmar Schorkowitz, John R. Chávez, and Ingo W. Schröder, 197–225. Singapore: Palgrave Macmillan.

Schieffelin, Bambi B., Kathryn A. Woolard, and Paul V. Kroskrity. 1998. *Language Ideologies: Practice and Theory*. New York: Oxford University Press.

Schneider, Cathy Lisa. 2008. "Police Power and Race Riots in Paris." *Politics & Society* 36 (1): 133–59.

Schuller, Gunther. 1989. *The History of Jazz. The Swing Era: The Development of Jazz, 1930–1945*. Vol. 2. New York: Oxford University Press.

Shipton, Alyn. 2007. *A New History of Jazz*. New York: Continuum.

Sigot, Jacques. 2010. *Ces barbelés que découvre l'histoire: Un camp pour les Tsiganes . . . et les autres, Montreuil-Bellay, 1940–1946*. Châteauneuf-les-Martigues, France: Wallada.

Silverman, Carol. 2000. Review of *Latcho Drom*, New Yorker Films. *Ethnomusicology* 44 (2): 362–64.

———. 2007. "Trafficking in the Exotic with 'Gypsy' Music: Balkan Roma, Cosmopolitanism, and 'World Music' Festivals." In *Balkan Popular Culture and the Ottoman Ecumene: Music, Image and Regional Political Discourse*, edited by Donna A. Buchanan, 335–63. Lanham, MD: Scarecrow Press.

———. 2012. *Romani Routes: Cultural Politics and Balkan Music in Diaspora*. New York: Oxford University Press.

———. 2013. "Global Balkan Gypsy Music: Issues of Migration, Appropriation, and Representation." In *The Globalization of Musics in Transit: Music Migration and Tourism*, edited by Simone Krüger and Ruxandra Trandafoiu, 185–208. New York: Routledge.

Silverstein, Michael. 1979. "Language Structure and Linguistic Ideology." In *The Elements*, edited by Paul R. Clyne, William F. Hanks, and Carol L. Hofbauer. Chicago: Chicago Linguistic Society.

———. 1992. "The Uses and Utility of Ideology: Some Reflections." *Pragmatics* 2 (3): 311–23.

———. 1993. "Metapragmatic Discourse and Metapragmatic Function." In *Reflexive Language: Reported Speech and Metapragmatics*, edited by John A. Lucy, 33–57. Cambridge: Cambridge University Press.

———. 2003. "Indexical Order and the Dialectics of Sociolinguistic Life." *Language & Communication* 23 (3–4): 193–229.

———. 2005. "Axes of Evals: Token versus Type Interdiscursivity." *Journal of Linguistic Anthropology* 15 (1): 6–22.

Silverstein, Paul A. 2018. *Postcolonial France: The Question of Race and the Future of the Republic*. London: Pluto Press.

Silverstein, Paul A., and Chantal Tetreault. 2006. "Postcolonial Urban Apartheid." *Items and Issues* 5 (4): 8–15. https://items.ssrc.org/from-our-archives/postcolonial-urban-apartheid/.

Simhandl, Katrin. 2006. "'Western Gypsies and Travellers'–'Eastern Roma': The Creation of Political Objects by the Institutions of the European Union." *Nations and Nationalism* 12 (1): 97–115.

Simon, Bill. 1957. "Charlie Christian." In *The Jazz Makers: Essays on the Greats of Jazz*, edited by Nat Shapiro and Nat Hentoff, 316–31. New York: Holt, Rinehart, and Winston.

Simon, Patrick. 2008. "The Choice of Ignorance: The Debate on Ethnic and Racial Statistics in France." *French Politics, Culture & Society* 26 (1): 7–31.

Simpson, Audra. 2014. *Mohawk Interruptus: Political Life across the Borders of Settler States*. Durham, NC: Duke University Press.

Smalls, Krystal A. 2020. "Race, Signs, and the Body: Towards a Theory of Racial Semiotics." In *The Oxford Handbook of Language and Race*, edited by H. Samy Alim, Angela Reyes, and Paul V. Kroskrity, 233–60. New York: Oxford University Press.

Smith, Andrea L. 2018. "Crisis France: Covert Racialization and the Gens du Voyage." In *Messy Europe: Crisis, Race, and Nation-State in a Postcolonial World*, edited by Kristin Loftsdóttir, Andrea L. Smith, and Brigitte Hipfl, 171–95. New York: Berghahn Books.

Sokolová, Vera. 2005. "Planned Parenthood behind the Curtain: Population Policy and Sterilization of Romani Women in Communist Czechoslovakia, 1972–1989." *Anthropology of East Europe Review* 23 (1): 79–98.

Spears, Arthur K., ed. 1999. *Race and Ideology: Language, Symbolism, and Popular Culture*. Detroit, MI: Wayne State University Press.

Spivak, Gayatri. 1985. "Criticism, Feminism and the Institution." *Thesis Eleven* 10–11: 175–87.

Stewart, Michael. 2013. "Roma and Gypsy 'Ethnicity' as a Subject of Anthropological Inquiry." *Annual Review of Anthropology* 42: 415–32.

Stocking, George W. 1968. *Race, Culture, and Evolution: Essays in the History of Anthropology*. Chicago: University of Chicago Press.

Stoever, Jennifer Lynn. 2016. *The Sonic Color Line: Race and the Cultural Politics of Listening*. New York: NYU Press.

Stoichita, Victor Alexandre. 2008. *Fabricants d'émotion: Musique et malice dans un village tsigane de Roumanie*. Nanterre, France: Société d'ethnologie.

———. 2016. "Appartenance ethnique et variations musicales selon les musiciens professionnels de Roumanie." In *Roms en Europe: Sous le regard de trois ethnologues*, by Patrick Williams, Martin Olivera, and Victor Alexandre Stoichita, 43–58. Nanterre, France: Société d'ethnologie.

Stokes, Martin. 2010. *The Republic of Love: Cultural Intimacy in Turkish Popular Music*. Chicago: University of Chicago Press.

Stoler, Ann Laura. 1997. "Racial Histories and Their Regimes of Truth." *Political Power and Social Theory* 11 (1): 183–206.

Strathern, Marilyn. 1996. "Enabling Identity? Biology, Choice and the New Reproductive Technologies." In *Questions of Cultural Identity*, edited by Stuart Hall and Paul du Gay, 37–52. London: SAGE.

Surdu, Mihai. 2016. *Those Who Count: Expert Practices of Romani Classification*. Budapest: Central European University Press.

Sweeney, Carole. 2001. "La Revue Nègre: Négrophilie, Modernity and Colonialism in Inter-War France." *Journal of Romance Studies* 1 (2): 1–14.

Szeman, Ioana. 2018. *Staging Citizenship: Roma, Performance and Belonging in EU Romania*. New York: Berghahn Books.

Taylor, Timothy D. 2007. *Beyond Exoticism: Western Music and the World*. Durham, NC: Duke University Press.

———. 2014. "Fields, Genres, Brands." *Culture, Theory and Critique* 55 (2): 159–74.

Ténot, Frank. 1988. "Reinhardt, Django." In *Dictionnaire du jazz*, edited by Philippe Carles, André Clergeat, and Jean-Louis Comolli, 851–52. Paris: Robert Laffont.

Tissot, Sylvie. 2011. "Excluding Muslim Women: From Hijab to Niqab, from School to Public Space." *Public Culture* 23 (1): 39–46.

Tournès, Ludovic. 1999. *New Orleans sur Seine: Histoire du jazz en France*. Paris: Fayard.

Trazegnies, Jean de. 1945. "Django Reinhardt: De la rêverie tzigane . . . à l'improvisation hot." *Jazz*, no. 9: 16–17.

Trehan, Nidhi, and Angéla Kóczé. 2009. "Racism, (Neo-)Colonialism and Social Justice: The Struggle for the Soul of the Romani Movement in Post-Socialist Europe." In *Racism, Postcolonialism, Europe*, edited by Graham Huggan and Ian Law, 50–73. Liverpool: Liverpool University Press.

Trehan, Nidhi, and Nando Sigona. 2009. *Romani Politics in Contemporary Europe: Poverty, Ethnic Mobilization, and the Neoliberal Order*. New York: Palgrave Macmillan.

Trouillot, Michel-Rolph. 1995. *Silencing the Past: Power and the Production of History*. Boston: Beacon Press.

———. 2003. *Global Transformations: Anthropology and the Modern World*. New York: Palgrave Macmillan.

Trumpener, Katie. 1992. "The Time of the Gypsies: A 'People without History' in the Narratives of the West." *Critical Inquiry* 18 (4): 843–84.

Tucker, Sherrie. 2002. "Big Ears: Listening for Gender in Jazz Studies." *Current Musicology* 71–73: 375–408.

———. 2012. "Deconstructing the Jazz Tradition: The 'Subjectless Subject' of New Jazz Studies." In *Jazz/Not Jazz: The Music and Its Boundaries*, edited by David Ake, Charles Hiroshi Garrett, and Daniel Ira Goldmark, 264–84. Berkeley: University of California Press.

Turino, Thomas. 1999. "Signs of Imagination, Identity, and Experience: A Peircian Semiotic Theory for Music." *Ethnomusicology* 43 (2): 221–55.

———. 2008. *Music as Social Life: The Politics of Participation*. Chicago: University of Chicago Press.

———. 2014. "Peircean Thought as Core Theory for a Phenomenological Ethnomusicology." *Ethnomusicology* 58 (2): 185–221.

Tuzet, Jean-Baptiste. 2007. *Jazz manouche: La grande aventure du swing gitan de Django Reinhardt à Tchavolo Schmitt*. Paris: Editions Dider Carpentier.

———. 2010. *Django Reinhardt et le jazz manouche, ou, les 100 ans du jazz à la française*. Paris: Éditions Dider Carpentier.

Ulanov, Barry. 1953. "Django Reinhardt, 1912–1953." *Metronome* 69 (8): 14.

"Un Manouche musicien et luthier: Matcho Sauzer." 1968. *Monde Gitan*, no. 7: 11–13.

Urciuoli, Bonnie. 1996. *Exposing Prejudice: Puerto Rican Experiences of Language, Race, and Class*. Boulder, CO: Westview Press.

———. 2003. "Excellence, Leadership, Skills, Diversity: Marketing Liberal Arts Education." *Language & Communication* 23 (3–4): 385–408.

———. 2008. "Skills and Selves in the New Workplace." *American Ethnologist* 35 (2): 211–28.

van Baar, Huub. 2014. "The Emergence of a Reasonable Anti-Gypsyism in Europe." In *When Stereotype Meets Prejudice: Antiziganism in European Societies*, edited by Timofey Agarin, 27–44. Stuttgart: Ibidem-Verlag.

———. 2015. "Enacting Memory and the Hard Labor of Identity Formation: Rethinking the Romani Movement and Its Historiography." In *The Identity Dilemma: Collective Identity and Social Movements*, edited by Aidan McGarry and James Jasper, 150–69. Philadelphia: Temple University Press.

van Baar, Huub, and Angéla Kóczé, eds. 2020. *The Roma and Their Struggle for Identity in Contemporary Europe*. New York: Berghahn Books.

van de Port, Mattijs. 1999. "The Articulation of Soul: Gypsy Musicians and the Serbian Other." *Popular Music* 18 (3): 291–307.

Vaux de Foletier, François. 1967. "Le Gala Tsigane et Gitan du 15 mars." *Études tsiganes*, no. 1–2: 30–33.

———. 1970. *Mille ans d'histoire des Tsiganes*. Paris: Fayard.

Vermeersch, Peter. 2005. "Marginality, Advocacy, and the Ambiguities of Multiculturalism: Notes on Romani Activism in Central Europe." *Identities: Global Studies in Culture and Power* 12 (4): 451–78.

———. 2006. *The Romani Movement: Minority Politics and Ethnic Mobilization in Contemporary Central Europe*. Oxford: Berghahn.

Violi, Patrizia. 2013. "How Our Bodies Become Us: Embodiment, Semiosis and Intersubjectivity." *Cognitive Semiotics* 4 (1): 57–75.

Volpp, Leti. 2007. "The Culture of Citizenship." *Theoretical Inquiries in Law* 8 (2): 571–602.

Warne, Chris. 1997. "The Impact of World Music in France." In *Post-Colonial Cultures in France*, edited by Alec G. Hargreaves and Mark McKinney, 133–49. London: Routledge.

Weidman, Amanda. 2009. "Listening to the Violin in South Indian Classical Music." In *Theorizing the Local: Music, Practice, and Experience in South Asia and Beyond*, edited by Richard K. Wolf, 49–63. New York: Oxford University Press.

Weil, Patrick, and John Crowley. 1994. "Integration in Theory and Practice: A Comparison of France and Britain." *West European Politics* 17 (2): 110–26.

Weiner, Melissa F. 2012. "Towards a Critical Global Race Theory." *Sociology Compass* 6 (4): 332–50.

Weiss, Erica. 2016. "Refusal as Act, Refusal as Abstention." *Cultural Anthropology* 31 (3): 351–58.

Wetherell, Margaret. 2013. "Affect and Discourse–What's the Problem? From Affect as Excess to Affective/Discursive Practice." *Subjectivity* 6 (4): 349–68.

Wieviorka, Michel. 1992. *La France raciste*. Paris: Éditions du Seuil.

Wiley, Eric. 2005. "Romani Performance and Heritage Tourism: The Pilgrimage of the Gypsies at Les Saintes-Maries-de-La-Mer." *TDR/The Drama Review* 49 (2): 135–58.

Wilf, Eitan Y. 2012. "Rituals of Creativity: Tradition, Modernity, and the 'Acoustic Unconscious' in a US Collegiate Jazz Music Program." *American Anthropologist* 114 (1): 32–44.

———. 2014. *School for Cool: The Academic Jazz Program and the Paradox of Institutionalized Creativity*. Chicago: University of Chicago Press.

Willems, Wim. 1997. *In Search of the True Gypsy: From Enlightenment to Final Solution*. Translated by Don Bloch. London: Frank Cass Publishers.

Williams, Patrick. 1994. "'Maro bravlepen i maro vàgo maro graj': Un répertoire de chansons manouches." *Études tsiganes*, no. 1: 28–39.

———. 1998. *Django Reinhardt*. 2nd ed. Marseille: Éditions Parenthèses.

———. 2000. "Un héritage sans transmission: Le jazz manouche." *Ethnologie française* 30 (3): 409–22.

———. 2003. *Gypsy World: The Silence of the Living and the Voices of the Dead*. Translated by Catherine Tihanyi. Chicago: University of Chicago Press.

———. 2004. "L'improvisation et le jazz manouche." In *L'improvisation du jazz: Actes du 2ième colloque de Monségur du 2 juillet 2004*, 29–40. Bordeaux: Presses Universitaires de Bordeaux.

———. 2015. "Cette chanson est pour vous, madame . . ." *L'Homme* 3 (215–16): 103–26.

Williams, Raymond. 1977. *Marxism and Literature*. Oxford: Oxford University Press.

Wilson, David Richard. 2015. "Music Making Space: Musicians, Scenes, and Belonging in the Republic of Macedonia." Ph.D. dissertation, University of California, Los Angeles.

Wirtz, Kristina. 2014. *Performing Afro-Cuba: Image, Voice, Spectacle in the Making of Race and History*. Chicago: University of Chicago Press.

———. 2016. "The Living, the Dead, and the Immanent: Dialogue across Chronotopes." *HAU: Journal of Ethnographic Theory* 6 (1): 343–69.

Woolard, Kathryn A. 2013. "Is the Personal Political? Chronotopes and Changing Stances toward Catalan Language and Identity." *International Journal of Bilingual Education and Bilingualism* 16 (2): 210–24.

Yúdice, George. 2003. *The Expediency of Culture: Uses of Culture in the Global Era*. Durham, NC: Duke University Press.

Zwerin, Mike. 2000. *Swing under the Nazis: Jazz as a Metaphor for Freedom*. New York: Cooper Square Press.

Index

accent, 146
accordion, 49, 116, 134, 200n10
activism. *See* cultural activism
advertising, 7, 28, 49, 55–57, 59–62, 81–83, 91, 123–24, 142, 154–56, 158, 167–68, 170, 175–76. *See also* marketing
African Americans, 17, 39, 55, 102, 138–40, 148–49, 186
Agha, Asif, 7, 157, 221n16
Alim, H. Samy, 9, 205n4
Alsace: as "cradle" of jazz manouche, 1, 142; *départements* of, 69, 86, 215n48; emblems of, 1, 142; and the genesis of jazz manouche, 49–59; guitar technique associated with, 142–45. *See also* APPONA; Festival International Tzigane; Festival Jazz Manouche de Zillisheim
amateurism, 32, 60, 137
ambivalent desire, 39
ambivalent essentialism, 6–8, 30, 31, 96, 101, 103–4, 126, 185–87
Andresz, Patrick, 50, 52, 94, 159
Angers, 27, 58, 154–56, 157–58, 172, 182
anti-anti-essentialism, 6, 101
antiracist organizations, 70
Antonietto, Alain, 16, 35, 36, 44, 46, 59, 105, 206n13
APPONA, 21–22, 29–30, 52, 65–66; afterlife of, 65–66, 85–97; dissolution of, 65, 85–86; founding of, 52, 65–66, 68–70; leadership of, 30, 52, 66, 69, 76–77, 80, 85, 147, 164, 204n40; membership of, 211n5; and music production, 66, 82–84; music school of, 52, 54–55, 56, 65, 78–82, 86, 88–90, 216n56, 216n57; violence toward, 211n8. *See also* Festival International Tzigane
APPONA 68, 86, 173, 178
Armstrong, Louis, 38
art world, 27–28
assimilation, 4, 11, 14, 30, 67–68, 70, 71, 90, 96
Association pour la Promotion des Populations d'Origine Nomade d'Alsace, L'. *See* APPONA
Astolfi, Christophe, 98, 116–17, 143
Ateliers Manouches d'Alsace, Les (ATEMA), 83–84, 86
aural pedagogy, 30, 56, 57–58, 78–82, 90, 149
authenticity, 4, 8, 27, 56, 57, 121–23, 124–25, 129, 135, 137, 142–45, 152, 175–76
autoexoticization, 103, 112–13, 201n13
AVA Habitat et Nomadisme, 69, 86, 95

Bakhtin, Mikhail, 157
Balibar, Etienne, 12
bal-musette. See *musette*
banjo-guitar, 37, 141, 206n9
bass, 2–3, 38, 50, 82, 91, 112, 178, 205n1, 219n2, 223n30
Bauman, Zygmunt, 7

Beaman, Jean, 15, 101–2
bebop, 38, 55, 57, 108, 124, 218n9
Becker, Howard, 27
Beissinger, Margaret, 22, 217n3
Belgium, 34, 37
Berish, Andrew, 206n5
Beriss, David, 14
Billard, François, 16, 46, 59, 105, 107, 206n13
Blackness, 6, 9, 17, 39, 130, 138–40, 151, 202n12, 204n30, 205n4, 220n10, 220n14, 221n22
blood, 36, 122, 149–51
blues, 17, 138–40, 148
bohemiens. *See* Romanies: stereotypes of
Bohlman, Philip V., 106–7
Bonilla-Silva, Eduardo, 12, 34
Bonneau, Pierre, 40
bossa nova, 6, 55, 57, 112, 123, 210n45
branding: ethnoracial, 12, 20, 22–23, 58, 67–68, 74–76, 112, 121–22, 129, 156, 158, 172–73, 175–76, 181, 186 (*see also* ethno-preneurialism); place-based, 1, 4, 24, 142, 154–59, 167–68, 170, 175, 199n2
Brubaker, Rogers, 204n34
Burrell, Kenny, 136

capitalism, 67, 185–87. *See also* neoliberalism
caravans, 37, 42, 69, 117, 147, 154–56, 165, 170, 174, 178–79, 204n35, 226n30. See also *roulottes*
Catholicism, 5, 51, 92, 168, 178, 179–80, 208n29, 209n38, 225n25
Central Europe, 47, 224n13
Chang, Denis, 223n31
Chaput, Roger, 38 205n1
C(h)œur des femmes, Le, 64–65, 68, 90–92, 96–97
chronotopes, 157–59, 160, 166–67, 170, 172–73, 179, 181, 224n3
Chumley, Lily, 131–32, 221n16
citizenship, 13, 14–15, 18, 24, 71, 74, 100–101, 160, 176, 180. *See also* cultural citizenship.
civic legitimacy, 79–81
class, 5, 7, 20, 21, 53, 67, 71–73, 84–85, 96–97, 102, 103, 109, 143, 148, 159, 181, 186. *See also* poverty
Cocteau, Jean, 207n17
Cœuroy, André, 207n16
colonialism, 9–10, 11, 13, 14, 187, 202n19
color blindness, 12, 13–14, 18, 34, 92, 93, 107, 172, 202n22. *See also* racism; republicanism; universalism
Comaroff, Jean, 20, 22–23, 67, 72–73, 94, 149–50
Comaroff, John L., 20, 22–23, 67, 72–73, 94, 149–50
commodification, 23, 35, 59–62, 72–73, 94–95, 112, 181. *See also* ethno-preneurialism
concentration camps, 13, 26, 29, 47, 49, 114, 226n31
cosmopolitanism, 24, 49, 101, 107, 109–11, 143, 160
Council of Europe, 1, 75, 161
Cruz, Jon, 139
csárdás, 6, 47–48, 50, 55, 56, 145, 210n45
cuisine, 1, 16–17, 111, 118, 223n32
cultural activism, 21–24, 27, 29–30, 34–35, 46–49, 51–59, 66–68, 70, 71, 73, 85, 91–96, 109, 158, 184–85, 186, 208n28, 225n20
cultural citizenship, 15–18, 20, 23–25, 30–31, 35, 63, 67–68, 71–73, 74, 81, 85, 90, 92, 96–97, 100–103, 117–18, 126–27, 159, 166, 180–82, 185; dialectical model of, 67, 71–72, 91–92, 96, 167
cultural expediency, 20–24, 34, 54, 66, 95, 113, 181, 185
cultural intimacy, 137

"Dark Eyes," 3, 50
Daval, Marcel, 50, 52, 55–56, 59, 69, 71–72, 79, 80, 121, 209n42, 222n24
decolonization, 14, 70
Delaunay, Charles, 37–38, 40, 41–42, 207n19, 207n20
Dick, Hilary, 12
disability, 37–38, 40, 206n12, 210n1, 212n10
Django. *See* Reinhardt, Django
Dollé, Marie-Paul, 205n42
Dregni, Michael, 33, 205n2, 222n24
Duranti, Alessandro, 136

Eastern Europe, ix, 15, 47, 49, 89, 109, 121, 134–35, 224n13
Eidsheim, Nina, 132–33, 205n3
Ellington, Edward "Duke," 38

employment, 7, 52, 66, 71–73, 83–85, 86, 93, 96, 114–15, 136–37, 212n12. *See also* labor
enculturation, 130, 133, 146–51
entrepreneurship, 23, 30, 46, 56, 67, 72–73, 85–86, 94–95. *See also* ethno-preneurialism
Espace culturel Django Reinhardt, 80, 88, 157
essentialism. *See* ambivalent essentialism
ethnicity, 10–12, 22–23, 45, 111, 133, 153
ethnocide, 52, 53, 73, 76–78, 91, 95–96
ethno-preneurialism, 22–23, 67, 72–73, 94. *See also* branding: ethnoracial
ethnorace, 10–12, 14
ethnoracialization, 31, 36–37, 44, 94, 99, 107, 115, 129–34, 187
ethnoracialness, 30, 66, 133–34, 140, 142, 149, 151–53
Études tsiganes, 46, 51, 208n28, 208n30
European Parliament, 1, 161
European Union, 160, 161, 203n26
evangelical Christianity, 5, 208n29
Ewing, Eve L., 199n3

Faudree, Paja, 201n16
Faure, Eric, 87–88, 108–9, 139–40, 215n52
Fédération Nationale des Associations Solidaires d'Action avec les Tsiganes et les Gens du Voyage (FNASAT), 28, 51
feeling, 30, 110, 133–43, 149, 151–52, 186
Feld, Steven, 107
Fellesz, Kevin, 102
Ferret, Jean "Matelo," 35, 45, 47, 59, 206n6, 208n30
Festival Django Reinhardt, 158, 167–73, 181
Festival Gipsy Swing, 22, 58, 154–56, 157–58, 172, 181
Festival International Tzigane, 158, 159–67
Festival Jazz Manouche de Zillisheim, 158, 173–81, 184
film, 42–43, 60, 75, 114, 162, 164–65, 178, 213n21, 215n53
flamenco, 87, 137–38, 139, 154–56
Fleming, Crystal, 12, 130
Flores, Nelson, 201n18
Foucault, Michel, 25
Fox, Aaron, 136, 143
Frankenberg, Ruth, 133, 220n13
freedom, 42–43, 54, 55, 122–24, 137, 146–47, 149
French jazz, 24, 34, 39, 55, 99–102, 114, 117–18, 206n5
French Ministry of Culture, 161
French racial policy. *See* racial policy in France
Front National, 70, 93, 199n2
Funaro, Stella, 28, 64, 65–66, 75, 78, 84, 86–87, 88, 90–91, 92, 161, 204n40, 215n50
funk, 112, 120

Gadjé, x, 5, 10, 25–26. *See also* Manouche-Gadjo relations
Gadjology, 25–26
Gal, Susan, 133–34, 222n28
Gastine, David, 98, 146
Gatlif, Tony, 60, 162, 215n50
Gelbart, Petra, 25, 26
genetics. *See* heredity
genre, 33, 34, 100–103, 126
Gens du voyage, 13–14, 16, 58, 69, 86, 138, 154–56, 158, 170–73, 181, 203n26, 203n27, 210n2, 223n1, 225n28, 226n29, 227n43; as "sedentarized," 14, 173
Germany, x, 34, 46–49, 52, 161, 163, 172, 199n1
Gille, Marie-Hélène, 95–96, 115
Gilroy, Paul, 6
Giniaux, Sébastien, 119–20
Ginsburg, Faye, 21
Gitans: as synonym for *Gypsy* or *Romani*, x, 5, 51, 74, 209n38, 211n8; as French-Spanish Romani group, x, 37, 46, 60, 74, 87–88, 164, 206n6, 208n30, 210n53. *See also* Romanies
Gitanos, 137–38, 139
Givan, Benjamin, 33, 35, 37–38, 107, 206n11, 206n12
Goldberg, David Theo, 9
gospel, 65, 124, 138
Grappelli, Stéphane, 38, 40, 108, 205n1, 206n7, 207n24
guitar: amplification of, 38, 56, 136, 140–41, 144, 178–79; Selmer, 5, 98, 154, 200n9; technique, 3, 47, 105, 107, 129, 140–45, 148–49, 206n12, 221n20. See also *pompe, la*.
Gypsies: as marketing term, 40, 59–61, 75, 110, 160; as synonym for *Romanies*, x, 1–2, 16, 35, 36, 39, 41, 42–43, 52, 69, 73–75, 114, 116, 123, 223n31. *See also* Romanies: stereotypes of

Gypsiology, 25
Gypsy jazz. *See* jazz manouche
Gypsylorism, 25–26
Gypsy stereotype complex, 217n4

Harkness, Nicholas, 131–32, 220n8, 221n16
Hauger, Pierre, 55–56, 59, 76, 79, 121, 209n42, 219n15
Helbig, Adriana, 21, 66, 110, 160, 225n17
Helmstetter, Engé, 78, 81, 91, 93, 123–24, 135, 164–66
Helmstetter, Louise "Pisla," 90–91, 216n59
Helmstetter, Railo, 91, 120, 141–42, 145
Helmstetter, Tchavo, 164–65
heredity, 11, 12, 13, 30, 36, 130, 133, 149–51
heritage, 3, 34, 156–59, 161, 181–82; French, 6, 16, 17, 20, 24, 100–101, 109, 111, 118; Manouche, 49, 72–73, 105–6, 109, 165
Herzfeld, Michael, 137
Hesse, Barnor, 202n19
Heyd, Pierre, 173–77, 184
Hill, Jane, 11
hip hop, 114, 121, 187, 200n12
Holocaust, 26, 28–29, 48, 114, 205n41
Holt, Fabian, 101
Horowitz, Michael, 218n9, 222n26
Hot Club de France, 37, 38, 39, 57, 205n1. *See also* Quintette du Hot Club de France
housing, 5, 68–70, 86–88, 173
"Hungarian" music, 47–48, 49–50, 51, 55, 121, 145, 166. See also *csárdás*
Hungary, 49, 57, 66, 75, 82, 161. See also *csárdás*; "Hungarian" music
hymnody, 180, 222n23, 225n25

iconicity, 132, 133–34, 221n16
iconization, 108, 133–34
immigration, 14–15, 70–71, 89, 203n26, 209n38, 212n10
improvisation, 2–4, 32, 44–45, 57, 107, 124, 136, 218n8, 221n17
indexicality, 101, 104–5, 132, 221n16
India, 160, 162, 164, 200n5
ineffability, 30, 126, 128, 129–30, 133, 135–36, 153, 186
Inoue, Miyako, 9, 129
insertion, 71–73, 78, 82–85, 90, 212n10, 212n12
integration, 53, 71–73, 82, 85, 88, 95–96, 212n10, 212n11
internment camps, 13, 87
intersubjectivity, 30, 101, 132, 138
Irvine, Judith T., 133–34, 222n28
Islam, 14–15, 70
Islamophobia. *See* xenophobia

Jackson, Travis, 17, 148–49, 221n21
Jalard, Michel-Claude, 43, 44–46, 208n26, 208n28, 221n17
jam sessions, 105–6, 172, 175, 177, 179
jazz: adoption by Sinti and Manouches, 47–51, 54–58; as African American, 17, 39, 55, 102, 138–40, 148–49; as high-prestige, 106–11; as "hot," 39, 49; and race, 18, 39–40, 109, 204n29, 218n7; as transnational, 6, 17, 103, 106–7, 109–11, 218n6; as universal, 17, 18, 30, 102, 106–7. *See also* bebop; bossa nova; French jazz; jazz manouche
jazz fusion, 102, 113, 120
jazz manouche: African American musics, comparisons to, 17, 55, 138–40; conflation with Django's music, 32–33, 35, 36–37, 43, 61, 99–100, 105–6, 119; and creativity, 102, 106, 107–9, 123; as "Django-style," 101, 108, 117–18; as "folkloristic," 4, 46, 47, 101, 107–11, 116; as "French jazz," 99–102, 115, 117–18; genesis of, 5–6, 29, 32–35, 36–37, 44–46, 49–51, 55–63, 93; intergenerational transmission of, 19–20, 32, 35, 37, 47, 50–51, 54–56, 58, 59, 78, 82, 146–49; Manouche listenership of, 49–50. 55–56, 88, 120, 164–65; online community of, 105; popularity of, 1–2, 6, 32, 57, 59–62, 93, 95, 113; repertoire and characteristic elements of, 2, 3, 5–6, 57, 98, 107, 112, 210n45 (see also *pompe, la*); as "serious," 109, 115; and the "Tsigane school," 44–46
jazz tsigane, 44–46
JEEP (Jeunes Equpies d'Education Populaire), 86–87, 88

Keane, Webb, 8, 153, 201n15
klezmer, 121
Krieg-Planque, Alice, 12

labor, 53, 84, 126, 152, 174, 185, 186–87, 211n6, 226n37. *See also* employment
Lafertin, Colette, 177, 178–79, 226n33

Lafertin, Fléco, 146–47, 175, 178–79
Lafertin, Zaïti, 175
Lagrène, Biréli, 60, 61, 113–14, 120, 210n52
language, music as, 45, 53, 54, 55, 57, 77–78, 79, 146
Latcho Drom, 162
Lefort, Michel, 45, 46, 58–59, 139, 141, 154–56, 172, 181, 222n23
Lemon, Alaina, 25, 26, 140, 223n33
Le Pen, Jean-Marie, 70
Le Pen, Marine, 93
"Les yeux noirs," 3, 50
listening subjects, 9, 129, 130, 134, 153
Loeffler, Cédric, 116, 123, 124, 128–29, 134, 142
Loeffler, Dorno, 175
Loeffler, Gigi, 2–4, 16–17, 56, 93, 109–11, 114, 118–19, 175, 176, 183–85, 187
Loeffler, Marcel, 49–50, 61, 116, 123, 124, 134–35, 143–45, 173
Loeffler, Mito, 145, 146–47, 173–75, 176, 178–81
Loeffler, Yorgui, 103, 110–11, 125–26, 148, 173, 183–85
Lowe, Lisa, 202n21
Luker, Morgan, 20
Lupovino, 87–88, 108
lyrics, 47–48, 65, 184

Maciejewski, Patrick, 69
Maeker, Siegfried, 46–49, 51, 52, 59
Mahon, Maureen, 21, 102
Manouche-Gadjo relations, 16–17, 18, 23, 25–26, 28–29, 41, 52–54, 56, 59, 60–61, 64–66, 69, 74–83 ,87, 89, 93, 95–96, 114–16, 153, 156, 163, 164–65, 170–4, 175–81
Manouches, ix–x, 1–2, 5; and artisanship, 72, 84, 211n6; community solidarity of, 3, 13, 66, 76–79, 96–97, 166, 180; cultural pride of, 19–20, 73, 76–79, 87, 91, 93, 122, 129, 137, 177, 186; and death, 168, 216n61, 225n25, 226n33; of mixed backgrounds, 27–28, 122, 153; and musical taste, 121, 165, 219n15; self-empowerment of, 53, 56, 72–73, 76–79, 81–82, 92, 164, 166; violence against, 5, 28–29, 52, 66, 68–69, 211n4; women, 64–65, 78, 87, 90–92, 96–97, 223n32. *See also* jazz manouche; racism: toward Romanies; Romanies: stereotypes of
Maré Sinté, 164–66
markedness, 10, 11, 15, 18, 25, 53, 102, 151, 185. *See also* Whiteness
marketing, 2, 7, 12, 23, 44, 53, 56, 59–62, 67, 81–83, 88, 94, 106, 110–13, 121–22, 142, 160. *See also* advertising
Marković, Alexander, 217n4
masculinity, 128–9, 133, 134, 142–45, 219n3
McGregor, Elizabeth Vihlen, 36, 40
MDZ. *See* Musik Deutscher Zigeuner
Mehrstein, Dino, 84, 86, 90, 94–95, 111–12, 118, 144
Mehrstein, Francko, 89–90, 111, 112, 216n56, 216n58
Mercier, Michel "Mitch," 60–61, 105–6, 108, 141, 210n53
migration. *See* Romanies: migration from India
Mirga-Kruszelnicka, Anna, 25–26
Moignard, Adrien, 141–42, 148
Monson, Ingrid, 18, 109, 120, 204n35
multiculturalism, 14–15, 70, 160
Munn, Nancy, 131
musette, 6, 37–38, 45, 99, 100, 200n10
music industry, 20, 24, 32, 59–62, 93, 94–95, 152, 200n12
music theory, 78, 82, 90, 137, 148, 149
Musik Deutscher Zigeuner, x, 34, 46–52, 145, 164, 166, 184, 208n31

Nakassis, Constantine, 201n18
National Front, 70, 93, 199n2
National Rally, 93, 199n2
Native Americans, 77, 186, 208n32
Nazism, 13, 26, 47, 49, 87, 114, 205n41
Nazi occupation of France, 13, 38
négrophilie, 39, 138
Negus, Keith, 61–62
neoliberalism, 20, 23, 56, 67, 72–73, 85, 94, 163, 202n20, 212n16
neorepublican discourse, 14–15
Neuhof, 52, 64–65, 78–80, 86–87, 88–90, 215n50
Neuhof Music School, 88–90, 92. *See also* APPONA, music school of
Niang, Mame-Fatou, 18
nonprofit organizations, 27, 32, 34, 44, 51–52, 59, 70, 83, 88, 93, 95. *See also* APPONA
Nourry, Pierre, 38, 205n1

Netherlands, 34, 161, 172
New York City, 26, 28, 99, 110–11, 148–49
nomades, 13, 210n2
nomadism, 13, 40, 41, 160, 165, 200n5, 210n2. See also *Gens du voyage*; Romanies: stereotypes of

Obadike, Mendi, 151, 220n14
Odéon, 38
Olivera, Martin, 13
Ong, Aihwa, 15
ontology, 103, 107, 126, 130

Panassié, Hugues, 39–40, 41–42
Parc de la Citadelle, 159, 161
Paris, 24, 27, 45, 60, 82, 103–4, 116, 128, 157; musical style of, 117, 142–45; periphery of, 37, 42
participatory discrepancies, 137
Pastor, Jean-François, 88, 216n54
Paviot, Paul, 42
Peirce, Charles S., 131, 201n14, 220n5, 220n6
Peircean semiotics, 131–32, 133, 201n14
Perman, Tony, 201n14
piano, 78, 141
Picker, Giovanni, 202n19, 225n28
Pierre, Jemima, 203n23
Plastino, Goffredo, 106–7
Polygone, 52, 74, 79, 87–88, 215n52
polyvalence, 4, 20, 61, 105, 185
pompe, la, 6, 47, 98, 112, 140–42, 143–44, 218n9, 222n26
poverty, 12–13, 51, 53, 66, 67, 68–73, 76, 89, 94, 102, 176–77, 186–87. *See also* class
Powell, Ryan, 202n20, 212n16
primitivism, 37, 39, 41, 77, 122, 137
professionalism, 2, 4, 22, 65, 81–85, 95, 102, 109, 114–15, 121–22, 126, 137, 141–42. *See also* professionalization
professionalization, 30, 52, 56, 72–74, 76–77, 81–85, 90, 94, 159, 163, 213n17, 215n45, 216n57. *See also* professionalism
Provot, Jacques, 204n40, 211n4, 214n29
public funding, 58, 79–81, 88, 92, 154, 160–61, 216n57, 224n7. *See also* welfare

QHCF. *See* Quintette du Hot Club de France
qualia, 131–34, 140, 142, 145, 151, 152–53, 220n6, 222n29
qualic transitivity, 131–32, 133, 144–45, 153, 220n8
qualisigns, 131–32, 133–34, 153
quantia, 222n29
Quieti, Laetitia, 88–89, 90, 91, 92, 216n56
Quintette du Hot Club de France, 5, 26, 32, 38, 40, 46–47, 48, 51, 55, 205n1, 206n13, 207n17, 209n41

racial avoidance, 12, 130
racialization, 9–14, 17, 20, 21, 25–26, 29, 34–44, 66, 96, 132–33, 138, 185, 186, 202n19
racialness, 133
racial policy in France, 11–15, 38–39, 66, 67, 70, 202n21, 211n7
raciolinguistics, 9–10, 201n18
raciosemiotics, 8–10, 14, 34, 129, 131, 186, 201n18
racism, 5, 9–10, 11–14, 93, 94, 202n19; color-blind, 12, 13–14, 34, 202n22; cultural, 12–13; toward Romanies, 5, 12–14, 15–16, 25–26, 28–29, 34, 52–52, 66, 68–70, 109, 118–19, 153, 170–73, 212n16; without races, 12. *See also* racialization; White supremacy
Radano, Ronald, 130, 140, 220n14
radio, 213n22
rap, 138, 219n15
Rassemblement National, 93, 199n2
Reed, Adolph, Jr., 13, 94, 203n23
refusal, 11–12, 22, 30, 103–5, 110, 112–13, 120, 124–27, 185, 187
Reinhardt, Babik, 42, 43, 139, 169, 208n30
Reinhardt, Django, 1, 5, 38; Black musicians, comparisons to, 36, 39–40, 55, 139; commemorations of, 41–44, 61, 62, 157, 158, 167–69, 183–84; death of, 5, 38, 40–41, 42, 43, 167, 168; early life of, 5, 37–38; improvisational technique of, 105, 136, 218n8; influence on other musicians, 16–17, 50, 54, 56, 57, 59, 99–100, 105–8, 111, 113, 119–20, 123–26, 209n42; injury to left hand, 5, 37–38, 206n12; as a "jazz musician," 33, 35, 105–7; literacy of, 206n7; original compositions of, 2, 6, 43, 47, 57, 136, 207n21; personality, characterizations of, 35, 36, 39, 41–44; recordings by, 5, 6, 32, 33, 38, 42, 46, 47, 51, 56, 61, 105, 134–35, 136; Romani influences in

the music of, claims to, 32–33, 35–41, 100, 105, 134–35; tour to the United States, 38
Reinhardt, Francky, 56–58, 93, 145
Reinhardt, Joseph, 38, 42, 205n1, 208n26, 208n27, 208n30, 221n17
Reinhardt, Mandino, 50, 52, 54–55, 56–57, 60, 61, 64–65, 75, 78, 82, 88, 89–91, 93, 111, 144, 148, 213n22, 215n50, 216n56, 219n1
Reinhardt, Naguine, 42, 43, 99, 158, 225n25
Reinhardt, Schnuckenack, 46–47, 48, 50, 147, 166, 209n35
religion, 5, 11, 14–15, 46, 92, 147, 150, 164, 176, 179–80, 200n5, 203n5, 222n23. *See also* Catholicism; evangelical Christianity; Islam
republicanism, 4, 11, 13, 14–15, 18, 34, 67, 70–73, 92, 93, 96, 101, 102–3, 106, 127, 172, 185. *See also* universalism
research methods, 26–29, 34
Reyes, Angela, 9, 152
rhematization, 133–34
right to difference, 70
RMI. *See* welfare
Roberts, T., 130, 205n3, 219n2
Robinet, Jean-François, 168–73, 225n27
Roma, ix–x, 15, 25–25, 33, 47, 160, 203n26; Manouche resistance to the term, x, 203n26. *See also* Romanies
Romania, 15–16, 22, 50, 124, 135, 161, 163, 203n26, 217n3
Romanies: definitions of, ix–x, 1–2, 5, 11, 25–26, 28–29, 162, 210n2; as European, 160–64; European policy toward, 69, 161–62, 201n20, 224n9, 224n13; French policy toward, 13–14, 15–16, 38, 203n26 (see also *Gens du voyage*); migration from India, 160, 161, 162–64, 166–67, 200n5; pan-Romani identity,19, 51, 103, 161–64; 209n43; stereotypes of, 5, 12–16, 39–45, 48, 54, 73, 77–78, 83, 101, 102, 108, 111, 114–15, 117, 122, 129, 137, 151, 156, 165, 186, 200n8, 204n35, 217n4
Romani language, x, 5, 29, 48, 65, 129, 166, 184, 219n15, 219n1
Romani music, 32, 44, 47–48, 49–50, 53–55, 57–58, 59, 77–78, 99–101, 105, 109–11, 121, 123–24, 134–35, 140, 159–60, 161–63, 174, 204n33
Romani rights movement, 48, 70, 204n33, 209n38
Romani World Congress, 70, 209n38, 211n8
Roms, ix–x, 164. *See also* Roma
Rosa, Jonathan, 9, 201n18
Rosaldo, Renato, 15
roulottes, 40, 42, 52, 174, 207n18. *See also* caravans
Roussin, Dider, 37, 206n9
Routhier-Faivre, Bertrand, 69
Russia, 3, 140, 163

Saintes-Maries-de-la-Mer, 65, 90–92
Salbris, 98–99, 158
Salgues, Yves, 42
Samois-sur-Seine, 42, 167–73, 178, 179
Samudaripen, 114
Samuels, David, 133, 136, 201n14
Sarkozy, Nicolas, 93, 203n26, 217n63
saxophone, 2–3, 27, 82, 110
Schmitt, Tchavolo, 60, 61, 84, 128–29, 134, 141–42, 144, 147, 215n50, 219n1
sedentarization, 13, 14, 53, 69–70, 147, 173, 210n2, 211n6, 225n27
Selmer guitar. *See* guitar: Selmer
semiotic ideologies, 8–10, 20, 30, 101, 126, 129, 131, 151, 153
Silverman, Carol, 5, 21, 26, 162
singers, 27, 46, 47–48, 64–66, 90–92, 184
Singh, Davindar, 27, 110
Sinti, ix–x, 5, 34, 35, 46–49, 55, 94, 114, 147, 164–66, 172, 184, 226n30
slavery, 12, 55, 139
Smalls, Krystal, 9
Social and Cultural Center of Neuhof, 64, 80, 88
social media, 27, 138
social workers, 13, 58, 64–65, 91, 95, 150, 180. *See also* APPONA
song, 6, 47–48, 65, 91, 164, 166, 184, 210n45
sonic space, 177, 178–79
sono-racialization, 130, 205n3, 219n2
Steinberger, Fabrice, 83, 147–48, 215n49, 223n33
Steinberger, Rigo, 80, 85, 147, 215n49
stereotyping. *See* Romanies: stereotypes of
Strasbourg, 16, 19, 27, 28, 50, 52, 60, 64, 66, 74, 79, 80–81, 82, 86–89, 111, 128, 142, 145, 148, 159–60, 163, 182

strategic anti-essentialism, 101, 109
strategic essentialism, 201n13
Strathern, Marilyn, 149
Swing (film), 60, 61, 215n50, 219n1
swing manouche. *See* jazz manouche
swing musette, 45, 47
Syntax, Baro, 138
Szeman, Ioana, 16

Ténot, Frank, 105
timbre, 128–29, 132, 141
tourism, 31, 156
Trazegnies, Jean de, 40
Trouillot, Michel-Rolph, 12
Tsiganes. *See* Romanies
Tucker, Sherrie, 102
Turino, Thomas, 201n14
Tuzet, Benjamin, 6
Tzigane Cultural Week, 53, 74–75, 80
Tziganes. *See* Romanies

Ukraine, 3, 21, 110
Ultraphone, 38
universalism, 11, 15, 17–18, 30, 70, 93, 102, 106–7, 127, 202n21. *See also* republicanism
Urciuoli, Bonnie, 10, 72

van Baar, Huub, 5, 202n20, 212n16
variety music, 55, 209n42
Vichy France, 13
Vigneron, Pierre, 148, 149, 152–53
violin, 26, 37, 38, 44, 46, 48, 49–50, 55, 56, 89, 124, 135, 180, 205n1, 209n35
virtuosity, 105, 113, 137, 141–42, 151–52
visual art, 19, 83, 146, 154–56, 174
voice, 9, 64–65, 132–33, 141, 205n3, 220n4
Vola, Louis, 38, 205n1

waltzes, 47, 55, 210n45
Weiss, Albert, 137, 139,
Weiss, Billy, 56, 98–100, 104, 114, 125, 128
Weiss, Gaga, 99–100, 104, 114
Weiss, Häns'che: 47, 49, 50, 184
welfare, 71–73, 84–85, 177, 212n12
Whiteness, 1, 6, 10–11, 15–16, 23, 25, 34, 38–40, 57, 70, 71,
White supremacy, 10–11, 34, 202n21. *See also* Whiteness
Williams, Patrick, 35, 37, 44, 46, 51, 59, 105, 134, 140–41, 216n61
Wilf, Eitan, 218n7
Wilson, David, 17
Wirtz, Kristina, 12, 220n10
world music, 33, 59, 60, 88, 216n54
World War II, 13, 38, 72, 87, 114, 184, 203n24, 207n16, 226n13

xenophobia, 1, 14–15, 70, 93, 203n26

Yéniches, 210n2
youth, 54–55, 56, 79, 78–82, 88–90, 149, 163–64
Yúdice, George, 20

Zigeuners, x. *See also* Musik Deutscher Zigeuner
Zillisheim, 146, 158, 173–82, 184